The Jewel of Liberty

Abraham Lincoln's Re-Election
and the End of Slavery

 **E. Long**

DA CAPO PRESS • NEW YORK

Library of Congress Cataloging-in-Publication Data

Long, David E., 1947–
    The jewel of liberty: Abraham Lincoln's re-election and the end of slavery /
David E. Long.
        p.   cm.
    Originally published: Mechanicsburg, PA: Stackpole Books, c1994.
    Includes bibliographical references (p.   ) and index.
    ISBN 0-306-80788-2 (alk. paper)
        1. Presidents—United States—Election—1864. 2. Lincoln, Abraham, 1809–
1865. 3. United States—Politics and government—1861–1865. I. Title.
E459.L85   1997
973.7′092—dc21   97-15672
                                                                                CIP

First Da Capo Press edition 1997

This Da Capo Press paperback edition of *The Jewel of Liberty*
is an unabridged republication of the edition published in
Mechanicsburg, Pennsylvania in 1994. It is reprinted
by arrangement with Stackpole Books.

Published by Da Capo Press, Inc.
A Subsidiary of Plenum Publishing Corporation
233 Spring Street, New York, N.Y. 10013

To my parents,
Paul Robinson Long and Blondina Ellison Long,
who never lost faith.

Also to David Riley,
my paternal great-grandfather, who wore blue;

and Samuel Wilkins,
my maternal great-great-grandfather, who wore gray.

In early 1864, as the efforts of Congress and the White House were increasingly directed toward the Reconstruction of some rebel states, several black men from Louisiana traveled to Washington, D.C., carrying a petition signed by more than a thousand "free people of color" of New Orleans. The memorial asked for the right to vote in reconstructed Louisiana. Abraham Lincoln invited them to the White House where he was so impressed that on March 13 he wrote Michael Hahn, the first governor of free Louisiana, the following letter:

> I congratulate you on having fixed your name in history as the first-free-state Governor of Louisiana. Now you are about to have a Convention which, among other things, will probably define the elective franchise. I barely suggest for your private consideration, whether some of the colored people may not be let in—as, for instance, the very intelligent, and especially those who have fought gallantly in our ranks. They would probably help, in some trying time to come, to keep *the jewel of liberty* within the family of freedom. . . .

Contents

Foreword

> "Do not mistake that the ballot is stronger than the bullet. Therefore, let the legions of slavery use bullets; but let us wait patiently till November and fire ballots at them in return; and by that peaceful policy I believe we shall ultimately win."
> —Abraham Lincoln, Bloomington, May 29, 1856

Facing defeat, did Lincoln still feel so democratic as the election of November 1864 approached? Some have expressed surprise that the election of 1864 *in the midst of civil war* was held at all. What is even more important is that in his entire utterance record and in the "auditors" who recorded their conversations with him, there is not one word of unwillingness by our sixteenth president to hold the election. To many leaders, such an election would have been an anathema, both in his day as well as ours. But not Lincoln, who continued to believe in the democratic processes even during a civil war. His behavior remains the American model for the world, especially today when executives suspend constitutional guarantees at whim, much less during civil war.

This may be explained in part, as Mark E. Neely, Jr., put it in *The Last Best Hope of Earth: Abraham Lincoln and the Promise of America* because the "continuity of robust two-party politics in the North throughout the war was a triumph of the American political system consciously sought by the President. . . ." Despite the loss of Stephen A. Douglas in 1861, leaving the Democratic Party leaderless, the Democrats proved to be highly competitive, though questions abound as to whether many Democrats constituted a "loyal opposition." Lincoln recognized that he had been elected by a minority of the electorate, so he never underestimated the Democrats. He worked hard to keep the Republican Party together to effectively garner votes—not necessarily to expound high-sounding moral principles.

Yet overall, 1864 was not a good year for the president. The nation had been entangled in the bitter civil war for four years. There was dissent against conscription. Nearly every home in the North was draped in mourning over the loss or wounding of a loved one. There were many in the North who wanted peace at any price—probably more than a million voters believed in the justice of the Confederate cause, or at least were unwilling to continue the war if this was necessary to defeat that cause.

Stephen B. Oates in *A Woman of Valor: Clara Barton and the Civil War* points out that even Lincoln supporters realized how unpopular he was in the North. Yet, Clara Barton morally supported Lincoln. "Who am I going to vote for?" she asked, even though women did not have the legal right to vote. "Why I thought for President Lincoln, to be sure. I *have* been voting for him for the last three years. I thought him honest, and true, and I believe that he sought the right with all his power, and would do it as fast as he saw it clearly, and I still think so." Despite seeing "a strong tide" for General John Charles Frémont, who was overruled by President Lincoln when he tried to free the slaves in Missouri in 1861,

> I *honor* Mr. Lincoln and have believed, and still do, that his election was ordained, that he was raised up to meet this crisis, but it may also be that *no one* man could be constituted who should be equal to both the beginning and ending of this vast, this mighty change, the same mind that could guide safely in the outset may be too slow now, for war has had its effects upon us, and our temper as a people, wiped out our conservativeness and touched us with the fire of the old nations. We have grown enthusiastic, and shout loud and long, where once we should have looked on in silence. I have said from the first that I believe this whole thing was directly in the hands of Providence, and that so it would continue, and that if we had *need* of our *appointed* and not elected, that if we had further need of him we should have him.

Barton sincerely hoped the Republican nominee would be Lincoln, whose "care worn face" had become very dear to her. His "face," through a moral commitment to the vision of the Framers of the Declaration of Independence, etched itself into the national psyche. The disfranchised (women and slaves, as well as up till now, soldiers) "felt" Lincoln's purpose.

While President Lincoln may have retained a "quiet confidence" that the military and economic resources of the North would eventually over-power the Confederacy, it is clear he knew that his chances of winning a second term were slim or nonexistent. He insisted that should he be re-elected, there must be restoration of the Union and the end of the Confed-eracy. The historical importance of the 1864 election cannot be overesti-mated. As Professor Long points out, "No previous nominee of a major party had afforded the population an opportunity to register a position on the issue of slavery in the United States. In 1864 that issue was before the voters, and they overwhelmingly rejected the institution as part of the postwar United States." It remains a primal vote in the annals of democracy.

David Long also raises and disposes of the notion, popular in some circles today, that Lincoln was a racial bigot who used emancipation merely as a political expedient while the slaves freed themselves. Long demonstrates that the Emancipation Proclamation was "an act of staggering importance" in the context of its time and place, and that it placed "a moral blockade" around the slave-based Confederacy. Long also convincingly argues that Lincoln never seriously considered retracting the promise of emancipation, not even during his lowest ebb in August 1864. The president would never have restored the rebellious states with slavery intact.

As does James M. McPherson's *Who Freed the Slaves?*, Long's account credits Lincoln, despite the self-emancipation theory, because Lincoln would not only have war but would continue the war rather than allow secession. Without a civil war, and its successful conclusion, there would have been "no Confiscation Act, no Emancipation Proclamation, no Thir-teenth Amendment, certainly no self-emancipation, and almost certainly no end of slavery for several more decades. . . ."

The Jewel of Liberty contains a brilliant analysis of Henry J. Raymond's peace plan and Lincoln's handling of it. Long points to the "illogic of the speculation" that Lincoln would have dropped emancipation if Jefferson Davis would have opened a dialogue with him about peace. Long rightly points to the 1864 election as "the most important electoral event in

American history." By sending Lincoln back to the White House for a second term, the Union electorate guaranteed that slavery would end in this country and that the United States would "enter the twentieth century undivided." What is provocative about this book is that it reveals the quality and style of Lincoln's leadership at a pivotal time in his presidency.

President Lincoln, according to Garry Wills, satisfies the definition of leadership. Wills believes "a leader does not just vaguely affect others," but "takes others towards the object of their joint quest." That object defines the *kind* of leadership at issue. To Wills, different types of leaders should be distinguished more by their goals than by the more common practice of using the personality of the leader to categorize them. Basing his policy on the moral claim of the Declaration of Independence, Lincoln led the people to union in the real sense (the United States *is* rather than *are*) and ensured such union would be devoid of involuntary servitude. To do this Lincoln had to show compromise and flexibility "appropriate for his kind of leadership."

Through Lincoln's perseverance, courage, and strength, the election proved that democratic government superseded "all other rights of a nation or individual citizen," and that holding an election was so basic that even civil war could not prevent it. The right to vote remained with all American citizens; in fact, it was expanded to include those in the field. It offers "a powerful example for the future." Ratification of a perpetual union and nullification of succession by a minority are indeed among Lincoln's greatest legacies.

Nonetheless, the 1864 election year was so bizarre that the country witnessed serious efforts to replace Lincoln as the Republican nominee. For example, radical Republican Senator Zachariah Chandler, who often disagreed with Lincoln, was forced to lead a major effort in aborting the independent third-party candidacy of his friend Frémont, but only after the president promised to replace Postmaster General Montgomery Blair. Lincoln's flexibility allowed him to maneuver in the political arena, trading minor concessions so that he might achieve his major goal, as Garry Wills might argue.

Lincoln's "blind memorandum" on August 23, 1864, always has puzzled historians and political observers. What did it mean? Long offers as plausible an explanation as ever has been given. Lincoln, in fear of defeat, retained his courage and stamina by "demanding a total effort by all members of his administration and the military." But why did he place his sentiments in writing on that fateful August day, seal the sheet, and have his cabinet members sign it without knowing its contents?

There is the humanistic Lincoln here too, with the president writing his own estimates of the November results after learning of the early October elections in some of the states. Despite the fact that in 1812 James Madison ran for president while the country was at war, 1864 was the year of the first national election while the country was in a state of civil war. It was the first election to allow soldier votes. Four out of five of those cast supported Lincoln's re-election. Except for the soldier votes cast in New York and Connecticut, the outcome would not have been different, but it still demonstrated the overwhelming support of soldiers for the commander-in-chief, who potentially might order them to their deaths.

Lincoln's calm decisiveness and lack of vindictiveness are amply demonstrated in this book, and must have been felt by the electorate. In large part, that leadership accounted for his receiving 55 percent of the final vote. Worried about the legality of the Emancipation Proclamation, Lincoln was assured that the election results would go a long way in approving the Thirteenth Amendment, permanently outlawing slavery everywhere in the United States. He was a leader, for the public came to understand the vision that he articulated in his speeches and his behavior.

Some point to military victories by Sherman in Atlanta and Farragut at Mobile Bay as the ultimate cause of Lincoln's victory. But, as Long points out, this ignores other facts, such as the peace platform of the Democratic National Convention. Even its candidate, George Brinton McClellan, disavowed the platform's appeasement plank. Both Lincoln and McClellan were in favor of pursuing the war to a successful conclusion. Was the real difference between Lincoln and the radicals of his own party, who after the election behaved as if they had won, rather than between Lincoln and those who tried to replace him?

Lincoln won the war but did not live long enough to secure the peace. He had to endure misstatements from his secretary of state, William H. Seward, who told an audience in Auburn, New York, "While the rebels continue to wage war against the Government of the United States, the military measures affecting slavery which have been adopted from necessity to bring the war to a speedy and successful end, will be continued. . . ." But when the war was over "all the war measures then existing, including those which affect slavery will cease also." Lincoln was forced to disavow the secretary's speech. If that were not enough, shortly before the nominating convention on May 18, the country read that President Lincoln had given up all hope and had issued a proclamation for a day of national prayer with a draft call for 400,000 men. A hoax initiated by a stock market manipulator, the vibrations remained with the public for some time.

As with his emancipation policy, the president refused to delay the draft call scheduled for September even at the urging of Governor Morton of Indiana, who feared electoral loss in his state. With Confederate agents stationed in major cities in the North, the Lincoln administration was forced to send Union troops to guard against any outbreak of mayhem.

Despite prevarication and intrigue, Lincoln's vision remained above the problems of everyday politics. No one better has expressed the American dream than Abraham Lincoln did to a group of soldiers in Washington that election year, when he said, "It is in order that each of you may have, through this free Government which we have enjoyed, an open field and a fair chance for your industry, enterprise, and intelligence; that you may all have equal privileges in this race of life, with all its desirable human aspirations. It is for this the struggle should be maintained, that we may not lose our birthright. The nation is worth fighting for, to secure such an inestimable jewel." For the first time, Professor Long details the public's recognition of President Lincoln's work toward that vision in the 1864 election. It's a story that deserves telling today.

Frank J. Williams
President, Abraham Lincoln Association

Preface

The 1864 election was the most important electoral event in American history. It determined the outcome of the Civil War. The freedom of millions of slaves depended on it and it did more to define and expand the meaning of democracy in the United States than any event since the adoption of the Declaration of Independence. It affirmed that the Union was perpetual and that the Constitution created a bond that was indivisible rather than a voluntary association of states existing at the whim of each of its individual members. It established that no principle of democratic government was more fundamental than the one that defined when and how elections would be held.

Yet, the 1864 election has been slighted by historians as a sideshow to the main event of the Civil War. More monographs have been produced on Abraham Lincoln and the Civil War era than any other U.S. history subjects, but the pivotal event of the war, and of the political career of the sixteenth president, has inspired only one specialized study, a 1953 work by William Frank Zornow. *Lincoln & the Party Divided* was of immense help in preparing this work, but Professor Zornow and most historians of his generation portrayed slavery as unimportant in bringing about the conflict and emancipation as an accidental and not-so-important result.

Later historians have challenged this interpretation. Slavery brought the conflict on (no other sectional issue would have caused the war); it could not long be kept from dominating the military and political policies of both sides. The war was fought almost exclusively in the South and slavery was omnipresent there. Despite ambivalent and racist feelings about slaves, most Northerners could see how the nearly four million slaves would either assist the rebellion or help to destroy it. Lincoln's Emancipation Proclamation was the overarching political act of the war; in addition to guaranteeing that Britain would remain neutral in the conflict, it inspired more opposition to Lincoln and the Republicans than any other act or event. It dominated discussion of the war, its goals, and what the country would be like afterward.

To understand the importance of the 1864 election, it is necessary to go back to the beginning of the Lincoln presidency. Almost from the moment he took office, slavery and the government's position on it in relation to the war began to impinge on his administration. That was disconcerting to Lincoln, whose first priority was to keep the border slave states from seceding. If Maryland, Kentucky, and Missouri had seceded, the North almost certainly would have lost the war. A precipitous blow struck against slavery before Federal authority was established in these states would have rendered moot any questions regarding the morality of human bondage, as it would then have existed only in an independent nation established in defiance of the United States.

Many themes beckon when one is writing about an event of this magnitude. It was, for example, the first election in which absentee ballot legislation permitted soldiers away from home to vote. In 1864 the prospect of Republican defeat became the centerpiece of Confederate military and political strategy, and the final hope of Southerners that summer and fall as they saw their beloved homeland destroyed. There was the racism in the North that was so blatantly and ruthlessly manipulated by the Democrats, and the domestic treason issue that the Unionists exploited with a vengeance. There were the events of the battlefield, from Cold Harbor to Peachtree Creek, where the verdict written in blood by the troops ultimately determined the outcome in the voting at the polls.

The most compelling theme that emerges out of this election, however, is that a fair and open plebescite was held at all in 1864. It became the acid test of democratic government; in the midst of a huge and destructive civil war, a violent challenge to the sovereignty of that government, the most basic function regularly performed by the institutions of the republic went forward in an orderly and peaceful way. No other government had held a truly free election while engaged in a rebellion or civil war. That there was never at any time serious thought of cancelling or suspending the election affirmed the belief in democratic government as defined by the Constitution. That affirmation was all the more resonant in light of what appeared until the end of August to be a probable administration defeat.

Will there be some future election more important than the one in 1864? It seems unlikely. Will there someday be a national crisis greater than the one posed by the American Civil War? It is improbable. Will there be a time when issues larger than freedom or slavery, union or disunion, and the continuation or dissolution of constitutional government, will face the electorate? It is nearly unimaginable. Might there in some future generation be an administration further behind in the popular opinion than the Lincoln administration was in August 1864, that will rally to gain not just a victory but an overwhelming mandate in the general election? Perhaps. But the intersection of all of these compelling circumstances in the same event could never again occur. At no time in the future will the United States be so vulnerable, or the nascent bonds of constitutional union so weak, or the germinating seeds of representative government so fragile, as they were in 1864. The re-election of Abraham Lincoln provided the glue that sealed the cracks in the foundation of representative government. It was a necessary rite of passage for a nation struggling to live up to its stated ideals while it tossed in a sea of violence. Its story has needed telling for the century and a third that has passed since then. Now, at last, it is told.

Acknowledgments

Too many people have contributed to this work for me to acknowledge each one. Some of them have been so important, however, that not to mention them would be unforgivable. Dr. Joe M. Richardson, the professor who directed the 1993 dissertation that became *The Jewel of Liberty*, demonstrated patience and insight in tempering my impetuousness and focusing my energies on what has been the most difficult project of my life.

Graduate Student Adviser Debbie Perry has been a good friend and constant supporter, even during times I had precious few of either. She is a person whose belief in me helped to sustain me through a difficult course of study. She will never know how much her efforts and support meant. This acknowledgment is a small, inadequate token of my appreciation. My good friends, Frank and Virginia Williams, made their substantial collection of Lincolniana available to me. Their support and encouragement were important to me as well. It was Virginia Williams' creative talent and nimble mind that led to placing a campaign ribbon on a couch pillow and producing an ektachrome slide. Tracy Patterson of Stackpole used the slide to produce the handsome bookcover that graces this text.

Linda Creibaum and Ed Foster, at the University of South Florida's Sarasota campus library, both performed far in excess of the line of duty in assisting me to obtain needed resources. Clark Evans, at the Rare Books Room of the Library of Congress, provided both assistance and encouragement. Dr. George Mayer, at the University of South Florida, assisted in identifying several important issues I needed to address. Laurence E. Hathaway, the division head of the Reference and Government Services Division of the Indiana State Library, made my trip to Indianapolis most productive and showed great patience in allowing me the extended use of some valuable resource materials. Steve Towne, in the Archives Division of the Indiana State Library, aided me in confirming several items of my research about the Copperheads in the 1864 election campaign. Tom Schwartz, the curator of the Lincoln Collection at the Illinois State Historical Library, was always available and helpful. Though he did not give me the shirt off his back, he did loan me the tie from his neck when I drove to Springfield for the 1993 annual dinner of the Abraham Lincoln Association, only to learn I had forgotten to bring a tie. Karen Kearnes, of the Reference Division of the Huntington Library in San Marino, California, was more than helpful while I was obtaining information from the valuable collections there. And Gary J. Arnold, head of the reference services at the Ohio Historical Society Library, helped me locate some useful documents when I was in Columbus.

This work would never have found its way into popular print had it not been for a fortuitous meeting several years ago. While a struggling graduate student completing my master's thesis, I chanced to meet William C. "Jack" Davis at a convention of the American Blue and Gray Association. Jack was a headliner on the program while I was but a plebeian attendee at the conference. Nevertheless, he was more than willing to retire to the local pub for a few rounds of "barley water" and some interesting repartee. When I asked if Jack would read a chapter of my thesis and render his opinion, he accepted without hesitation. Several weeks later I received a package from Mechanicsburg, Pennsylvania, consisting of my manuscript and a letter from Jack, who is coincidentally an editor at Stackpole Books. He liked what he had read (the chapter on the race issue in the 1864 election) and was interested in reading the entire text for the possibility of publication.

The result of Jack's interest and support is *The Jewel of Liberty*. Thank you, Jack. He also introduced me to those people at Stackpole who have helped bring this project to fruition. Sylvia Frank, the managing editor, helped bring order and style to my disorganized efforts. At a time when we were having trouble choosing a title (previous choices such as *A New Birth of Freedom* and *The Last Best Hope* have appeared on recent works regarding Lincoln), Sylvia was the one who located the phrase *The Jewel of Liberty* from the little-known letter Lincoln wrote to Michael Hahn in

March 1864. Thank you, Sylvia. Also a word of thanks to my copy editor, Mark Ferguson, who reduced my often wordy prose to a much tighter and better organized story. His reading of the text must have been a real struggle; however, because he did, it will read better for everybody else. My thanks as well to all of the other folks at Stackpole who made this possible . . . Dick Frank, Marianne Baier, and anybody else I have neglected to mention.

The single most important acknowledgment is to my mother, Blondina Long, who has been typist, copy editor, support staff, and general source of encouragement during the long struggle to bring this project to completion. Without her indefatigable efforts this would not have been possible. Thank you, mom.

To all of these people I owe a debt of gratitude for assisting this often inept researcher to locate and explore some of the many resources available regarding this important event in the political history of the United States. Thank you to all of you.

The Jewel of Liberty

1

"In Giving Freedom to the Slave"

When Abraham Lincoln ran for the presidency in 1860, he was relatively unknown to most of the nation. Though he had garnered significant press coverage during his tours of the Midwest in 1859 and New England in 1860, his national presence did not compare with those of his three better-known opponents. This had served him well during the nominating convention, where he had been relatively obscure compared with better-known candidates from New York, Pennsylvania, Ohio, and even Missouri. Among many of the pundits who weighed the relative chances of the candidates, Lincoln was not even a dark horse to be considered in the event of a brokered convention.[1]

Lincoln was very well known in his home state, however, and the convention was held in Illinois, where he had accumulated significant political capital. Lincoln's absence from the national stage had prevented the formation of a coalition of opponents. All of the other candidates had been in the national spotlight long enough to create a sizable opposition to their candidacies. Their lack of nationwide appeal and Lincoln's own relative anonymity were largely responsible for his victory in 1860. That situation had changed by 1864, as he had become the best-known politician in the country. He had also unintentionally developed a large cadre of political enemies within his own party. During his first term Lincoln saw the nation he had been chosen to lead descend into a frenzy of violence from which it was his duty to deliver it. The situation was so precarious that the president-elect disguised himself and stole into Washington in the middle of the night. To reach it, he had to pass through Maryland, in which there were nearly as many disloyal as loyal people. In 1860 he had received only 2,000 of the 93,000 votes cast in that state.[2] From the White House, he could look across the Potomac River into Virginia, where within a couple of months he would see banners of rebellion flying from rooftops. He knew already that this was not going to be an ordinary presidency.[3]

Slavery was still legal in the District of Columbia, and many Washingtonians were openly hostile to the president. While rebel armies were forming to the south, Lincoln could not assemble a full regiment from the Federal soldiers stationed in and around the capital. Rebel governments in seven states (by early February, South Carolina, Alabama, Florida, Georgia, Mississippi, Louisiana, and Texas had seceded) were seizing Federal arsenals and other property, and he could do little about it. Lincoln had won the nomination and the presidency without fully stating his political positions. But now he was president and if he did not act soon, there would no longer be a Federal presence in the seceded states. Regaining the lost property would require an invasion that might provoke European powers and enhance the rebels' chances of winning the diplomatic recognition they so desperately sought. Even symbolic acts took on enormous significance, while the failure to act at all only encouraged further encroachments. The cautious man, the man of logic, reason, and ideas, was being tested as no other American president had ever been. He could not provoke, yet had to restore respect for the U.S. government. For five weeks following his inauguration, Lincoln proceeded with deliberate caution.[4]

On April 12, 1861, rebel guns ringing the harbor in Charleston, South Carolina, opened fire on Fort Sumter. On April 15 Lincoln declared that an insurrection existed, called on the states to raise 75,000 volunteers, and convened Congress in special session effective July 4. Within a short time, Virginia, Arkansas, Tennessee, and North Carolina followed the other Confederate states out of the Union. On April 19 a pro-southern mob in Baltimore attacked a passing Massachusetts regiment, killing at least four soldiers. The soldiers fired back, killing nine civilians. The mob destroyed railroad tracks, bridges, and telegraph lines leading north, and many Marylanders joined regiments that would serve in the Confederate army.[5]

Since all troops traveling to Washington by train from the Northeast had to pass through Baltimore, the situation was serious. The capital was virtually defenseless, so on April 27, Lincoln suspended the writ of habeas corpus along the communication lines between Philadelphia and Washington at the discretion of the commander of the Army, Major General Winfield Scott.[6] A number of military arrests in Maryland followed, including the Baltimore chief of police, several members of the General Assembly, four police commissioners, and a grandson of Francis Scott Key. After the Union defeat at Bull Run near Manassas, Virginia, on July 21, reports began to circulate of a plot for a simultaneous Confederate invasion of Maryland, insurrection in Baltimore, and enactment of a secession ordinance by a special session of the Maryland legislature. Federal troops responded by arresting thirty-one secessionist legislators, including Mayor George Brown of Baltimore, and many other people suspected of conspiring in the plot.[7]

Early in his presidency, Lincoln's primary concern was for the safety of the nation and the continuation of the government. He wrote later that a limb must often be amputated to save a life, but a life must never be given to save a limb. "I felt that measures, however unconstitutional, might become lawful by becoming indispensable to the preservation of the Constitution, through the preservation of the nation," he explained.[8] He extended the area in which the suspension applied on several occasions, primarily because of Copperhead ("Copperhead" was the term applied to opponents of the war by supporters of the war) activity, or resistance to the draft, which included attacks on conscription officers. By the fall of 1862 the suspension order applied to all parts of the country. The suspension led to the arbitrary arrest of thousands of Northern citizens during the war who had one thing in common—they all stood in political opposition to the president. Most of those arrested were influential men, which made their detention newsworthy and created the general impression that the policy was invoked far more than it actually was.[9]

Lincoln disliked ordering arbitrary arrests, but he knew well the disruptive effect of eloquent speakers and editors who encouraged young men to resist conscription or desert from the army. Agitation and desertion became two of the most nagging problems of the Lincoln administration and loomed large in every Democratic campaign from May 1861 until the end of the war. "The Constitution as it is, the Union as it was" became the slogan chanted by virtually every Democratic candidate in 1862, and it was repeated many times over in the next three years. It summed up all the themes that the opposition party sought to exploit against the Republican administration and Congress: suspension of the writ and arbitrary arrest; suppression of rights of free speech, press, and assembly; turning the war into a crusade to end slavery; and the passage of confiscation and conscription legislation that expanded Federal authority without constitutional sanction.[10]

After Bull Run showed that the war would be protracted and bloody, there was increasing sentiment that the government should make emancipation a specific goal and one without which the administration would not make peace. The sentiment picked up momentum as newspaper editors such as Horace Greeley urged the president to issue an emancipation proclamation. However, in the late summer and fall of 1861, Lincoln was still concerned for the safety of the capital, and his highest priority was to assure that the border states remained in the Union. He could not risk an action that might cause thousands of loyal Unionists to become instant rebels. He remained intransigent on the issue, repeating the promise of his inaugural address that "I have no purpose, directly or indirectly, to interfere with the institution [of slavery] in the states where it exists. I believe I have no lawful right to do so, and I have no inclination to do so."[11]

However, the Lincoln exterior, usually simple and folksy, belied a man who constantly struggled with the philosophical implications and practical consequences of the positions he assumed on issues. He began his first term earnestly assuring Southerners that he would not interfere with their "peculiar institution" and avoided making any public judgments on its morality. Was this the same man who had crisscrossed the Northwest and Northeast in 1859–60, railing against the immorality of slavery and the moral bankruptcy of politicians who claimed not to care whether it was voted up or down? The easy answer is that Lincoln had changed, either because of the job he now held or because he had seen the error of his former position. It is more likely that Lincoln held his same views but had new priorities because of the changed circumstances.

It was not surprising that Lincoln appeared inconsistent about slavery and its role as the principle cause of disunion. Many in the free states were ambivalent toward slavery. It contradicted many principles upon which the country was founded and morally it made both owner and slave victim to a class structure that depended on violence and intimidation. In spite of these sentiments, most white Americans regarded blacks as inferior and also feared that freed slaves would move north and take jobs from working-class whites. Had the purpose of the war at the outset been the destruction of slavery, many Northerners would not have volunteered for military service.

As it was, they saw the war as a case of unprovoked attack on the national honor.

Many of the Radical Republicans (those antislavery Republicans demanding immediate action against slavery) in Congress were less patient than Lincoln on emancipation. As summer 1861 turned to fall, they became more vocal in their denunciations of the chief executive. On August 30, Major General John C. Frémont, commander of the Western Department in St. Louis, placed Missouri under martial law and ordered that the rebels' slaves be seized and freed. Lincoln told him to make the order conform to the confiscation bill recently passed by Congress. Frémont refused to obey unless Lincoln made the order public, which he did.[12]

Lincoln did not countermand Frémont's order because he opposed in principle what the general was attempting to do. It was the right order, but the wrong time and place. In August 1861, Missouri was not securely in the Union camp, nor was Kentucky or Maryland. Support for the war was delicately balanced on the narrow policy that the Union was perpetual and that states were not free to secede. Lincoln's message to the special session of Congress convened on July 4 referred to the policy of armed neutrality claimed by many in the border states who were not yet prepared to secede, but who also chose not to fight against those who had seceded.

> This would be disunion completed . . . it would be the building of an impassable wall along the line of separation. . . . Yet, not quite an impassable one; for, under the guise of neutrality, it would tie the hands of the Union men, and freely pass supplies among them to the insurrectionists, which it could not do as an open enemy. . . . It would take all the trouble off the hands of secession, except only what proceeds from the external blockade. It would do for the disunionists that which . . . they desire most—feed them well, and give them disunion without a struggle of their own. It recognizes no fidelity to the Constitution, no obligation to maintain the Union; and while very many who have favored it are, doubtless, loyal citizens, it is, nevertheless, treason in effect.[13]

In this message, one of the most important state addresses during his presidency, Lincoln defined the purpose of the war.

What is now combatted, is the position that secession is

consistent with the Constitution—is lawful and peaceful. It is not contended that there is any express law, which leads to unjust, or absurd consequences. The nation purchased, with money, the countries out of which several of these states were formed.[14]

He asked rhetorically if it was just that states formed from lands purchased by the national government could leave the Union without refunding the monies used in their purchase, and if one state could so leave, why could not any other, so that eventually no states would remain to be responsible for the obligation.

> If we now recognize this doctrine, by allowing the seceders to go in peace, it is difficult to see what we can do, if others choose to go, or to extort terms upon which they will promise to remain. . . . It is now for them to demonstrate to the world, that those who can fairly carry an election, can also suppress a rebellion—that ballots are the rightful, and peaceful, successors of bullets; and that when ballots have fairly, and constitutionally, decided, there can be no successful appeal, back to bullets; that there can be no successful appeal, except to ballots themselves, at succeeding elections. Such will be a great lesson of peace; teaching men that what they cannot take by an election, neither can they take it by a war. . . .[15]

It was a theme Lincoln returned to often in defending the government's prosecution of the war.

While Lincoln was carefully trying to manage the Union war effort to assure the maximum possible public support, Frémont's precipitous action could only undermine the base of support Lincoln needed to defeat the insurrection. Lincoln's action countermanding him was justified and restrained. The border states applauded, but Radicals in Congress did not. Senator Charles Sumner of Massachusetts moaned that Lincoln "is now a dictator," and Benjamin F. Wade of Ohio said that the president's views on slavery "could only come of one born of 'poor white trash' and educated in a slave state."[16]

The rift between Lincoln and the Radicals created by the Frémont episode proved to be a great embarrassment and source of concern to the president. He repeatedly assured the Radicals—chiefly through Sumner, who had become his primary liaison with Congress—that they had a common purpose and that only his position restrained him from acting as rapidly as they wanted. Sumner wrote Governor John A. Andrew of Massachusetts that Lincoln "tells me that I am ahead of him only a month or six weeks."[17] Nevertheless, the Radicals became more and more outspoken in their denunciations of Lincoln's indulgence of slavery and generals who would not fight.

The liberation of slaves was of profound legal and historical significance. To emancipate by any means other than those with the strongest constitutional sanction and the broadest base of support would only jeopardize the attempt by undermining the war effort and diminishing the credibility of the government. To attempt emancipation and fail would cripple the liberation effort. The only alternative to a constitutional amendment was an executive decree under Lincoln's authority as a wartime commander in chief. Thus, when Congress passed the first confiscation act in July 1861— it freed slaves used by the South in its war effort—Lincoln approved the measure, though he would have preferred that the border states had been more secure first.[18] In May, Major General Benjamin F. Butler refused a demand to return slaves who had escaped to Union lines at Fortress Monroe, Virginia, declaring them contraband. Lincoln approved Butler's *de facto* policy regarding fugitive slaves.[19]

Between July 1861 and July 1862, Lincoln moved ever closer to the Radicals' position on emancipation. Still concerned about the border states, he settled on a plan for gradual and compensated emancipation approved by a vote of the people or their representatives as a viable solution for those sensitive regions. He also advocated colonization of emancipated slaves, since they would not be accorded equal citizenship. If he could implement such a plan in one of the border states, then perhaps the others would follow. Since Delaware had the fewest slaves and was the border state most securely in the Union camp, he drew up two plans for compensated emancipation there and presented them to its congressman, George P. Fisher. The state legislature did not cooperate. "Our main work is to save the Union and not to meddle with slavery," the Democrats declared. They defiantly denied that Congress had the right to buy slaves, claimed that Delaware could not guarantee a debt depending on the mere pledge of the Federal government, and that when Delawareans concluded to abolish slavery, they would do it in their own way.[20]

Lincoln was discouraged by the Delaware rebuff. Could these people not see the handwriting on the wall? He was trying to represent their best interests while stimulating what would be the most revolutionary act in the history of the presidency. In an April 4, 1864, letter the president explained his thinking regarding his urging the scheme of compensated emancipation on the border states.

> When, in March and May, and July 1862 I made earnest, and successive appeals to the border states to favor compensated emancipation, I believed the indispensable necessity for military emancipation, and arming the blacks would come, unless averted by that measure. They declined the proposition; and I was, in my best judgment, driven to the alternative of either surrendering the Union, and with it, the Constitution, or of laying strong hand upon the colored element. I chose the latter. In choosing it, I hoped for greater gain than loss; but of this, I was not entirely confident. . . . In telling this tale I attempt no compliment to my own sagacity. I claim not to have controlled events, but confess plainly that events have controlled me.[21]

By the end of 1861, the president was clearly undergoing a political metamorphosis. Since July, several Republican senators—chief among them Sumner, Wade, and Zachariah Chandler of Michigan—had sequestered themselves with Lincoln and implored him to free the slaves. They maintained that since the Confederate states were in rebellion, they could no longer rely on the legal protection of the government for their "peculiar institution." They argued that as commander in chief, Lincoln could eradicate slavery, thereby maiming the Confederacy and hastening the end of the war.[22]

The Radicals maintained that slavery was the primary cause of the war, something the president had not yet acknowledged publicly because of the situation in the border states as well as the many loyal unionists whose fervor would be dampened by focusing on emancipation. The Radicals argued that it was absurd to fight a war without attacking slavery. Otherwise, the next time the South felt the institution was threatened, it would simply secede again.[23]

In his State of the Union address on December 3, 1861, Lincoln for the first time as president publicly criticized slavery and the planters who brought on the war. He characterized the insurrection as a war upon the rights of the people, maintained by a minority that had imposed its will upon the many who owned no slaves. He intimated that this policy would eventually lead to despotism. He extolled the virtues of capitalism and its built-in incentives to the hired laborer to become first an independent contractor, and eventually an employer himself. "This is the just, and generous, and prosperous system, which opens the way to all, and consequent energy, and progress, and improvement of condition to all."[24]

Lincoln also called for the diplomatic recognition of Haiti and Liberia, both of which he was considering for his colonization idea, and suggested colonization would provide for slaves who would become wards of the government under the Confiscation Act.[25]

The philosophical dilemma that dominated Lincoln's thinking at this point also was revealed in this address:

> In considering the policy to be adopted for suppressing the insurrection, I have been anxious and careful that the inevitable conflict for this purpose shall not degenerate into a violent and remorseless revolutionary struggle. I have, therefore, in every case, thought it proper to keep the integrity of the union prominent as the primary object of the contest on our part, leaving all questions which are not of vital military importance to the more deliberate action of the legislature. . . . I have adhered to the act of Congress to confiscate property used for insurrectionary purposes. If a new law upon the same subject shall be proposed, its propriety will be duly considered. The Union must be preserved, and hence, all indispensable means must be employed. We should not be in haste to determine that radical and extreme measures, which may reach the loyal as well as the disloyal, are indispensable.[26]

Lincoln had revealed himself as a constitutional purist. Social and political change were within the realm of Congress. Whether or not he agreed that it helped the war effort, Lincoln approved the first confiscation act. He also suggested that if Congress passed a second confiscation act that extended to the property of all those "adhering to the rebellion," as opposed to merely those whose slaves supported the rebel war effort, then he would consider approving it as well, though it would violate his notions of due process.[27] This was significant, since Lincoln was committing himself to a policy that would reach the overwhelming majority of slaves. The earlier measure affected only those slaves who were actually being used by the Confederate military.

At any rate, Lincoln continued to push his plan for gradual compensated emancipation in the border states to be followed by colonization. On March 6, 1862, he asked Congress to consider this measure:

> Resolved that the United States ought to cooperate with any state which may adopt gradual abolishment of slavery, giving to such state pecuniary aid, to be used by such state in its discretion, to compensate for the inconveniences public and private, produced by such change of system.[28]

This was the first emancipation proposal ever submitted to Congress by a president, and it created a sensation.[29] Even if Lincoln had not directly linked the war with slavery, he implied the connection. Read with his veiled threat in December that "the Union must be preserved, and hence, all indispensable means must be employed," it suggested that he was prepared to go much further than his modest proposal for Delaware. All but the most radical Republicans welcomed the message. Horace Greeley on March 7 expressed the attitude of the antislavery community:

> This message constitutes of itself an epoch in the history of our country. It has no precedent; we trust it may have many consequences. It is the day-star of National dawn. . . . The 6th of March will yet be celebrated as a day which initiated the Nation's deliverance from the most stupendous wrong, curse and shame of the Nineteenth Century. Years may elapse before the object boldly contemplated in this Message shall be fully attained; but let us never harbor a doubt that it will ultimate in a glorious fruition.[30]

Three times between March and July, the president met with border state congressmen to urge them to endorse his program. At their last meeting on July 12, he warned them that it was now impossible to restore the Union with slavery intact and that his plan was the only alternative to a more drastic move against slavery. He listened in disbelief as they claimed the plan would cost too much, that it would only whip the flames of rebellion, that Congress lacked the constitutional authority to compensate slaveholders, and that it would cause dangerous discontent within their states.[31]

Lincoln had learned that even loyal slaveholders would never voluntarily give up slavery. If abolition was to be realized, he would have to act himself. He could no longer avoid the responsibility and, after the events of the first half of 1862, he was no longer so inclined toward toleration and understanding. The war was taking its toll on him as well as the nation.[32]

The military situation was not going well, either. In April, word arrived of the Battle of Shiloh in West Tennessee. The casualties were seven times those at either Bull Run or Wilson's Creek, a Union defeat fought in Southwestern Missouri in August 1861. Few people, certainly not Lincoln, had envisioned such slaughter. The seemingly endless patience and tolerance of this president was being severely tested. Shiloh had surpassed every previous armed struggle in the country's history and both sides continued to escalate the conflict.

Lincoln's biggest headache during this time was the general in chief of the Army, Major General George Brinton McClellan, who would oppose him in the 1864 election. McClellan, thirty-five, had risen rapidly through the officer corps to the highest office in the military. At the moment of the nation's greatest peril, he commanded the best-equipped and most literate army that had ever been assembled. He had the support of an adoring public and a desperate government. But McClellan had an ego that knew no bounds.[33]

Following his appointment as general in chief in August 1861, McClellan whipped the Army of the Potomac into shape and streamlined its organization with the skill and precision of a symphony conductor. Unfortunately, he was reluctant to commit it to battle, and the more Lincoln gently prodded him, the more aloof McClellan became.[34]

The Radicals who attacked Lincoln on the slavery issue now joined in on military affairs. Wade, chairman of the Senate Committee on the Conduct of the War, had developed a barely restrained contempt for the president and his administration. He wrote Chandler that "you could not inspire Old Abe, [William H.] Seward, [Salmon P.] Chase, or [Edward] Bates with a galvanic Battery," referring respectively to the secretaries of state and the treasury, and the attorney general. It might be useful, he suggested, if the rebels seized the capital and captured the president and his Cabinet. Wade wrote that Lincoln was a fool and Chandler called him "timid, vacillating, and inefficient."[35]

On December 31, the committee met with the president regarding McClellan. Wade told Lincoln, "You are murdering your country by inches in consequence of the inactivity of the military and the want of a distinct policy in regard to slavery."[36] Members of the committee were not the only ones who leveled criticism, often publicly, at the president. Pennsylvania Representative Thaddeus Stevens described Lincoln's plan for compensated emancipation as "the most diluted, milk-and-water gruel proposition that was ever given to the American nation."[37]

On the other hand, Democrats, conservative Republicans, and even McClellan attacked Lincoln for any steps he took that linked slavery with the war. On November 17 McClellan wrote, "I went to the White House shortly after tea, where I found 'the original gorilla' about as intelligent as ever. What a specimen to be at the head of our affairs now!"[38] He often referred to Lincoln as a gorilla and criticized his abilities and motives. Ironically, Lincoln was at the same time defending McClellan from the Radicals, who were calling for a more energetic replacement. It did not help matters when the Army of the Potomac finally demonstrated against the Confederate defenses at Manassas, only to find empty trenches and "quaker guns," logs that had been painted and then erected so as to resemble large artillery pieces.[39]

McClellan had for months deferred attacking south from Washington because, according to his intelligence, the Confederate positions were extremely formidable.[40] Now the anti-McClellan faction raised an even greater cry for his removal. At one point Wade and others confronted Lincoln and demanded McClellan's removal. When Lincoln asked Wade who he should put in command, the senator responded, "Well, anybody." Lincoln countered, "Wade, anybody will do for you, but not for me. I must have somebody—I must use the tool I have."[41]

Then McClellan proposed an unorthodox plan to float his entire army down to Tidewater, Virginia, and land it on the Peninsula, which runs between the York and James rivers. The army would then be only seventy miles from Richmond and southeast of the city, while much of the Confederate army would have to remain north of the capital to protect it from attack by forces remaining in Washington. Lincoln, unimpressed with the plan but eager to get McClellan into action, approved it on the condition that sufficient troops be left in Washington to assure its safety.[42]

McClellan got his ponderous army onto the Peninsula but still refused to engage the inferior Confederate forces, instead performing maneuvers preparatory to a massive artillery barrage. A month after the Army landed on the Peninsula, when McClellan was finally ready to begin the cannonade, the Confederates simply withdrew from their positions. By late June, McClellan had finally maneuvered to within a few miles of Richmond. The Army of Northern Virginia, under General Robert E. Lee, then launched a series of sledgehammer attacks. The Seven Days battles that resulted drove the Union army in an eastward arc from the outskirts of Richmond to

Harrison's Landing on the James River, where it huddled under the protection of Navy gunboats. Assuming that McClellan would never attack under such circumstances, Lee headed north and inflicted a serious defeat on Union forces at the Second Battle of Manassas in August.[43]

Lincoln, who had ordered McClellan and his army to return to Washington before Second Bull Run, once again began preparing the capital for an anticipated Confederate assault. Although there had been significant Union victories in the West, including the capture of such cities as New Orleans; Memphis and Nashville, Tennessee; and Corinth, Mississippi, international attention was focused on Virginia, where the North had not won a single victory. Britain was seriously considering recognizing the Confederate government, and if it did, France and other European nations could follow suit.

The Seven Days battles had resulted in more than 35,000 casualties. The northern press printed accounts of thousands suffering in field hospitals, small mountains of amputated limbs outside of surgical tents, and an army of screaming and dying wounded lying for days untended between the lines.[45] Depending on its political persuasion, the press variously blamed Lincoln, Secretary of War Edwin M. Stanton, McClellan, or the Radicals. However, with each reverse, the demand to change the goal of the war increased. Lincoln continued to move toward attacking slavery as the root cause of the rebellion. On April 8 the United States joined in a treaty for greater suppression of the international slave trade; on April 13 Lincoln approved a new article of war prohibiting the return of fugitive slaves; and on April 16 he signed the bill for the abolition of slavery in the nation's capital, which recognized and applied the principles of compensation and colonization that he had encouraged.[46] This last piece of legislation was close to Lincoln's heart, since he as an unknown first-term congressman in 1847 had attempted to bring about the reform. Now, at last, a major blemish on the capital of the foremost democratic nation in the world had been eliminated. A few months later, he signed a measure establishing diplomatic relations with Haiti and Liberia as well as a bill abolishing slavery in the territories.[47]

Lincoln, however, was not yet prepared to support general emancipation. When Major General David Hunter in May 1862 declared martial law and freed all the slaves within his jurisdiction in South Carolina in the Department of the South, Lincoln revoked the order. Again, however, he gave evidence of his approach toward a sweeping executive order regarding slavery in the rebellious states.

> I further make known that whether it be competent for me, as Commander-in-Chief of the Army and Navy, to declare the slaves of any state or states, free, and whether at any time, in any case, it shall have become a necessity indispensable to the maintenance of the government, to exercise such supposed power, are questions which, under my responsibility, I reserve to myself, and which I can not feel justified in leaving to the decision of commanders in the field.[48]

The Radicals, particularly Sumner, were disturbed. He despaired that the president was reverting to his save-slavery policies of 1861. Chase wrote to Greeley, "I have not been so sorely tried by anything here . . . as by the nullifying of Hunter's proclamation." Lyman Trumbull, senator from Illinois, Sumner, and others now sponsored another confiscation bill that would liberate the slaves of all who supported the rebellion. It was an implied threat that if Lincoln did not strike at slavery, Congress would. Lincoln threatened a veto because the act would forever extinguish the title to property of the person charged, thus constituting a bill of attainder in violation of the Constitution. He also objected to forfeiting an individual's property "without a conviction of the supposed criminal, or a personal hearing given him in any proceeding."[49] When a joint resolution of Congress was rushed through declaring that the legislation did not apply to acts prior to its passage, nor did it allow "a forfeiture of the real estate of the offender beyond his natural life," Lincoln signed it, despite its continued legal questionability.[50]

It appears likely that when Lincoln revoked Hunter's order, he was considering an emancipation proclamation of his own. Nevertheless, on May 19, 1862, he still clung to the narrow hope that the border states, where he did not have the authority to act unilaterally, might still accept his plan for gradual and compensated emancipation. On July 12 Lincoln met with border state representatives to plead with them one last time to consider his plan. His remarks hinted at his true feelings on the issue. There was division between those pressing for the war to be prosecuted to destroy slavery, he said, and those who supported the Union while opposing the attack on slavery. This division threatened the security of the government, he suggested, but he made it clear that slavery would effectively be extinguished by the war even without specific government interference. Then he spoke of the Hunter incident.

Gen. Hunter is an honest man. He was, and I hope still is, my friend. I valued him none the less for his agreeing with me in the general wish that all men everywhere, could be free. He proclaimed all men free within certain states, and I repudiated the proclamation. He expected more good, and less harm from the measure, than I could believe would follow. Yet in repudiating it, I gave dissatisfaction, if not offence, to many whose support the country cannot afford to lose. And this is not the end of it. The pressure, in this direction, is still upon me, and is increasing. By conceding what I now ask, you can relieve me, and much more, can relieve the country, in this important point. Upon these considerations I have again begged your attention to the message of March last. Before leaving the capital, consider and discuss it among yourselves. You are patriots and statesmen; and, as such, I pray you, consider this proposition; and, at the least, commend it to the consideration of your states and people. As you would perpetuate popular government for the best people in the world, I beseech you that you do in no wise omit this. Our common country is in great peril, demanding the loftiest views, and boldest action to bring it speedy relief. Once relieved, its form of government is saved to the world; its beloved history, and cherished memories, are vindicated; and its happy future fully assured, and rendered inconceivably grand. To you, more than to any others, the privilege is given, to assure that happiness, and swell that grandeur, and to link your own names therewith forever.[51]

Most of the border men rejected his plan, so Lincoln was left with only one choice. The next day on a carriage ride, the president stunned Seward and Navy Secretary Gideon Welles with the announcement that the war could not be won by showing further tolerance toward the rebels. He said that it was "a duty on our part to liberate the slaves," that presidential emancipation was "the last and only alternative," and that it was a military necessity, absolutely essential to the preservation of the union."[52]

Lincoln had actually concluded at least a month earlier to issue an emancipation proclamation. He had been working on a draft he kept in a drawer at the telegraph office where he frequently sought news on military campaigns. He wrote a few sentences each time he was there, then returned it to the drawer when he left. On June 20, he invited Vice President Hannibal

Hamlin for supper at the Soldier's Home. Afterward, the president took Hamlin into the library and informed him that he had decided to liberate the slaves. Then, inviting Hamlin's criticism, he read him a draft of the proclamation and accepted several comments made by the delighted Hamlin.[53]

At a July 22 Cabinet meeting, Lincoln read a draft of the proclamation abolishing slavery in areas currently in rebellion. He also promised as part of the proclamation to enforce the confiscation acts. The proclamation was more far-reaching than anything Congress had attempted. It affected not just the slaves of secessionists in areas of rebellion, but freed those of unionists as well.[54] When Lincoln invited comments, Postmaster General Montgomery Blair pointed out that the country was not ready for such a step and that it would hurt the party in the fall elections. The president was surprised to learn that Chase, the Cabinet Radical, was apprehensive. He feared that it would cause profound financial instability and thereby disrupt the government. Seward vehemently opposed an immediate proclamation because the Union had won no battlefield victories in the East and Europe might view it as "our last shriek on the retreat."[55]

Lincoln accepted Seward's argument and decided to postpone issuance of the proclamation until the Union won a major battle. The man who had at long last concluded to mandate the single most important change in U.S. history could afford to wait a little longer. More important, Lincoln's ideas had evolved into a new way of viewing the nation and what it stood for. He had begun to wonder whether the war raised larger questions than the simple ability of the government to sustain itself. The Radicals had demanded immediate action and condemned his tortoise-like pace, but Lincoln had acted as deliberately as necessary to ensure that this revolutionary act would not be well-intentioned but unsuccessful. When he did act, the stakes were the freedom and dignity of more than three million human beings. His actions also sent a message to the world that the American experiment in free government could survive, perpetuate itself, and come ever closer to the ambitious ideals proclaimed at its birth.

Between July and late September, when the proclamation was finally announced after the Battle of Antietam, Lincoln deliberately gave no indication that a dramatic political event was imminent. On August 14 he had addressed a committee of free black men regarding colonization.

We have between us a broader difference than exists between almost any other two races. Whether it is right or wrong I need not discuss, but this physical difference is a great disadvantage to us both, as I think your race suffer very greatly, many of them by living among us, while ours suffer from your presence.[56]

He pointed out that even the free blacks enjoyed nothing close to equality with white men in any section of the country. He told them that as leaders of the black community in the United States, their support was necessary if he was to establish a nation. He was willing to expend "money intrusted to me," and even though the "Government may lose the money . . . we cannot succeed unless we try."[57]

Perhaps Lincoln foresaw the oppression, subjugation, and exploitation that the freed slaves and their descendants would suffer. For whatever reason, he genuinely believed that the best interests of the nation and both races called for a permanent separation, and his soliciting the voluntary participation of those most likely to make the plan work was typical. His approach appealed to the reason and compassion of others and he assumed that the minds of others worked like his own. Lincoln eventually realized, long before the 1864 election and possibly before the Emancipation Proclamation, that Americans of African descent had roots in American soil as deep as those who were descended from Europeans—that they could no more be uprooted and returned to the mother country (at least not voluntarily, and Lincoln insisted that colonization had to be voluntary) than could the entire population that had descended from settlers who arrived after 1492.

Between the July Cabinet meeting and his announcement of the preliminary Emancipation Proclamation in September, Lincoln's intentions remained secret. From every quarter came entreaties to act, but he continued to respond based upon previous principles. A careless remark made at such a critical juncture could result in the loss of support from tens of thousands of Americans and several important states and, in light of the military situation, the country could not afford to compromise the loyalty of its people at that particular moment.

On September 13, two Protestant ministers representing "Chicago Christians of all denominations" called on Lincoln at the White House. Only a week earlier, as the nation was still recovering from the defeat at Second Bull Run, Lee had led his army into Western Maryland. Now a rebel army was on Union soil, less than two days' march from the capital. It was the darkest moment of the war thus far and Lincoln immediately had to find a commander to drive Lee back into Virginia. To the dismay of many Republican congressmen, Cabinet members, and Republican newspaper editors, he reaffirmed McClellan as commander of the Army of the Potomac. Lincoln apparently believed that only McClellan could restore the confidence of a defeated and dispirited army. After meeting with McClellan, Lincoln made a vow to himself, a covenant with God, he later claimed, that if the Union army won the upcoming contest, he would consider it "an indication of Divine Will" that God had "decided the question in favor of the slaves," and that it would be his duty to "move forward in the cause of emancipation."[58] By the thirteenth, the messages from the army indicated it was closing on the rebel force and a great battle was about to take place. Under such trying circumstances, Lincoln was uncharacteristically but understandably short with the Chicago ministers.

The clergymen presented him with a memorial calling on him to emancipate the slaves. Lincoln responded that religious men of opposite opinions and advice, all purporting to represent divine will, had been approaching him for months claiming to know the proper course to take on slavery. "I am sure that either the one or the other class is mistaken in that belief, and perhaps in some respects both . . . for, unless I am more deceived in myself than I often am, it is my earnest desire to know the will of Providence in this matter. And if I can learn what it is, I will do it!"[59] Lincoln's additional remarks to the ministers raise interesting questions about his thoughts on the eve of issuing the proclamation.

> What good would a proclamation of emancipation from me do, especially as we are now situated? I do not want to issue a document that the whole world will see must necessarily be inoperative, like the Pope's bull against the comet! Would my word free the slaves, when I cannot even enforce the Constitution in the rebel states? Is there a single court, or magistrate, or individual that would be influenced by it there? And what reason is there to think it would have any greater effect upon the slaves than the late law of Congress, which I approved, and which offers protection and freedom to the slaves of rebel masters who come within our lines? Yet I cannot learn that the law has caused a single slave to come over to us. And suppose they could be induced by a proclamation of freedom from me to throw themselves upon us, what should we do with them? How can we feed and care for such a multitude? . . . If, now, the pressure of the war should call off our forces from New

Orleans to defend some other point, what is to prevent the masters from reducing the blacks to slavery again; for I am told that whenever the rebels take any black prisoners, free or slave, they immediately auction them off! They did so with those they took from a boat that was aground in the Tennessee River a few days ago. And then I am very ungenerously attacked for it! For instance, when, after the late battles at and near Bull Run, an expedition went out from Washington under a flag of truce to bury the dead and bring in the wounded, and the rebels seized the blacks who went along to help and sent them into slavery, Horace Greeley said in his paper that the Government would probably do nothing about it. What could I do? . . . Now, then, tell me, if you please, what possible result of good would follow the issuing of such a proclamation as you desire?[60]

Lincoln's decision would affect the lives of millions, and although he had committed himself to act, he still struggled with the awful responsibility. He was therefore impatient with the Chicago ministers, who claimed to be emissaries of the Almighty, while he knew the real decision was about to be made on some battlefield in Western Maryland where thousands more young Americans would die. Lincoln returned to character before parting company from the clergymen.

Do not misunderstand me, because I have mentioned these objections. They indicate the difficulties that have thus far prevented my action in some such way as you desire. I have not decided against a proclamation of liberty to the slaves, but hold the matter under advisement. And I can assure you that the subject is on my mind, by day and night, more than any other. Whatever shall appear to be God's will, I will do. I trust that, in the freedom with which I have canvassed your views, I have not in any respect injured your feelings.[61]

On September 17, nearly 100,000 Americans clashed along Antietam Creek near Sharpsburg, Maryland. By sunset they had recorded the bloodiest day in American history, as more than 4,000 lay dead. In the next two weeks, 4,000 more died of wounds received on that field. On the evening of September 18, Lee quietly abandoned his positions and slipped back across the Potomac River. The invasion had been turned back. The Union had its victory. In Lincoln's view, God had decided the issue in favor of the slaves.[62]

He called a Cabinet meeting for September 22. The excited and tense secretaries knew the historic moment had arrived. The president, perhaps to provide some comic relief, began by reading a chapter from Artemus Ward, a popular humorist of the day.[63] He loved Ward's homespun humor and often used it to fight the melancholy he frequently experienced in the White House. When he finished, he became serious, told the secretaries about the vow he had made to himself "and to his Maker,"[64] and then read from his preliminary Emancipation Proclamation. He said that when Congress convened in December, he would again push for gradual and compensated emancipation in the loyal states along with his voluntary colonization project. As for the Confederate South, if the rebels did not stop fighting and return to the Union by January 1, he would free all slaves in areas that were still actively engaged in rebellion against the government. Further, the executive branch would recognize and maintain the freedom of black people in those states and the Army would enforce the slave liberation sections of the second Confiscation Act. Lincoln invited comments and criticism from the Cabinet members and made several minor changes. The next day, the draft was published.[65]

After that, nobody in the United States looked at the war in the same way. Within six weeks, important elections would be held in every loyal state, particularly in the five most populous ones from Illinois to New York. Republican prospects had already been doubtful. Now a new issue had been injected into the campaign, one that would potentially dwarf all the others. Would Americans continue to support a party that had raised the standard of emancipation next to the guidon of Union as the banner its legions would carry into battle? The outcome of the war, the future of the nation, and the freedom of more than three million people could depend on the answer.

2

"We Assure Freedom to the Free"

The wartime and early postwar activities of the Republican Party revolved around a constant rivalry between two wings. The more active and controversial wing contained the Radicals, also known as Jacobins, Ultras, Vindictives, Unconditionals, and Liberals.[1] Historian T. Harry Williams described them as "aggressive, vindictive, and narrowly sectional" for their frequent stands for social reform, especially their opposition to slavery and their determination to prevent its spread to any new territory. Their vehemence caused them to be dubbed as Radicals. During the war, "they advocated complete emancipation and vigorous prosecution of the war," with the official acknowledgment that "slavery was at the root of the conflict" and therefore justified "the confiscation of so-called 'rebel' property and the employment of Negro troops."[2]

Radicals had no official organizational status and they differed widely on numerous matters, but once the war came, they closed ranks on the issue of immediate and uncompensated emancipation. They distrusted generals who were Democrats, who did not aggressively carry the war to the rebels, or who disagreed with them on slavery. Some of them welcomed the war as enthusiastically as the Southern fire-eaters, and saw it as the only way to destroy slavery. In pursuit of this, they jealously sought to control government and military policy and to a significant degree they succeeded. Though they never were a majority in either chamber of Congress, they played a major role in shaping and implementing government policy during the war.[3]

Non-Radicals were even less monolithic than their Radical contemporaries. They believed the war was being fought primarily to save the Union and that consideration should shape wartime policies. They agreed that slavery was morally wrong and resisted its extension, but they were reluctant to tamper with it unless abolition would directly influence the salvation of the Union. They believed any attack on slavery should involve the voluntary participation of slave states, particularly those that did not secede, and they preferred gradual, compensated emancipation followed by colonization of the freed slaves outside of the United States.[4]

It is difficult to make such statements strongly, since many moderates became increasingly radical as the war dragged on and some of the most doctrinaire Radicals early in the war held moderate positions on compensation and colonization. Most of these party members also were racists to some degree and even though Radicals worked closely with Abolitionists before and during the war, few believed that blacks were the social and intellectual equal of whites or deserved equal rights and opportunities. Most Radicals believed in the efficacy of the Constitution, and felt that short of a domestic insurrection or constitutional amendment, nothing could be done to interfere with slavery in those states where it already existed.

The toughest Radicals in Congress included Senators Charles Sumner of Massachusetts, Benjamin F. Wade of Ohio, Zachariah Chandler of Michigan, and Lyman Trumbull of Illinois, and Representatives Thaddeus Stevens of Pennsylvania, George W. Julian of Indiana, Owen Lovejoy of Illinois, James M. Ashley of Ohio, and later George S. Boutwell of Massachusetts and Henry Winter Davis of Maryland. Leading moderates are more difficult to identify, but included Orville Browning of Illinois in the Senate and Francis P. Blair, Jr., of Missouri in the House. Lincoln has usually been associated with the moderates, though he would have taken issue with that characterization, as his biographer Stephen B. Oates points out:

> Since Lincoln had no ideological image within the party, several people wanted to know where he stood. But Lincoln refused to pin an ideological label on himself—and rightly so. For in 1860 the difference between "radicals," "moderates," and "conservatives" were largely rhetorical, more of degree than of kind. . . . Lincoln himself resisted being categorized as anything but a Republican. If he often called the Republicans a "conservative" party, he meant that in a historical sense—

that they held the same ground as the Founding Fathers when it came to slavery and the inalienable rights of all men to life, liberty, and the pursuit of happiness.[5]

Actually, Lincoln often sympathized with the Radicals and admired them as the genuine patriots and freedom fighters of the Civil War. Once when he was asked to intervene in a spat between Missouri Radicals and conservatives, he took the side of the conservatives. Discussing the matter later with his secretary, John Hay, he said, "I know these Radical men have in them the stuff which must save the State and on which we must rely. If one side must be crushed out & the other cherished, there could be no doubt which side we would choose as fuller of hope for the future. We would have to side with the Radicals."[6] Lincoln told the border state representatives in July 1862 that when he overturned General Hunter's proclamation freeing all slaves in the Department of the South, he "gave dissatisfaction, if not offence, to many whose support the country can not afford to lose."[7] His closest adviser in the Senate, the man he asked to accompany him and Mrs. Lincoln to the second inaugural ball, was Sumner, while one of his closest friends in the House was Lovejoy. It was Sumner who repeatedly went to the White House during the spring and summer of 1862 urging the president to issue the Emancipation Proclamation and whose criticism and cajoling Lincoln always welcomed.

Lincoln's admiration of the Radicals was not generally reciprocated. By the war's end, he had enacted virtually every program, reform, policy, and principle urged by them except for Reconstruction. Most Radicals, nevertheless, vilified Lincoln at one time or another in terms usually reserved for the most dangerous members of the opposition.[8]

It was the tension between the president and the Radicals that defined the political landscape during the war. Without the Southerners, the political process worked with remarkable smoothness and efficiency as a substantial amount of significant progressive legislation was enacted. Almost without exception, Congress enacted proposals the president sought; vetoes were rare. Highly controversial but necessary laws such as the Confiscation Acts, the Militia Act of 1862, the Conscription Act of 1863, the "West Virginia" bill, the Indemnity Act of 1863, and the Thirteenth Amendment, were enacted because of the commonality of purpose between the overwhelmingly Republican Congress and the president.[9] However, the war provoked tremendous emotional strains and many Union leaders knew its consequences would determine the nation's direction far into the future. Therefore, the nuances of when and how political actions were taken and who bore the primary responsibility for them had much greater significance than would be the case in peacetime.

The Radicals' ire was first stimulated before Lincoln took office. He selected Cabinet members who had been his primary competitors for the nomination. The only appointee the Radicals claimed was Salmon P. Chase, the Treasury secretary. One reason Chase lost the nomination in 1860 was that many delegates considered him too radical. William H. Seward, secretary of state, who was later despised by the Radicals because of the conservative influence they felt he exerted on Lincoln, lost the nomination largely because of the radical reputation he had gained as a senator.[10]

When the war began, Lincoln did little the Radicals considered timely or sufficient. Even before Congress convened in July 1861, certain members began lobbying for a statement defining slavery as the cause of the war and for using the insurrection as a means of abolishing slavery in the Confederacy. They also urged the use of the military to liberate runaway slaves and the recruitment of black soldiers. When Lincoln overturned the proclamation of John C. Frémont in Missouri, the Radicals "reacted with fury."[11] The general was later dismissed for incompetence and malfeasance, charges that even Chandler acknowledged, but the Radicals continued to denounce the president at mass meetings.[12]

In December 1861, Secretary of War Simon Cameron, soon to be dismissed for incompetence and fraud, called for arming slaves and enlisting them in the military. This came while the president was preparing to propose compensated emancipation and colonization to border state congressmen. Also at the time, Kentucky and Missouri were more under rebel control than Union.[13] Lincoln had already agreed to enlist blacks in the Navy, because it was not a presence in the border states, but he would not risk offending border state unionists by the presence of armed blacks in uniform. The Radicals adopted Cameron as their newest hero, fully realizing that his administration of the War Department was questionable. When Lincoln replaced him on January 15, the president was saved from further Radical criticism only by the appointment of Edwin M. Stanton, a man of decided Radical persuasion.[14]

The Radicals also faulted the president in his conduct of the war. The Committee on the Conduct of the War, an ad hoc group created late in 1861, became the Radicals' vanguard for questioning the military activities of commanding officers and the loyalty of soldiers and civilians alike. The committee castigated Lincoln for his failure to relieve McClellan and later

Major General George Gordon Meade, the victor at Gettysburg, but it warmly embraced such commanders as Irvin McDowell, John Pope, and Joseph Hooker, who were in charge when the Union suffered three disastrous defeats.[15] The Radicals in general and the committee in particular unrelentingly pursued a more vigorous and purposeful prosecution of the war. That was understandable, but they often acted on the notion that Lincoln was incompetent, weak, and influenced by conservatives such as Seward, Postmaster General Montgomery Blair, and Thurlow Weed, the Republican political boss of New York and editor of the Albany *Evening Journal.* When Lincoln took political action of which they approved, such as issuing the Emancipation Proclamation, the Radicals and the Abolitionists gladly accepted the credit and assumed that the president would never have acted had it not been for their constant pressure.[16]

The Radicals credited Lincoln with limited political courage, and whenever he refused to accommodate them, they assumed it was because of conservative advice. Since Seward was Lincoln's closest friend in the Cabinet, and since he had advised Lincoln to postpone issuing the Emancipation Proclamation in July 1862, he became the target of Radical wrath. The impression of Seward's undue influence over the president was reinforced by the resident Radical in Lincoln's Cabinet, Salmon Chase, who "had long been complaining that the Cabinet did not meet as a unit."[17] Chase intimated to his Radical Congressional friends that Seward was a malignant influence on the president and was responsible for administrative bunglings.[18] The confrontation came on December 18, 1862.

Union morale was low after the disastrous defeat at Fredericksburg, Virginia. The press began casting about for scapegoats, and Republicans in Congress took up the cause. On December 16 and 17 Republican senators met and, fortified with information provided by Chase and Sumner, determined that Seward was to blame for the government's failures and must be replaced. That the senators concluded that Seward, whose duties were limited to foreign policy, was primarily responsible for the failure of the nation's armies, indicated their desperation or the extent to which Congress and the Radicals tried to influence the president in his conduct of the war. Probably it was both. A delegation of the committee met with the president on December 18 and presented a litany of offenses against the administration in general and Seward in particular. Insisting upon a more vigorous prosecution of the war, the committee presented a paper calling for unity in the Cabinet and the concurrence of ministers and generals. Wade blamed recent defeats on the presence of so many Democratic officers in the army, and James Grimes, a republican senator from Iowa, remarked that the secretary of state had lost the confidence of the country.[19]

The next day Lincoln called his secretaries together, minus Seward, and described the previous night's meeting. He then said that "he'd consulted with them all on questions of fundamental policy and there had been no lack of unity on the measures they had adopted. They all conceded this was so, including Chase."[20]

That evening the president invited the committee to the White House to meet with the Cabinet—again minus Seward. Lincoln opened the meeting with a speech about Cabinet harmony, saying there had been "no want of unity or of sufficient consultation." He then asked the secretaries individually to back him up.

Chase was trapped. He couldn't change his position now, lest Lincoln and the other secretaries think him the schemer, him the liar. Yes, he confessed, the Cabinet was generally in agreement on important matters. He even admitted that Seward was in earnest in his conduct of the war, that in Cabinet he'd favored the Emancipation Proclamation and hadn't "improperly interfered" in anything.[21]

The senators were surprised and impressed. "Old Abe promises to stand firm & I think he will," wrote Chandler to the governor of Michigan shortly afterward. "We shall get rid of his evil genius, Gov. S., eventually if not now. . . . Without him Old Abe is naturally right."[22]

Lincoln's insistence on making all military policy decisions was reasonable and necessary in his role as commander in chief. Had he allowed military commanders, such as Frémont and David Hunter, to set policy, he would have abdicated his constitutional authority. This would have invited contempt for his administration and insubordination, both civilian and military. The Radicals in Congress realized this but Lincoln never begrudged their criticism, always regarding these men as well-intentioned and loyal patriots. He never challenged them publicly for second-guessing his administration.[23]

The more important consideration for overturning the orders of Frémont, Hunter, and Cameron was the danger of losing the border states. Closely associated with this consideration was the effect a change of the stated purposes for fighting the war would have in the states of the lower North. This region included the five most populous Union states, and the validity of Lincoln's concern was demonstrated in the results of the fall 1862 midterm elections which occurred just weeks after the preliminary Emancipation Proclamation. Four of those five states had returned Republican majorities in 1860. Illinois, with four Republicans and five Democrats, was the exception. These five states had sent sixty-seven Republicans and only thirty-two Democrats to Washington. In the 1862 election, four of the five states returned Democratic majorities to Congress and the fifth, Pennsylvania, returned twelve Republicans and twelve Democrats. The cumulative totals following the 1862 ballot were forty Republicans and fifty-nine Democrats.[24] Despite the evidence that Lincoln's stance on slavery was well-founded, the Radicals never forgave or forgot what they considered to be his tardiness in proclaiming slavery the focus of the Union war effort.

The larger reason behind Radical antagonism toward Lincoln was more likely his constant effort to develop policies jointly with Republicans and War Democrats. War Democrats were those members of the Democratic Party who consistently supported the government's war effort. Lincoln made appointments, primarily in the military sphere, on a non-partisan basis. This was wise and perhaps inevitable, since in 1860 most regular Army officers were Democrats. Lincoln also encouraged the cooperation of many Democrats early in the war, when local enlistment and fund-raising were so important. Though many Democrats who supported the administration in 1861 had become political opponents by the time of or as a result of the Emancipation Proclamation, some War Democrats continued to cooperate with the Republican majority throughout the war. A number of Democrats even changed parties. Nevertheless, the Radicals repeatedly accused the president of preferring to appoint Democrats and conservative Republicans to military command and to many patronage positions.[25]

The Radicals' concern surfaced during the long and painful marriage between the administration and McClellan as the commander of the principal Union army. McClellan was outspoken about his Democratic roots and his determination to defeat the rebels without disturbing slavery. Had McClellan actually inflicted some of the punishing defeats he so often promised, the Radicals might have been able to overlook his political views. However, while McClellan commanded the Army of the Potomac, the only actual attack he launched against the rebels was at Antietam, where he outnumbered Lee by more than two to one, and even then he failed to follow up the battle with a spirited pursuit that might have pinned the rebel army against the Potomac and brought an end to the war. The same complaint was raised against Meade in 1863 after Gettysburg. Both of these generals were Democrats and therefore, suggested the Radicals, they did not seek to defeat the rebels and punish the traitors. The Radicals failed to recognize that these two commanders provided the only two major battlefield victories achieved by the Union in the East.[26]

Lincoln was no less concerned about this lack of aggressiveness; he was infinitely more tolerant than the Radicals, just as he had been when he had declined to dismiss Frémont and Hunter. He did not believe military commanders were traitors because of either their political views or their failures on the battlefield. Yet this issue, and the Radical insistence that they participate in military decision-making, was a constant source of friction, particularly during the first two years of the war.[27]

After Lincoln issued the Emancipation Proclamation, much of the tension between the administration and the Radicals subsided, though it never disappeared. The Radicals sometimes seemed as interested in why commanders fought against the rebels as in how they fared in battle. This was the sort of infighting that Lincoln feared most in his attempts to unify the country. Policies that demanded strict adherence to Radical philosophy were provocative and divisive and endangered the political coalition necessary for victory.

Lincoln primarily sought to prevent his party from splintering. Although the Republicans maintained control of Congress throughout the war, the intensity of feelings about emancipation and the role of blacks in the war and their status in the postwar society led to squabbles that made for some curious political coalitions. Many of the 1862 elections for local and national offices pitted coalitions of moderate Republicans and War Democrats against Radical Republicans, with each side nominating its own candidate and splitting the vote. In some instances, the result was a Democratic victory for a man who could never have won a majority on his own. More often, it resulted in the election of a Republican or "Union" candidate of one persuasion that the other wing refused to support.

In the New York gubernatorial election, for example, the Republicans nominated James S. Wadsworth, who had always been sternly antislavery and who was the overwhelming choice of the New York Radicals. He was nominated on the first ballot over the moderate choice, John A. Dix, a much more experienced politician. Wadsworth was provided a defiantly Radical platform, "hailing emancipation and urging a relentless prosecution of the war."[28] The Democrats nominated an attorney and former governor of the state, Horatio Seymour. Seymour was a moderate who supported the war but "was fiercely hostile to the more advanced administration measures:

the attacks on slavery, the confiscation laws, the draft, and all restrictions on civil rights."[29]

Most of the War Democrats who had been at the Republican/Union convention either split with the party because of Wadsworth or sat the election out. The moderate Republicans, a powerful group led by Thurlow Weed, William Seward, and James Gordon Bennett, editor of the influential New York *Herald*, offered little or no support for the candidate. Seymour, who expected to lose the election, intemperately attacked the administration, assailing emancipation as "a proposal for the butchery of women and children, for scenes of lust and rapine, and of arson and murder, which would invoke the interference of civilized Europe."[30] Wadsworth made his first political appearance in the state only a week before the election, and then he promptly delivered a strongly emancipationist speech. The split among the Republicans and the alienation of many of the War Democrats enabled Seymour to win by a margin of 11,000 votes. Seymour's presence in the New York statehouse during 1863 would prove very discomforting for Lincoln. In this instance Republican infighting had hurt the government's war effort more than the Democratic opposition had. After the 1862 elections, this was precisely the sort of dangerous squabble Lincoln sought to avoid.[31]

1863 ushered in a period of relative harmony between the White House and Congress. The Radicals were generally pleased with the Emancipation Proclamation on January 1, which went even further than its draft by providing that freed slaves could serve in the armed forces. Moreover, in his State of the Union message, Lincoln had proposed three constitutional amendments that would encourage the areas not covered by the proclamation to proceed with voluntary emancipation. More important, he defined the expanded Union war effort and made it clear that the war was now a struggle for the freedom and dignity of all people.

> The dogmas of the quiet past, are inadequate to the stormy present. The occasion is piled high with difficulty, and we must rise with the occasion. As our case is new, so we must think anew, and act anew. Fellow citizens, we cannot escape history. We of this Congress and this administration, will be remembered in spite of ourselves. The fiery trial through which we pass, will light us down, in honor or dishonor, to the latest generation. We say we are for the Union. The world will not forget that we say this. We know how to save the Union. The world knows

we do know how to save it. We—even we here—hold the power and bear the responsibility. *In giving freedom to the slave, we assure freedom to the free*—honorable alike in what we give, and what we preserve. We shall nobly save, or meanly lose, the last best, hope of Earth. Other means may succeed; this could not fail. The way is plain, peaceful, generous, just—a way which, if followed, the world will forever applaud, and God must forever bless [italics added].[32]

Greater harmony between Lincoln and Congress could not prevent growing war weariness. The conflict was entering its third year and the sacrifices were imposing genuine hardships in addition to the terrible casualties. The absence from farms and shops of a million young men was causing tremendous strains on families. As the year began, there also seemed to be little progress in the war. The impression that many sacrifices had been in vain and that the country was no closer to victory than it had been a year earlier was only strengthened when Hooker's "best army on the planet" was whipped in May by Lee and Stonewall Jackson at Chancellorsville.[33]

Then fortunes seemed to change. A Union army achieved a bloodless victory when it outmaneuvered a rebel army in Tullahoma, Alabama, and forced it back into Chattanooga, the last toehold of the Confederacy in Tennessee. In Pennsylvania, the Army of the Potomac under Meade finally defeated Lee and his Army of Northern Virginia at Gettysburg, inflicting nearly 30,000 casualties and permanently rendering it incapable of mounting a major offensive. Ulysses S. Grant finally captured Vicksburg, Mississippi, the last major stronghold on the Mississippi River. In a display of courage and proof that black soldiers could perform as well as their white counterparts, the 54th Massachusetts Infantry, a regiment of black enlisted men and white officers, led a spectacular assault on Battery Wagner guarding the entrance to Charleston Harbor. The 54th, which had distinguished itself in several encounters along the coast of South Carolina and Georgia, led the doomed attack and lost nearly half of its complement, including its commander.[34]

Northerners who had been skeptical of how blacks would perform in battle now read glowing accounts of the conduct of this model black regiment. "Through the cannon smoke of that dark night, the manhood of the colored race shines before many eyes that would not see."[35] This contrasted starkly with the scenes from several days earlier in which white Democratic rioters in New York lynched black people and burned the

Colored Orphan Asylum. As historian James McPherson noted, "Few Republican newspapers failed to point out the moral: black men who fought for the Union deserved more respect than white men who fought against it."[36]

All of the previous confrontations between Lincoln and the Radicals served as background for the split that came over Reconstruction. By mid-1863, it was clear that the North was winning the war. Large portions of Louisiana, Arkansas, and Tennessee were under Union control and as early as the fall of 1862, Lincoln had appointed military governors in those states. He had instructed them to hold congressional elections.[37] Lincoln maintained that secession was not constitutionally possible and the rebellious states had never been out of the Union; the task of Reconstruction was to restore loyal citizens to power.[38] Under this interpretation, the president could prescribe restoration under his authority to suppress insurrections and to grant pardons and amnesty.[39]

Radicals in particular believed that Reconstruction was a function of Congress. Unlike Lincoln, they assumed that these states had sacrificed their rights and had reverted to the status of territories. This idea first arose in December 1860, when Congressman James Hamilton characterized South Carolina's secession as "state suicide."[40] From the moment that Reconstruction arose as an issue, there was a battle over which branch of government would control it. At the heart of the battle was the question over the tone and character of Reconstruction. Should it be stringent and punitive, as many Radicals demanded, or should it be mild and forgiving, as Lincoln and many moderates urged? The manner in which Reconstruction was ultimately implemented would influence the lives of the freedmen after the war. Their ability to survive and flourish in a society where their status had changed from that of property to people would in large measure depend on the extent to which the government committed itself to their protection. Reconstruction became part of the larger issues of emancipation and freedom.

The serious rift, and the one that jeopardized Republican chances in the 1864 election, was initiated by the State of the Union message in December 1863, and finally exploded the following August. In his message, Lincoln announced that a Proclamation of Amnesty and Reconstruction was being issued that day. He granted amnesty to rebels if they would take a loyalty oath, with the exception of high-ranking civil and military officials. The oath included language that indicated Lincoln's commitment to the freedom of the slaves:

> I will . . . abide by and faithfully support all acts of Congress
> passed during the existing rebellion with reference to slaves,
> so long and so far as not repealed, modified, or held void by
> Congress, or by decision of the Supreme Court; and that I will,
> in like manner, abide by and faithfully support all proclamations
> of the President made during the existing rebellion having
> reference to slaves, so long and so far as not modified or
> declared void by decision of the Supreme Court. So help me
> God.[41]

The message was generally well-received by Radical and moderate
Republicans. John Hay wrote, "I never have seen such an effect produced
by a public document. Men acted as if the millennium had come. Chandler
was delighted, Sumner was beaming, while at the other political pole Dixon
and Reverdy Johnson said it was highly satisfactory. . . . None can fail to
realize the regretful tenderness and kindly charity wherewith the Rebel
masses are contemplated by the President."[42]

The New York *Tribune* editorialized, "Though his official term of
service has been rendered anxious and troubled by their treason, he has never
ceased to regard them as deceived and misled, and to desire their speedy
return to loyalty and peace."[43] The *New York Times* suggested that "the
closer it is examined, the more it will be discovered to be completely adapted
to the great end desired. The public mind . . . will accept it as another signal
illustration of the practical wisdom of the President."[44]

Actually, the president had little chance of winning over all of the
Radicals, particularly Sumner, despite Hay's impression of the senator as
"beaming" at the address. In October 1863, in an unsigned article in the
Atlantic Monthly, Sumner denounced the appointment of military governors
in Tennessee, Louisiana, and the Carolinas.[45]

> But if this can be done in four States, where is the limit?
> It may be done in every Rebel State, and if not in every other
> State of the Union, it will be simply because the existence of
> a valid State government excludes the exercise of this
> extraordinary power. But assuming, that, as our arms prevail,
> it will be done in every Rebel State, we shall then have eleven
> military governors, all deriving their authority from one source.
> . . . And this imperiatorial dominion, indefinite in extent, will
> also be indefinite in duration; for if, under the Constitution and
> laws, it be proper to constitute such governors, it is clear that
> they may be continued without regard to time . . . and the whole

region which they are called to sway will be a military empire, with all powers, executive, legislative, and even judicial, derived from one man in Washington. Talk of the "one-man power." Here it is with a vengeance. Talk of military rule. Here it is, in the name of a republic.[46]

Sumner compared Lincoln to Oliver Cromwell, without hinting that the president was trying to restore civil government. Apparently, Sumner planned to bring the chief executive into a debate. Since he and the other Radicals had decided that Lincoln could not be the party nominee in 1864, anything the president could be baited into doing could only help the Radical candidate, whoever he might be.[47] Lincoln was not unaware of Sumner's tactic. "I can do nothing with Mr. Sumner in these matters.... He is making his history with me on this very point.... I think I understand Mr. Sumner; and I think he would be all the more resolute in his persistence . . . if he supposed I were at all watching his course."[48]

Reconstruction was likewise dividing the Cabinet, where the two principal antagonists were, as usual, Seward and Chase. Seward supported the restoration of the seceded states as they were, while Chase adopted the Radical position of treating them as conquered provinces. The timing of this squabble coincided with a rise in the presidential aspirations of the Treasury secretary. Chase had never stopped believing that he had been the best qualified Republican contender in 1860, and had throughout the first term harbored a barely concealed desire to succeed Lincoln.[49] Since he was the only Radical who had a positive national reputation, this longing was not necessarily unrealistic. He had made good use of the substantial patronage available through his Cabinet post and had placed his own portrait on the $1 greenback, millions of which were printed.

As early as October 1863, Attorney General Edward Bates took note of Chase's ambition for the presidency: "I'm afraid Mr. Chase's head is turned by his eagerness in pursuit of the presidency. For a long time back he has been filling all the offices in his own vast patronage, with extreme partisans, and contrives also to fill many vacancies, properly belonging to other departments."[50] Bates' impression was shared by Navy Secretary Gideon Welles: "I think there are indications that Chase intends to press his pretensions as a candidate, and much of the Treasury machinery and the special agencies have that end in view. This is to be regretted. The whole effort is a forced one and can result in no good to himself, but may embarrass the Administration."[51]

The Chase groundswell among the Radicals began to grow after the first of the year. He was the only genuine Radical with any hope of success against the president. The leading Radicals would back Chase if it appeared he could beat Lincoln at the convention and the Democratic nominee in the election. He was a microcosm of the Radical program. He would make no concessions to the South as a basis for peace. Slavery would have to be abolished unconditionally before any peace proposal were considered. Congress, not the president, should dictate the terms of readmission, according to Chase, and determine what measures to take to prevent future secession.

Chase had extensive patronage as secretary of the treasury, and his appointees were active in pursuing his candidacy.[52] James B. Bingham wrote to Governor Andrew Johnson of Tennessee:

> The Secretary of the Treasury has numerous appointees down at Memphis, all whom are understood to be active in labors looking to his selection as the next candidate for the Presidency. Favors are granted with that object in view.[53]

Chase vehemently denied that he had used his position to further his ambitions. "I should despise myself if I felt capable of appointing or removing a man for the sake of the Presidency," he wrote.[54] Yet, his appointments revealed a different story, as on March 5, 1864, George Dennison, a Chase appointee in New Orleans, wrote, "We are forming a Chase Club here and meet for organization next Monday. It will comprise some of the best men of the city of different interests and political affinities. I believe we can control the election of delegates to the National Convention."[55]

As secretary, Chase could seek the support of financial leaders. His business relations with the Cooke brothers, Henry and Jay, were cordial, and Henry Cooke had been a political ally in Ohio. He had devised the bond subscription that financed the war, and Chase could claim him as a tutor in finance and a supporter in politics.[56] He also enjoyed the support of C. H. Ray, a prominent Chicago business executive and part owner of the *Tribune*; John Austin Stevens, president of the Bank of Commerce of New York; and William P. Smith of the Baltimore and Ohio Railroad. Because the Legal Tender Act of 1862 empowered Chase to select certain banks as depositories for public funds, he could curry the favor of major banking interests.[57]

Chase claimed that he was indifferent to the nomination and that he acted only for the public good. Nevertheless, while protesting his personal lack of ambition, he wrote many letters that branded the administration as lacking leadership or purpose. He wrote to the editor of a religious newspaper:

> Had there been here an Administration in the true sense of the word—a President conferring with his cabinet and taking their united judgments, and with their aid enforcing activity, economy, and energy in all departments of public service—we could have spoken boldly and defied the world. But our condition here has always been very different. I preside over the funnel; everybody else, and especially the Secretaries of War and the Navy, over the spigots—and keep them well open, too. Mr. Seward conducts the foreign relations with very little let or help from anybody. There is no unity and no system, except so far as it is departmental. There is progress, but it is slow and involuntary; just what is coerced by the irresistible pressure of the vast force of the people. How, under such circumstances, can anybody announce a policy which can be made respectable by union, wisdom, and courage?[58]

On January 27, he wrote:

> The administration cannot be continued as it is. There is, in fact, no Administration, properly speaking. There are departments and there is a President. The latter leaves administration substantially to the heads of the former, deciding himself comparatively few questions. These heads act with almost absolute independence of each other.[59]

Chase also deluded himself as to his own popularity with the people. In a February 2 letter to an Ohio supporter, he wrote:

> I cannot help being gratified by the preference expressed for me in some quarters, for those who express it are generally men of great weight, and high character, and independent judgment.[60]

In addition to overestimating his own popularity, Chase and many other Radicals underestimated Lincoln's grass-roots strength. Lincoln was so secure about his status that even though he was fully aware of Chase's activities and candidacy, he judged the secretary on the performance of his job, which was outstanding, and discouraged conversation relative to

Chase's other activities. "I have determined to shut my eyes, so far as possible, to everything of the sort," Lincoln wrote. "Mr. Chase makes a good Secretary, and I shall keep him where he is. If he becomes President, all right. I hope we may never have a worse man."[61] The president also wrote, "I am entirely indifferent as to his success or failure in these schemes so long as he does his duty as the head of the Treasury Department."[62]

Early in 1864, a central committee officially launched the Chase candidacy. It soon became apparent that his strength lay primarily in his home state of Ohio. The central committee expanded and became known as the Republican National Executive Committee, with Senator Samuel Pomeroy of Kansas as chairman.[63] Chase was fully aware of the activities of the committee, but the choice of Pomeroy was unfortunate and showed Chase's sloppiness in choosing political intimates. Pomeroy was openly hostile to Lincoln and, as chairman of the Chase committee, orchestrated the drafting and distribution of a confidential circular intended to block the president's renomination. The circular solicited the reader to join in the Chase movement and thereby "elevate the standard of public and private morality, vindicate the honor of the Republic before the world, and in all things make our American nationality the fairest example for imitation which human progress has ever achieved."[64]

On February 22, the circular was printed in the *National Intelligencer*.[65] Chase immediately wrote to Lincoln, assuring him that he had no knowledge of it before seeing it in print.

> I have never wished that my name should . . . be continued before the public a moment after the indication of a preference by the friends of that cause for another. . . . If there is anything in my action or position which in your judgment will prejudice the public interests under my charge, I beg you to say so. I do not wish to administer the Treasury Department one day without your entire confidence.[66]

Lincoln responded that he had not and would not read the circular, that he saw no need to assault Chase's character publicly or to countenance such attacks by anyone else, and assured the Treasury secretary that his continuation in service was not in question.[67]

The Pomeroy Circular effectively destroyed Chase's candidacy. A week after it appeared, Frank Blair, Jr., on leave from the Army to take a seat in Congress, delivered a blistering anti-Chase speech in the House, which among other things charged widespread Treasury Department corruption.[68] Republican state committees, legislatures (including Ohio's), newspapers, and organizations rushed to endorse Lincoln's renomination.[69] Ohio congressmen who had used their franking privilege to send out the circular to constituents now found it necessary to dissociate themselves from the document. A friend wrote to John Sherman, who had mailed out the circular, that "if you were to resign tomorrow, you could not get two votes in the legislature provided it could be shown that you have been circulating such stuff as this."[70] Sherman published a letter in the Cincinnati *Daily Gazette* explaining that he had been the victim of an unfortunate mistake or of a deliberate deception.[71]

The pro-Lincoln declaration of the Ohio General Assembly was the final blow to Chase's hopes. On March 5, Chase wrote to James C. Hall, a home-state supporter: "I wrote to you briefly not long ago . . . that, should our friends in Ohio manifest a preference for another, I should accept their decision. . . . The recent action of the Union members of our Legislature indicates such a preference. It becomes my duty, therefore, . . . to ask that no further consideration be given to my name."[72]

Chase continued to harbor aspirations for the candidacy, however, and some Radicals continued to promote him. But as a potential Republican nominee, he was out of the running. Horace Greeley of the New York *Tribune*, recognizing the inevitability of Lincoln's renomination at the June convention, had as early as February 1864 sought the postponement of the convention until September, insisting that winning the war should take precedence over winning the election. At the same time, Greeley was promoting the candidacies of Chase and Generals Benjamin F. Butler and Frémont.[73] He had enlisted the support of William Cullen Bryant of the New York *Evening Post*, and such prominent Republicans as Governor John Andrew of Massachusetts, war correspondent Whitelaw Reid of the Cincinnati *Daily Gazette*, Richard Henry Dana, and Governor Andrew G. Curtin of Pennsylvania.[74] However, by May these men had accepted the inevitable and until the controversy created by Lincoln's veto of the Wade-Davis bill in July, efforts toward a September convention for the most part ceased.

Probably Grant was the only man in the country who enjoyed sufficient reputation and popularity to challenge the president going into the convention. Conservative editor James Gordon Bennett of the New York *Herald* proposed Grant as a nominee, but Grant said that the country needed Lincoln and that his defeat would be a "great national calamity."[75] Some of the

Radicals considered Butler, the politician-turned-general, but he was too uncertain. Although most Radicals would have supported him as general in chief to replace Major General Henry W. Halleck, they would not seriously consider him for the presidency.[76]

When the Republicans assembled in Baltimore, it was as a show of support for the incumbent. Lincoln did not attend the convention, but his secretary John Nicolay did, and he made clear the president's wishes on important questions. The first major issue arose when, in the opening address, Senator Edwin D. Morgan of New York called for a constitutional amendment prohibiting slavery. This was greeted by applause and cheering. Lincoln had suggested the amendment to Morgan several days before the convention.[77] The platform, which was adopted without serious opposition, also called for "harmony . . . in our national councils," declared that only those who "cordially endorse the principles proclaimed in these resolutions and which should characterize the administration of the Government" were worthy,[78] and urged the protection of black troops, who were dealt with harshly under Confederate policy.[79]

Lincoln was nominated on the first ballot, 484 to 22. The Missouri delegation, which had voted for Grant, changed its vote, making the nomination unanimous. The only remaining business was the nomination of a vice presidential candidate. The candidates were the incumbent, Hannibal Hamlin; Governor Andrew Johnson of Tennessee; Congressman Daniel S. Dickinson; and former Secretary of War Joseph Holt. Though Lincoln's wishes are still unclear and remain the subject of a continuing controversy today, the convention chose Johnson, a War Democrat and the only member of Congress who did not leave when his state seceded. He was a compromise candidate, as he had dealt harshly with rebels in Tennessee but shared Lincoln's approach to Reconstruction.[80] The Union Party, as it was called, now had a ticket. It was nearly three months before the nation learned of the Democratic candidate and what platform he would run on. Also, as the party was nominating Lincoln and Johnson, nobody knew that less than 150 miles from the convention site, the Army of the Potomac had just suffered the worst defeat of the war by a Federal army at Cold Harbor, Virginia. Bad news would continue to visit the Union candidates until it appeared that neither they nor the party stood any prospect of winning.

3

"And the Niggers Where They Are"

In 1864 the Democratic Party well understood the twin concepts of defeat and demoralization. After having dominated politics during most of the nineteenth century, the slavery controversy had resulted in defections beginning in the 1840s. The party leadership had tried to be noncommittal, since more than a third of its strength was in slave states, and no issue could divide a group more quickly.[1]

Democratic fortunes reached their lowest point in 1860–61 with the election of Lincoln and the secession of the deep South. When Congress convened in July 1861, "Democratic senators and congressmen held no caucus, offered no candidate for speaker, and supported the drastic war measures taken by Lincoln calling forth the militia, increasing the regular army and navy and proclaiming a blockade of southern ports." After the Southern senators and representatives departed, fewer than one-fourth of each house were Democrats. In 1861, they lacked the political strength to form even a loyal opposition. Moreover, the Democrats were without a prominent national leader.[2]

The last loyal Northern Democrat of any national prominence in 1861 was Senator Stephen A. Douglas of Illinois, the star-crossed candidate in the 1860 presidential contest. His last important political act was a series of addresses to Democrats in Ohio and Illinois, including one delivered to a large crowd in Chicago on May 1, 1861, in which he said, "Every man must be for the United States or against it. There can be no neutrals in this war; only patriots or traitors." Previously he had said of Lincoln's inaugural address, "I am with him." He told the Illinois General Assembly, "Whoever is not prepared to sacrifice party and organizations and platforms on the altar of his country, does not deserve the support or countenance of honest people."[3]

Douglas died on June 3, 1861. His final addresses had been perhaps the most important service he rendered to his country as a statesman, for numerous Democrats eagerly adopted the view. Many War Democrats merged with the Republican Party; others retained their political independence but supported the administration's war measures and supplied their share of officers and men to the Army. Alexander K. McClure, a journalist and Republican Party boss in Pennsylvania during the war, claimed that Douglas had rendered Lincoln "the greatest service of all at the beginning of the war. When the Republican leaders were hesitating and criticizing their president, Douglas came to the front with all his characteristic courage and sagacity, and was probably the most trusted of all the Senators at the White House." During his speaking tour, Douglas converted to the administration's position such important Illinois Democrats as congressmen John A. Logan and William Richardson and editor Cyrus McCormick of the Chicago *Times*. In the Indiana Assembly, Democratic Minority Leader Horace Heffren not only reversed his position on the war but, "as a gesture of cooperation, he nominated for re-election the Republican Speaker of the previous session."[4]

Douglas's death left a void in the Democratic leadership. Most Northern Democrats of national prominence who had not previously defected to the Republicans had retired or were dead. The Democratic Party became splintered and ineffective. Swept from office throughout the North, it operated primarily on the local level during most of the war. Relegated to the unfamiliar position of a minority party, it was much less effective than the Republican Party in working out its divisions and presenting a united front. The major division was over the war itself and spawned two wings— the Peace Democrats and the War Democrats. Even within these two groups, there were splits, prominently among the War Democrats, a number of whom formed coalitions with the Republicans. Many other Democrats supported the administration's war effort but differed sharply on racial policy, confiscation, conscription, suppression of civil rights, economic and fiscal policies, and Reconstruction.[5]

The War Democrats who did not align with the Republicans represented the party's best hope to unseat the majority party which they felt was mishandling the war. Willing to prosecute the war to restore the Union, these Democrats readily denounced the Republicans for their revolutionary racial policy, bungling of military operations, and the suppression of constitutional rights. This group has generally been referred to as the Regular Democrats or as Conditional War Democrats.[6] Regular Democrats rejected any coalition with the despised Republicans and attempted to re-establish the traditional Democratic majority minus members who had entered into a Union coalition.

However, Regular Democrats had little opportunity to woo back Union Democrats because a third faction threatened the party's existence. As the party had grown and assumed a dominant role in politics, one branch of the family tree had developed in an aberrant manner. While the various schools of free-state Democrats had branched separately, all generally accepted the perpetuity of the Union and the illegality of secession—all save one. They were known as Doughfaces before the war—Northern men with Southern sympathies—and Copperheads during the war because they were compared to the deadly snake. This group was based largely in the Ohio River Valley of the Midwest and most members had Southern roots. They strongly sympathized with the South's racial policy and assumed a right of secession, or at the least they opposed forceful suppression of the rebellion. They existed from the beginning of the war but had remained largely silent during the patriotic outpouring following Fort Sumter. It was only after the initial military reverses and the arrest of many Northerners that the Copperheads, or Peace Democrats, publicly began condemning the Republicans, the administration, and the war.[7]

Peace Democrats ranged from the fifth columnists of the Knights of the Golden Circle and the Sons of Liberty to vehement vocal opponents of the war and administration. They were not limited to the Midwest; they also were active in New York, Pennsylvania, New Jersey, and New England. Still, they were strongest among Midwesterners, who had shared social and economic interests with the South before the war.[8]

Nearly all of the party leaders identified with the War Democrats or Regular Democrats early in the war, so Peace Democrats exercised little real national leadership. They were despised by the war supporters in Congress and in turn castigated the opposition, often walking a tightrope between legitimate political opposition and outright sedition. For example, there was a fine line separating the condemnation of the conscription policy from the outright encouragement of draftees to desert or resist induction into the army. Throughout the war, Copperhead politicians and editors pressed such limits to the extreme, then protested loudly the violation of their civil and constitutional rights. It was this constant lurking in the shadowy area separating legitimate dissent from treason that made them vulnerable to the label of "traitors."[9]

Though arbitrary arrests and suppression of rights gave the Copperheads effective weapons to use against the Republicans, the preliminary Emancipation Proclamation provided them with a new issue. They unleashed vitriolic racist rhetoric designed to stimulate the fears of Northerners. During the 1862 campaign, a supporter of Copperhead leader Clement L. Vallandigham expanded on the Democratic campaign theme of that year: "The Constitution as it is, the Union as it was, *and the Niggers where they are.*"[10] This flagrantly negative campaign tactic may have offended more voters than it won. Nevertheless, it became the predominant theme in Democratic politics throughout the remainder of the war, particularly in 1864.

The leadership of the Peace Democrats devolved primarily upon the editors of the anti-war press, as the war supporters often silenced particularly effective Copperhead politicians in Congress and the statehouses. This was accomplished by expulsion, as in the case of Indiana senator Jesse Bright, who had corresponded with Jefferson Davis, or by gerrymandering, as was done to Vallandigham in 1862. There were many Northern newspapers that, if not outright pro-Southern, were opposed to the war as a means of restoring the Union. Since few Northern newspapers were actually suspended during the war, editors largely said what they wanted. Because newspapers were the major source of news beyond word of mouth, they were widely read and tremendously influential on public opinion.[11]

Several Copperhead newspapers had sizable followings. Perhaps the most virulently anti-Lincoln, anti-war, pro-slavery newspaper of the North was the weekly Columbus (Ohio) *Crisis*, published by Samuel Medary, an elderly but fanatical pacifist, Quaker, and Democrat. In Pennsylvania, the *Jeffersonian* was the most blatant and pro-slavery Copperhead journal, and the Philadelphia *Age* was a consistent and partisan opponent of the administration and the war effort. In Michigan, the Detroit *Free Press* was the leading newspaper of the Peace Democracy, and no Northern newspaper engaged in more rhetorical abuse of the administration than the La Crosse

(Wisconsin) *Democrat,* whose editor once expressed a willingness to himself assassinate Lincoln. In New York City the *Freeman's Journal,* the *Daily News,* the *Journal of Commerce,* and the *Weekly Day-Book* were all organs of Peace Democrats.[12]

Democratic political fortunes during the war peaked in the 1862 midterm elections. Democrats scored impressive gains in Congress and statehouses, particularly in five of the most populous states. They returned Democratic majorities to Congress in Illinois, Indiana, Ohio, and New York, and divided equally with the Republicans in Pennsylvania. In New York, the Democratic gubernatorial candidate, Horatio Seymour, bested Republican James S. Wadsworth. Fortunately for the Republicans, the governors' mansions and statehouses in Ohio and Pennsylvania were not at stake in 1862; however, the Democrats did gain legislative majorities in the Illinois and Indiana statehouses. Historians have regarded the elections as a near disaster for the Republicans and have declared that "the verdict of the polls showed clearly that the people of the North were opposed to the Emancipation Proclamation."[13] However, the Democratic celebrations may have been based upon a false reading of the results.

There were several reasons for the Democratic gains. First, during the 1862 elections, the Union war fortunes were at their nadir and, in spite of successes at Antietam and Perryville, Kentucky, the atrocious casualties and Mathew Brady's widely viewed photo collection, "The Dead of Antietam," had contributed to the growing Northern malaise. Many war supporters, unable to bring themselves to vote for Democrats, reflected their loss of faith in the Republicans by not voting at all. The Cincinnati *Gazette* concluded that the people were depressed by the conduct of the war and by the squandering of national resources without progress.[14]

Second, in 1862 few of the nearly one million Union troops participated in state elections. Absentee voting had not yet been enacted by state legislatures and the furloughing of troops in the midst of Confederate invasions in both theaters of the war was impossible. Thus hundreds of thousands of probable Republican voters did not vote. It was an interesting irony that occurred to many Republicans that the one group of eligible voters almost universally denied participation in the election were those who daily risked their lives for the republic. Union politicians stated this argument repeatedly in seeking absentee voting legislation before the 1864 election.[15]

Also, the outcome of nearly all of the elections in the critical states in

1862 was very close. In Pennsylvania, the Democratic margin of victory was less than 4,000 votes; in Ohio, less than 6,000; and in Indiana, less than 10,000. Even in New York, where more than 600,000 votes were cast, Seymour won by less than 10,000. The participation of a fraction of the Union soldiers from each of these states could have more than overcome these margins.[16]

The reliance of so many historians on the administration's revolutionary change in racial policy as an explanation for the Democratic successes does not square with the facts. Undoubtedly many people were upset by the Emancipation Proclamation. Most of them, though loyal citizens who supported the war, probably would not have voted Republican anyway. Though some voters switched to the Democrats or did not vote at all, others rallied to the Republican banner because of the Proclamation. The former group was probably more numerous than the latter, but not so much so as to account for a major alteration of political alignments in these important states.[17]

Probably the arrest of citizens was as important as the Emancipation Proclamation in influencing the vote against the Republicans. The Democratic gubernatorial candidate of New York wrote, "I am glad to see that you follow up the subject of illegal arrests. It must be made the issue."[18] Most Americans in 1862 were jealously protective of their civil and constitutional liberties and inherently suspicious of a government that claimed they must be sacrificed because of the conflict. Attacks on arbitrary arrest, the suspension of the writ of habeas corpus, the closing of opposition newspapers, and the proposed conscription of young men proved to be fertile ground for attacking the administration in 1862 and the remainder of the war. A lively political campaign featuring constitutional issues would have been valuable, informative, and stimulating. Sadly, many Democratic bosses ignored this tactic and took up racist harangues intended to frighten and mislead voters.

The greatest Northern fear was that once freed, former slaves would migrate north in large numbers. Two days before the preliminary Emancipation Proclamation was issued, the Philadelphia *Inquirer* pointed out that while New England and upper New York would receive few liberated slaves, states further south might get many. The Ohio legislature in early 1862 had tabled legislation prohibiting further movement of blacks into that state by a vote of only fifty-three to fifty-one. Samuel Sunset Cox, an Ohio congressman who became a Peace Democrat in the wake of the Emancipation Proclamation, trumpeted a warning that Ohio would become the chief haven for the slaves of Virginia and Kentucky. That summer, race riots broke out in Cincinnati and Toledo, where people feared competition for jobs of poor white laborers.[19] There also were riots in Illinois and Indiana.

Seymour's election in New York was the most significant Democratic electoral gain in 1862. He became the chief executive of the most populous Union state, with enormous potential for helping or hindering military recruitment. The respect Lincoln accorded him was indicated by a letter dated March 23, 1863. Lincoln pointed out that though they did not know each other, their respective positions called for them to become better acquainted. Lincoln as the head of a nation in peril and Seymour as the head of the biggest state of that nation had to share an interest in maintaining the nation's life. Whatever differences they had, cooperation was necessary if the nation were to survive.[20]

Seymour was a Regular Democrat and though he supported the war to restore the Union, he agreed with the president on little else. An attorney from Utica, he was "a gentleman of wide reading, winning manners, and pure life" who was "hard-working, conscientious, and talented." However, Seymour could be intemperate, acrid, fiercely partisan, and unrestrained in his hostility toward the opposition. At the state Democratic Convention in 1862, he called emancipation "a proposal for the butchery of women and children, for scenes of lust and rapine, and of arson and murder, which would invoke the interference of civilized Europe."[21] Seymour quickly discovered just how much he and the president differed.

On March 3, 1863, Lincoln signed legislation providing for the first draft in U.S. history. The Confederate government, which felt the manpower shortage earlier than the Federal government, had acted similarly almost a year previously. Though the bill became effective in March, the first enrollment was delayed until May 25. In New York, it was postponed until July 11, 1863, and then it resulted in a riot.[22]

The timing was particularly bad for an urban uprising, for virtually every militia, volunteer, and regular Army unit near New York had been sent toward Pennsylvania in response to Lee's invasion. Thus, on the thirteenth when the riot began, the city depended upon police and private volunteers. For four days, a mob of chiefly Irish laborers ransacked the city, hanging or beating black people, gutting and burning the Colored Orphan Asylum, murdering soldiers in uniform home on leave, and plundering and burning tenements and boarding houses in the black ghetto.[23]

Troops eventually arrived and ended the riot, but not before at least a dozen free blacks had been murdered and hundreds more had lost their homes and property. At the height of the riot, Seymour expressed sympathy for the rioters. "Let me assure you that I am your friend," he told them, and "I am here to show you a test of my friendship. I wish you now to separate as good citizens and you can assemble again whenever you wish to do so." He assured them that he would see to their rights.[24] In addition to this ill-considered statement, the city's Democratic press encouraged the rioters. Manton Marble's *World* said the draft law "could not have been ventured upon in England even in the black days when press gangs were filling the English warships."[25] In like manner, by printing seditious newspaper articles, the *Daily News* of Ben Wood, brother of former Mayor Fernando Wood, was tiptoeing that tightwire between legitimate opposition and treason.[26]

The draft was suspended in New York City for more than a month. On August 3, Seymour wrote Lincoln, charging that the administration was hostile to New York, that the draft was harsh and unfortunate, that the quotas assigned to New York districts were disproportionate, and that he was convinced the law was unconstitutional. He asked the president to suspend conscription in his state until the courts could examine the validity of the law.[27]

On August 8, Lincoln responded in his measured and practical manner. Though much of the communication related to the issue of New York's quotas, the president's conclusion showed how illogical was the governor's request.

> I can not consent to suspend the draft in New York, as you request, because, among other reasons, time is too important. . . . I do not object to abide a decision of the United States Supreme Court . . . on the constitutionality of the draft law. In fact, I should be willing to facilitate the obtaining of it; but I cannot consent to lose the time while it is being obtained. We are contending with an enemy who, as I understand, drives every able-bodied man he can reach, into his ranks, very much as a butcher drives bullocks into a slaughterpen. No time is wasted, no argument is used. This produces an army which will

soon turn upon our now victorious soldiers already in the field, if they shall not be sustained by recruits, as they should be. It produces an army with a rapidity not to be matched on our side, if we first waste time to re-experiment with the volunteer system, already deemed by Congress, and palpably, in fact, so far exhausted, as to be inadequate; and then more time, to obtain a court decision, as to whether a law is constitutional, which requires a part of those not now in the service, to go to the aid of those who are already in it; and still more time, to determine with absolute certainty, that we get those, who are to go, in the precisely legal proportion, to those who ask not to go. . . . My purpose is to be, in my action, just and constitutional; and yet practical, in performing the important duty with which I am charged, of maintaining the unity, and the free principles of our common country.[28]

The correspondence between the two continued until draft enrollment resumed in New York City on August 19. Though Lincoln had justified his position, he twice reduced that state's quota. It was vintage Lincoln, responding to an unfair accusation in respectful and logical terms, and then allowing the opposing party to achieve a partial victory. Throughout the rest of the war, Seymour was a leading spokesman of the Regular Democrats. He served as the permanent chairman of the Democratic nominating convention in 1864 and was urged by some to present himself as a candidate. He was not interested.[29]

The Democrat who most obstructed the war effort from beginning to end was Congressman Clement L. Vallandigham of Ohio, the "handsome, fluent exhibitionist, and a life-long dissenter on all kinds of questions" who was "swayed more by southern sympathies and love of notoriety than by any patriotic considerations."[30] This eloquent Peace Democrat was one of the first members of Congress to speak out against the war. He epitomized "the fire in the rear" that Lincoln told Charles Sumner in January 1863 he feared most—referring to the Peace Democracy, especially that of the Northwest.[31] Republican antipathy toward Vallandigham was so great that before the 1862 mid-term election, Ohio Republicans gerrymandered his district so as to guarantee his defeat. Though Ohio returned fourteen Democrats among its nineteen representatives to the Thirty-Eighth Congress, Vallandigham was not one of them. He did, however, return for the lame-duck session in December 1862 and vaulted into national prominence.

On January 14, he delivered before the House the most conspicuous Copperhead attack on the Lincoln administration up to that point.

> But the reign of the mob was inaugurated only to be supplanted by the iron domination or arbitrary powers. Constitutional limitation was broken down; *habeas corpus* fell; liberty of the press, of speech, of the person, of mails, of travel, of one's own house and of religion; the right to bear arms, due process of law, judicial trial, trial by jury, trial at all; every badge and muniment of freedom in republican government . . . all went down at a blow.[32]

Vallandigham proclaimed that "whatever pleases the President, that is law!" After setting forth his litany of violations, he stated, "From the beginning, the war has been conducted like a political campaign, and it has been the folly of the party in power that they have assumed that numbers alone would win the field in a contest not with ballots but with musket and sword." He accused the administration of waging the war "with an arbitrary power which neither the Czar of Russia nor the Emperor of Austria dare exercise." But despite "two years of more vigorous prosecution of war than ever recorded in history . . . you have utterly, signally, disastrously—I will not say ignominiously—failed to subdue" the outnumbered rebels "whom you had taught the people of the North and West not only to hate but to despise."[33]

Vallandigham, descended from a Virginia family, had married the daughter of a Maryland planter. He strongly sympathized with the South and firmly believed in the Jeffersonian philosophy of limited government. His arguments were powerful, if rhetoric-laden and provocative. Although he inspired little but antipathy in Congress, his public speeches generated intense feeling in many of his listeners. Republican fanaticism had provoked "this ruinous war," he charged, and after winning public support on the premise that the war was to save the Union, Republicans had furtively converted it into a war for abolition. And with what result? "Let the dead at Fredericksburg and Vicksburg answer."[34]

But Vallandigham had an answer. The South could not be conquered militarily, so the Union should withdraw from the seceded states and begin negotiations for reunion. When told that his solution would preserve slavery, Vallandigham retorted, "I see more of barbarism and sin, a thousand times, in the continuance of this war . . . and the enslavement of the white race by debt and taxes and arbitrary power" than he did in black slavery. "In considering terms of settlement, we should look only to the welfare, peace, and safety of the white race, without reference to the effect that settlement may have on the African."[35]

Upon his return to Ohio after the lame-duck session, Vallandigham was in demand as a speaker. However, his actions agitated Major General Ambrose E. Burnside, commanding the Department of the Ohio. On April 13, 1863, Burnside issued an order stating:

> All persons found within our lines who commit acts for the benefit of the enemies of our country will be tried as spies or traitors, and, if convicted, will suffer death. . . . The habit of declaring sympathy for the enemy will not be allowed in this department. Persons committing such offenses will be at once arrested, with a view to being tried as above stated, or sent beyond our lines into the lines of their friends.[36]

Vallandigham defied the order and on May 1 delivered a fiery speech at a Democratic mass meeting in Mount Vernon. Four days later, Burnside's agents arrested him at his Dayton home and hauled him before a military commission convened by the general, where he was found guilty and sentenced to imprisonment. This assured Vallandigham's political martyrdom. The prisoner on May 5 issued from "a military bastille" in Cincinnati a stirring appeal "to the Democracy of Ohio" in which he declared that he was imprisoned because "I am a Democrat—for the Constitution, for law, for the Union, for liberty. That is my only crime." This was the most prominent military arrest during the war and it quickly became an embarrassment for Lincoln.[37] On May 29, Burnside offered to be relieved if that would reduce the pressure on the president.

Lincoln refused to deflect blame from himself at the expense of a decent and patriotic warrior. Yet to leave Vallandigham imprisoned would only magnify his political aura, which had already been increased by his arrest and conviction.

In his response to Burnside's telegram, Lincoln noted the language of the original order and fixed on a solution that might limit the damage. The concluding sentence had provided banishment to the Confederacy as an alternative to trial and imprisonment. The president chose banishment as the best of several undesirable alternatives. This avoided humiliating Burnside and rendered Vallandigham vulnerable to charges of disloyalty. No sooner had the Copperhead leader arrived behind Confederate lines than he met with high-ranking officials, which seemed to confirm Republican accusations that he had been a rebel sympathizer and traitor from the start. Thus Lincoln turned an embarrassing situation to his advantage.[38]

In the meantime, Vallandigham's martyrdom had won him the Ohio Democratic gubernatorial nod in 1863, at a state central committee gathering at which the nomination was made by acclamation. The committee, before Vallandigham's arrest, had unanimously favored moderate Hugh J. Jewett. But thousands of Democrats, mostly farmers and workers, flocked to Columbus to demand the nomination of "Valiant Val." Vallandigham had since gone to Canada and did not return to Ohio for more than a year.

He soon realized that he would not be reimprisoned and again began stumping the state. However, thousands of Ohioans who had formerly regarded him as the eloquent and courageous defender of civil and constitutional rights now considered him to be a dangerous Confederate agent. Sneers often greeted his efforts, but Vallandigham continued to be the spiritual and political leader of the Peace Democrats throughout the war, particularly in the Midwest.[39]

In the 1863 gubernatorial election, Vallandigham had been defeated by Union candidate John Brough, a War Democrat who had broken with the party, by more than 100,000 votes. Ohio had gone Democratic in a majority of national elections since 1800, but Vallandigham received less than 40 percent of the vote.

Important, but not critical, to this result had been the absentee votes of 53,000 Buckeye soldiers and sailors. The General Assembly had recently enacted an absentee ballot law, and ten other loyal states followed suit before the 1864 election. The results of soldier voting in that critical year provided a practical and symbolic boost for the government and the Republicans. Of the Ohio military personnel who voted in 1863, more than 51,000 went for Brough.[40] Vallandigham almost singlehandedly destroyed Democratic prospects in the third most-populous Union state and, remarkably, a year later performed the same service on a national level.

The Ohio gubernatorial contest was the most important election in 1863 because it served as a plebiscite on Vallandigham and his policies. However, there also was a gubernatorial election that year in neighboring Pennsylvania, pitting Republican incumbent Andrew G. Curtin against George W.

Woodward, a Peace Democrat and justice of the State Supreme Court. Not only was a Lincoln supporter opposing an anti-war candidate, but the Democrat was backed by General McClellan, the hero of Antietam, the beloved former commander of the Army of the Potomac, and the brightest star on the Democratic horizon. Though Woodward was a more attractive candidate than Vallandigham, many suspected he was a Copperhead attempting to pass himself off as a conventional Democrat. Regardless, he was decidedly an opponent of emancipation. Peace Democrat Heister Clymer, a state senator, suggested that Woodward, if elected, would join with Vallandigham, Seymour, and Governor Joel Parker of New Jersey to compel the administration to abandon its antislavery policies.[41]

Despite McClellan's endorsement and the activity of an energetic and efficient state Democratic machine, Curtin won re-election by 15,000 votes. This boded well for the administration. Republicans claimed that the 1863 elections had been a stunning ratification of their war policy. Although the returns were largely the results of Union field victories and growing public support for emancipation and black military service, they also reflected a growing bond between a people and president sharing the agonies and victories of the nation's greatest trial.[42]

The most important Democrat as the 1864 conventions and campaign approached was a man who had no official political experience. McClellan emerged early in the war as the most attractive and electable Democrat in the country. As his disputes with the Republican president and Congress increased following his appointment to the highest command position in the Army, he grew in stature among Democratic leaders across the country.

McClellan's parents were of the best of Philadelphia society, as was his wife's family. A bright child, he entered West Point at fifteen. He achieved a virtually flawless record, graduating second only because of a technicality, and received a degree and commission at an age when most young men were just beginning their careers there. Before the age of thirty, he had been selected by Secretary of War Jefferson Davis to serve on a three-man commission that inspected the armies of France and Russia and observed warfare in the Crimea. His portion of the report was considered the definitive work of that period on siege ordnance. The prospects for the dashing young man appeared unlimited.[43]

Before the war, McClellan retired from the Army and became president of a railroad headquartered in Cincinnati, employing his considerable skills as an engineer and administrator. When hostilities began, he was commissioned as a major general, first in the Ohio Volunteers, and later in the Regular Army by commission from President Lincoln. He raised a small army of Ohio volunteers in 1861. He was instructed to take this force across the Ohio River and rid Western Virginia of rebels. This area, like other mountainous portions of the South, was strongly pro-Union.[44]

In a campaign that brought the government its only victories in 1861, McClellan defeated rebel forces at the battles of Philippi and Rich Mountain. These victories were welcomed by a jubilant Northern press and public. McClellan was dubbed "The Young Napoleon" by the Northern press, a nickname that stuck despite subsequent events.[45]

McClellan loved the adulation and never corrected any misstatements made to his benefit. He had not been on the field at Philippi and did not arrive until the day after the battle. Actually, it was Brigadier General William S. Rosecrans who had led the Union attacks in both battles. However, McClellan's correspondence and reports only make a minor mention of his role. He did, however, on several occasions call Rosecrans "a silly goose" and said Rosecrans "is at Buckhannon, very meek now after a severe rapping I gave him a few days since."[46]

As a result of this campaign, McClellan was summoned to Washington as the capital reeled from the defeat at Bull Run. He was first given command of the primary Union field army, which was to defend the capital and also bear the primary responsibility for driving on Richmond. But the aging general in chief of the Army, Major General Winfield Scott, obstructed McClellan's attempts to mold his new Army of the Potomac.[47] McClellan regarded Scott as a senile old man. He often refused to communicate with him, going directly to the president and secretary of war.

If Lincoln, who respected Scott's military record, was reluctant to release the old soldier, McClellan harbored no such sentimentality. On August 2, 1861, McClellan wrote to his wife:

> General Scott has been trying to work a traverse to have Emory made Inspector Genl of my army & of the army—I respectfully declined the favor and perhaps disgusted the old man, who by the by, is fast becoming very slow & very old. He cannot long retain command I think—when he retires I am sure to succeed him, unless in the mean time I lose a battle—which I do not expect to do.[48]

Then on the fourth:

> It made me feel a little strangely last evening when I went in to the Presdt's with the old General leaning on me—the old veteran [Scott] & his young successor; I could see that many marked the contrast.[49]

On August 8, McClellan wrote Scott, dictating to him that "military necessity demands that the Departments of Northeastern Virginia, Washington, the Shenandoah, Pennsylvania including Baltimore, and the one including Fort Monroe should be merged into one Department under the immediate control of the Commander of the main army of operations and which should be known and designated as such."[50] McClellan was making his grab for power. The rave press reviews he had received across the North convinced him he possessed so much political and popular support that he could make his move.

On August 8 he also described the events of the day in a letter to his wife. He told her he was being "pestered to death" by members of Congress and had engaged in "a row with Genl Scott until about 4 o'clock." Then he had to endure a meeting with Seward about his "pronunciamento" against Scott's policy. McClellan was frustrated by the inability of anybody to see the burdens he was laboring under. "How does he think that I can save this country when stopped by Genl Scott—I do not know whether he is a dotard or a traitor! The old general was entirely unequal to the emergency" and "if he cannot be taken out of my path, I will not retain my position, but will resign & let the admin take care of itself." Despite his best efforts to prepare his understrength army for the attack, McClellan imminently expected "that confounded old Genl always comes in the way—he is a perfect imbecile. He understands nothing, appreciates nothing & is ever in my way."[51] On August 15 he wrote, "Genl Scott is the most dangerous antagonist I have—either he or I must leave here—our ideas are so widely different that it is impossible for us to work together much longer";[52] and the next day he wrote, "I am here in a terrible place—the enemy have from 3 to 4 times my force—the Presdt is an idiot, the old General in his dotage—they cannot or will not see the true state of affairs." In the same correspondence he also said, "I am weary of all this. I have no ambition in the present affairs—only wish to save my country—& find the incapables around me

will not permit it!"[53] Much of McClellan's correspondence indicated that
he genuinely believed he was surrounded by unintelligent people, and that
only he was qualified to protect the honor of the capital.[54] Eventually he
forced Scott's resignation.

Then McClellan's real problems with the president and Congress began.
Curiously, McClellan was without peer in getting ready for battle but when
the time came, he could not take the final step. Having done everything
to maximize his advantage in battle, he was unable to fight. He was so afraid
of losing that he could not exercise the quick and decisive leadership that
would make victory possible.

His willingness to take credit for a subordinate's victory at Philippi was
not the sole instance of McClellan's lack of integrity. During the summer
of 1862 and earlier, particularly following Second Bull Run, there was much
grumbling among officers in the Army of the Potomac about the administration, and some felt the need for a military dictator who would not
undermine the army's efforts. Some high-ranking officers had actually
discussed this with McClellan. He had hinted at the thought as early as
August 9, 1861, in a letter to his wife.

> I receive letter after letter—have conversation after
> conversation calling on me to save the nation—alluding to the
> Presidency, Dictatorship &c. As I hope one day to be united
> with you forever in heaven, I have no such aspirations—I will
> never accept the Presidency—I will cheerfully take the
> Dictatorship & agree to lay down my life when the country is
> saved.[55]

That the general in chief countenanced even a hint of a military dicta-
torship was a gross violation of his constitutional duty. Yet after the Battle
of Antietam, McClellan not only countenanced a discussion of the matter,
he called together several of his corps commanders to solicit their opinions.[56]
His raising such an issue with his highest-ranking subordinates, even if only
to solicit their opinions, was justification for convening a court-martial and
ordering his summary dismissal from the Army.

When McClellan received word of the preliminary Emancipation Proclamation, he was furious. On September 25, 1862, he wrote:

> It is very doubtful whether I shall remain in the service after
> the rebels have left this vicinity. The Presdt's late Proclamation,

the continuation of Stanton & Halleck in office, render it almost impossible for me to retain my commission & self respect at the same time. I cannot make up my mind to fight for such an accursed doctrine as that of a servile insurrection—it is too infamous.[57]

The next day, he invited an old friend, William Aspinwall, a wealthy New York merchant, to visit him. McClellan asked him what he should do regarding the proclamation. Aspinwall was more than a little surprised that McClellan asked advice on how to respond to a political decree of the president. Apparently, McClellan was considering the suggestions that he either march on the capital and install himself as a dictator or refuse to take any further military action against the rebels. Perhaps he was uncertain and again wanted the advice of someone he respected. Aspinwall carefully explained that McClellan, as an Army officer, owed the same loyalty to Lincoln as commander in chief that he would expect of his own corps commanders. If McClellan differed with the president on a political matter, he was to act absolutely in accordance with the president's orders and take up the political matter at the next election. Young Napoleon acknowledged that Aspinwall was, of course, correct, but the businessman must have left camp wondering what McClellan might have done if his advice had been different.[58]

It was possible for McClellan to envision himself marching on the capital and installing himself as the executive authority. Then he could restore sanity and order to a government that, carried away by its intoxication with Republican principles and revolutionary doctrines, had espoused freedom for slaves. During the Peninsula Campaign, Lincoln had gone to Harrison's Landing, Virginia, to meet with the commanding general and observe the condition of the army. McClellan gave him a memorandum presenting what should be the purposes of the war and said that the president must decide and follow through on a civil and military policy or the cause would be lost. He gratuitously offered his commander advice regarding slavery.

> Neither confiscation of property . . . or forcible abolition of slavery should be contemplated for a moment. . . . Military power should not be allowed to interfere with the relations of servitude, either by supporting or impairing the authority of the master. . . . A declaration of radical views, especially upon slavery, will rapidly disintegrate our present Armies.[59]

On October 5, 1862, he wrote to his wife regarding his meeting with Aspinwall the previous day.

> Mr. Aspinwall is decidedly of the opinion that it is my duty to submit to the Presdt's proclamation & quietly continue doing my duty as a soldier. I presume he is right (& am at least sure he is honest in his opinion.) I shall surely give his views full consideration.[60]

That McClellan was uncertain before talking with Aspinwall about how he should proceed in light of the president's proclamation, and even after the meeting simply "presumed" that Aspinwall was correct, reveals a lack of devotion to the Constitution and the American principle of civilian authority over the military. McClellan was a dangerous man in 1862 as the leader of the Army of the Potomac, and in 1864 as the candidate for president. His potential for undermining and reversing the nation's drive toward freedom could destroy all the gains that Lincoln had made. In 1864, McClellan was on the threshold of achieving legitimately that which in 1862 he had considered taking in contravention of the Constitution.

Lincoln did not lose faith in McClellan; he had been remarkably patient with other commanders who made rash political statements, as long as they were competent on the battlefield. Lincoln finally removed McClellan from command because he failed to pursue Lee in the two months after Antietam, and ordered him to Trenton, New Jersey, to await further orders.[61]

Between November 1862 and October 1863, McClellan made the transition from military leader to political candidate. Though he was the senior general on active duty during this time, "he performed no military duties beyond writing a lengthy report of his fifteen months as commander of the Army of the Potomac and helping organize a militia call-up in New York State." He believed that he would at some point be recalled to resume command of the Army of the Potomac or again to serve as general in chief. This seemed even more likely after terrible Union defeats at Fredericksburg in December 1862 and Chancellorsville the next May.[62]

While waiting to resume his command, McClellan spent much of his time in the company of leading Democrats, wealthy and powerful individuals who had an economic interest in seeing the war ended. Among them were Aspinwall; August Belmont, the American agent of the wealthy Rothschild family; and the national chairman of the Democratic Party,

S. L. M. Barlow, one of the great corporation lawyers of New York. Also included were editors Manton Marble and William C. Prime of the New York *World* and *Journal of Commerce*, the two leading Democratic newspapers.[63]

Wherever McClellan went, he was surrounded by adoring crowds. The New York *Express* described his arrival in New Jersey: "No such demonstration, political or otherwise, was ever before witnessed in Trenton." When he relocated to New York a week later, "newspapers began to carry regular features headed 'McClellan's Movements,' listing his attendance at the theater and the opera and at dinner parties and grand balls." A number of the prominent Democrats with whom he associated were viewed as Copperheads. Thus Regular Democrats, many of whom had long envisioned McClellan as their candidate in 1864, became concerned about his frequent attendance at soirees in the company of these men and the front page coverage it was receiving all across the country.[64]

Among those who were reading these news stories were the soldiers of the Army of the Potomac, and their reverence for their former commander began to diminish. The general feeling in the army was that his dismissal had been wrong and politically motivated, and that McClellan had good reason to be upset. However, his consorting with prominent Copperheads disappointed the troops he had nurtured and trained so devotedly. If he had any promise as a national political candidate, he had to retain the support of his army. The Army of the Potomac represented not merely the votes of 100,000 men, but also the votes of relatives and friends who relied on these men for news from the front. The soldiers were heroes to those they left behind and any action that hindered their effort was looked upon as disloyalty.[65] Had McClellan been as astute a politician as he was a military organizer and theorist, he would have realized that the military vote represented his best chances of being elected and could have been more circumspect in his associations.

Many New York Democrats had viewed McClellan as a potential candidate for president since 1861. Of the many Democratic generals who had been commissioned at the beginning of the war, he alone had been successful. He had worked a miracle with the Army of the Potomac, which even the most rabid Radicals had to concede, and had fortified Washington to virtual impregnability. Most important, McClellan had turned back the invasion of a Southern army and "saved the nation for a second time," by his own immodest account of the situation. Finally, the North had a genuine military hero. He was the only national figure in the party with a genuine chance of unseating the Republican nominee and stopping the revolutionary programs being enacted by the congressional Radicals.[66]

Historians differ over when McClellan decided to become a presidential candidate. His first overt act was the endorsement of George W. Woodward for governor of Pennsylvania. Woodward was a conservative and at the time of secession had been more than willing to allow the Southern states to leave. He had also opposed the Legal Tender and Draft acts. Therefore, Republicans portrayed Woodward as a peace-at-any-price Democrat, a Copperhead just as much as Vallandigham and others who had garnered more attention. The Republican press tried to capitalize on McClellan's popularity, claiming that he had worked closely with Curtin while in command of the Army of the Potomac and was committed to the governor's reelection. In response, McClellan published a letter denying that he had supported Curtin and said that if he were in a position to do so, he would both campaign and vote for Woodward. It was his "earnest endeavor, heretofore," he added, "to avoid participation in party politics," but it was obvious now that "I cannot longer maintain silence under such misrepresentations." McClellan stated that he had spoken with Judge Woodward and found "that our views agree and I regard his election as Governor . . . called for by the interests of the nation."[67]

Woodward lost, and McClellan lost as well. He had offended soldier voters, particularly those of the Keystone State. McClellan, aware of this likelihood, had discussed it with S. L. M. Barlow and Manton Marble of the *World.* Marble had told him, "Without a plump authoritative word from you we shall certainly be beaten," in which event "your silence will certainly be deemed by the leading Democratic politicians as the cause of the defeat. The effect of this in the future is obvious enough."[68]

That McClellan had eyes on the White House in late 1863 is obvious. His first written acknowledgment of this was in a December 6, 1863, letter to his mother, Elizabeth B. McClellan. "I feel very indifferent about the White House—for very many reasons I do not wish it—I shall do nothing to get it & trust that Providence will decide the matter as is best for the country." McClellan was responding to a letter from his mother in which she had written, "The Democrats say, the War Democrats, that George B. McClellan, is to be the next President."[69]

From this time, McClellan's correspondence became increasingly political. He was in constant contact with Barlow, Prime, Marble, and other

Democratic leaders. Interestingly, the only significant political activity of that winter and spring that involved McClellan grew out of Republican strife. Francis P. Blair and his son, Montgomery, undertook a campaign to defeat the Radicals, their mortal enemies within the party. The Radicals were casting about frantically for a candidate to replace Lincoln. The Blairs wished to frustrate the Radicals and Montgomery wrote to Barlow on May 1 proposing that the best interests of the country dictated that Lincoln should be re-elected and that McClellan should be reinstated as general in chief. If McClellan would agree to refuse the Democratic nomination and support the president, Blair felt confident that Lincoln would want McClellan to be in "a military place in which he could be most useful."[70] Barlow approached the general with Blair's proposal, but McClellan refused to consider it. He would not endorse Lincoln's policies, particularly those regarding slavery.

In July, Lieutenant General Jubal A. Early led a rebel corps on a raid through the Shenandoah Valley that brought it on July 11 to the outskirts of Washington. Many called for McClellan's recall. Francis Blair conferred with McClellan at his residence at Astor House on July 21, where he renewed his son's earlier offer. McClellan was noncommittal. Blair returned to Washington and told Lincoln what he had done and what McClellan had said. The president, who had not authorized Blair to act, "neither expressed approval nor disapprobation of what I had done," Blair noted.[71]

In a July 22 response to Blair that McClellan prepared but never sent, he wrote that he was "not an aspirant for the Presidency," although he believed that "no true man should refuse it, if it is spontaneously conferred upon him, and he is satisfied that he can do good to his country by accepting it." He said that the original purpose of the war, which was "the preservation of the Union, its Constitution and its laws, has been lost sight of, or very widely departed from, and that other issues have been brought into the foreground which either should be entirely secondary, or are wrong or impossible of attainment." McClellan thought that the war had taken a course that "unnecessarily embitters the inimical feeling between the two sections, and much increases the difficulty of attaining the true objects for which we ought to fight." Those "true objects," of course, were reunion on conservative principles, leaving slavery intact and a matter of state choice. He complained that emancipation "far from tending to that end tends in the contrary direction."[72]

As the year passed, McClellan's popularity soared. Grant's army had suffered horrendous casualties in the Wilderness and Spotsylvania battles and by summer the two armies had settled into siege lines stretching from easternmost Richmond to below Petersburg. By August, the Federal casualties in the 1864 campaigns had hit 90,000, with no imminent prospect for an end to the killing. Calls for peace were rising, even a Copperhead peace with the South gaining its independence. The president and his advisers, discouraged and frustrated by the events of the war and suffering from the public reaction to a draft call for yet another 500,000 men, did not believe it was possible for him to be re-elected.[73]

Where did McClellan stand on a cease-fire and negotiations? It is unclear whether he would have honored the Copperhead demand for an immediate cease-fire in the event of Democratic victory or whether he would have continued to prosecute the war, albeit for different reasons than his predecessor. The evidence can be interpreted to support either position. New York businessman S. L. M. Barlow, McClellan's principal adviser during this period, assured other Democratic leaders that "the General is for peace, not war. . . . If he is nominated, he would prefer to restore the Union by peaceful means, rather than by war." And according to a St. Louis businessman, on August 24, less than a week before the Democratic convention, McClellan told him, "If I am elected, I will recommend an immediate armistice and a call for a convention of all the states and insist upon exhausting all and every means to secure peace without further bloodshed."[74] If McClellan said this, it represented a change in position from several weeks earlier, when he had responded to advice that he should write an open letter suggesting an armistice. On that occasion he had written, "These fools will be the ruin of the country."[75]

On Monday, August 28, the Democrats gathered in Chicago, jubilant in the expectation that they would be returning to the White House. So good did McClellan's prospects appear that on August 10, Manton Marble had told him, "This is your only fortnight of peace & quietness for four years." He assured the general that he had to do nothing and say nothing for nineteen more days and the nomination was his. Barlow told Marble, "I have no doubt of our ability to elect McClellan and to restore the Union."[76]

However, it soon became apparent that the Democrats had problems. Two in particular threatened to derail McClellan. First, McClellan supporters were primarily from the East. The only McClellan advocate not from New York was Samuel Sunset Cox of Ohio, and though the McClellan managers knew that a number of Midwestern delegates were from the peace wing, they badly underestimated this group's strength. They were a far more numerous minority, if they were a minority at all, than any of the McClellan people anticipated, and they closed around Vallandigham.[77]

Democratic leaders knew that Vallandigham was tainted and that his reputation could seriously damage their prospects. Without Vallandigham (who had only recently returned from exile), the Copperheads might be controlled and mollified; with him, the convention could develop into an ugly and politically embarrassing fight.[78]

The second problem was that former Governor Horatio Seymour of New York, having previously announced his unavailability, was now willing to be drafted. Seymour was a formidable candidate and the Copperheads preferred him to McClellan. McClellan's managers immediately began attempting to hold the first-ballot commitments they had, to seek favorite-son delegates who would promise second-ballot support, and assure an early McClellan nomination with as little friction as possible. In the process, they completely neglected what would prove to be the most important aspect of the convention, the Committee on Resolutions or, as it was more commonly known, the platform committee.[79]

Vallandigham was on the platform committee. The only McClellan man there was Samuel Tilden, a veteran of legislative wars who had long since learned that disputes were best handled by compromise and accommodation. He proved to be no match for the forceful, eloquent, uncompromising Prince of Copperheads. Vallandigham not only got a platform plank declaring the war a failure, but also one calling for peace at any price, the old Vallandigham solution for ending the war—simply pulling back your armies and then sitting down at a conference table with the other side and amicably working out your differences.[80]

Though the McClellan men on the committee tried to insert a substitute plank that would call for reunion as a condition, the Vallandigham majority held. Tilden could have led a fight against the plank in the full committee or once it reached the floor of the convention, but he judged that that would lead to an open fight and possibly a rupture within the party. Vallandigham evidently used the threat of a bolt by the peace men as a weapon to save his second plank. He made his position clear in a letter to McClellan a few days later: "If anything implying war is presented, two hundred thousand men in the West will withhold their support, & may go further still."[81] The

Vallandigham contribution to the platform became known as the "war-failure" plank, or the "second" plank, but in fact it was the plank that the Democratic Party had to walk to its death in 1864.

The platform was adopted on August 30, 1864. On August 31, the convention nominated McClellan for president. Seymour's candidacy was never a factor. McClellan garnered 174 votes on the first ballot, comfortably more than the 151 required for nomination. On the motion of Vallandigham, the nomination was made unanimous.[82]

In a final act of political self-destruction, the convention provided its war candidate for president with a peace candidate for a running mate. The New York delegation, making a further ill-considered attempt to unify the party, led the movement for George H. Pendleton of Ohio as the vice presidential nominee.[83] Pendleton's opposition to the war was almost as vehement and well-known as Vallandigham's.

The discouragement of many McClellan supporters did not dampen the celebration in the streets of Chicago after the convention. The Democratic press for days afterward painted scenes of unrestrained joy and celebration. However, the day after the convention, Republican newspapers began featuring another news item—an account of what would prove to be the most important Union victory of the war, the fall of Confederate Atlanta, and one that would dramatically dampen McClellan's prospects.

4

"You Say You Will Not Fight to Free Negroes"

In the North, significant anti-administration sentiment had developed by 1864, more so in some regions than others. In areas where many Confederate sympathizers resided, there had been numerous arrests of civilians by the military. Since these regions were usually in or near border states, the people there had to endure the almost constant presence of troops. In some instances, martial law had been imposed by these occupation forces, and the civil government and courts had ceased to operate. Most of the civilian arrests during the war were based on the suspension of the writ of *habeas corpus* by Lincoln.[1]

The Northern states along the Ohio River were among the most populous. Ohio, Illinois, and Indiana ranked third, fourth, and fifth in population of non-rebel states. The southern parts of those states contained many former Southerners. They were called Butternuts because of the home-dyed clothing they commonly wore. They were Democrats whose towering hero was Andrew Jackson, and they were much closer politically to their Southern brethren than they were to New England Yankees.[2]

When anti-administration sentiment developed in many areas of the North early in the war, it was strongest in the Butternut region. There had also been significant opposition to the war effort among first- and second-generation Irish immigrants in seaboard cities such as New York and Boston, and in the coal fields of eastern Pennsylvania. Likewise, many of the German immigrants who had settled in the Midwest opposed enlistment efforts. However, violence erupted in these regions only when troops were sent there in significant numbers or when conscription officers attempted to conduct the selections ordered by Lincoln. Otherwise, these people did not pose an ever-present danger of civil unrest. The Butternuts in the Midwest were a different story.[3]

The opposition to the war in the Ohio River states was greater and more active than in any other part of the North. Initially, anti-government sentiment took no concrete form and merely seethed beneath the surface in the flush of the patriotic outpouring after the surrender of Fort Sumter. But when Union armies began assembling on or near the Ohio River, many civilians suspected of being Confederate agents were arrested by the military, usually without benefit of specific charges, a fact the Democratic press exploited.[4]

Farmers in these states had become disillusioned with the war effort as early as the fall of 1861. This area was the nation's breadbasket and the food it grew had fed the country before the war. According to historian James McPherson, "The war had cut off their normal trade routes along the Mississippi and its tributaries, forcing them into dependence on Yankee railroads and canals feeding an east-west pattern of trade." Samuel Medary, the Copperhead editor of the Columbus *Crisis,* asked, "Shall we sink down as serfs to the heartless, speculative Yankees, swindled by his tariffs, robbed by his taxes, skinned by his railroad monopolies?" The longstanding animosity that the Butternuts felt toward New England developed into a raw nerve when they were forced to rely upon railroads charging inflated rates and owned by Eastern capitalists.[5]

What ultimately moved many Butternuts in the Midwest to engage in outright, sometimes violent, opposition to the war effort, however, was the Emancipation Proclamation. Before September 1862, the Democratic press and politicians had mounted only sporadic and disjointed opposition to the war. After that, the protests changed.[6]

In February 1863, the Indiana House of Representatives, controlled by the Democrats as a result of the 1862 election, resolved that the war would no longer be supported unless it was waged "solely for the preservation of the Union, with all the rights, dignity, and equality of the states unimpaired." A Democratic convention in Greene County, Indiana, resolved that, "Our soldiers went to save the Union, not to free the slaves." And when the Army was used to free blacks, "the war ought to cease." The opposition press called Lincoln's action a gross betrayal of the public trust because of his repeated promises not to interfere with slavery. The papers decried a "black wave" which would invade the state, thereby requiring Indiana to support "a horde of black paupers, idlers and thieves."[7]

An Indiana soldier received a letter from his parents that said:

> "I am sorry that i have a son in the servic [sic] to help to uphold the old traitor's Emansapation [sic] Proclamation Bill. . . . Lay down your arms and come home if you can. . . . Tell your friend soldiers not to fight anymore to free the slaves."[8]

In Congress, Representative Daniel Vorhees of Indiana accused Lincoln of buckling under pressure from Horace Greeley, "that political harlot, who appeared in a praying attitude in behalf of twenty millions of people." The Indiana *Sentinel* called the proclamation "a confession of weakness—an acknowledgment that twenty millions of white people, with every advantage on their side, can not conquer six millions of whites." It warned that the results of emancipation would be disastrous.[9]

In Illinois, a Democratic majority also had been elected. These legislators gathered at the capitol on January 5, 1863, after the first day's session of the legislature, to discuss the Emancipation Proclamation. A Springfield correspondent to the Chicago *Daily Tribune* wrote: "We are in revolutionary times, and for my part I should not be surprised at anything that may be done here."[10]

Throngs from every section of the state also gathered. Richard T. Merrick, one of four speakers who addressed the crowd, demanded that Lincoln withdraw the proclamation and, if he did not, then Merrick would favor severing the West from New England. Merrick called for hanging all Abolitionists and "did not know which were the greatest traitors, those at Washington or Richmond." Another speaker declared that he was for marching an army to Washington and turning out the administration.[11]

As the meeting concluded, a resolution was approved.

> *Resolved,* That the emancipation proclamation of the president of the United States is as unwarrantable in military as in civil law; a gigantic usurpation . . . the present and far-reaching consequences of which to both races cannot be contemplated with the most dismal forebodings of horror and dismay . . . and which we denounce, as an ineffaceable disgrace to the American name.[12]

The meeting had generated so much popular support that the Democrats called for another on January 8.[13]

At this gathering, Circuit Court Judge Harvey Omelveny chastised Lincoln for unconstitutionally perverting the war by altering its original purpose of restoring the Union and substituting in its place the obnoxious goal of freeing the slaves. Representing a soldier's viewpoint, Theophilus Dickey, formerly a colonel with the Fourth Illinois Cavalry, claimed that this alteration of purpose would magnify the will of rebels and prolong the war "equal to fifty-thousand bayonets against us." That meeting concluded with a resolution calling for a national peace convention to be held at Louisville, Kentucky, "at the earliest practicable period."[14]

The reaction in the ranks to Lincoln's decree was also strongest among troops from the Ohio River states. Twenty-three hundred soldiers from Indiana deserted in December 1862. This was one-fourth of the total from that state who deserted during the war, and even though the defeat at Fredericksburg contributed to this, much of it was the result of disaffection with the proclamation announcement. Similar rates of desertion were not witnessed following the defeat in 1864 at Cold Harbor, a military setback even more one-sided than that which occurred at Fredericksburg.[15]

The Democratic nominee for governor of New York, Horatio Seymour, spoke for many soldiers when he declared, "If it be true that slavery must be abolished to save this Union, then the people of the South should be allowed to withdraw themselves from the government which cannot give them the protection guaranteed by its terms." One Ohio editor insisted that if "the despot Lincoln tried to ram abolition and conscription down the throats of white men," then "he would meet with the fate he deserves: hung, shot, or burned." Referring to Ohio troops, he declared, "A large majority can see no reason why they should be shot for the benefit of niggers and Abolitionists." When Colonel Frank Wolford opposed the enlistment of black soldiers, this veteran of numerous battles was dishonorably discharged from the 1st Kentucky Cavalry. An entire regiment of Illinois troops was arrested because when a high-ranking officer called for them to cheer the president's "Negro policy," they hissed and booed instead.[16]

In Ohio the announcement of the preliminary Emancipation Proclamation had an unintended effect: it cloaked the most outspoken and eloquent opponent of the war, Clement L. Vallandigham, with an aura of credibility. Prior to September 1862 Vallandigham had attracted Republican wrath for his antiwar oratory and bombastic attacks on the party in power. Republican denunciation continued after the proclamation; but within the ranks of the Democratic Party, he ascended from being a minor embarrassment to a leading spokesman. Vallandigham's phrase "to maintain the Constitution as it is and to restore the Union as it was" was adopted as the slogan of the Democratic Party for the 1862 midterm election, and would become a centerpiece of Democratic strategy for the remainder of the war.[17]

The results of the 1862 midterm elections seemed to confirm popular support for Democratic opposition to the proclamation. Had Lincoln run for president in 1862, he could well have been turned out of office. Having sniffed success, the Democrats exploited the issue with greater intensity and demagoguery in the post-election period.

With Vallandigham as the new darling of Peace Democrats and the proclamation causing most Democrats who had initially supported the war to break with the administration, the party of Jackson appeared to have common ground on which to unite in opposition to the war. No issue drove more Democrats to outright opposition to the administration than emancipation. Those War Democrats who remained in coalition with the Republicans after September 1862 were decidedly a minority of what had been the antebellum Democratic Party.[18]

The Democrats most affected by the Emancipation Proclamation were those who had supported the war as long as it was waged to suppress the rebellion. In the early months, their support was increasingly compromised by such acts as arbitrary arrest of civilians, the suspension of the writ of habeas corpus, the suppression of anti-war newspapers, and finally conscription. Almost invariably, Democrats were most affected by these measures. Democrats who supported a limited war were forced to choose between backing a government that was dividing and weakening their party or opposing the government by defending those who were working against the war irrespective of why it was being waged. Whichever choice these Democrats made, they would be working at cross-purposes with their own stated goals.[19]

At the point that the Lincoln administration officially approved the Abolitionist demand that the war also be waged to end slavery, the ambivalence ceased. Many who had supported the war were now converted to outright opposition. Some became Peace Democrats while others chose to place a higher priority on the defeat of Lincoln and the Republicans than they did on the defeat of the rebels. If the Democrats had any hope of ousting the party in power, it could only be achieved by again embracing that sizable portion of their party that by late 1862 had reached the point of absolute opposition to the war. Of the compromises that were necessitated by this reunion, most would be made by Democrats who at some point had supported the war.[20]

Thus the Emancipation Proclamation had a staggering impact not just on the future of slavery but also on the alignment of political parties. In its wake, the oldest and most successful political party in early American history, which in 1861 and early 1862 had seemed on the verge of extinction, now rose to again become a force in national politics. Based on the 1862 midterm election, the resurrection appeared to be a resounding success. The scent of victory in 1864 became intoxicating, and whatever ambivalence many pro-war Democrats had felt before the 1862 election, their marriage with the pro-Southern wing of the party became more palatable afterward.[21]

Any support for the war that this sizable middle of the Democratic Party might still have nurtured was killed when Lincoln issued his first draft call. On August 4, 1862, he ordered a draft of 300,000 militiamen to serve for nine months. This was done under the Militia Draft Act, which had become law July 17. A howl of protest from the Democrats was sounded across the country. But the legislation was poorly conceived and unenforceable, leaving implementation up to the state governments. In October, attempts to conduct the selection were opposed in several states, and particularly in the anthracite region of eastern Pennsylvania, where many Irish coal miners lived. Like the poor everywhere, these miners saw the draft as being aimed chiefly at them, while the wealthy could escape service by paying bounties or hiring substitutes. Eventually, attempts to enforce this draft were suspended.[22]

The actual Conscription Act was enacted in February 1863, and signed by the president on March 3. This turned anti-emancipation sentiment into violent resistance in many places. Enrollment for the first draft under this act began in June 1863, and hostility toward it immediately erupted into violence. An enrollment officer in Indiana reported an attempt on his life.[23] On July 17, another enrollment officer, a Republican active in local politics in Sullivan County, Indiana, was killed in an ambush. On August 24, a mob in Danville, Illinois, tried to overpower a provost marshal, and five people were killed. In Monroe County, Indiana, a force of armed men took a list of names from a conscription officer. As a result, state officials dispatched troops to force a showdown with the reported 1,500 men there who were determined to resist the draft.[24]

The proclamation and the draft drove many Northerners to the point of desperate opposition to the war. Historian James McPherson has noted, "Scarcely any other issue except emancipation worked such clearcut partisan division. Indeed, Democrats linked these two issues in their condemnation of the draft as an unconstitutional means to achieve the unconstitutional end of freeing the slaves." Lincoln's promise to free slaves in states still in rebellion "was denounced as a gross betrayal of the people because of his previous promises not to interfere with slavery." When Congress mandated conscription, it affected the poor and working classes disproportionately because of provisions for substitution and commutation that permitted the wealthy to buy their way out of serving. Since the poor and working classes were overwhelmingly Democratic, "it was regarded as a means of compelling men to fight for principles in which they did not believe."[25]

Conscription became a partisan issue in 1863. Democrats exploited it by illustrating the irony of a war to free black slaves being waged by white soldiers who had no choice in the matter and who would never have volunteered to fight for these people. The Conscription Act had been supported by every Republican in Congress but few Democrats. The expression "rich man's war, poor man's fight," first heard in the South in response to the Confederate Conscription Act, now came into vogue in the North. Democratic editors and politicians manipulated the poor and working classes by attacking the commutation provision of the legislation, which permitted individuals to hire a substitute for three hundred dollars—almost as much as some unskilled laborers earned in a year. In Iowa, a newspaper proclaimed, "The rich are exempt! Did you ever know aristocratic legislation to so directly point out the poor man as inferior to the rich?"[26]

On the Fourth of July, virtually on the eve of the beginning of enrollment in New York City, Governor Seymour spoke to the city's Democrats. He addressed the Republican claim that emancipation and conscription had been dictated by military necessity, and warned, "The bloody and treasonable doctrine of public necessity can be proclaimed by a mob as well as by a government." It was tantamount to an invitation for what happened little more than a week later. An editorial in the New York *Journal of Commerce* asked, "What right has any man, or any class of men, to use this war for any purpose beyond its original object?" The writer proclaimed that if a man or class of men had indeed diverted the war's purpose "from its original object" or had "prolonged it one day, added one drop of blood to its sacrifice" because of an effort "to use it for other ends than its original design, then they are responsible before God and man for the blood and cost."

James McMasters, editor of the leading Catholic periodical of New York, said at a mass meeting that "when the President called upon them to go and carry on a war for the nigger, he would be d___d if he believed they would go." A resolution of the Van Buren County, Michigan, Democratic Party stated that "an armistice and national convention" was the "only means by which our present national differences can be adjusted."

Historian Wood Gray referred to this as the "Period of Despair." He theorized the conservative wing of the Democratic Party essentially abdicated its role as the loyal opposition. In doing so, it forfeited to the Peace Democrats, whose loyalty to the Union was subject to legitimate question in 1863–64, the role of shaping party goals and allowed it to implement peace strategies that often smacked of treason.

Republican campaign strategy in 1863–64 focused on domestic treason and, in trumpeting that theme to the people, the party in power enjoyed the windfall of an opposition party that sacrificed principle for political unity. Gray wrote:

> The more conservative Democratic papers . . . by continued harping on shortcomings in the conduct of the war . . . gave tacit assistance to the peace faction. Few attempted to reprove even the most extreme statements of that group, and virtually none made any effort to reinvigorate their readers' enthusiasm for the war.[27]

The newspapers that were demanding peace were at the same time reprinting editorials from Southern papers that insisted upon nothing less than independence as a condition for any peaceful settlement. "They must have known, therefore, that a voluntary reunion would come, if at all, only after a lapse of years." However, for expediency, they did not mention this to their readers. "Much of their talk about the possibilities of an immediate reunion by negotiation must have been intended merely to mislead the gullible, to provide a sugar coating for the unpalatable reality that permanent disunion was the price of immediate peace."[28]

The zenith of the violent resistance to emancipation and conscription hit during July 1863. On July 11, a Saturday, the first draft under the

Conscription Act was conducted in downtown New York. A number of enrollees in each district of the city were to be chosen by lot from the list of eligible men; this would proceed until each district's quota was met. The idea was to call up 20 percent of the men on the lists. However, the share of draftees from each district varied according to the number of men who had already enlisted from that district. James McPherson points out, "There were numerous opportunities for fraud, error, and injustice in this cumbersome and confusing process." Ultimately, because of the numerous means for avoiding actual service, only 7 percent of those chosen ever served in the Union military.[29]

On that Saturday morning, draft officers began drawing the names. There were few troops around the city at the time; most of those normally stationed there had been called to Pennsylvania in response to Lee's invasion. Nothing happened that morning as 1,200 names were drawn. However, that evening and on Sunday, in pubs and on street corners of the city's tenement districts, groups of working-class men imbibed alcohol and anti-black rhetoric in generous doses. Their mood grew increasingly ugly.[30]

According to author Joseph Fried, when the enrollment officer arrived to begin selecting names again on Monday morning, he found a mob "jammed outside his office in an ugly, booing, cursing mass," much too large a crowd to be controlled by police. When a pistol shot was fired, the crowd began pelting the office with stones, and some people forced their way into the building. The officer and his aides escaped out the back door as the mob doused the building with kerosene and set it ablaze. Within minutes, the fire spread to adjoining buildings, and when firemen arrived, they were assaulted with bricks and rocks. Police from the local precinct were routed within minutes. An attempt was made to call police headquarters, but the telegraph lines had been cut, one of many indications that there had been careful planning behind the outbreak of violence.[31]

The incident ignited the worst urban violence in U.S. history. Although the rioting could be attributed to many things, it was foremost a race riot. The mobs sometimes looted and destroyed indiscriminately, but there were a number of specific targets. Author Adrian Cook, writing of the riot, said, "Draft offices and other federal property went up in flames early in the rioting" and black people who had the misfortune of being near one of the mobs were beaten, lynched, or terrorized. Early in the rioting, the Colored Orphan Asylum became a target. As the 237 children who lived there, all of them under twelve, were rushed from the rear of the building, they could hear the invective of the mob—"Down with the niggers!" "Burn the niggers' nest!" The rioters ransacked the building before setting it afire. Repeated efforts to put out the fire were thwarted by the mob. Lt. Colonel Arthur Fremantle, the officer of Her Majesty's Coldstream Guards, was in New York City from July 13 to 15, 1863. He was walking near his hotel when he saw

> a negro pursued by the crowd take refuge with the military; he was followed by loud cries of "Down with the b____y nigger! Kill all niggers! & c." Never having been in New York before, and being totally ignorant of the state of feeling with regard to negroes, I inquired of a bystander what the negroes had done that they should want to kill them? He replied civilly enough—"Oh sir, they hate them here; they are the innocent cause of all these troubles."[32]

The riot lasted for four days and resulted in at least 105 deaths. A dozen or so of these were blacks, most of whom had been beaten to death or hanged. Many others' homes or businesses were destroyed, and businesses that employed blacks also were targeted.

Eventually, several Union regiments recalled from Pennsylvania put down the rioting.[33] The scenes symbolized the deep and widespread resentment of emancipation and the unwillingness to pursue that goal through conscription.

But there were other lessons to be learned. Democrats such as Horatio Seymour, Ben and Fernando Wood, James McMasters, and others had spewed enough rhetoric to create an atmosphere ripe for explosion. Harangues about the right of the people to resist a tyrannical government straddled the boundary between political opposition and encouragement of treason. Wood Gray wrote, "They indirectly fostered resistance to conscription by constantly endeavoring to cast doubts upon its legality. They did not oppose the war; they merely indulged themselves in fussy constitutionalism and in irresponsible criticism, with the determined purpose of making party capital."[34] That their actions might lead to the dissolution of the Union was apparently less important to them than the success of the Democratic Party.

New York was not the only place where violence was directed against blacks in 1863. In Detroit, in response to a rape case, thirty-five homes were burned and many blacks were beaten. Simultaneously with the New York riot, mobs gathered, in Boston; Jersey City, New Jersey; and Troy and

Jamaica, New York; but swift action by local authorities dispersed the crowds before sustained violence erupted. In Illinois, employers of "contrabands," who had entered the state illegally, were threatened with arson or mob action unless they discharged the workers.[35]

Democrats expressed their displeasure at the war measures at the official level as well. The Indiana legislature entertained a motion that declared that until the Emancipation Proclamation was withdrawn, "Indiana will never contribute another man or another dollar" in support of the war. Other anti-war and anti-black resolutions were introduced, and the lower house passed one calling for a six-month armistice. One measure was described by a newspaper as calling for "hanging every negro, he or she, who came into the state till he or she be dead." When the Democrats began a legislative scheme intended to transfer control of the state militia from the governor to the legislature, the Republicans withdrew from the assembly, so the majority lacked the quorum it needed to conduct business. For the next two years, Indiana operated without a legislature.[36]

Illinois Governor Richard Yates grew increasingly irritated with the Democratic majority in the state legislature that dominated the proceedings with peace proposals. One resolution proposed that a commission be sent to Washington to confer with the president and Congress about a national peace convention. In addition, Democrats took up a measure to revise control of the state militia and a habeas corpus bill intended to offset extralegal arrests, then proposed an inquiry into Yates' private and public conduct, insinuating that he was unfit to govern. When the two Houses were unable to agree on a date for adjournment, on June 10 Yates took advantage of a never-before-used section of the Illinois Constitution to suspend the legislature for two years.[37]

Thus, by the summer of 1863, the coalition of 1861 that had featured most Democrats closing ranks with the Republicans to defeat the rebellion had ruptured into bitter and partisan division. Democrats who regarded the war effort as demanding the highest priority suppressed their political and policy differences with Republicans and adopted the moniker of the Union Party until the end of the war. Many remained Republican even after the rebellion was defeated. Though they were but a small minority of the antebellum Democratic Party, their participation in the Union coalition was critical to the successes of the government after 1862.[38] A strong argument has been made by historian Christopher Dell that "without their assistance, the Federal government would have been powerless to restore the union by force of arms."[39]

The War Democrats broke with the regular party structure during the second half of the Civil War. The Peace Democrats benefited because the absence of the War Democrats gave them proportionately greater representation in party councils. Regular Democrats suffered the most; they were that middle portion that represented those who had initially supported the war effort, but whose support had progressively waned with the various Republican enactments they regarded as unconstitutional. Many had openly disavowed support for a war for emancipation and they became committed opponents. They were less doctrinaire than party members who advocated either of the more extreme views of the war. Because they were inclined to place party success ahead of philosophical or ethical considerations, this group tended to control the leadership and pursestrings. These were the "pragmatic" Democrats, the ones most sensitive to shifts in the popular mood.

In the midst of the strife occurring within the loyal states and the party, this was the faction of the party forced to make a Hobson's choice in 1863–64.[40] If they continued to support the war after emancipation had been decreed, it would have to be on Republican terms. They could not associate themselves with a war to end slavery without alienating millions of traditional Democrats. But to oppose the war as it was being waged while condemning those who called for an immediate peace convention was to divide the party yet again. These were the Democrats who appreciated most keenly the fatal error of 1860 when the party split at its convention in Charleston, ensuring Lincoln's victory. They were determined not to repeat that error.[41]

There was never really a choice for these Regular Democrats. The 1862 mid-term elections had demonstrated the explosive potential of the emancipation issue. They had to embrace the racist rhetoric of the peace wing just to preserve their standing among the millions of working-class and immigrant voters who had increasingly become the backbone of the Democratic Party. Likewise, they needed to maintain their appeal to the Butternuts of the Midwest. The common bond that united these groups was a deep-seated fear and hatred of blacks, whether they were free or slave. They violently resented the prospect that they could be compelled to fight to free people they loathed. In order to retain these voters, the Regular Democrats would have to minimize any support for the war. Either adoption of the demand for a peace convention, or at the least a discreet silence, had to drive the Regular Democrats in 1863–64. They would not be the policy-making faction of the party during this critical period.[42]

The characterization of this element of the party as War Democrats after 1862 is not supported by the evidence. Though they spoke and wrote of their continued support of a war to rejoin the sections without affecting slavery, they were addressing a situation that no longer existed. By the mid-point of the Civil War, hundreds of thousands of blacks had already been freed simply by the occupation of large areas of the South by Union armies. Many of these people were working for the government and more than 100,000 were Union soldiers or sailors. Many others were in the North and though many people in the areas where they worked or settled were often hostile to them, it was unlikely that they could ever be forced back to the plantations. Had emancipation never been decreed, slavery would have been crippled because the war was waged in the slave states. In the form and magnitude it had known before the war, slavery would never be restored in the United States.

Democrats who complained about a war against slavery were desperately clinging to a way of life that was forever gone. A war waged solely to restore Federal hegemony in the seceded states without mitigating the scope and influence of slavery was simply an impossibility. War Democrats realized this and embraced the president's emancipation policy as an act of military necessity. Regular Democrats continued to believe that they could support a limited war to restore the Union and simultaneously resist emancipation and conscription. This inconsistency would make them vulnerable to accusations of treason during the last two years of the war.

5

"Must I Shoot a Simple-Minded Soldier Boy?"

By 1862, Copperheads had become a power to be reckoned with, especially in the country along the Ohio River and in areas with substantial Catholic immigrant populations. When emancipation and conscription were added to the government's wartime program, many Northerners who already sympathized with the South or opposed the war were moved to active opposition. Almost all were Democrats or voted a straight Democratic ticket. Therefore, from 1863 to the end of the war, domestic treason became a highly partisan issue that played a major part in the outcome of the war.[1]

Clement Laird Vallandigham had been the first and best-known Copperhead early in the war. Because of his high profile and influence as a member of Congress, he had become the most conspicuous target of Republican attacks during the Thirty-Seventh Congress. Even while sweeping most of the congressional seats in Ohio in 1862, the Democrats lost the voice of the most eloquent and best-recognized Copperhead in Congress when Vallandigham was defeated.

The period of Vallandigham's political life that most affected the 1864 election was between his banishment in May 1863 and his return to Ohio a year later.

While in the Confederacy, Vallandigham became a major object of concern for several high-ranking officials of the Confederate government (including Jefferson Davis), and he spent much time in interviews with important officers of the Confederate States Army. Though he frequently and publicly expressed his commitment to reunion through a cease-fire and negotiated settlement, Vallandigham must have realized the oxymoronic nature of his proposal. Southern newspapers and officials repeatedly told him that the Union could not be restored through peaceful settlement and that nothing short of independence would be acceptable to the South. If Vallandigham knew that a cease-fire could never lead to reunion, then any claim that he made otherwise was simply posturing for political purposes. He knew that a suspension of hostilities for more than a brief time would result in the widespread desertion of soldiers. This would render the government impotent if it needed to summon the enormous citizen participation required to again commence hostilities.[2]

Confederate officials, who were taken by surprise when Vallandigham was delivered into their lines, proceeded cautiously with respect to their new prisoner. Since no arrangement for this highly unorthodox exchange had been discussed, no Confederate soldier or officer wanted to take the responsibility for accepting him. General Braxton Bragg, commander of the Confederate Army of Tennessee, finally authorized the outpost to accept him hours after his delivery. Bragg was afraid to do anything official about his sensational prisoner until he received specific instructions from Richmond. President Davis and Secretary of War James A. Seddon recognized the danger of welcoming an involuntarily exiled man to the Confederacy while he still claimed loyalty to the United States. If they were too friendly, Lincoln could claim that this proved that Vallandigham was now among friends. The stain of disloyalty could then be extended by implication to all anti-war Democrats, thereby discrediting them in the eyes of the voters. However, as the leading Copperhead in the country, Vallandigham could also provide valuable information about the pulse of the Peace Democracy in the North, and he might serve as a valuable conduit for covert operations.[3]

Thus when General Bragg suggested to Confederate Adjutant General Samuel Cooper that either Cooper or some "confidential agent" should conduct a personal interview with Vallandigham, Jefferson Davis approved. Davis wired Bragg that he should appoint an officer in his command to conduct Vallandigham to Wilmington, North Carolina. Meanwhile, Secretary of War James A. Seddon assigned Colonel Robert Ould, the officer responsible for prisoner exchanges, to interrogate him in Lynchburg, Virginia. After a reasonable delay for Vallandigham to rest, Ould was to escort him to Wilmington, where he would be delivered to the charge of Major General Whiting, the commander of the military district that included

Wilmington. Ould's mission during this week-long trip was to interview Vallandigham. Immediately upon returning to Richmond, Ould penned a memorandum to Seddon summarizing their meetings.[4]

John Jones, a clerk in the Confederate War Department who kept a detailed diary during the war, saw the memo and, on June 22, 1863, summarized what Ould wrote. Vallandigham said that if the South could hold out for another year, the peace party in the North would sweep "the Lincoln dynasty out of political existence." However, a Confederate invasion of the North would "unite all parties" and strengthen Lincoln's standing with the people. It would justify him in even greater infringements of the constitutional rights of his political opposition. Vallandigham proffered that the Confederate cause was in decline and that the peace movement in the North would also be destroyed "if Northern arms triumphed." The only interpretation one could make from these remarks is that Vallandigham was suggesting that the Confederates and the Peace Democrats shared a common interest in working against Northern arms. There is no suggestion that Vallandigham was hostile to the Confederate cause. The idea that a negotiated reunion might follow a cease-fire could not have been realistically entertained by Vallandigham after his twenty-four days in the rebel states. Any suggestion otherwise made by him after June 17, 1863, showed that Vallandigham was deluded or engaging in political chicanery.[5]

The importance of Vallandigham's banishment was twofold. First, it allowed rebel officials, who were already considering covert activities against the North, to confer with a prominent politician sympathetic to their cause. Second, it caused an outpouring of support for Vallandigham across the loyal states, including most Regular Democrats, many of whom had objected to his tactics and tone before his arrest. The full extent of what was discussed between Ould and Vallandigham will never be known because Ould did not record it. Also, Vallandigham, whose wartime activities were not excused by the Amnesty Act of 1865, did not later record the subjects broached. Perhaps Ould was sent for the sole purpose of determining Vallandigham's status and intentions while in the Confederacy. If such were the case, he spent a lot of time learning something that could have been gleaned in minutes. Clearly Jefferson Davis devoted more time and attention to this "alien enemy" than he did to any other supposedly loyal Northerner who was in the Confederacy during the Civil War. During Vallandigham's exile, Davis had made clear that no loyal Northerner was welcome to remain in the South. Yet he also sent a vital government official to spend more than a week with this supposedly unwelcome guest. Vallandigham even departed from Wilmington, North Carolina, aboard the *Lady Davis*, a blockade runner owned by Secretary of War James A. Seddon. "Through Seddon's influence, Vallandigham received a priority rating on the passenger list," also calling into question whether the rebels really regarded him as an "alien enemy." Upon his departure, a Richmond editor expressed his approval of the way officials had dealt with Vallandigham: "We are glad indeed that the matter was managed [in a way] most likely to frustrate Lincoln's amiable designs."[6]

Vallandigham's arrest, trial, and banishment in May 1863 had a clearly unintended consequence: It made him a martyr. He suddenly became the darling of many Democrats, many of whom had considered him a political liability. Before his arrest, party leaders in Ohio had unanimously determined to block any attempt by Vallandigham to regain important political office, because his bombast and rhetoric tended to provoke accusations of disloyalty that hurt all Democrats.[7]

But after his arrest, even national party leaders joined in the protest against Lincoln and Burnside. Manton Marble, owner of the New York *World*, had disapproved of Vallandigham's anti-war views. In May 1863, however, Marble wrote several articles criticizing Burnside's high-handed tactics and condemning the general's defense of the arrest.[8] Henry N. Walker of the Detroit *Free Press* wrote

> Vallandigham was arrested for no crime known to law, tried
> by no tribunal recognized as having any cognizance of crimes
> committed by man in civilized life, sentenced to a punishment
> never heard of in any free country, and arbitrarily changed by
> the President to one not recognized in the Constitution.[9]

Protest rallies were held, with the finest Democratic orators calling Vallandigham their friend and deploring the assault on the First Amendment. Even some prominent Republicans, sensing the popular mood, chastised Burnside, calling the arrest and trial a blunder. A perceptive Republican editor wrote, "Vallandigham was fast talking himself into the deepest political grave ever dug, when Burnside resurrected him."[10]

Subsequent to his arrest, Vallandigham promoted his own martyrdom with righteous indignation and bombastic expression. He was savvy enough to realize that before his arrest, he had little chance of being nominated in

1863 as the Democratic candidate for governor of Ohio. Most leading Democrats supported the nomination of Hugh J. Jewett. Samuel "Sunset" Cox, one of the most important Democrats in the House of Representatives, and George W. Manypenny, who owned the influential *Ohio Statesman*, were convinced that Vallandigham's nomination would seriously damage the Democratic Party in the Buckeye State. When Jewett realized that the demand for his competitor's nomination was snowballing among the rank and file of Ohio's Democracy, he offered to withdraw from the canvass. Cox and Manypenny, desperate to untrack the Vallandigham engine, then urged George B. McClellan to enter the race. But McClellan still expected to receive yet another call from the president to save the country, and he declined the offer.[11]

At every stage, from the moment soldiers arrived to arrest him at his home in Dayton, through his trial before a military court where he refused to enter a plea, and up to his delivery to the Confederate outpost in Tennessee, Vallandigham did whatever was possible to force his captors into actions that would appear excessive under normal circumstances. In order to arrest him, the soldiers who came to his home on May 5 had to break down three different doors. When they finally reached him, he was armed with a loaded pistol. Standing terrified behind him were his wife and sister-in-law. Vallandigham had forced a maximum effort from these troops so that it would play much better in the Democratic press.[12] Vallandigham knew that the more sensational the circumstances of his arrest, the more explosive would be the rhetoric of the Democratic press and the conduct of any mobs that gathered in protest.

The Dayton *Daily Empire* that day ran headlines that fueled the passion of Vallandigham's hometown supporters:

Vallandigham KIDNAPPED
A DASTARDLY OUTRAGE!!!
WILL FREE MEN SUBMIT?
THE HOUR FOR ACTION HAS ARRIVED

The editorial column exhorted Democrats to action, blaming the arrest on the "cowardly, scoundrely abolitionists," and calling what had happened to Vallandigham "a hellish outrage." It called upon Democrats to defend their "endangered liberties" and suggested that in so doing, they should cause "blood and carnage." The *Empire*'s editor got his wishes when a mob of Vallandigham's supporters rioted and burned down the office of the *Daily Journal*, the city's Republican newspaper. A rioter was shot when a soldier saw him cutting the water hose being used by firemen on the scene. Burnside then suspended publication of the *Empire*, arrested its editor, and placed Dayton under martial law.[13]

While in confinement the same day, Vallandigham drafted an address "To the Democracy of Ohio" and a visitor smuggled it out. The "military bastille," in which the visit took place, was a room in Cincinnati's Burnet House, the most luxurious and best-known hotel in the Midwest. It was not exactly the draconian confinement Vallandigham claimed. But the vision of a martyred hero being held in close confinement in a luxury hotel suite, eating catered meals, was not the sort of image that would summon his supporters to the streets.[14]

In the aftermath of Vallandigham's arrest and trial before a military court, Democratic protests were held in numerous cities. Several meetings, including one in Albany, New York, adopted resolutions censuring the administration. In a reply addressed to Hon. Erastus Corning and others, Lincoln demonstrated the qualities that had made him such an effective appellate lawyer back in Springfield. He pointed out that "he who dissuades one man from volunteering, or induces one soldier to desert, weakens the Union cause as much as he who kills a Union soldier in battle." But the government, in trying to prevent such conduct through the existing civil courts, was hampered by the fact that the criminal codes were adopted to define unacceptable behavior based upon a peacetime standard.

Vallandigham had used the Constitution to portray himself as the champion of Union and liberty. Lincoln parried each allegation "Valiant Val" had raised in this promotion. In his "To the Democracy of Ohio" letter, Vallandigham claimed that he violated no law, uttered no word, gave no sign or gesture of sympathy with the Southern disunionists, yet he had been incarcerated "in obedience to their demand, as well as the demand of Northern Abolition disunionists and traitors." Vallandigham's suggestion that he had been arrested and imprisoned at the behest of the Confederate government was misleading and ridiculous. Implicit was the characterization of a government conspiring *in pari delicto* with the hated rebels, to suppress him, the true patriot and champion of free government. It was the most incredible of all the martyred pleas made by the Prince of Copperheads, and it was to this claim that Lincoln delivered his most effective volley.[15]

The president knew that no symbol of the United States was more beloved and respected than the civilian soldier who had left home and family to serve his nation in its hour of peril. Vallandigham, who encouraged and fostered desertion and resistance to the draft every time he spoke, could have no greater liability than the people's belief that he was endangering the soldiers of the republic. That he was doing exactly that was eloquently stated by Lincoln in a few short sentences.

> He was not arrested because he was damaging the political prospects of the administration or the personal interests of the commanding general, but because he was damaging the army, upon the existence and vigor of which the life of the nation depends. He was warring upon the military, and this gave the military constitutional jurisdiction to lay hands upon him. . . .
>
> I understand the meeting, whose resolutions I am considering, to be in favor of suppressing the Rebellion by military force— by armies. Long experience has shown that armies cannot be maintained unless desertions shall be punished by the severe penalty of death. . . . *Must I shoot a simple-minded soldier boy* who deserts, while I must not touch a hair of a wily agitator who induces him to desert? This is none the less injurious when effected by getting a father, or brother, or friend, into a public meeting, and there working upon his feelings till he is persuaded to write the soldier boy that he is fighting in a bad cause, for a wicked administration of a contemptible government, too weak to arrest and punish him if he shall desert. I think that in such a case to silence the agitator, and save the boy is not only constitutional, but withal a great mercy [italics added].[16]

Lincoln would have preferred that Vallandigham had never been arrested. He was wiser than Burnside; he realized that Vallandigham wanted to be arrested, so that martyrdom would breathe life once again into a political career that had been near death. Burnside had acted without consulting the War Department or the president. Under those circumstances, Lincoln could have mitigated the damage by ordering Vallandigham released and publicly upbraiding Burnside, who had already served as the scapegoat for Fredericksburg. Burnside was no stranger to being humiliated in public.[17]

But Lincoln was not cruel. He assured the general of his continued support, then drafted an eloquent defense of the arrest. His statement seemed to satisfy all but the Copperheads that Lincoln had parried the challenge of an articulate antagonist and had again taken the day. The failure of the Peace Democrats to appreciate this sentiment helped spell their defeat in 1864.

A week after Vallandigham's arrest, Lincoln demonstrated that he could exercise a moderating influence on his generals when it came to infringements of civil liberties. On June 3, Burnside seized the office of the virulently racist and anti-war Chicago *Times* for "the repeated expression of disloyal and incendiary sentiments." Editor Wilbur Storey had called emancipation "a criminal wrong," and Governor Richard Yates had reported to Stanton the previous year that the suppression of the *Times* was the "urgent and almost unanimous demand" of the "loyal citizens" of Chicago. Yates feared that if nothing were done, people might take vigilante action. Navy Secretary Gideon Welles recorded in his diary that Lincoln and every other Cabinet member regretted Burnside's act in suppressing the *Times*. Stanton had advised Burnside that such an act would undermine his stature within his own command.[18] Several days later, after the *Times* had been suppressed, Stanton wrote Burnside:

> Since writing the above letter the President has been informed that you have suppressed the publication or circulation of the Chicago *Times* in your department. He directs me to say that in his judgment it would be better for you to take an early occasion to revoke that order. The irritation produced by such acts is in his opinion likely to do more harm than the publication would do. The Government approves of your motives and desires to give you cordial and efficient support. But while military movements are left to your judgment, upon administrative questions such as the arrest of civilians and the suppression of newspapers not requiring immediate action the President desires to be previously consulted.[19]

Lincoln was reluctant to overrule Burnside, as he sought to avoid weakening military authority. However, he was influenced by a telegram from two of Illinois's most prominent sons, Senator Lyman Trumbull and Representative Isaac N. Arnold, who asked the president to suspend the order. There had not been the national uproar over the suppression of the *Times* that had followed Vallandigham's arrest, and Lincoln could act without destroying Burnside's credibility. Having been shut down for a day, the *Times* was allowed to resume operation. When he had opted to defend Burnside's course of action in the Vallandigham matter, Lincoln knew it would prove much more difficult for him to do so than simply to overturn the order.

Several weeks after responding to the Albany Resolutions, Lincoln expanded on the Corning letter in writing to a delegation of Ohio Democrats. The "Committee of Nineteen" had met with him on June 25, 1864, to present their protest over the Vallandigham affair. In contrast to the Albany committee, the majority of the Ohio group were Peace Democrats. The difference in Lincoln's attitude toward the two groups was reflected in his response. He pointed out that since they had made use of his reply to the Albany Resolutions, he wanted to be certain that they used his statements "with accuracy." The Ohio delegation had said, referring to his Corning letter, "The undersigned are unable to agree with you in the opinion . . . that the constitution is different in time of insurrection or invasion from what it is in time of peace & public security." Lincoln retorted that what he had said was "the constitution is different, *in its application* in cases of Rebellion or Invasion, involving the Public Safety, from what it is in times of profound peace and public security."[20]

Lincoln said that his position was adopted in order to assist those who were engaged in combatting "a giant rebellion," whereas the Ohio delegation defended the right of a man to embarrass "those whose duty it is" to defeat that rebellion. They claimed, according to Lincoln, that a man who hindered the military from performing its duty could expect to be dealt with as if there were no rebellion. This was a view that "the constitution itself rejects." Vallandigham's was but one of many arrests and detentions, and his was "not different in principle from the others." They had "been for *prevention*, and not for *punishment*—as injunctions to stay injury, as proceedings to keep the peace" and were "to prevent injury to the Military service only."[21]

Then Lincoln shamed the committee for having nominated Vallandigham, an act that would not have occurred but for the arrest.

> I am unable to perceive an insult to Ohio in the case of Mr. V. Quite surely nothing of the sort was or is intended. I was wholly unaware that Mr. V. was at the time of his arrest a candidate for the democratic nomination for Governor until so

informed by your reading to me the resolutions of the convention.
I am grateful to the State of Ohio for many things, especially
for the brave soldiers and officers she has given in the present
national trial, to the armies of the Union.[22]

What remained unwritten, but by implication fairly leaped from the paper,
was that Lincoln was not grateful to Ohio for giving Clement Laird
Vallandigham the appearance of legitimacy and credibility by nominating
him for governor. His reference to being "wholly unaware that Mr. V. was
at the time of his arrest a candidate for the democratic nomination for
Governor" was a not-so-subtle reminder that without his arrest, Vallandigham
had no chance of garnering the nomination.[23]

The president was less benevolent with this group than he had been with
the Albany delegation. The contempt with which he regarded Vallandigham
carried over to his supporters. The New Yorkers had merely been party
loyalists speaking out against the perceived suppression of the rights of a
fellow Democrat. But the Ohioans knew Vallandigham and had rewarded
his wrongdoing. Their nomination of him had increased his stature exponentially and had been an unprincipled act. "Both they [the members of the
convention who were not part of the delegation] and you, have declared
the purpose to sustain the national Union by all constitutional means."
However, they had reserved to themselves the right to decide what "constitutional means" were.[24]

He compared them with the Albany group and found the Ohioans lacking
because they failed even to recognize that "an army is a constitutional means
of saving the Union against a rebellion," or to acknowledge that they were
"conscious of an existing rebellion being in progress with the avowed object
of destroying that very Union." And while they remained conspicuously
silent as to those matters, they were making an appeal on behalf of their
nominee for governor who "is known to you, and to the world, to declare
against the use of an army to suppress the rebellion." As a result their attitude
"encourages desertion, resistance to the draft and the like, because it teaches
those who incline to desert, and to escape the draft, to believe it is your
purpose to protect them, and to hope that you will become strong enough
to do so." He told them that the result of their conduct, even if unintended,
"was a real strength to the enemy."[25]

While Lincoln was completing the response to the Albany resolutions,
Vallandigham was preparing to go to Canada aboard the blockade runner.

In transit, two enormous events considerably dimmed his popularity and prospects for election. Robert E. Lee was turned back in his second invasion of the North, losing more than a third of his army at Gettysburg. As he began his march back to Virginia, Lieutenant General John C. Pemberton surrendered his army and Vicksburg, Mississippi, to Major General Ulysses S. Grant. In terms of military events, it was the greatest day of the war for the Union. Combined with Lincoln's defense of Vallandigham's arrest and other measures to inhibit anti-war activity, these events doomed Vallandigham's candidacy for governor of Ohio.[26]

In August 1863, an old friend of Lincoln, James Conkling of Springfield, Illinois, invited the president to speak at a massive Union rally at the Illinois Capitol on September 3. Lincoln could not attend, but he sent a letter for Conkling to read at the rally. It began by addressing those who were dissatisfied because the nation was still at war:

> You desire peace; and you blame me that we do not have it. But how can we attain it? There are but three conceivable ways. First, to suppress the rebellion by force of arms. This, I am trying to do. Are you for it? If you are, so far we are agreed. If you are not for it, a second way is, to give up the Union. I am against this. Are you for it? If you are, you should say so plainly. If you are not for *force*, nor yet for *dissolution*, there only remains some imaginable *compromise*. I do not believe any compromise, embracing the maintenance of the Union, is now possible. All I learn, leads to a directly opposite belief.[27]

There was no doubt where those of the first or second group stood, but those who wished to maintain the Union *and* opposed the use of force had seized upon the prospect of a compromise that would make both goals possible. Lincoln was unaware of any one man having the authority to control the rebel army who also was willing to strike a peace compromise that included reunion. This part of Lincoln's letter was referring to Vallandigham and generally to those who defended him.[28]

Then Lincoln addressed the heart of the subject. "But, to be plain, you are dissatisfied with me about the negro. Quite likely there is a difference of opinion between you and myself upon that subject." Now he was speaking to those Regular Democrats who had claimed to support a war for the Union but had disowned the war since his proclamation.

You dislike the emancipation proclamation; and, perhaps, you would have it retracted. You say it is unconstitutional—I think differently. I think the constitution invests its commander-in-chief, with the law of war, in time of war. The most that can be said, if so much, is that slaves are property. Is there . . . any question that by the law of war, property, both of enemies and friends, may be taken when needed? And is it not needed whenever taking it, helps us, or hurts the enemy?[29]

He pointed out that more than a year and a half of war before the proclamation was issued, "the last one hundred days of which passed under an explicit notice that it was coming," had not succeeded in quelling the rebellion.

The war has certainly progressed as favorably for us, since the issuance of the proclamation, as before. I know as fully as one can know the opinions of others, that some of the commanders of our armies in the field who have given us our most important successes, believe the emancipation policy, and the use of colored troops, constitute the heaviest blow yet dealt to the rebellion; and that, at least one of those important successes, could not have been achieved when it was, but for the aid of black soldiers.[30]

Lincoln then made a compelling point that some military commanders who supported the proclamation and use of black troops had never been Abolitionists or Republicans.[31] Their views were strictly based upon their observations as commanders.[31] This strongly supported his original claim that emancipation was undertaken to strengthen the Federal armed forces.

In closing, the president wrote perhaps the most salient defense of the Emancipation Proclamation to appear during the war.

You say you will not fight to save negroes. Some of them seem willing to fight for you; but, no matter. Fight you, then, exclusively to save the Union. I issued the proclamation on purpose to aid you in saving the Union. Whenever you shall have conquered all resistance to the Union, if I shall urge you to continue fighting, it will be an apt time, then, for you to declare you will not fight to free negroes.

I thought that in your struggle for the Union, to whatever

extent the negroes should cease helping the enemy, to that extent it weakened the enemy in his resistance to you. Do you think differently? I thought that whatever negroes can be got to do as soldiers, leaves just so much less for white soldiers to do, in saving the Union. Does it appear otherwise to you? But negroes, like other people, act upon motives. Why should they do anything for us, if we will do nothing for them? If they stake their lives for us, they must be prompted by the strongest motive—even the promise of freedom. And the promise being made, must be kept.[32]

After praising the Army and Navy for recent victories, he wrote hopefully of a peace that "does not appear so distant as it did." He emphasized the importance of assuring that when it did come, it should be a peace that would last, one that made the sacrifice a thing of value. It should be a peace that was achieved only after the triumph of free men, which proved that in a democratic society, "there can be no successful appeal from the ballot to the bullet; and that they who take such appeal are sure to lose their case, and pay the cost."

And then, there will be some black men who can remember that, with silent tongue, and clenched teeth, and steady eye, and well-poised bayonet, they have helped mankind on to this great consummation; while, I fear, there will be some white ones, unable to forget that, with malignant heart, and deceitful speech, they have strove to hinder it.[33]

A nation still struggling to adjust to the discomforting notion of armed black men in uniform now witnessed its elected leader's confirmation that these soldiers had upheld the Army's finest tradition. Lincoln had been greatly troubled on January 1, 1863, when he had feared that later generations would sense some ambivalence on his part about signing the proclamation, and they might believe that a document of such importance written in such lifeless prose had to come from an author struggling over whether he was doing the right thing. Nobody who heard Conkling read Lincoln's words to a crowd on September 3, 1863, could have had any doubt that the author had recorded his sincerest thoughts.

He had shamed those who had fallen by the wayside in the struggle simply because the war had been expanded to include the liberation of enslaved human beings. He gave nobility and meaning to the country's terrible suffering. Many who heard or read his words came to feel a greater trust and affection for their captain. Two and a half months later, at the dedication of a cemetery in Gettysburg, Pennsylvania, he read ten sentences that reinforced those feelings further.

In the fall of 1863, it had become important to Lincoln to define what was happening to his country, so that people whose lives had been disrupted, whose friends and loved ones had been killed or maimed, might not lose heart.[34] In doing so, he eased concerns about the revolutionary changes the war was causing to the nation's social and political fabric. Things would never be the same, but the nation would be better than the country that had naively gone into war several years before. He appealed to their better nature. By his words and conduct, he subtly encouraged the racially prejudiced to become a little kinder and fairer in their attitudes toward black people and encouraged a more democratic ideal of justice and equal opportunity.

Though most white Northerners had strong negative feelings about blacks, Lincoln recognized in them a quality in himself—the capacity to rise above his prejudices by trusting his instincts for fair play and decency. If whites were not prepared to accept blacks as their equals in 1863, perhaps they needed a different perspective. In 1858, Lincoln had countered Douglas' appeals to racism with the simple question, "Is the black man not equally entitled to enjoy the benefits earned by the sweat of his own brow?"[35] By changing the question, he increased the ground he shared with those willing to continue fighting the war knowing that slavery would be a victim. His intelligence and sensitivity had elevated the war effort. He had reduced his detractors in the eyes of many who would make the important choices between war and peace at the ballot box in 1863 and after.

As 1863 ended, Lincoln was in firm control. His leadership had been tested by two and a half years of war and agony, and he had grown in understanding and vision. He had never deviated from his course. But the effort was far from over and 1864 would determine whether the United States remained one nation or whether it dissolved into a collection of nation-states, some condemning and others condoning slavery. Though he had effectively silenced detractors for the moment, Lincoln knew his most difficult trial still lay ahead.

6

"With Malice toward None, with Charity for All"

As 1863 closed, prospects for ending the war looked brighter than they had at any time since the early summer of 1861. No general in the field had done more to diminish the prospects of Confederate victory than Lincoln, with his mighty pen and steady stewardship. Even many of the Radicals had by 1864 developed a grudging respect for this lawyer from the Plains because of his powerful acts of statesmanship in defense of the war. As one Radical wrote in a letter to Senator Lyman Trumbull of Illinois:

> In the early stages of the war, as you are aware, I did not like some things that were done, and many things that were not done, by the present administration. Like every body else . . . as among earnest, loyal men, I too was a grumbler, because as we thought, the Gov't. moved too slow. But now . . . it is pretty generally conceded that . . . Mr. Lincoln's administration has done well. I think I am not mistaken . . . in saying this is the general sentiment out [side] of Copperhead Circles, and to such reptiles we don't propose to cater. . . .
>
> We have tried [Lincoln and] . . . know what he is: that he is both honest and patriotic; that if we don't go forward as fast as some of us like, *he never goes backwards.* . . . Very many say . . . "we can't risk a change of Administrators." Some go so far as to say, "this re-election is a political necessity." I would . . . say, if the war is so conducted as to satisfy the reasonable

expectations of the friends of the war, it would seem to be the dictate of prudence to continue him four years more.[1]

In the South, however, the hatred and contempt for Lincoln had increased as Union armies brought ever-greater death and destruction. The Emancipation Proclamation had raised to a new level the greatest fear of most Southerners—a bloody slave uprising. Lincoln was regarded by many as a kind of apocalyptic reincarnation of John Brown, determined to rain death, famine, pestilence, and destruction on the South. Southerners who were watching their world being destroyed knew him only as a satanic figure chosen by the despised Yankees to direct armies and fleets against them.[2]

When Lincoln issued the Emancipation Proclamation, he struck the nerve of Southern society. A man who would encourage slave rebellion, Southerners believed, was without moral restraint. When ex-slaves were enlisted into the Union army, the South saw it as tantamount to granting them a license to murder, rape, and pillage their former owners. The Confederate fight for independence became, in the minds of most Southerners, a struggle for survival. The most desperate resistance was now called for.[3]

This attitude is found in the correspondence and speeches of Confederate leaders in late 1862 and early 1863. It was generally known, even before the new year, that Lincoln would sanction new black units in the armed forces. He had not done so in the draft of the proclamation, but he added it before issuing the final document. In October, General P. G. T. Beauregard, the Confederate hero of Bull Run, called for the garroting of black Federal prisoners taken after the first of January. Jefferson Davis called the proclamation "the most execrable measure recorded in the history of guilty man." Unless Congress advised him otherwise, he said, he would turn over all Union officers captured while commanding black troops to state governments to be prosecuted under anti-insurrection laws.[4] The punishment in all Confederate states was death. In an article on the exchange of prisoners, the Richmond *Enquirer* said:

> The Yankees are not going to send their negro troops in the field; they know as well as we do that no reliance can be placed upon them; but as depot guards, prison guards, etc., they will relieve their white troops. This is the use that will be made of them. Should they be sent to the field, and be put in battle, none

will be taken prisoners—our troops understand what to do in such cases.[5]

Northerners who claimed that the proclamation turned the war into a relentless, remorseless conflict were absolutely correct.

Southern hatred of Lincoln intensified as a result of an 1864 incident. On February 28, a Union cavalry force attempted to raid Richmond to free Federal soldiers in the Belle Isle and Libby prisons. In this instance, Lincoln probably intervened directly in the planning of a military operation.[6] Part of it involved Colonel Ulric Dahlgren, son of Rear Admiral John A. Dahlgren, whom Lincoln greatly admired.[7] Lincoln's friendship with the elder Dahlgren gave rise to Confederate accusations that the former had personally sponsored the raid. Brigadier General Judson Kilpatrick, commander of the raid, had left much of the detailed planning to the younger Dahlgren. The raid failed and a number of Federal troopers were captured; the young colonel was killed in an ambush.[8]

The failed raid would have been a back-page story except that Confederate authorities claimed they found incriminating papers on Dahlgren's body. The papers, in the colonel's handwriting, purported to be the orders and instructions for the raiders once they had gained control of Richmond. They contained a grisly message:

> The bridges once secured, and the prisoners loose and over the river, the bridges will be burned and the city destroyed. The men must be kept together and well in hand, and once in the city it must be destroyed and *Jeff Davis and Cabinet killed* [italics added].[9]

Controversy over the authenticity of the document was front-page news both North and South for weeks following the raid.[10] It was widely believed that Lincoln had not only sponsored the raid but that he had approved of the goals to be carried out by the raiders once they had entered Richmond.[11]

James Headley, an officer who rode with Morgan's raiders, wrote after the war:

> It appears that General Kilpatrick and Colonel Dahlgren came directly from a conference in Washington with President Lincoln and acted by his authority and approval, just as the army

commanders were doing who were burning the homes and property of the citizens of the South.[12]

The Richmond press had no doubt who was to blame. "Let Lincoln and Kilpatrick remember that they have bidden their subordinates give no quarter to the Confederate chiefs," wrote one editor. In a disparaging reference to the disguised and undignified manner in which Lincoln had entered Washington in 1861, a Richmond writer warned, "Perhaps even a scotch cap and a military cloak will not prevent a just and stern vengeance from overtaking them."[13] The Richmond *Sentinel*, a frequent critic of Jefferson Davis, took advantage of the occasion to chastise him and his advisers for not pursuing a more punitive war policy. "If the Confederate capital has been in the closest danger of massacre and conflagrations; if the President and the Cabinet have run a serious risk of being hanged at their own doors, do we not owe it chiefly to the milk-and-water spirit in which this war has hitherto been conducted?" The *Sentinel* spoke for many Southerners in the aftermath of the raid.

> To the Washington authorities we are simply criminals awaiting punishment, who may be hanged or who may be pardoned. In their eyes our country is not ours, but theirs. The hostilities which they carry on are not properly war, but military execution & coercion. . . . What then, would we practically suggest? First, to put to death all "raiders" caught in the fact; secondly, to insist upon the most scrupulous carrying out of retaliation for murders, robberies, and other outrages, with the most punctual exactitude.[14]

And the Richmond *Whig* editorialized, "What more have we to dread from Yankee malice or brutality than we know now awaits us if success attends them?"[15] The answer seemed obvious to all.

It was probably more than coincidence that March 1864, the month of the Dahlgren revelations, was also the genesis of Confederate covert operations out of Canada designed to undermine the Northern war effort. A flurry of activity at that time committed the rebel government to a campaign of fifth column activity during 1864. Though it would be a gross oversimplification to give the failed cavalry raid a preponderant role in shaping Confederate strategy after March, many historians have neglected it altogether. It has basically gone unmentioned in examinations of Cabinet-level policy decisions for that period. Since Confederate military and diplomatic policies in 1864 were driven mostly by consideration of the November election in the North, anything that influenced their implementation also would have an important bearing on the election campaign. Nothing so rocked Richmond officialdom at that time as the Dahlgren papers.[16]

The papers offered the stark reality of future war of apocalyptic proportion. They were a warning of impending destruction by Major General William T. Sherman's armies in Georgia and South Carolina, and Major General Philip H. Sheridan's army in the Shenandoah Valley of Virginia. They were a warning of Southern cities in flames and refugees wandering a wasteland made desolate by "war so terrible."[17]

Lincoln had made clear his intention to prosecute the war until the states were reunited and slavery was abolished. Though it has never been shown that he knew about the purpose of the Dahlgren raid and the authenticity of the papers has never been firmly established, his role was really irrelevant. What was important was that Southern leaders believed that he knew and that Dahlgren's orders represented a new policy. That perception drove the Confederacy to respond desperately as defeat became increasingly apparent.

Some Confederate officers and many soldiers had for more than a year routinely killed wounded black Union soldiers or summarily executed those who attempted to surrender. Those not killed were usually returned to slavery. The white officers who led black soldiers often received similar treatment. At a dozen different sites, from Fort Pillow, Tennessee, to Olustee, Florida, and the sea islands of South Carolina, reports of the battlefield execution of black soldiers and their white officers had posed a problem for Lincoln.[18]

On July 31, 1863, he ordered "that for every soldier of the United States killed in violation of the laws of war, a rebel soldier shall be executed, and for every one enslaved by the enemy or sold into slavery, a rebel soldier shall be placed at hard labor on the public works, and continued at such labor until the other shall be released and receive the treatment due to a prisoner of war."[19]

Lincoln, who had placed black soldiers in the position to suffer those atrocities, did not follow through on the order. The Cabinet struggled with an appropriate response during several meetings following the Fort Pillow massacre. Welles insisted that the government not follow such a "barbarous

. . . inhuman policy." Lincoln agreed that "blood can not restore blood, and governments should not act for revenge."[20] It was a source of tremendous frustration to him, however, that he could not do more to protect these soldiers for whom he felt a personal accountability. That he gave serious consideration to retaliation is an indication of the extent to which the war by 1864 had diminished the humanity of all involved.

Even if Lincoln could not justify an eye-for-an-eye policy on rebel prisoners, he might have felt no such restraint toward their leaders. Davis and Seddon, after all, had authorized the vicious policy of executing black troops and their officers. The assassination of Davis and Seddon was a more humane response to the barbarism than the slaughter of helpless prisoners of war. And if it discouraged the rebel policy toward black prisoners, then the lives of untold numbers of near-citizens might very well be saved.[21]

All of this related to the 1864 election, because it signaled a new direction in the methods and measures each side would employ to win. Everybody, North and South, knew that the signal event in 1864, the one meaningful prospect for Confederate victory that remained, was the presidential election in November. A realistic appraisal of the manpower and resources available convinced Southern officials that their best chance of victory rested with the defeat of the Republicans at the polls.[22]

Larry E. Nelson has provided a well-documented look at Southern policy toward the 1864 presidential contest in *Bullets, Ballots, and Rhetoric.* He plays down emancipation as a driving force in Confederate election-year strategy, but his analysis adds significantly to the scholarship on a subject that remains largely unexplored. Nelson illustrates how Confederate military and diplomatic policy were influenced more by the upcoming election in the North than by any other consideration. Writing after the war, Davis said of the prospects the election posed:

> Political developments at the North [in 1864] . . . favored the adoption of some action that might influence popular sentiment in the hostile section. The aspect of the peace party was quite encouraging, and it seemed that the real issue to be decided in the Presidential election of that year was the continuance or cessation of the war.[23]

Davis had appreciated the possibilities that elections in the North presented well before 1864. Part of the reasoning behind the September 1862 invasions of Kentucky and Maryland by the armies of Generals Braxton Bragg and Robert E. Lee was to influence the congressional midterm elections that fall. The presence of Confederate armies on pristine soil would make the unspoken point. Davis blamed Lincoln for the war and urged Northern voters "to prevail on the government of the United States to conclude a general peace" or to prevail on their state governments to make separate peace treaties with the Confederacy.[24]

The military results of the 1862 effort had been far from encouraging, but the significant Democratic gains in the states of the lower North—the population centers of the Union—had seemed to bode well. The vocal part played by Copperheads and the appearance of growing dissension between the Northeast and the Northwest were also promising. And the spring and summer of 1863, with the outbreaks of violence in Northern cities and the rallies of support for Vallandigham, had raised the possibility of an uprising against the Federal government that would cripple its ability to wage war.[25]

Several Southern officers who had served in Brigadier General John Hunt Morgan's command and had been in the North during the cavalry raid in July 1863 reported significant anti-war sentiment in the Northwest. They wrote about what historian Frank Klement referred to as "dark lantern societies," with memberships of more than half a million. These reports were confirmed by Confederate agents in the North. Lieutenant Colonel R. A. Alston wrote the War Department about "a perfect organization all over the North, for the purpose of revolution and the expulsion or death of the Abolitionists and free negroes." Captain Thomas Henry Hines was summoned to Richmond during the first week of March to discuss a plan for releasing Southern soldiers from Northern prisons as part of a larger effort to start a rebellion in the Northwest. One Confederate agent who worked behind Union lines reported an organization, "the most perfect and most secret the world has known," with a membership of 490,000 men, who favored recognition of Confederate independence, the right of Kentucky, Missouri, and Maryland to join with other slave states, and vowed a willingness to take up arms against the United States to achieve these goals.[26]

Several Confederate military officials proposed actions designed to influence the presidential election. The famous raider Morgan, back in the South after having escaped confinement from a prison in Columbus, Ohio, advocated a new raid into Kentucky to counter articles in the Northern press that suggested the South was close to defeat. Navy Secretary Stephen R. Mallory stressed to a Confederate naval officer that if rebel cruisers appeared simultaneously along the New England coast and in the fishing waters around the Grand Banks, in the West Indies, and in the South Atlantic, the Pacific, and East Indies, New England merchantmen would pressure the Federal government to sue for peace. Mallory concluded that he was "exceedingly anxious to do this."[27]

Benjamin H. Hill, a Confederate senator from Georgia, in a speech given March 1, 1864, said:

> The presidential election in the United States in 1864, then, is the event which must determine the issue of peace or war, and with it, the destinies of both countries. . . . I say we can control that election.[28]

First, the Confederates had to "defeat Mr. Lincoln's armies in the fast-approaching campaigns. Without this, nothing else we can do will, or can avail."[29] If it could defeat the Yankee armies and give an open endorsement to the Peace Democracy, the South could define the decisive issue of the campaign, which was, according to General Morgan, "Whether the people of the United States will elect Mr. Lincoln and continue the war, or whether they will defeat him and accept an honorable peace."[30]

The widespread perception of a powerful anti-war movement in the Northwest fostered by secret societies became a source of hope for Southerners. After the Chicago *Tribune* published an article revealing the existence of the Knights of the Golden Circle, the Augusta *Constitutionalist* reprinted the article:

> This organization has a double object in view, first, the election of a Copperhead like McClellan or Vallandigham to the Presidency, by which the independence of the rebels may be secured, with slavery restored to them; or, failing in that, the kindling of the flames of civil war in the North, which shall compass the same object, and to this end these clubs are being extended all over Illinois, and will rapidly spread through the other states.[31]

When a Copperhead newspaper in the Northwest told its readers to arm themselves against imminent attack by Abolitionist mobs, the Augusta (Georgia) *Chronicle & Sentinel* felt that it signaled an imminent eruption of violence in the Ohio River states. The newspaper encouraged its readers to have faith that "the little speck of trouble which has now appeared in the Northern political sky" was just "the forerunner of a tempest of blood and ruin which will sweep over that section of the old Union."

On April 8, 1864, Congressman Alexander Long of Ohio delivered a House speech in which he pronounced the war unconstitutional and predicted that it would destroy the Union forever. However, what most cheered Southerners was when Long expressed his willingness to recognize Confederate independence and called upon the Democratic Party to embrace immediate peace. Long's speech created a sensation in the South; many newspapers published it in its entirety. One Texas newspaper correspondent described it as "the most important speech in the United States since the commencement of the war, and by far the most honest and able." The editor of the Richmond *Examiner* wrote, "The political cauldron is beginning to bubble, and expectation is aroused to see what will emerge from its agitated depths."[32]

Reprinting articles from the Northern press particularly revived Southern spirits as the Confederacy braced for what everybody knew would be a bloody spring campaign. The Richmond *Sentinel* reprinted an article from the New York *Daily News*:

> It is not to be disguised that the wisest men at Washington, as well as throughout the country, look with fear and dread upon the issues of the coming Presidential canvass. The temper of the people is so excited, the issues so vital, the disturbances—civil, social, and political—created by the war are so profound, that it is feared an excited Presidential canvass will plunge the nation into chaos.[33]

And employing the rationale of Clement Vallandigham, the same clerk in the Confederate War Department who had recorded in his diary the contents of the Ould memorandum (describing his interview with Vallandigham in June 1863) now wrote:

> We have heard to-day that Lincoln was nominated for re-election at Baltimore. . . . Fremont is now obliged to run also, thus dividing the Republican party, and giving an opportunity for the Democrats to elect a President. If we can only *subsist* till then, we may have peace, and must have independence at all events.[34]

Davis attempted to harness all of the hope and desperation felt by Southerners in 1864 to carry out covert operations from Canada. Those, combined with some Confederate battlefield successes, were designed to maximize the opportunity presented by the Northern election. However, the differences between Davis' official pronouncements and his unofficial agenda (the one he promoted in closed sessions with his Cabinet and Congress) were often radically different. Initially, Davis encouraged the belief that the election held great promise for the South. However, he never publicly associated himself with proposals for peace negotiations. This led to divisions within the Confederacy that rivaled the dissension Lincoln was facing in the North.[35]

During its Fourth Session, the Confederate Congress had appropriated money for a covert operations corps. A number of legislators also were directly involved in planning and implementing these activities. However, the defiant and warlike official posture of the rebel government by no means represented all of Southern officialdom. A Georgia representative, Augustus R. Wright, introduced a resolution seeking to shift the onus for the continuation of the war to Lincoln. Since Lincoln had recently stated that the South had never proposed peace terms to the United States, the resolution declared that the Confederacy had attempted negotiations that the Northern president had avoided. The resolution further called for the two governments to convene a peace conference at which they would consider "formation of a new government, founded upon the equality and sovereignty of the States." Wright said this resolution would justify the Confederacy and its policies "in the sight of Conservative men of the North of all parties, and strengthen Lincoln's opponents by inspiring them in their belief that the South would be willing to accept reunion through peaceful negotiations." That had been the position of the Peace Democrats for the past year.[36]

The ubiquitous clerk in the War Department, John Jones, wrote that the resolution was a good political card for Northern Democrats because it would "give the Abolitionists trouble in the rear while we assail them in the front." Though the resolution was not adopted, its introduction sparked a public debate that grew into serious popular dissension before the summer was out. Supporting the proposal, the Selma *Daily Reporter* wrote, "It should be our business to hold aloft the olive branch to our implacable foe, and thus put ourselves in sympathy with the anti-war party at the North, thereby facilitating the overthrow of the Black Republican party."[37]

The Confederate Congress did adopt a public statement (aware that it would also be read by anti-war forces in the North) that opposed negotiation because previous such efforts had been spurned by the Federal government. Therefore, "unless some evidence is given of a change of policy" by the Northern administration, "any direct overtures for peace would compromise our self-respect, be fruitless of good, and interpreted by the enemy as an indication of weakness." The statement urged the "powerful political party" in the Northern states to resist Lincoln's tyranny:

> Many sagacious persons at the North discover in the usurpations of their Government the certain overthrow of their liberties. A large number revolt from the unjust war waged upon the South and would gladly bring it to an end. Others look with alarm upon the complete subversion of constitutional freedom by Abraham Lincoln, and feel in their own persons the bitterness of the slavery which three years of war have failed to inflict on the South. Brave and earnest men at the North have spoken out against the usurpations and cruelties daily practiced. The success of these men over the radical and despotic faction which now rules the North may open the way to peaceful negotiation and a cessation of this bloody and unnecessary war.[38]

Though Wright's resolution failed, it represented the position of three very powerful Georgia politicians: Alexander H. Stephens, the diminutive Confederate vice president; his brother, Linton; and Governor Joseph E. Brown. They sought to make the election the centerpiece of Confederate policy in 1864 and favored an overt and public strategy in doing so. That spring, Stephens proposed his ideas to Davis, whose relations with him were less than cordial. Davis tersely rejected them, failing even to address Stephens' labored argument. Stephens became a powerful opponent of Davis before the spring was over.[39]

There was no disagreement between Davis and his opponents on the importance of the 1864 election and the prospects it presented. There was a serious disagreement over strategy. The president wanted to initiate widespread covert operations from Canada to influence Northern public opinion, free Confederate prisoners, undermine the Union war effort, aid the campaigns of peace candidates, and eventually defeat the Republicans at the ballot box. This would involve an extensive, unofficial fifth column. While sponsoring these agents, the Confederate government would maintain a public posture of vigorous prosecution of the war as though certain of victory. Davis' detractors wanted a policy of overt, direct support of the Peace Democrats while maintaining a strong defensive posture militarily designed to deny Federal battlefield victories. They repeated calls for peace negotiations and a cease-fire.⁴⁰

Davis appointed Thomas H. Hines to carry out his verbal orders, the specific nature of which were never revealed by either.⁴¹ A bright young officer, Hines had been a scout for Morgan's raiders and had been with the general when he and several other officers escaped from the Ohio Penitentiary. Hines was dispatched to Canada to form a command of escaped rebel prisoners and then to conduct "appropriate enterprises of war against our enemies." Unlike most Confederate agents who went to Canada, Hines did not travel by blockade runner. He was to pass "through the United States under such character and in such mode as you may deem most safe," and to "confer with the leading persons friendly or attached to the cause of the Confederacy, or who may be advocates of peace." He was to encourage "our friends to organize and prepare themselves to render such aid as circumstances may allow" and also "those favorable to a peaceful adjust-ment to the *employment of all agencies calculated to effect such consum-mation on terms consistent always with the independence of the Confederate States*" (italics added). He was also "at liberty to employ such of our soldiers as you may collect in any hostile operation." (These were the rebel prisoners held in the Northwest.) Hines was to orchestrate a Northwest conspiracy in which thousands of Copperheads, having been armed by the Confederate agents in Canada, would liberate the rebel prisoners in Camp Douglas in Illinois, Camp Morton in Indianapolis, and Johnson's Island in Lake Erie.⁴²

Davis selected Jacob Thompson of Mississippi, a former U.S. secretary of the interior, and Clement C. Clay, a former U.S. senator and a strong defender of the Confederate president, to direct the secret mission in Canada. There they met James P. Holcombe, who was already in Canada on other business for the Confederacy. Of the three, Thompson was clearly in charge; like Parliament and Congress, he controlled the pursestrings of the generous fund that had been authorized by the Confederate Congress.⁴³

During the summer and fall, these civilian "directors," Hines, and a motley crew of Confederates who had been rounded up tried to damage the Lincoln administration and hinder the Union war effort. Their pet project was to be the spontaneous rebellion in the Northwest.⁴⁴ The Confederates were convinced that a large organization of committed peace men were prepared to rise up, on signal, and storm prisoner of war camps, engage in pitched battle with Federal troops, and release thousands of rebel prisoners to wreak havoc in Northern communities. On five occasions, scheduled uprisings failed to materialize, which has led many historians to conclude that the organization was never as large or as rebellious as claimed by members and by Union officers and spies. Lincoln dismissed the problem with his characteristic humor. It was one thing to take "oaths against the Government; to declare in their secret councils they were ready to shed the last drop of their blood to abolish it. . . . Shedding the last drop of one's blood is a comparatively easy sacrifice—it is shedding the first drop that costs."[45]

There was also contact between the rebel agents and Vallandigham, who had been chosen as supreme commander of the Sons of Liberty. His stay in the Confederacy had contributed significantly to Southern leaders' belief that there was a strong element of pro-Confederate Westerners in the Ohio River states. He had created an impression of sympathy, if not outright support, for the Confederate cause. Thus it was logical that the rebel agents would contact Vallandigham upon their arrival in Canada. Hines did so on June 9. On June 11, Thompson met with Vallandigham in Windsor, Ontario, and asked about the Sons of Liberty. The content of the conversation has long been disputed. In testimony before the Cincinnati Military Commission on March 29, 1865, Vallandigham denied that he had been a member of any organization involved in any way with the Camp Douglas conspiracy, which was an attack on the camp planned to coincide with the Democratic nominating convention in August 1864. Yes, he had been the supreme commander of the Sons of Liberty, but that was only a political organization, an auxiliary for the Democratic Party, similar to the Republican Union League. He acknowledged meeting with Thompson in Windsor, but said they had only discussed peace, compromise, and Reconstruction. When Thompson asked about the Sons of Liberty, Vallandigham claimed he brought him up short because Thompson was not a member and only members were entitled to know about the organization.[46]

Thompson remembered the meeting differently. Vallandigham told him the Sons of Liberty had 300,000 members, including 85,000 in Illinois, 50,000 in Indiana, and 40,000 in Ohio. Thompson claimed he offered the Copperhead $25,000 to arm his followers, but Vallandigham made a great show of righteousness in refusing. However, Vallandigham introduced

James J. Barrett, adjutant general and grand lecturer of the Sons of Liberty, who accepted the money. The primary reason for the last meeting, when Thompson gave Barrett the $25,000, was to discuss plans for the Sons of Liberty to attack Camp Douglas and free the rebel prisoners there. And Thompson said that Vallandigham initiated him into the Sons of Liberty.[47]

Vallandigham's claim that the Sons of Liberty never had a paramilitary aspect is incredible. Felix Stidger, Horace Heffren, and others testified that the organization definitely did, and that members planned espionage of various sorts. Could Vallandigham have been unaware of the most important characteristic of the organization he headed? If there was any truth to what Hines, Thompson, Headley, and other Confederate agents wrote regarding the meetings with Vallandigham, then he was lying.[48]

When Vallandigham testified at the Cincinnati trials in March 1865, the information that Thompson, Hines, Castelman, Headley, and others revealed after the war was not there to challenge the testimony. If what Thompson later said was true, then Vallandigham had engaged in treason. Klement pointed out that Thompson was implicated after the war on charges of corruption related to his postwar handling of the appropriation given him to conduct covert operations. According to Klement, this must be weighed when considering his credibility against Vallandigham's. The charge of misfeasance against Thompson still did not explain why he would intentionally lie about Vallandigham. What did he have to gain by concocting an elaborate fiction? On the other hand, if what Thompson said were true, then Vallandigham had a great deal to lose by answering honestly. The rebel commissioner simply had no good reason to manufacture such a ruse.[49]

Not only had Vallandigham and other leaders of the Sons of Liberty met with Confederate agents, they had planned a violent rebellion against the government. Their plans included armed attacks on camps guarded by Federal troops and marching on Indianapolis and killing or capturing Governor Oliver P. Morton. Then the Sons of Liberty would presumably either join the Northwest with the South in its bid for independence, or at the least take the Northwest out of the war. That none of these plans materialized does not alter the significance of what did take place. Weapons were purchased and shipped to leaders of the Sons of Liberty, and to what purpose if not to be used against the government? The rebel agents and commissioners were not stupid or delusional. Could they all have misjudged the potential for violent rebellion that badly? Were those Union authorities, civilian and military, who firmly believed in the existence of the conspiracy, similarly deluded? A number of historians have suggested just that as the explanation for why the Northwest Conspiracy never came to fruition.[50] However, there is another factor to consider. Wood Gray, James McPherson, and others have pointed out that all of the dates scheduled for the uprising came between early June and the end of August, which was the darkest period of the war for the North militarily. Between Lincoln's nomination and the Democratic National Convention, almost nothing good happened for Union armies. Staggering numbers of men were dying in a bloodbath that far exceeded the losses during any previous spring campaign. The administration's war effort was self-destructing, and the best thing Democrats could do was to sit back and stay out of harm's way. Nothing would have polarized the country so quickly as outbreaks of violence by those seeking to release Confederate prisoners. Northern citizens who were not already either "total war" or "total peace" would be driven into the arms of the government. Though the Copperheads were probably one of the most impractical political groupings in American history, on this occasion even they could see that precipitous action might easily undo all the gains of the summer.[51]

With each day, the Democrats were growing in strength. Because of this, and in order to have the best possible perspective when they nominated a candidate, they moved their convention back nearly two months to the end of August. Victory by the regular process seemed imminent so long as they did nothing to alter drastically the popular perception. They were not likely to try to destroy a government they were about to take control of legitimately.

Thompson's courtship of Clement Vallandigham did not end with Vallandigham's return to Ohio. The Peace Democrats had succeeded in getting one of their own the nomination for governor in Illinois. James C. Robinson was unabashedly for peace at any price. In a public letter to his constituency, reprinted by many Southern newspapers, Robinson said that the Confederacy was still strong and resilient, that the Lincoln government was destroying the Constitution, and that the nation was fast approaching bankruptcy. Unless there were drastic changes at the top of the government, and in the policy pursued by the national leaders, the Union would be lost.[52]

In September, after the Confederates failed to spark an uprising at the Chicago Convention, a committee of Peace Democrats journeyed to Canada to visit Thompson. They carried a note from Vallandigham, who wrote that the election of Robinson as governor of Illinois was of "the first importance," and funds for his campaign were needed for victory. That

Vallandigham was soliciting support from a source currently at war with the United States was of a treasonous ilk in itself. Author James Horan claims that Vallandigham promised that Robinson, if elected, would turn over control of the state militia and arsenal to the Sons of Liberty.[53]

The Confederate agents were by now somewhat skeptical of Copperhead promises. Hines advised Thompson to obtain a written guarantee from Robinson. Among the Thomas Henry Hines Papers is a note, signed by Hines, about this transaction.

> Robinson was Peace Democratic candidate for the Governor of Illinois. Application had been made to the Confederate Commissioner for funds to carry on the canvass. Desiring, before giving pecuniary aid, some written evidence as to the course Mr. Robinson would pursue if elected, this letter was written to satisfy the Confederate Commissioners on that point. Verbal assurances from Mr. Robinson, fully committing himself to our movement had already been had. A large amount of money was furnished on these assurances.[54]

In a subsequent letter addressed to Copperhead leaders in Indiana and Ohio, Robinson wrote:

> I would state that if I am elected governor of the state I will see that its sovereignty is maintained, the laws fully enforced and its citizens protected from arbitrary arrest, and if necessary for these purposes will, after exhausting the civil, employ military force of the state.
> I will also be happy to avail myself of the counsel and aid of the Executive Committee of the Peace Democracy in the conduct of the organization of the militia of the state, recognizing the fact that a well-equipped militia is necessary for the maintenance of states' rights as well as the rights of people.[55]

Those who have claimed that Republican accusations of domestic treason against Copperheads in 1864 were simply hyperbolic campaign tactics turn a deaf ear to such evidence as the Robinson letter. If it was not treasonous for an Illinois gubernatorial candidate to do business with enemy agents, then the definition of treason has been narrowed tremendously.[56] Thompson contributed significant sums in gold to Robinson's campaign.

Of the various state Democratic Committees, Illinois was the one most solidly in the camp of the Peace Democracy. Contributions made by the Confederate Secret Service identified the South's last hope of success.[57]

Many other activities were attempted and projects funded from Canada. Confederate agents subsidized Copperhead newspapers, in particular the New York *Daily News*, which received $25,000 and thereafter conveyed messages between Richmond and Canada in its columns. Peace rallies were subsidized, with the emphasis on the notion that peace could be had if only Lincoln were not president. A plan, apparently suggested by Confederate Cabinet Secretary Judah P. Benjamin, to drive up the price of gold by buying it in large quantities and then shipping it out of the country, was attempted by Thompson (the price of gold did rise by nearly $100 per ounce that spring and summer). Weapons were purchased, as was "Greek fire," a new incendiary substance. Confederate agents damaged or destroyed a half-dozen military steamboats in St. Louis; an Army warehouse in Mattoon, Illinois; Grant's port facilities in City Point, Virginia; and several hotels in New York City. There was a plan to shell and burn Maine's coastal cities. An attempt was made to capture the Federal gunboat *Michigan* on Lake Erie as part of the plan to liberate the prisoner of war camp on Johnson's Island. The plot went awry, as did so many Confederate intrigues, because an informant tipped off authorities.[58]

The most conspicuous success of Confederate covert operations, however, came when the Confederates mounted a peace offensive. Their efforts were aided considerably by Horace Greeley's contact with Lincoln, urging him to push for peace. Based upon communication from a highly unreliable source, Greeley initiated correspondence and activities that nearly led to Lincoln's defeat. It must have struck Clay and Holcombe, two so-called Confederate commissioners in Canada, as a remarkable windfall that Greeley had suddenly provided them a legitimacy that their best efforts had been unable to achieve.

In *Bullets, Ballots, and Rhetoric*, Larry Nelson described how these commissioners utilized the perception in the North that peace with the restoration of the Union was plausible. He pointed out that "despite the complexities of Northern peace philosophy, the commissioners still hoped to employ it (Democratic willingness to yield much to restore the Union) in the cause of the Confederacy." In private correspondence, Clay wrote, "The Demos will yield a great deal, almost anything, for reunion." On August 11, 1864, Clay informed Secretary of War Judah P. Benjamin that when questioned about whether the Southern states would consent to reunion, he would typically respond:

> Not now. You have shed so much of their best blood, have desolated so many homes, inflicted so much injury, caused so much mental and physical agony, and have threatened and attempted such irreparable wrongs, without justification or excuse, as they believe, that they would now prefer extermination to your embraces as friends and fellow-citizens of the same government. You must wait till the blood of our slaughtered people has exhaled from the soil, till the homes which you have destroyed have been rebuilt, till our badges of mourning have been laid aside, and the memorials of our wrongs are no longer visible on every hand, before you propose to rebuild a common government. But I think the South will agree to an armistice of six or more months and to a treaty of amity and commerce, securing peculiar and exclusive privileges to both sections, and possibly to an alliance defensive, or even, for some purposes, both defensive and offensive.[59]

Clay and Holcombe had never presented themselves as accredited peace commissioners and claimed this characterization arose from the "fervid and fanciful imagination" or the "ignorance, folly, or knavery" of the originator of the scheme or the creative talents of "Dame Rumor." However, as they sought to cooperate with Northern peace advocates, stimulate discontent in the Northwest, and convince the voters of that region that no peace was possible as long as Lincoln was president, they allowed rumors to spread that the South might agree to reunion if slavery were permitted to continue. When Lincoln issued a memorandum on July 18, stating that emancipation was a condition of any negotiated peace, it magnified this impression in the public mind. Clay wrote to Benjamin, "We have not felt it our duty to declare . . . that reunion was impossible. . . . We have not dispelled the fond delusion . . . that some kind of common government might at some time hereafter be re-established." This impression, Clay added, had benefited the Confederacy, because "if we can credit the asseverations of both peace and war Democrats . . . our correspondence with them has been promotive of our wishes." Clay declared, "I am satisfied that the correspondence has tended strongly towards consolidating the Democracy and dividing the Republicans and encouraging the desire for peace." This seemed to verify the position of those peace men who questioned the wisdom of Lincoln's emancipation policy, claiming that it alone stood in the way of reconciliation and reunion. It was the strongest argument the Democrats could muster to support the position that the president and his "abolition party" were the sole cause of the continuation of the war. It posed a powerful obstacle to Lincoln's re-election in the summer of 1864.[60]

The South was buoyed by the news from Canada. Mallory wrote Mrs. Clay several weeks after the revelation of the Niagara correspondence that he was satisfied with the Northern political situation as it was. "Our weak brothers in N.C. & Geo., who have clamored so loudly that peace propositions should be made by us, cannot fail to see that, at present, peace with Lincoln means degradation."[61] In the North, many were disheartened by the news. Clay reported to Benjamin that "all the Democratic presses denounce Mr. Lincoln's manifesto in strong terms, and many Republican presses admit it was a blunder." Governor Zebulon Vance of North Carolina was able to exploit the correspondence in his closely contested campaign for re-election against peace candidate William Holden.[62]

The Columbus *Crisis* untypically stated a position that was shared by many Northerners in the aftermath of the Lincoln memorandum concerning peace conditions:

Tens of thousands of white men must yet bite the dust to allay the negro mania of the President. . . . A half million more are called for and millions in debts are yet to be saddled upon the people to carry out this single negro idea, while the negroes themselves will be literally exterminated in the effort to make them equals with the white man.[63]

Even Lincoln's secretaries and biographers, Nicolay and Hay, who normally cast positive light on his every act or statement, admitted that the Confederate response to the memorandum "formed a not ineffective document in a heated political campaign."[64]

Clay and Holcombe had scored a major public relations success for the Confederacy, and if they were at times halting and uncertain, it was because nobody had ever imagined they would actually draw the direct attention of the president and the editor of the leading Republican newspaper. Direct communication between the commissioners and their government was impossible, so they either had to take advantage of the unexpected opportunity or probably lose the chance permanently. They knew they were acting without authority and were probably concerned about doing something that might have far-ranging consequences.[65]

It was incredible that Lincoln had involved himself in such a potentially damaging situation. He was facing re-election and had to project accessibility to reasonable peace proposals. Perhaps he was driven to run risks that jeopardized his ability to wage the relentless and seemingly interminable war that the American conflict had become in 1864.

However, it is difficult to understand why Davis felt impelled to meet with Colonel James F. Jaquess and James R. Gilmore, two Union agents who had come to Richmond. It is even more difficult to understand why he then very candidly rejected any consideration of reunion and established that nothing short of independence would do. It seemed profoundly inconsistent with the best Confederate interests. Although he could not have known when he met with Jaquess and Gilmore just what was taking place at Niagara, his act in officially meeting with these unauthorized emissaries and making bellicose statements could only weaken the cause of those arguing for peace and negotiation in the North. Davis was not facing a vote of confidence by the people and though he too had a problem with a peace movement, he had to know that such candor and bravado would hurt his position. Also it had to deflate a rapidly growing peace movement in his enemy's rear.

The editor of the Augusta *Constitutionalist* wrote, "Lincoln was the prime mover of the whole affair, and engineered it with no other object than to promote his chances for re-election." The Richmond *Dispatch* claimed that had Davis refused an audience with the negotiators, "this would have been repeated through five hundred newspapers, and its consequences would have been fatal to the Peace party of the North." This interpretation did not square with the facts. Davis' refusal to meet with a couple of Northerners who claimed no authority other than their own personal interest in peace would not have been a newsworthy event. However, his meeting with them and stating very stern demands for recognition of Confederate independence played right into Lincoln's hands.

Thus Davis had inexplicably undone much of what had been achieved by the commissioners. Clay wrote to Davis, asking him to soften his stance, explaining the importance of not upsetting the impression in the North that peace could be had if only Lincoln were removed. But by the time this letter reached Davis, he was more concerned with other problems, particularly the crisis in the Army of Tennessee. It had by then retreated to the defenses of Atlanta, whose loss the Confederacy could not afford. The opportunity of July was gone by the end of August, and with it the last significant prospect of Southern independence.[66]

The Niagara Falls peace offensive was the only Confederate covert operation that had any influence on the Northern election, promoted the Southern cause, or hampered the Northern war effort. It might have done much more but for a couple of events at the end of August and beginning of September. The Democrats convened in late August, meaning they had to expose their vulnerabilities by adopting a platform. Then, on September 2, Atlanta fell.

The news hurt the rebel covert operations. Had the convention taken place a week later, when Atlanta's capture had deflated the certainty of Democratic success, many more Copperheads might have been desperate enough to undertake the assaults on camps Douglas and Morton that were supposed to occur during the meeting. As it was, timing and luck saved Lincoln's candidacy and re-election.

During September and October, several attempts by rebel operatives from Canada resulted in failure. In mid-September a plan to capture the gunboat *U.S.S. Michigan* came to naught when Captain Charles Cole, the Confederate officer who had gained access to the warship by charming the Federal officers, was arrested at the dinner party he had thrown for them.[67]

It had been a good plan, but Cole was betrayed. The gunboat had been tipped off, and an armed crew was waiting for the arrival of a Confederate steamer. But the members of the rebel band assigned to conduct the takeover grew suspicious as their boat neared, and threatened to mutiny if their commander did not call off the operation. He finally, grudgingly, relented, and another Confederate covert operation failed.[68]

Several miles from the Canadian border is the sleepy city of St. Albans, Vermont. It was far removed from the fighting of the Civil War, and nobody there imagined they would ever see any Confederates. On October 19, 1864, twenty raiders who had just ridden across the border suddenly pulled guns and their leader announced, "This city is now in the possession of the Confederate States of America." The raiders stripped three banks of gold worth $175,000, stole some horses, and burned a number of buildings, farmhouses, and bridges. They killed one person who had fired at them from a porch and generally turned a place that had had little to do with the war previously into a bastion of Unionism. The governor declared an emergency, Canadian officials arrested the raiders, and diplomatic relations between the United States and Canada became strained.[69]

A final plan for a rebellion by the Sons of Liberty was pressed by Hines, the irrepressible rebel agent who was designated to be the military commander of the Northwest uprising. Despite repeated disappointments, Hines' vision of a Northwest Confederacy had grown. His new day of destiny was to be November 8, 1864, election day in the United States. The uprising was to begin at noon and this time would not be limited to one city or area. It would erupt spontaneously in New York, Chicago, Cincinnati, and every place where Sons of Liberty organizations existed. If prisoner of war camps were in or near a city, then they would be primary targets for local Copperhead organizations.[70]

Hines was probably one of the last people to accept the defeat of his beloved South. With great energy and optimism, he had clung to his dream of a Northwest Confederacy. He attended secret sessions of the society and instructed members on how to cut telegraph lines, storm prison compounds, and set fire to government buildings.[71] He also dispatched an agent to Missouri to help arm guerrilla fighters there. Hines may have lost some of his high hopes for the Midwestern wing of the Sons of Liberty, because his grand plan for the November uprising included Eastern cities as well. New York, Boston, Chicago, and Cincinnati were to be burned. In those cities, prominent Copperheads worked with the rebel agents in planning the uprising.

In New York, one such ally was the "peace at any cost" editor of the *Freeman's Journal*, James A. McMasters. McMasters was closely affiliated with Fernando Wood, one of the leaders and managers of the Sons of Liberty in that city. The Sons had been armed and organized for the uprising, and 20,000 could be expected to turn out on the appointed day. In assigning John W. Headley his responsibilities for this mission, Jacob Thompson had said that "the New York managers" had suggested taking possession of the city on the afternoon of election day. They had also advised that fires should be set to create confusion and minimize resistance.[72]

By Headley's account, he and Colonel Robert Martin, the officer in command of the New York mission, met with McMasters to discuss the uprising. Headley indicated that McMasters promised he would request that Governor Horatio Seymour send a confidential agent to New York with whom Martin and Headley could confer. McMasters "understood that the Governor would not use militia to suppress the insurrection in the city but would leave that duty to the authorities at Washington." Then, in the only highlighted sentence in the chapter, Headley wrote, *"Indeed, we were to have the support of the Governor's official neutrality."*[73]

Four days later McMasters sent for Martin and Headley and introduced them to Seymour's private secretary. The Confederates were assured that "our expectations would be lived up to by the Governor and we could prosecute our plans accordingly." If what Headley said was true, then the most important elected Democrat in the country was conspiring with rebel agents who were committed to the defeat of the Federal government. It is inconceivable that Seymour's personal secretary met with Confederate officers without the governor's knowledge and approval. If the governor was vouchsafing any espionage activities of rebel agents, then he was engaged in treasonous conduct.

A parallel plan being orchestrated in Chicago involved no Democrat of Seymour's stature, but it involved a brigadier general of the Sons of Liberty, Charles Walsh. The uprising was to coincide with an attack by the more than 8,000 Confederate prisoners in Camp Douglas on the prison guards. According to a later government investigator, "Chicago was to be sacked, burned, looted and turned into an enemy city."[74]

Loose tongues apparently doomed all the election day plots. In New York, Benjamin F. Butler and 10,000 Union soldiers showed up several days before the election. The *New York Times* wrote, "The wisdom of the Government in selecting the man who scattered the howling rabble of New Orleans like chaff, and reduced that city to order most serene, approved itself to the conscience of every patriot and made Copperheads squirm and writhe in torture."[75]

In Chicago, Colonel Jeffrey Sweet, commandant of Camp Douglas, learned of the plot several days before the election from a Confederate officer in the compound. Likewise in Boston, Cincinnati, and elsewhere, troops hastily arrived in response to information from agents or spies. There was no violence of any significance on election day. The last covert operation designed to take advantage of the national election in the United States failed as miserably as nearly all of its predecessors.[76]

The last operation of the Confederate espionage program was not designed to influence the election. It was not carried out until nearly three weeks after the results were in, and it was done in spite. The rebel agents who had been in New York since the beginning of November were feeling all the frustration of their failed efforts. Using the "Greek fire" supplied by Copperheads, on November 25 they burned a number of fine hotels and P. T. Barnum's famous museum. It was one last futile act.[77]

In 1864, the national election was perhaps the only remaining prospect for Confederate victory. If the Confederates could have helped defeat Lincoln, they would have greatly increased the prospect of Southern independence. Combined with military success on the battlefield, clandestine operations could have convinced the loyal population that the war could not be won or that the price of victory would be too great. Through the spring and most of the summer, the two-pronged strategy seemed to be eminently successful. However, Atlanta's fall was the last turning point of the war. Union victory was just a matter of time and, with that revelation, Lincoln's re-election was assured.

7

"We Shall Nobly Save or Meanly Lose"

At the height of the crises in the spring and summer of 1864, Horace Greeley decided he had divined the means for bringing the war to an early and satisfactory conclusion. He claimed there were negotiators in Canada authorized by the Confederate government to discuss peace terms. To fully understand the almost unbelievable events that followed, one must understand this unpredictable man and his history with the Republican Party. For a decade, Greeley had been the leading figure of one faction in a bitter party dispute that had influenced Republican politics in New York State. The other faction was led by Secretary of State William H. Seward and his patron, the influential Albany newspaperman Thurlow Weed. Both factions were powerful, and no Republican who wanted to succeed in national politics could afford to offend either.[1]

The parties to the dispute were peevish and the squabble did not stop at the state line. Both sides sought the support of the administration. Lincoln attempted to stay aloof, but often had to intervene to avert ugly disagreements over patronage and other political concerns. Years of experience in Illinois politics had taught him the value of compromise, but Greeley was not a politician. He was a dreamer, a visionary, and such men abhor the pragmatism of politics. Compromise was the sacrifice of principle for expediency, and Greeley despised this quality in Lincoln's character.[2]

In 1860, Greeley had supported Lincoln because he was the only

Republican who had a chance of denying the nomination to Seward. Greeley's role had caused a permanent and bitter rift in New York Republican politics. It also made Lincoln somewhat beholden to Greeley, without whom he never would have become president. This was important in 1864 because of the diplomatic dance the president and editor performed over the peace issue. It had been the bloodiest season of the war, and the mere mention of "peace" raised the hopes of all but the most cynical. Though Lincoln was skeptical of Greeley's claim of peace negotiators in Canada, he knew that a failure to respond would find its way onto the front page of the *Tribune.*

Apart from Greeley, two other men played major roles in the Confederate "peace panic" of 1864. William Connell "Colorado" Jewett, a strange man descended from a prominent Maine family, spent the war chastising both Davis and Lincoln for continuing it. He traveled back and forth from the United States to Europe as a self-appointed peace emissary, lobbying heads of state and prominent Americans to intervene and end the conflict.[3] Kentuckian George N. Sanders had operated as an independent contractor for the Confederacy, arranging the construction of ships. Before the war, he had been involved in politics and had obtained an appointment as consul in London. There he had thrown lavish parties and become known for his "rabid republicanism," which led him to become associated with Victor Hugo, Ledrou Rollin, Giuseppe Garibaldi, and Joseph Mazzini in a scheme to overthrow the monarchies of Europe and establish republican principles.[4] In 1864, Sanders was in Canada as an unofficial intermediary between Copperheads and Clement C. Clay and James P. Holcombe in Saint Catharines, Ontario.

Jewett and Sanders had been organizing meetings of influential Northerners with Clay and Holcombe. Greeley had in the past publicized Jewett's peace efforts and on at least one occasion had commended Jewett for his efforts to save the Union.[5] On July 5, Jewett wrote to Greeley:

> I have to advise having just left Hon. Geo. N. Sanders of Ky on the Canada side. *I am authorized to state to you—for your use only—not the public—that two ambassadors—of Davis & Co are now in Canada—with full & complete powers for a peace* & Mr Sanders requests that you come on immediately to me at Cataract House—to have a private interview, or if you will send the Presidents protection for him & two friends, they will come on & Meet you. He sayd the whole matter can be

comsummated by me and you—them & President Lincoln. Telegraph me in such form—that I may know—if you come here—or they come on—with me.[6]

On July 7, Greeley wrote to Lincoln, enclosing the "letter and telegraphic dispatch that I received yesterday from our irrepressible friend, Colorado Jewett, at Niagara Falls. I think they deserve attention." Greeley's disarming overture did not beguile the president into underestimating the situation. Lincoln moved immediately to blunt the editor's initiative. Greeley's ego had not suffered in the slightest from previous embarrassments. He now advised Lincoln:

> I venture to remind you that our bleeding, bankrupt, almost dying country also longs for peace—shudders at the prospect of fresh conscriptions, of further wholesale devastations, and of new rivers of human blood. And a wide-spread conviction that the Government . . . are not anxious for Peace, and do not improve proffered opportunities to achieve it, is doing great harm now, and is morally certain, unless removed, to do far greater in the approaching Elections.[7]

Greeley felt that a substantive overture by Lincoln would benefit the peace candidate in the gubernatorial election in North Carolina. It would also offset the draft call Lincoln would have to make sometime that summer. Greeley implied that the president was unaware of the extent of peace sentiment in the country and demonstrated how the national desperation could lead individuals to confuse their priorities; "it may save us from a northern insurrection."[8]

In response, Lincoln again displayed his knack for turning situations to his advantage. He made Greeley his agent to proceed to Niagara Falls and present the commissioners with a safe-conduct letter so they could come to Washington. If they had any proposition in writing from Davis, "for peace, embracing the restoration of the Union and abandonment of slavery, whatever else it embraces, say to him he may come to me with you."[9] Greeley was apparently surprised and disoriented by the unexpectedly forthcoming response and seemed miffed at Lincoln's attempt to bring him into the negotiations.

Lincoln knew enough of Greeley's style that whatever the president's response, it would soon become the subject of public scrutiny. If he answered in writing, anything he said would also find its way into the newspaper, but at least that way he would have some control over the content and thus might influence the response of the people. In his written response to Lincoln's letter of July 9, Greeley displayed his usual audacity by rebuking Lincoln for not having received Alexander Stephens' Confederate peace overture in 1863, and then set out in detail exactly what terms the president should set for any discussions of peace. Among them were:

> 1. The Union is restored and declared perpetual. 2. Slavery is utterly and forever abolished throughout the same. 3. A complete amnesty for all political offenses. 4. Payment of $400,000,000 to the slave States, pro rata, for their slaves. 5. The slave States to be represented in proportion to their total population. 6. A National Convention to be called at once.[10]

Lincoln maintained the initiative, responding to the Greeley letter with a proposition:

> If you can find, any person anywhere professing to have any proposition of Jefferson Davis, in writing, for peace, embracing the restoration of the Union and abandonment of slavery, what ever else it embraces, say to him he may come to me with you, and that if he really brings such proposition, he shall, at the least, have safe conduct . . . (and without publicity, if he choose) to the point where you shall have met him.[11]

The president had deflected what could have been a damaging public assault on his war policy, by appointing his attacker as the government's agent in such negotiations. He also had significantly deflated any effect of refusing to accede to the demand for an immediate national convention by agreeing to Greeley's first two conditions. It was that public concession to the unpredictable Greeley, however, that nearly cost him the election.

Responding on July 10, Greeley claimed that if the rebel agents were empowered to commit their government, "they would decline to present their credentials to me." Likewise, they would not "open their budget and give me their best terms." In an uncharacteristic moment of self-deprecation, the editor wrote, "Green as I may be, I am not quite so verdant as to imagine anything of the sort. I have neither purpose nor desire to be made a confidant, far less an agent, in such negotiations."[12]

Greeley was free to compromise the position of the president he had played such a prominent role in nominating and electing. When the president did the same thing to him, the editor took offense. But Lincoln understood Greeley better than did the newspaperman his president. On this occasion, he was unwilling to let Greeley control correspondence that he knew would eventually reach the voting public. Lincoln was most vulnerable in the summer of 1864 to the accusation that because of his unwillingness to withdraw emancipation as a condition of peace, he was responsible for continuing the war. By drawing out of Lincoln a formal statement of his conditions for negotiations, Greeley had forced him to reveal his position on this sensitive issue to a public still greatly ambivalent regarding emancipation.

On July 13, Greeley again wrote Lincoln:

> I have now information on which I can rely that two persons, duly commissioned and empowered to negotiate for peace, are at this moment not far from Niagara Falls, in Canada, and are desirous of conferring with yourself or with such persons as you may appoint and empower to treat with them. Their names, (only given in confidence) are Hon. Clement C. Clay of Alabama, and Hon. Jacob Brown of Mississippi.[13]

The editor's source was George N. Sanders, whom only Greeley would consider reliable. There was no Jacob Brown representing the Confederacy in Canada. Since Greeley was obviously referring to Jacob Thompson, it is significant that Thompson was in Toronto and had nothing to do with the so-called Niagara Falls peace negotiations that summer. The second Confederate agent involved was James P. Holcombe, but accuracy was of little matter to Greeley when such issues as war or peace were involved.[14]

The actual correspondence from Sanders to Greeley read as follows:

> I am authorized to say that the Hon. Clement C. Clay, of Alabama, Prof. James C. Holcombe, of Virginia, and George N. Sanders, of Dixie, are ready and willing to go at once to Washington, upon complete and unqualified protection being given either by the President or Secretary of War. Let the permission include the three names and no other.[15]

This was the reliable information upon which Greeley was willing to hinge the future of the Lincoln presidency and perhaps the Union. Then, having vouched for the information, Greeley added a disclaimer:

> You will of course understand that I know nothing, and have proposed nothing, as to terms, and that nothing is conceded or taken for granted by the meeting of persons empowered to negotiate for peace. All that is assumed is a mutual desire to terminate this wholesale slaughter if a basis of adjustment can be mutually agreed on. And it seems to me high time that an effort should be made. . . .

Lincoln responded immediately. Determined not to be blamed for a failure of negotiations, he maintained his course. He made Greeley his agent for pursuing what Lincoln felt was probably a dead end. He telegraphed Greeley, chastising him for not having acted more vigorously with respect to Lincoln's earlier missive:

> I suppose you received my letter of the 9th. I have just received yours of the 13 and am disappointed by it. I was not expecting you to *send* me a letter, but to *bring* me a man, or men. Mr. Hay goes to you with my answer to yours of the 13th.[17]

He also dispatched his secretary, John Hay, with the following letter:

> Yours of the 13th. is just received; and I am disappointed that you have not already reached here with those Commissioners. . . . I not only intend a sincere effort for peace, but I intend that you shall be a personal witness that it is made.[18]

It was Lincoln's attempt to defuse the issue Greeley had raised. If there was even a remote possibility that the rebel agents might be able to initiate peace negotiations, then Lincoln had made a good-faith effort to explore the possibility.

The reluctant Greeley consented on the condition that he be given a safe-conduct pass for four people to be named by him. Lincoln agreed and again urged haste. He instructed Hay to "write the Safe-conduct . . . without waiting for one by mail from me. If there is, or is not, any thing in the affair, I wish to know it, without unnecessary delay." Hay wrote the pass to cover Clay, Thompson, Holcombe, and Sanders, and notified Lincoln by telegram on July 17. "Gave the order yesterday. He promised to start at once and I supposed did so. I return this evening if connections can be made."[19]

On the same day, Greeley telegraphed the commissioners that Lincoln had offered safe conduct to Washington.[20] Greeley was shocked by the reply from Clay and Holcombe:

> The safe conduct of the President of the United States has been tendered us, we regret to state, under some misapprehension of facts. We have not been accredited to him from Richmond as the bearers of propositions looking to the establishment of peace. We are, however, in the confidential employment of our Government, and are entirely familiar with its wishes and opinions on that subject; and we feel authorized to declare that, if the circumstances disclosed in this correspondence were communicated to Richmond we would be at once invested with the authority to which your letter refers.[21]

Greeley had still not informed his correspondents of the conditions to any negotiations. A straightforward statement that the proposition had to be in writing from Jefferson Davis and had to include abolition would have brought the farce to an end.[22]

In addressing this incident in their history of Lincoln's presidency, Nicolay and Hay wrote, "It is incomprehensible that a man of Mr. Greeley's experience should not have recognized at once the purport of this proposal." However, nothing seemed to shame the newspaperman and he simply acknowledged receipt of the letter from the agents "and then telegraphed to Mr. Lincoln the substance of what Clay and Holcombe had written."[23] The president, "with unwearied patience," then drew up the document that nearly destroyed his chances of re-election.

> TO WHOM IT MAY CONCERN: Any proposition which embraces the restoration of peace, the integrity of the whole Union, *and the abandonment of slavery,* and which comes by and with an authority that can control the armies now at war against the United States, and will be met by liberal terms on other substantial and collateral points, and the bearer or bearers thereof shall have safe conduct both ways.[24]

This message was given to Greeley at Niagara Falls on July 20. It was dated July 18, the day Lincoln had issued a 500,000–men draft call for September 5. As if he were attempting to deal with all his adversities simultaneously, Lincoln issued the two most controversial documents of that campaign season within a matter of hours, and only two weeks after having vetoed the Wade-Davis Act, a plan for Reconstruction put forth by Benjamin F. Wade and Henry W. Davis. And during the correspondence between Lincoln and Greeley, a Confederate army under Lieutenant General Jubal A. Early, after defeating or driving out Federal forces that had been wreaking havoc in the Shenandoah Valley that spring, pushed down the Valley, crossed the Potomac, and drove southeast toward Washington. The rebels pushed aside a hastily assembled force of Federals at the Monocacy River in Maryland and arrived at the outskirts of the capital on July 11. About 15,000 Confederates faced fortifications that had been stripped almost bare to reinforce Grant's army.[25]

The irony was that a government that had been saying the enemy was nearly defeated now found its capital in jeopardy. Grant dispatched the best corps of his army to Washington, but the London *Times* wrote that "the Confederacy is more formidable than ever." On July 20, the new editor of the Columbus (Ohio) *Crisis* surmised, "I just hear that a new call has been made for 500,000 men. If so, Lincoln is *deader* than dead." On July 12 the New York *World* posed the question, "Who shall revive the withered hopes that bloomed on the opening of Grant's campaign?"[26]

But the farce being acted out at Niagara Falls was not over. Perhaps feeling like the buffoon at this point, Greeley proposed to bring Jewett into the negotiations, which Hay vetoed immediately. Then Greeley refused to cross the border to deliver the president's terms unless Hay went with him. They entered Canada together and went to the Clifton House, where Clay and Holcombe were staying. Before they even entered the hotel, they were accosted by George Sanders. As they were waiting to be taken up to the commissioners' suite, Sanders conversed with Greeley in the bar.[27]

Clay was gone, so Hay and Greeley delivered Lincoln's "To Whom It May Concern" message to Holcombe, who promised a reply the following day. As they were leaving the hotel, Greeley, according to Hay's diary, told Sanders, "I expect to be blackguarded for what I have done, and I am not allowed to explain. But all I have done has been done under instructions." Greeley returned to New York and withdrew from further involvement in the negotiations, but not before naming Jewett to act as his agent. The following day, the Confederate agents gave their response to Jewett, who delivered a duplicate to the Associated Press. Thus, the man whose letter to Greeley had started the whole ridiculous episode revealed to the world the information his effort had yielded.[28]

The response, addressed to Greeley, contained the vitriol the commissioners wanted to heap on Lincoln.

> We feel confident that you must share our profound regret that the spirit which dictated the first step toward peace had not continued to animate the councils of your President. Had the representatives of the two Governments met to consider this question . . . who is there so bold as to pronounce that the frightful waste of individual happiness and public prosperity which is daily saddening the universal heart might not have been terminated[?] . . . Instead of the safe conduct which we solicited, and which your first letter gave us every reason to suppose would be extended for the purpose of initiating a negotiation in which neither Government would compromise its rights or its dignity, a document has been presented which provokes as much indignation as surprise. . . . Addressed "to whom it may concern," it precludes negotiation, and prescribes in advance the terms and conditions of peace. It returns to the original policy of "no bargaining, no negotiations, no truce with rebels except to bury their dead, until every man shall have laid down his arms, submitted to the Government, and sued for mercy. . . . It is enough for us to say that we have no use whatever for the paper which has been placed in our hands.[29]

Knowing the reply would be reprinted in newspapers across the North, they concluded with a splash of bravado intended to reinforce the popular Democratic theme that Lincoln was responsible for the remorseless, relentless nature of the war.

> This correspondence will not, however, we trust, prove wholly barren of good result. If there is any citizen of the Confederate States who has clung to a hope that peace was possible with this administration of the Federal Government it will strip from his eyes the last film of such delusion; or if there be any whose hearts have grown faint under the suffering and agony of this bloody struggle, it will inspire them with fresh energy to endure and brave whatever may yet be requisite to

preserve to themselves and their children all that gives value
and dignity to life or hope and consolation to death.[30]

This exchange was the one Confederate project in Canada that summer
that damaged Lincoln's re-election prospects. Except for Greeley's role,
it would have come to nothing.

After the breakdown of the negotiations, Greeley became very defensive
and self-conscious about his part. When other Republican newspapers,
particularly the *New York Times*, criticized him, he implied that Lincoln
caused the misunderstanding. He claimed that the safe-conduct letter given
him on July 16 had constituted a waiver by Lincoln of any conditions stated
in previous correspondence. He figured this freed him from announcing the
conditions in Lincoln's letters of July 9 and 15. Greeley's shallow and
transparent argument did both the president and the country a disservice.
His unwillingness to accept responsibility for his part in the unfortunate
affair damaged the prospects of an already troubled administration. It stood
in contrast to the kindness with which Lincoln had treated Greeley.[31]

Henry Raymond, editor of the *Times*, was a major competitor of Greeley
and was the manager of Lincoln's re-election campaign. Raymond disliked
Greeley even before the Niagara Falls debacle, and it only deepened his
contempt. When the commissioners' letter to Greeley hit the front pages,
Raymond exploded. The hypocritical Greeley's failure to disclose to the
Confederates the conditions that Lincoln had insisted upon, Raymond
charged, had caused the fiasco. Then when the commissioners blamed
Lincoln for the breakdown of the negotiations, "Greeley not only failed to
relieve him from it by making public the facts, but joined in ascribing to
Mr. Lincoln the failure of negotiations for peace and the consequent
prolongation of the war." Raymond felt there was no limit to Greeley's
perfidy, pointing out that according to Jewett's statement, Greeley "also
authorized him to express to the rebel commissioners his regrets, that the
negotiation should have failed in consequence of the President's 'change
of views.'"[32]

Raymond wanted to show that the Democrats and Confederates were
on common ground as they shrieked about Lincoln as a warmonger.
Southern newspapers said it was evidence of Northern determination to
destroy the Confederacy.

Lincoln could have regained some public confidence simply by exposing
all of Greeley's hypocrisy and petulance, but he chose to bear the blame

for the breakdown of negotiations. He did, however, learn much about Greeley from this affair. If he had believed the editor to be a man of character, he was disabused of the notion. Secretary of the Navy Gideon Welles recorded the discussion about Greeley at the August 19 Cabinet meeting.

> Concerning Greeley, to whom the President clung too long and confidingly, he said to-day that Greeley is an old shoe— good for nothing now, whatever he has been. In early life, and with few mechanics and but little means in the West, we used, said he, to make our shoes last a great while with much mending, and sometimes, when far gone, we found the leather so rotten the stitches would not hold. Greeley is so rotten that nothing can be done with him. He is not truthful; the stitches all tear out.[33]

For his part, Greeley returned to campaigning for a new convention at which a candidate other than Lincoln could be nominated. As a final insult, he argued that the president had bungled the peace negotiations by changing the conditions at just the point when agreement seemed imminent. He claimed this was additional proof that Lincoln was not the right man to lead.[34]

Another peace conference took place that summer at the same time as the nonsense at Niagara Falls. The coincidence was remarkable and would lead some to suggest that the peace mission to Richmond was coordinated by some evil genius in the White House. Although such an interpretation requires an active imagination, at least one historian has suggested the plausible theory that Lincoln knew of the Confederate peace offensive, possibly from a double agent, and initiated a Northern peace offensive as a countermeasure. If so, one has to accept that the president was possessed of a remarkable kind of sixth sense, because it is difficult to imagine that even Lincoln could have anticipated that Horace Greeley would make himself such a witting accomplice to a scheme intended to erode support for the war.[35]

Two peace emissaries went to Richmond that July. The first was Colonel James F. Jaquess, a Methodist minister whom Governor Richard Yates had commissioned to raise the 73rd Illinois Volunteer Regiment. In May 1863, he had written to Brigadier General James A. Garfield, also a fundamentalist Christian, who was then an aide to Major General William S. Rosecrans. The letter was a labored explanation of the history of the antebellum split of the Methodist Episcopal Church over slavery. Jaquess said he had spoken with members of the Methodist Episcopal Church South, the Southern church resulting from the break, who were in Southern territory under Union occupation. They had told him:

> They consider the rebellion has killed the Methodist Episcopal Church South; that it has virtually obliterated slavery, and all the prominent questions of difference between the North and the South; that they are desirous of returning to the "old church" (Methodist Episcopal); that their brethren of the South are most heartily tired of the Rebellion; and that they most ardently desire peace, and the privilege of returning to their allegiance to church and state, and that they will do this on the first offer coming from a reliable source.[36]

He concluded with an offer to "go into the Southern Confederacy and return within ninety days with terms of peace that the Government will accept."

Garfield showed the letter to Rosecrans, who forwarded it to Lincoln with a note that read, "I do not anticipate the results that he seems to expect, but believe that a moral force will be generated by his mission that will more than compensate us for his temporary absence from the regiment."[37] Lincoln was impressed enough by the correspondence to write back:

> Such a mission as he proposes I think promises good, if it were free from difficulties, which I fear it can not be. First, he can not go with any Government authority whatever. This is absolute and imperative. Secondly, if he goes without authority he takes a great deal of personal risk—he may be condemned and executed as a spy. If, for any reason, you think fit to give Colonel Jaquess a furlough, and any authority from me for that object is necessary, you hereby have it for any length of time you see fit.[38]

Jaquess talked his way through Confederate lines and actually reached Richmond, but Davis refused to see him and the colonel was back in Baltimore a week later. He returned to the Army of the Cumberland and proved himself to be a better soldier than diplomat during the fall campaigns of that army.[39]

The second member of the peace commission was James R. Gilmore, co-editor of a monthly antislavery periodical called the *Continental* during the war. Before the war, he had been involved in cotton exporting and had traveled extensively in the South. Gilmore was an acquaintance of Greeley and the *Tribune* had published a number of his articles and books. It was because of this association that he met Jaquess in the spring of 1863. Greeley had by then already begun his relentless search for an alternative to Lincoln for the 1864 Republican presidential nomination, and Rosecrans was just then riding the crest of military success and popular acclaim. Greeley commissioned Gilmore to travel to Tennessee and learn where Rosecrans stood on slavery. If he was right on the subject, the *Tribune* editor would begin promoting his candidacy. It was while Gilmore was with the Army of the Cumberland that the letter from Jaquess arrived at headquarters.[40]

Probably no general in either army during the war was more open with the press than Rosecrans. There were few secrets in the Western army during his command. Thus Gilmore, a journalist, knew about the Jaquess proposal almost as soon as Rosecrans did. Though Gilmore was not initially impressed with Jaquess, the colonel's persistence and idealism were infectious and within a short time he had won over Gilmore plus most of the general staff. Gilmore became friendly enough with Jaquess that Rosecrans commissioned him to deliver the colonel's proposal plus Rosecrans' note to Lincoln in person. That would also make it possible for Gilmore to present his own arguments in favor of the proposal. The colonel's letter and the reporter's arguments were compelling enough to persuade the president to sanction the effort in 1863.[41]

In the aftermath of the unsuccessful Jaquess mission in 1863, press coverage had been unfavorable. Gilmore felt that the mission had probably failed because Jaquess had no experience in diplomacy. In April 1864, Gilmore met with Lincoln again and urged him to allow Jaquess to approach Davis a second time. Gilmore argued that some explicit statement from Davis defining separation as a condition for peace would kill the Copperhead movement, remove any illusions about Southern willingness to compromise, and restore faith in the administration. Again Lincoln was convinced, but this time he wanted Gilmore to conduct the mission. Jaquess would accompany him as the "ticket of admission." The president was clearly more comfortable with the pragmatic Gilmore than Jaquess in charge of the mission. Reportedly he told the journalist that Jaquess "couldn't draw

Davis' fire; he is too honest. You are the man for that business."[42] Gilmore, as pragmatic as Jaquess was idealistic, convinced Lincoln that Davis would this time meet with these Federal peace commissioners if they went to Richmond.[43]

Lincoln was well aware of the damage caused by the peace offensives of the Copperheads and the Confederates. However, he was caught in a dilemma. It was important to get Davis officially to acknowledge that the South was unwilling to consider reunion. Otherwise, Northern voters would continue to consider the claims of peace advocates that the rebels were amenable to reunion if only Lincoln would agree to a cease-fire or would withdraw emancipation as a condition for peace. According to his secretaries:

> President Lincoln saw clearly enough the futility of all such projected negotiations. But he also understood the necessity of silencing clamors for peace. He therefore again gave Jaquess leave of absence, and to both permission to pass the lines; refusing, however, all authority, instruction, or any promise of protection. He would not even give the colonel a personal interview.[44]

If Lincoln had sent official emissaries or negotiators, under international law he would have effectively recognized Confederate sovereignty. All claims based on the war as an internal rebellion rather than a clash of sovereign nations would be rendered meaningless. The threat to treat recognition of the Confederacy by Britain or France as an act of war would become hollow.[45]

To apprise Jaquess and Gilmore of the terms they could discuss if they were granted an audience with Davis, plus to insulate himself against criticism from the Radicals, Lincoln consulted the recently deposed Salmon P. Chase. Chase then met with Gilmore and Jaquess and explained that the conditions had to be generous if their rejection were to cause public indignation. They were "the immediate dissolution of the Southern Government," including its armies, and the recognition of the sovereignty of the Union; the abolition of slavery; amnesty for all those who engaged in rebellion; the states restored "as if they had never attempted to secede from the Union"; and compensation to the owners of fifty or fewer slaves based on half of the value of the slaves they had owned in 1860, this from a total of $400,000,000 to be authorized by the government. Also, a national convention would be called to ratify this settlement.[46]

Gilmore and Jaquess set sail for City Point (now Hopewell, Virginia) on July 7, the day Greeley initiated his correspondence with Lincoln that led to the Niagara Falls meeting. They got an interview with Davis and Judah P. Benjamin on July 17, probably about the time that Lincoln was drafting his call for 500,000 troops and his "To Whom it May Concern" memorandum. Gilmore made it clear that they were private individuals but professed to be "acquainted with the views of the United States Government, and with the sentiments of the Northern people relative to an adjustment of the differences existing between the North and South."[47] Davis was charming and cordial, but he stated an initial ultimatum that set the tone for the conference: "This war must go on till the last of this generation falls in his tracks and his children seize his musket and fight our battle unless you acknowledge our right to self-government. We are not fighting for slavery. We are fighting for independence, and that, or extermination, we will have."[48]

On the day Greeley published his account of the Niagara conference in the *Tribune*, a "card from Edmund Burke" (Gilmore's pen name) appeared in the Boston *Evening Transcript* giving a brief account of the trip to Richmond and primarily quoting Davis' ultimatum, with key words and phrases italicized or in capital letters. Although this mission and the pro-administration sentiment it fostered did not entirely compensate for the setback from the Niagara initiative, it did blunt its effect. For genuinely undecided voters, this certainly made a difference. If it did not win many of them over to the president's cause, it probably at least kept many of them from turning against him.[49]

Nevertheless, Lincoln's "To Whom It May Concern" memorandum, exposing his insistence upon abolition, raised a new and potentially fatal factor in his re-election equation. Rather than making him seem willing to enter into genuine peace negotiations, the memo had made it look like the war was continuing because of his insistence upon it. People reasoned that since the Southern states left because of threats against slavery, they surely would not return to a Union with emancipation. Even a staunch Republican such as George Templeton Strong could see the enormous damage that had been done to the administration. On August 19 he wrote:

Lincoln's blunder in his letter "to all whom it may concern" may cost him the election. By declaring that abandonment of slavery is a fundamental article in any negotiation for peace and settlement, he has given the disaffected and discontented a weapon that doubles their power of mischief. It's wonderful what an ill savor the word Abolition has acquired during our long period of constitutional subjugation by the slaveholding caste. One would think it a good word, and likely to be popular with a free people, but it isn't. I never call myself an Abolitionist without a feeling that I am saying something rather reckless and audacious.[50]

Attacks on Lincoln continued as Northern armies and fleets were stymied or frustrated, the price of gold continued to soar, the day for conscription approached, growing numbers of Radicals and Germans announced their support of Frémont, and members of Lincoln's own party plotted to hold a convention to nominate another candidate. The resolve against slavery was becoming more and more difficult to maintain.[51]

8

"With Malignant Heart and Deceitful Speech"

"Opposition to the Government by constitutional means
was not enough to gratify the vehement and resentful feelings
of those Democrats in the North whose zeal for slavery seemed
completely to have destroyed in their hearts every impulse of
patriotism."[1]

Thus wrote Nicolay and Hay about those Peace Democrats who formed
secret associations during the Civil War "for the purpose of resisting the
laws, of embarrassing in every way the action of the Government, of
communicating information to the rebels in arms, and in many cases of
inflicting serious damage on the lives and property of the Unionists."[2]

This was a serious indictment by the president's secretaries, and yet in
their ten-volume history of Lincoln's administration, they scrupulously
avoided the term that was almost universally applied during the Civil War
to these anti-war activists—Copperheads.

It has long been debated as to whether some members of Lincoln's
political opposition engaged in treasonous activities during the 1864 campaign season. The dispute has been influenced by the unique circumstances
of the Civil War, which in its fourth year achieved new levels of horror.
Tolerance of dissent in a free society invariably shrinks as the concern for
national security increases; no external threat triggers the self-defense
instinct as strongly as a powerful internal uprising. Only a few rebellions
in history have achieved the magnitude of the American Civil War.

A government that might otherwise remain tolerant of internal dissent, even in wartime, is apt to become anti-libertarian when the enemy is its own people. Such was the case in the United States from 1861–65, when civil liberties were often subordinated to the perceived demands of internal security. In some cases, the perceptions were imaginary, vastly overstated, or even contrived, but they often were valid. Some of the most prominent Democrats in the country acted recklessly in 1864. They met with Confederate agents in Canada to discuss insurrection.[3] According to Nicolay and Hay, "a constant system of communication with the rebels in arms was kept up across the border" and "arms, ammunition and in some instances, recruits, were sent to aid the Confederates."[4] Several Democratic newspapers castigated Lincoln to the point of calling for his assassination;[5] secret societies in the border states and Midwest discussed plots to free Confederate prisoners and to engage in other treasonous activities;[6] and a very active and well-funded Confederate secret service, acting on direct orders of Confederate officials, engaged in widespread espionage and plotted to kidnap Lincoln.[7]

Few debates regarding the Civil War have incited as much disagreement as the question of the loyalty of the Peace Democrats who participated in secret societies during the conflict. Some historians have put forth that the Copperheads were Confederate guerrillas working to destroy the government's war effort; apologists take the position that Copperheads were merely Jacksonian Democrats who disagreed with the Republican administration, performing the traditional role of a loyal opposition during a national crisis.[8]

Most of the primary evidence on this issue was destroyed by the end of the war or went to the grave with various participants. People who planned or orchestrated such activities during the war were reluctant to memorialize or testify about their roles. Most Confederate records were lost in the Richmond fire in April 1865. Even if they were extant, they probably would reveal little, since the Confederates did not usually document covert operations.[9]

The escape of Judah P. Benjamin, Jacob Thompson, Thomas Henry Hines, and others who could have provided firsthand information prevented investigators from discovering the nature and extent of any plots. However, this constraint abated when President Andrew Johnson signed the Amnesty Act on May 29, 1865, pardoning ex-Confederates who would take an oath of allegiance. This allowed Southerners to reveal much about the activities of the secret societies. In 1882, Hines decided to publish the full story of the Northwest Conspiracy. In 1863–64, he had been assigned to work with Copperheads in the Northwest to provoke an uprising. He had traveled from Ohio to Missouri, meeting with Democratic leaders who were sympathetic to the Confederacy and arranging for the transfer of funds and weapons to the secret societies.[10]

Publication of Hines' memoirs would obviously have provided significant information about the Northwest Conspiracy. However, before proceeding, he wrote to his second in command, John Breckenridge Castelman. Apparently, he envisioned Castelman as the primary author and offered him "all my private papers bearing on the matter, including original orders, etc. What say you?"[11]

Castelman suggested that they first confer with Jefferson Davis, who apparently felt that the information could have subjected some Northerners to prosecution for treason. Though the secret societies had been a major disappointment to the Confederacy during the war, at least they had not waged terrible war against the South. When Davis never responded to their letter, Hines and Castelman must have understood his disapproval. They took no further action for several years.[12]

In 1885, Basil Duke, a publisher of *Southern Bivouac*, again asked Hines for his memoirs. Hines, busy with a successful law practice, simply sent all of the papers from his wartime service to Castelman with a note urging him to write the article. In 1886, Castelman did so, but when the *Bivouac* previewed the story, Davis sought to stop the series.[13]

In *Confederate Agent*, James D. Horan concluded that, "Hines, Castelman and Duke must have conferred together and decided to respect once again the wishes of Davis, who wanted to protect the names of Northern traitors."[14] When the two articles finally appeared in 1887, the names of a number of Copperheads were conspicuously absent. This was not lost on Southern newspaper editors, who urged Hines and Castelman to publish the whole story.[15] They refused. A delegation of Kentucky Confederate veterans urged Castelman in 1890 to publish a full account of the 1864–65 intrigues. Though Hines endorsed the idea unqualifiedly, Castelman again wrote without naming the men in the North who had plotted with them to instigate an uprising in 1864.[16]

Therefore, what is known about Northern plots to disrupt the war effort is limited primarily to the testimony from treason trials, correspondence between the Confederate commissioners in Canada and their government, a book written about twenty years after the war by a Confederate agent, and the Hines/Castelman accounts of their activities that spring and summer. That information at least suggests that a number of well-placed Democrats in 1864 conspired with Confederate agents. Some went so far as to plan the forcible release of Confederate prisoners of war, the armed capture of several state governments along with chief executives and legislative officials, or the forcible secession of those states.[17]

Among the highly placed Democrats who were implicated were the governor of New York, the 1864 Democratic candidate for governor of Illinois, the defeated candidate for governor of Ohio in 1863, a former mayor and member of Congress from New York City, and the editors of three New York newspapers. That is not to say most leading Democrats were prepared to engage in armed resistance against the Federal government, but many of them were reluctant to condemn those who did. Their unwillingness to dissociate themselves from such elements of their party implied a sanctioning of the Copperheads and contributed to their political defeat in 1864.[18]

The virulent anti-administration rhetoric, the coziness with rebel agents, the strong defense of Vallandigham and Alexander Long (a Lincoln critic in the U.S. House), the attempted actions of the Democratic majorities in the Illinois and Indiana state legislatures—all suggested a political party working to defeat the government's war effort. In one sense, it was the absence of conflict between the Regular Democrats and the Copperheads that helped to deflate the prospect of a violent uprising that summer. The more victories the Peace Democrats won on the local and state levels, the more their program prevailed in the party councils. The more leadership positions the Copperheads garnered, the greater was the likelihood they would prevail through the legitimate democratic processes. Throughout that spring and summer Copperhead victories continued to bolster the standing of the peace-at-any-price Democrats and to lend an air of legitimacy to their movement. Since the prospect of a fall Democratic victory had become a very strong probability by mid-summer, the Copperheads now eschewed violence and turned their attention toward gaining control of the party apparatus.[19] They did not want to provide the Lincoln administration with justification for suspending the election. There was no reason to take by force what they could win by popular election.[20]

By the time of the Democratic National Convention in late August, Vallandigham seemed almost embarrassed about his leadership of the Sons of Liberty. Though at least three of the largest state delegations (Ohio,

Illinois, and Indiana) were overwhelmingly controlled by the peace faction, delegates were sensitive about the association of the party with a possibly treasonous organization. The Republicans had stepped up accusations against all Democrats; now, in the eleventh hour, they became much more damaging as the Confederates accelerated their campaign of espionage. When delegate Edson B. Olds of Ohio sought the floor to read a communication from the Sons of Liberty, he was howled down and had to withdraw. Other party leaders who were in contact with the secret society sought to prevent any conduct that might harm the party and provide political capital to the Republicans.[21]

In the months before the convention, the peace men called local meetings across the Midwest and adopted resolutions demanding an immediate end to the war. The Ohio state convention had on March 23 chosen delegates-at-large to the national convention. At that time, when the prospect of Union victory still seemed imminent, a slate of mostly moderates or Regular Democrats was chosen. Also, a platform was adopted that was noncommittal on peace. However, when the elections were held in the various Ohio congressional districts, the spring military offensives had begun. The military outlook for the government had rapidly deteriorated. Many of these conventions adopted resolutions or platforms calling for immediate peace and instructing their delegates to vote for none but peace men.[22]

The Columbus *Crisis*, the most outspoken Copperhead newspaper in Ohio, ran an article under the headline "OHIO FOR PEACE—THE PEOPLE HAVE SPOKEN AND THE VICTORY IS WON! Let the Democrats of Ohio rejoice—let the friends of peace everywhere rejoice that Ohio will stand in the Chicago Convention almost unanimous for PEACE— a peace candidate and a peace platform."[23] The newspaper estimated that of the forty-four delegates from the Buckeye State, no more than eight would support "Sunset" Cox's plan to nominate George McClellan on a platform advocating the continuation of the war while calling for a peace convention.[24]

The editorial in the *Crisis* concluded, "Ohio may, therefore, be set down as triumphantly for the peace policy, and as goes Ohio, so will go the Union." In a half-dozen Ohio counties, resolutions opposing conscription were also adopted. In Grant's hometown in Illinois, the Democratic Club unanimously voted its approval of the position stated in Congress by Alexander Long, and exclaimed "that it is to such men we look for leadership." Long had charged Lincoln with deliberately provoking war, subverting civil liberties in the North, and resorting to harsh measures to subjugate the South. Long supported Southern independence and declared that under any circumstances the Union was lost, never to be restored.[25]

At a Democratic meeting in Hendricks County, Indiana, Harrison H. Dodd, state commander of the Sons of Liberty, called for a Northwest Confederacy as a step toward reuniting with the South. He threatened civil war if the government attempted to impede or obstruct any action the party carried on through the regular political channels. An Illinois congressman speaking to the Young Men's Democratic Union Association of New York told his listeners that Illinois would insist upon a peace platform for the party.[26]

On August 1, the Chicago *Times* predicted Confederate victory and said that a Northwest Confederacy would likely follow.[27] Such a prediction was not as absurd as it appears in retrospect. Less than two weeks earlier, Lincoln had issued a call for 500,000 volunteers, with deficiencies to be made up by a draft call on September 5. The same day, he had released the "To Whom It May Concern" memorandum, which revealed that the abolition of slavery had become his primary wartime goal. For two years, the volatile combination of conscription and emancipation had been the cause of the most dangerous anti-war violence. On July 18, the president for the first time presented them together, undiluted. If he was trying to remove any uncertainty about the goals of the war and the effort that victory would require, he had done so dramatically. He must have known that there would be a major public reaction.[28]

The Copperheads exploded, and their virulence exceeded only in degree the outcry from the rest of the Democratic Party. The La Crosse *Democrat* said:

> If the people of Wisconsin were not natural born cowards
> . . . if they were not as great slaves as the blacks this war is
> now being conducted to benefit, they would stand shoulder to
> shoulder and swear by the living God that not a man nor a dollar
> should be sent to war from the West until the East had filled
> her quotas.[29]

A southern Illinois newspaper addressed the issue this way:

> Before making this last call, Mass. was advised that it would
> be made, and the provisions were arranged to suit her case
> exactly. She had time to hunt up negro substitutes for her quota,

as if they were deemed good enough to stand side by side with the brave sons of Indiana and Illinois!

The article criticized Massachusetts Governor Andrew for so vocally supporting the war and black equality, and then hypocritically finding "negro substitutes for the *brave* boys of the old Bay State."[30]

The reaction across the Midwest frightened state officials. On August 20, Ohio Governor John Brough pleaded with Stanton to reduce his state's quota. He feared that 10,000 to 15,000 soldiers might be necessary to carry out the draft in his state. Major General Samuel P. Heintzelman, commander of the Northern Department and generally a level-headed officer, predicted that 25,000 troops would probably be required to enforce conscription in Ohio, Indiana, and Illinois. The acting assistant provost marshal general for Wisconsin on September 1 predicted trouble across the state and recommended that soldiers be assigned to each congressional district.[31]

In August a Copperhead speaker at a mass meeting in Peoria, Illinois, was cheered when he said:

> In September next a heartless and relentless call for five hundred thousand more men—a heartless and relentless conscription—is to be enforced throughout the State. One of Lincoln's Provost Marshals will cross your threshold, drag you from your home, tear you from your loved ones to die under the torrid Sun of the South or be stricken down in battle. . . . Let us no longer crouch at the feet of power with our petitions. Let us stand up and *demand* that the rights and liberties bequeathed us by our fathers be respected, and proclaim if they are not respected, we will maintain them as our fathers achieved them.[32]

A gathering at Hamilton, Ohio, on August 15 adopted a resolution that mimicked Lincoln's July 18 memorandum as it pronounced a very sobering message:

> We but perform a natural and social duty in declaring "to all whom it may concern," that no citizen of Ohio, resident of Butler county, shall be compelled to join the Federal army to consummate the avowed designs of the enemies of State rights, even should it prove necessary to give effect to this decision *by force and with arms.*
> Resolved that the citizens of this county, who are opposed

to a further prosecution of the war, *should prepare for such a contingency.*[33]

And a meeting at Fort Wayne, Indiana, produced a resolution "that the honor, dignity, and safety of the people demand that against ruin and enslavement, they must afford to themselves the protection which usurpation and tyranny denies them."[34]

The unrest was reaching a boiling point at the same time that various uprising plots were supposed to come to fruition. It now seems remarkable that the timber of public unrest and the spark of Confederate agents working with the Sons of Liberty did not combine to result in major violence. It only makes sense that the prospect of success for the Democratic Party in the election and the incorporation of the Copperheads into party councils preempted a revolution until September. Then the fall of Atlanta effectively reversed the public perception to one of imminent victory, averting such a possibility.

The initial plan for an uprising had been scheduled to coincide with Vallandigham's return to Ohio from Canada. His arrest was taken for granted and it was assumed that this would provoke widespread protests across the country, leading to an uprising. It did not occur to Jacob Thompson or the Sons of Liberty that Vallandigham might not be arrested.[35]

In mid-June, a disguised Vallandigham crossed the border between Windsor and Detroit. He had to attend a Democratic district convention in Hamilton, Ohio, on June 15, at which delegates to the national convention from that congressional district were to be elected. Since the at-large slate of peace men, which included Vallandigham, had been rejected by the state convention the previous March, this was his last chance to qualify as a delegate. If he weren't a delegate, it would appear that he was abandoning his cause. To make a strong statement after a year's absence, his return had to be dramatic.[36]

When delegates in Hamilton were told that Vallandigham would speak that afternoon, a long ovation erupted. When order was restored, the convention named its two delegates to go to Chicago, one of which was Vallandigham.[37]

When he spoke, it was the old Vallandigham, cocksure and defiant, but he was careful not to say anything that could justify his arrest. "I am here for peace, not turbulence; for quiet, not convulsions; for law and order, not anarchy." However, he also suggested that if he were again arrested, his supporters should riot and rebel against authorities. He defended his link to the Sons of Liberty and denied that it was anything more than "a lawful Democratic society" created as a foil to the Republican-sponsored Union Leagues. He denied that it existed to aid Southern rebels or to form a Northwest Confederacy.[38]

The government knew of Vallandigham's return almost from the start. A detective was in Hamilton when he spoke. Brough asked the military to arrest the returned exile, but Heintzelman refused. He did not want to repeat Burnside's blunder and was reticent to act until he heard from Washington.[39]

Other Republicans were also outraged by Vallandigham's return. Murat Halstead, the editor of the Cincinnati *Gazette*, threatened to make a citizen's arrest if the authorities did not do so. However, the editor of the New York *Tribune* wrote, "It would be a great mistake *now* to arrest Vallandigham. Sensible Republicans without exception say the best thing to do is to let him alone." Greeley, never shy about sharing his advice with the president, suggested, "Better let him alone. He will do good here. His running for Governor last year was worth fifty thousand votes to the Unionists of Ohio." On this occasion, Lincoln determined that Greeley's advice was well-founded. He told Brough and Heintzelman to stay in touch with each other while watching Vallandigham and others closely. If there was "any palpable injury, or imminent danger to the Military, proceeding from him, or any of them, arrest all implicated. Otherwise do not arrest without further order." Lincoln also decided that he would not acknowledge the Copperhead's return. This would deny Vallandigham the publicity he yearned for. In private, Lincoln said that since he had no official knowledge of Vallandigham's return, until he committed some objectionable act, the president would continue to know nothing of it.[40]

Vallandigham's arrest was to have triggered the uprising, but nobody had planned for his not being arrested. The next occasion for the uprising was to be July 4, during the Democratic National Convention, but party leaders had rescheduled it to the end of August in order to take maximum advantage of the battlefield reverses the Federal armies were suffering. According to Jacob Thompson, Confederate covert operations chief in Canada, the next scheduled date for some kind of action was July 20. Many three-year enlistments were expiring that summer and Lincoln probably would have to issue a substantial draft call in July. The uprising could be planned to coincide with the public reaction to such a proclamation. It was anticipated that legions of Copperheads would be ready to revolt. A Chicago leader of the Sons of Liberty had promised two regiments of "eager, ready, organized, and armed" soldiers to "join in the play." In Indiana, Sons of Liberty were prepared "to seize and hold Indianapolis and release the prisoners there." But by the time Lincoln issued the draft call on July 18, Copperhead leaders were having second thoughts in light of their improved prospects for the fall election. One confessed that he was "overwhelmed with the responsibility of speedy action on so momentous a subject."[41]

The Northern conspirators called off the July 20 revolt and an exasperated Thompson summoned leading members of the Sons of Liberty to Saint Catharines, Ontario, on July 22 to discuss a new date. He was still convinced that with the right encouragement and financial aid, the Sons of Liberty could incite a revolution that would culminate in a Northwestern Confederacy. He wrote to Confederate representatives in Europe, "I am addressing every energy that is practicable and reasonable to assist the Northwestern people, and everything justifies the belief that success will ultimately attend the undertaking." The Confederates urged August 16 as the new date, but several weeks after the Saint Catharines meeting, the Sons of Liberty leaders again equivocated when Southern agents couldn't promise a simultaneous rebel invasion of Kentucky and Missouri. Gatherings were scheduled on August 3 in Peoria, Illinois, and several weeks later in Springfield and Chicago. Thompson paid large sums of travel money for the Peoria meeting and later reported to Benjamin that this gathering was a major success.[42]

By August 16, the full impact of the Niagara Falls diplomacy had taken hold. In later describing the impact of Lincoln's "To Whom It May Concern" memorandum, coming during attempts by Confederates and some Copperheads to spark a rebellion, Thompson wrote:

> About this time that correspondence between our friends and Horace Greeley made its appearance. Lincoln's manifesto shocked the country. The belief, in some way, prevailed over the North that the South would agree to a reconstruction, and the politicians, especially the leading ones, conceived the idea that on such an issue Lincoln could be beaten at the ballot-box. At all events they argued that the trial of the ballot-box should be made before a resort to force, always a dernier resort.[43]

In Indiana, the Democratic Central Committee, including some members of the Sons of Liberty, moved to rescind the efforts of Harrison H. Dodd to hold a party mass meeting in Indianapolis on August 16. Dodd was the grand commander of the Sons of Liberty in Indiana and had accumulated weapons in anticipation of an uprising on that date. On August 13, the committee urged Indianians not to resist conscription, but rather to obtain redress through the political process. The arrest of some Sons of Liberty from Kentucky who had just returned from meeting with Confederates in Canada added to the sudden Democratic sensitivity about being too closely linked with the secret societies. It also told Democrats that Federal spies had penetrated deeply into the organization and knew about the activities of its leading officials.[44]

By that point, all but the lunatic fringe of Copperheads had foresworn a violent rebellion to bring about a Northwest Confederacy. They had risen to be among the respectable leaders of the oldest political party in the United States. Those who had participated in clandestine activities now felt self-conscious about the pledges they had made in Canadian hotel rooms. But the zeal of rebel agents had only increased with each failure, and the last scheduled date for an uprising coincided with the Democratic convention in Chicago. It seemed a perfect opportunity. Throngs from across the country would descend on the city at the end of August, providing cover for the seventy or so Confederate commandos and the numerous Sons of Liberty who would attend. Thompson wanted to be sure that the spark was ignited this time; thus the contingent of Southern soldiers who were dispatched with the irrepressible Captain Hines. The primary object was the release of Confederates in Camp Douglas, a compound normally guarded by fewer than 800 men.[45]

But as the convention assembled, 3,000 Union troops marched into Chicago and reported to Camp Douglas. The Confederates had been betrayed, probably much to the relief of most of the Sons of Liberty. Though the Confederates wanted to go ahead with the plan, the Northern conspirators refused. The sudden presence of soldiers and arrests of Sons of Liberty in Missouri and Kentucky had unnerved them and proved that much of what they thought was secret was known by the government. Probably many of the leaders were already starting to feel nervous about their own futures.[46]

Throughout that spring and summer, the administration had been apprised of the existence of massive secret societies formed to rebel against the government and provide aid to the Confederate cause. These reports were the result of efforts by a governor, several military officers, and one very enterprising spy, all of whom have been attacked as incredible by numerous twentieth-century historians. Colonel John P. Sanderson, provost marshal general for the Department of the Missouri and staff officer to the department commander Major General William Rosecrans, revealed in June that there was a secret society working for the defeat of the government. He claimed that Clement Vallandigham was the leader of the Northern wing of the organization and that membership numbered in the hundreds of thousands. Sanderson was the protégé of Rosecrans, who had fallen from grace because of his dismal performance at Chickamauga. Rosecrans, having failed in June to convince Lincoln that the situation called for harsh measures, in late July turned the results over to the press. On July 28, the Missouri *Democrat* published Sanderson's exposé, titled "Conspiracy to Establish a Northwestern Confederacy," which was reprinted along with indignant editorials in Republican newspapers across the country. The Chicago *Tribune*, the Cincinnati *Gazette*, and the Illinois *State Journal* made the report an overnight sensation. The New York *Tribune* not only published the report in its entirety, but also condemned Vallandigham and the 200,000 "McClellan Minutemen" of New York as being guilty of conspiring in the treasonous plot. Republican newspapers lashed out at the Democrats, glad to assume the offensive after months of defending emancipation, conscription, the conduct of the war, and violations of civil liberties.[47]

The Sanderson exposé provided the spark that finally allowed the Republicans to take the offensive in the political campaign. Though Sanderson's was the first information about secret societies to be publicly released that summer, Brigadier General Henry B. Carrington, commander of the military district of Indiana, had long been investigating treasonous groups operating in Ohio and Indiana.[48]

Indiana Governor Oliver Morton and General Henry Carrington made a powerful and ruthless political team. Morton's resort to extralegal means to govern during the war and Carrington's suppression of Copperheads and Democrats assured that state's continued role as a major contributor to the war effort. The two cooperated closely to prevent the strong anti-war movement in Indiana from obstructing the government's war effort.[49]

In December 1862, Carrington wrote a long report blaming the appalling desertion rate of Indiana soldiers on treasonous secret societies. In a second report in March 1863, he said the situation was bordering on open revolt. He claimed the societies were planning to seize the arsenals, the railroads, and the telegraph, then they would "assert independent authority as a state" and withdraw Indiana from the war. According to Carrington they were communicating with Confederates, particularly John Hunt Morgan, who would soon become a terror to the citizens of southern Indiana.[50]

Four days after submitting the March report, Carrington was promoted to brigadier general and placed in command of the newly created Indiana District of the Department of the Ohio. General-in-Chief Henry Halleck objected to the promotion, claiming that Carrington was not fit for such a responsibility. Carrington's promotion, Halleck added, was due "entirely to political influence," and suggested sending the new general to the front to test his mettle as an officer. Following an exchange of communications between General Ambrose Burnside, commander of the Department of the Ohio, and Carrington's immediate superior, he was told to remain in Indianapolis.[51]

Carrington had repeatedly tried to obtain summary powers over all of Indiana when he was the chief mustering officer and post commander for Indianapolis. As commander of the Indiana District, his authority was greatly enhanced, and now he only needed to obtain permission from Burnside. Burnside, as shown by his record of dealing with anti-war newspapers and individuals, was not likely to keep a tight rein on a subordinate who was perhaps overly zealous in suppressing anti-war sentiment. Yet Carrington sent a dispatch to his commander on April 21, 1863, that was such as to draw an admonition even from Burnside. Perhaps because of this dispatch (its contents are unknown), on April 22, 1863, Carrington was relieved of command and slated for active service. The general immediately appealed to Governor Morton, who had rescued him from a similar fate the previous December. Morton was unsuccessful at keeping Carrington in Indianapolis this time, but he was able to save him from a battlefield command. Even though the general had to spend a couple of months at temporary assignments in Ohio, Morton continued to pressure the War Department until Carrington was returned to Indianapolis in July.[52]

Carrington proved to be an able and aggressive enforcer for Governor Morton in the highly partisan political warfare of wartime Indiana. Carrington had begun investigating the secret societies shortly after arriving in Indianapolis in 1862. He depended heavily on his spy network, which kept him well informed of the group's activities and members. One particularly effective spy was a young man named Felix Stidger, a Kentuckian who penetrated the Sons of Liberty and became its grand secretary for Kentucky. Stidger's prominence within the organization made him privy to the planning sessions of high–ranking officers.[53]

Information from Stidger during May and June 1864 provided Carrington with much of the foundation for his third report to Morton on June 28, in which Carrington claimed the Sons of Liberty were engaged in treasonable activities designed to form a Northwest Confederacy. Indiana had for several years been a battleground over emancipation and conscription. When the Republicans prevented the state legislature from achieving a quorum and thus made it possible for Morton to rule the state without legislative constraint, the tension had increased. Numerous clashes between troops and Peace Democrats had inspired a number of Democratic leaders to conclude that an organization for their protection was necessary. Joseph Bingham of the Indianapolis *Daily Sentinel* wrote on January 16, 1863, "Is it not time that the people should openly organize for their own protection?"[54] When Republicans claimed the existence of a subversive secret society known as the Knights of the Golden Circle, Harrison H. Dodd of Indianapolis claimed that if they continued to be treated badly Democrats might form such an order:

> And if some men wished to find out its objects and aims further than this, they have only to do as they have done before, place arms in the hands of their sons and send them to the polls in company with hired ruffians to intimidate and overawe peaceful citizens in the exercise of their constitutional right. Let them try this again, and they might find out what the secret order meant.[55]

When troops guarded against guerrilla activities at the polls in Kentucky, some Democrats feared that soldiers might prevent anti-administration voters from casting their ballots in Indiana. One Democratic editor wrote, "No Burnside or bayonets shall stand between the people of Indiana and the expression of their will. They must vote their sentiments, even if they have to clear a path to the polls with their swords."[56]

Morton, whose campaign for re-election was in serious trouble, chose to use Carrington's June 28 report to his political advantage. Most of the information contained in the report was unsubstantiated and could not be verified without compromising or endangering operatives like Stidger, but the Democrats' fortuitous decision to postpone their national convention permitted Morton additional time to corroborate the allegations and still make the report public before the convention. It was the end of July before Morton turned it over to the Indianapolis *Daily Journal,* which published it on July 30. Like the Sanderson report that had appeared two days earlier, this exposé received extensive coverage in the Republican press. Probably any meaningful possibility of an organized uprising in the Northwest ended with the publication of these investigative findings. Democratic leaders shrank from any affiliation with the secret societies as the potential damage to party and career became apparent. Also those who held leadership positions in both the Democratic Party and the Sons of Liberty now found their standing in the former seriously compromised by their association with the latter. Since most believed that the prospects of Democratic success at the polls were greater than the chances of successfully conducting a violent uprising, they now either distanced themselves from the secret society or, in some instances, intervened to defuse any activities by the more militant members of the organization.[57]

No arrests were made at that time, and apart from embarrassing some individuals named, little changed as an immediate result of the Carrington report. After all, Carrington was seen as Oliver Morton's agent, and no Republican governor during the Civil War was more partisan in his support of the war or more willing to forgo democratic principles in battling his political enemies. When the report was released, Morton had been ruling Indiana for more than a year as a virtual dictator. The Democratic press furiously lashed back at Morton and Carrington in the aftermath of the report's publication. The somewhat cavalier attitude these Republicans had demonstrated toward democratic principles made their credibility suspect to the public. Like the Sanderson report, Carrington's exposé lacked the evidence to smear the Democrats with the taint of disloyalty. Carrington's resourceful detective, Stidger, soon cured this evidentiary problem.[58]

On July 20, 1864, one of the dates that had been designated for the outbreak of revolution in the Northwest, a "Council of 16," drawn from the ranks of the Sons of Liberty, met in Chicago. They concluded that an uprising at that time was premature, as no event was scheduled that would bring large numbers of Democrats together before August. "The 16th of August was fixed upon for a general uprising," according to Jacob Thompson, who met with Harrison H. Dodd, John C. Walker, and Judge Joshua Bullitt in Canada on July 22. Those three, representing probably the most militant faction of the council, agreed to call for mass meetings of Democrats in the various Northwestern states on the condition that the Confederates would provide diversions by mounting invasions of Kentucky and Missouri. Unfortunately, the commissioners could not promise the requested diversions, and the Northern conspirators could not pledge definite action. Although perhaps unrelated to these negotiations, it is nevertheless interesting that in September, General Sterling Price invaded Missouri with

12,000 cavalry, and in November, General John Bell Hood led the Army of Tennessee into Tennessee intending to push George H. Thomas' army out of the way and invade Kentucky.[59]

Although Dodd, Walker, and Bowles began preparations for the August 16 uprising, Indiana authorities knew about it before the conspirators had even returned from Canada. Carrington strengthened the guard at Camp Morton and placed several artillery pieces on platforms facing the compound, where the increasingly restive prisoners had been apprised of the role they were to play in the uprising. On August 2 or 3 Dodd met with Joseph J. Bingham, chairman of the Democratic State Central Committee, and asked him to call a mass meeting near Indianapolis on August 16. When Bingham asked why, Dodd swore him to secrecy and told him the plans for revolution that had been hatched in Canada. The chairman refused the request for the meeting. When Dodd left, Bingham was still uncertain that he had disabused his visitor of the idea of trying to spark an outburst of violence on the eve of the Democratic National Convention. He consulted the leading Democrats in the state: the attorney general, the state auditor, the secretary of state, and Democratic gubernatorial nominee Joseph E. McDonald. Though all of them were members of the Sons of Liberty, they were as ignorant of the plot and as appalled as Bingham had been. They met with Dodd and Walker and sternly insisted that the plans be canceled. Though the two plotters argued earnestly that the old government could not be restored without forcible revolution and that a revolution was certain whether they did anything to assist it or not, they finally gave their word.[60]

Apparently, however, Dodd and Walker had no intention of keeping their promise. Dodd met with the executive council of the Sons of Liberty several days later to convince them of the need for action on August 16. He found little more support from them than he had from the Democratic leaders. Their hopes for winning at the polls were brighter in August 1864 than at any other time during the war, and responsible Democrats were terrified that important individuals in the party would be plotting an activity that could destroy those prospects. Moreover, on August 1 the leaders of the Sons of Liberty in Kentucky had been arrested, indicating that administration spies knew of these plans.[61]

One administration spy most certainly knew about the plot and had informed his superiors. Felix Stidger learned about it from Dodd at the end of July while in Indianapolis. On the train, he met up with Joshua Bullitt, who was returning to Kentucky from a meeting with Jacob Thompson in

Canada. Bullitt was the chief justice of Kentucky's highest court and grand commander of that state's Sons of Liberty. As the two men traveled together, Bullitt confirmed the plans for an August uprising. Immediately upon arriving in Kentucky, Bullitt was arrested. He was carrying several large drafts drawn on a Canadian bank account, which had been provided by Thompson.[62]

Morton and Carrington had wished to arrest the Indiana leaders of the Sons of Liberty for some time, but General Heintzelman had learned from the Vallandigham matter that acting precipitously could be harmful to the government. An unprovoked arrest of a Copperhead leader might be the very spark that would ignite rebellion. Therefore, the Indiana conspirators were instead kept under close surveillance. The governor and district commander were prepared to crush the proposed August 16 uprising, but it never occurred. What actually arrived came several days later, in crates addressed to "J. J. Parsons" and delivered to Dodd's printing business. According to his biographer, Morton received a letter August 20 from a woman in New York who wrote that she had reliable information that "the Copperheads of Indiana have ordered and paid for thirty thousand revolvers and forty-two boxes of fixed ammunition, to be distributed among the antagonists of our government." She also noted that thirty-two of the boxes addressed to "J. J. Parsons" and marked "Sunday-school Books" had already been sent.[63]

John C. Walker had purchased the guns in New York using mostly state funds. He was the state agent for Indiana in New York and his correspondence with commissioner Clement C. Clay requesting reimbursement was almost desperate in tone.

> It has been very difficult for me to arrange with the fund in my office to prevent trouble. I shall expect you to send me a draft to Indianapolis. . . . This I wish you to send immediately to square my account. My reputation is involved in this, and I trust that you gentlemen in whom I have confidence will not leave me to suffer.[64]

Morton now had the evidence to indict the Democrats for domestic treason. The facts of the seizure appeared in Republican newspapers the next day, including some compromising letters from Clement Vallandigham and others. The public outcry was overwhelming. Resolutions were passed and speeches were made across Indiana condemning the conspirators, and a mass meeting was announced for August 22 in Indianapolis. The crowd called for Morton and he took advantage of the opportunity. In self-vindication he reminded the people that for eighteen months he had been telling them that guns and ammunition had been entering the state to be used in resisting state and federal authority.[65]

Morton further proclaimed that a central committee (the "Council of 16") claiming to represent the Democratic Party had called upon other Indiana Democrats to organize an army to revolt against the government. And he raised the issue of the secret political correspondence:

> Look at some of these letters. As an example, take one written by the present Auditor of State, a candidate before the people for re-election. The letter was written three years ago, before the inauguration of Mr. Lincoln's anti-slavery policy, which these men now assert to be the great source of dissatisfaction. What does he say to his friend, Mr. Voorhees? 'Our salvation is in the success of the Southern arms. If they are crushed then woe betide us.' What think you, my fellow-citizens, of that, coming from the Auditor of this State?[66]

Morton told his listeners that if they wished to be safe from "the torch and the robber," they should condemn those who allowed the shipment to be sent, effectively opening the door to the arsonist and the thief. Concluding, he stated, "The question has been asked me this evening what money it is that has been expended in the purchase of these arms and munitions of war, and where it came from." After a dramatic pause he continued, "In answer to that question I must say that I do not know. . . . I believe, however, . . . that the money . . . has been supplied by the rebellion." He reminded them that "it is all one thing to Jefferson Davis whether we fail by means of a defeat at the coming elections or by the overthrow of the Union arms in the field."[67]

The Democrats were staggered by what had happened. The primary party newspaper in Indiana tried to make light of the seizure, editorializing about the right of the people to bear arms and referring to the whole controversy as a "tempest in a teapot." It suggested that Morton and Carrington must have shipped the revolvers to compromise the Democratic Party. Nevertheless, this tempest would not dissipate. Public opinion ran so high against the Sons of Liberty that all the Democratic candidates who were members published a card in the Indianapolis *Sentinel* claiming they had never belonged to a society of a *treasonable or disloyal* character, and had never entertained a purpose to inaugurate a movement of a *treasonable or revolutionary* character against the government.[68]

Dodd and Walker would have been arrested immediately, but both were out of town. The only person arrested at the time was William M. Harrison, grand secretary of the Sons of Liberty in Indiana. Harrison was rather a small catch compared with Dodd, Walker, or Bullitt, and his arrest was probably made to justify the search of his home. Dodd arrived in Indianapolis September 3 and was arrested immediately. Walker never returned to Indianapolis and was never arrested. From Chicago he fled to Canada, "where he was reported as late as February, 1865."[69] What he did, however, "with incredible presumption" in the words of Morton's biographer, was address "a demand upon Governor Morton for the evangelical literature of which Dodd had been so unceremoniously deptived."

> Chicago, August 25, 1864
> *To His Excellency, O. P. Morton, Governor . . .*
> Sir—A few days ago, I purchased, in the city of New York, a few hundred pistols, with accoutrements and ammunition, and shipped them to Indianapolis for the purpose of supplying the orders of friends in Indiana.
> I am now informed that on the 20th or 21st of this month, this property was seized by the military authorities at Indianapolis. . . .
> Having the legal right to the custody of the property which has been forcibly and illegally taken from the possession of my consignee, I now call upon you, the chief executive officer of the state of which I am a citizen, to fulfill your promise to the people, obey the requirements of your oath of office, and see that the laws are faithfully executed.
> Hoping that you will feel it to be your duty to rebuke the attempt made to subordinate civil to military power, and in the protection of citizens to vindicate the honor and dignity of the state, I am,
> Respectfully yours, etc.,
> J. C. Walker[70]

The seizure of the weapons cache in Indianapolis, the arrest of Harrison, the sensational press accounts of this startling new evidence that seemed clearly to support the claims of Sanderson and Carrington, and the public outcry against the Sons of Liberty and the Democratic Party drove the final nail into the coffin of the Northwest Conspiracy.[71]

A number of other Indiana members of the Sons of Liberty were arrested in October, including Joseph J. Bingham, editor of the state Democratic Party organ, the *Daily Sentinel*. Bingham, along with gubernatorial candidate Joseph McDonald, had been responsible for convincing Dodd and Walker to abandon their plan to attack Camp Morton on August 16. For that reason his arrest and prosecution have been criticized as being politically motivated. Yet it was Bingham's testimony at the trial of the conspirators that definitely established the existence of a conspiracy. Still, immediately after the seizure of the weapons on August 20, Bingham attempted to debunk the Republican claims of a conspiracy, though he knew very well that one existed. Eventually, however, Bingham and virtually every other Indiana Democrat interested in success at the polls joined in the chorus of condemnation against the conspirators. Dodd, Walker, Bowles, and the others became pariahs to the party in those final weeks before the state election in October. When Dodd requested that Bingham, his longtime friend and political ally, publish "An Address By the Committee of Thirteen," a tract that sought to justify and explain the purposes of the Sons of Liberty, the editor refused.[72]

Walker escaped arrest by going to Canada, but the rest of the conspirators went to trial before a military court based upon a proclamation of President Lincoln suspending the writ of habeas corpus for citizens charged with disloyalty. (That policy had been implemented on September 24, 1862, sanctioned by Congress in March 1863, and applied in the case of Clement L. Vallandigham.) The timing of their trials was undoubtedly motivated by political considerations. Harrison H. Dodd's trial began on September 27, 1864, two weeks before the scheduled state election in Indiana. It did not hurt Republican prospects that a prominent Democrat was on trial for treason when that election took place. Nor did it harm the Union cause when in the early morning hours of October 7, Dodd escaped from his confinement in the federal courthouse. His escape was cited by Republicans as evidence of his guilt.[73] Bowles and the others were convicted and sentenced to be hanged but were eventually released after the war.

At the same time that the treason trials in Indiana were beginning, Judge-Advocate General Joseph Holt released yet another report on the Sons of Liberty. He described the organization as well armed, with rigorous internal discipline, commanding large numbers of devoted followers, and financed by and in collusion with Jefferson Davis. Judea had produced only one Judas Iscariot, Holt concluded, but "there has arisen together in our land an entire brood of such traitors . . . all struggling with the same relentless malignity for the dismemberment of our Union."[74]

When Sanderson and Carrington published their reports, they were both unknown, employed by superiors who had repeatedly proclaimed their partisanship. Personal quests for promotion had influenced their findings, and their credibility was subject to attack. On the other hand, Joseph Holt was the judge-advocate general of the United States. There was no higher position he could attain within the JAG Corps, and it was unlikely that he was bucking for promotion to a battlefield command. His superior was Abraham Lincoln, who had discouraged sensational reports about treasonous societies bent on the destruction of the government. Holt's credibility stood above that of Sanderson and Carrington, or for that matter, of Rosecrans and Morton. Holt's report was dispersed widely by the Republican Party and Union Leagues, and he was often quoted by Union campaign speakers who equated "the Democratic party with copperheadism and copperheadism with treason."[75]

The Democrats had been rocked by the Sanderson and Carrington exposés; the Holt report disoriented them even further. They were caught in the ambivalent tug-of-war between the need to condemn the reports and testimony from the trial of the conspirators and the necessity to put as much distance as possible between the party and the accused conspirators. Some Democratic newspapers denounced the reports and testimony of government detectives as "absolute falsehoods and fabrications . . . too ridiculous to be given a moment's credit." Because Lincoln was inclined to assume the same position, the government's prosecution of these charges never had the blessing of the White House or the War Department. Lincoln regarded the Sons of Liberty as "a mere political organization, with about as much of malice [as of] puerility." A senator claimed that Lincoln once said to him, "Nothing can make me believe that one hundred thousand Indiana Democrats are disloyal." His attitude helped to spawn the revisionist position that "the great Civil War myth of conspiracies and subversive secret societies" was nothing but a "fairy tale," a "figment of Republican imagination" compounded of "lies, conjecture and political malignancy."[76]

This revisionist history is as guilty of selectively emphasizing the weaknesses of the reports and testimonies while ignoring the irrefutable evidence that supported the investigative findings as Sanderson, Carrington, and Holt were of overstating the size and scope of the treasonous conspiracy in the North. By focusing on the exaggerations and the often suspect nature of the investigators and their agents, it is possible to lose focus of the foundation on which much of the questionable superstructure was constructed. That this foundation was solid and certain was established not just by government agents, but by conspirators who wittingly or unwittingly found themselves involved in the activities. To meet with agents of the nation's enemy during time of war; to discuss with those agents ways in which the government can be defeated; to accept money from those agents to use in weakening the nation's ability to conclude that war successfully; to solicit citizens to violate the law and to defy agents of the government, often by violence—these are acts of treason. It must further be remembered that what is known of the activities of the Copperheads in collusion with Confederate agents is merely the tip of the iceberg. As Jacob Thompson wrote in his final report from Canada, "I have so many papers in my possession, which would utterly ruin and destroy very many of the prominent men in the North."[77]

The Sanderson and Carrington reports, the seizure of the weapons shipment addressed to Dodd's business, the plot by the "Council of 16," and most important, the failure of the rest of the Democratic Party to muzzle those disloyal elements within their ranks changed the public perception of the parties in the final months of the 1864 campaign season. Though it was not decisive itself, the domestic treason issue certainly influenced the outcome of the election. It also provided the Republican/Union coalition with a powerful issue to hammer home to the voters, one that voters would become more receptive to as the fortunes of war underwent a dramatic change on the battlefield.

9

"I Am Aware That the Subject Creates Prejudice"

Race has played an important part in many presidential elections. It has been particularly important in influencing voters in the second half of the twentieth century, but the manipulation of the issue during the 1864 campaign surpassed anything seen in any other national poll in American history.

Historian Forrest G. Wood, referring to the 1864 presidential election, wrote that it was "to the racist fanatic, a national referendum on the government's Negro policies in general and the Emancipation Proclamation in particular." Leading Democratic politicians and much of the press exploited the question during the 1864 political season far beyond the rough and tumble normally associated with nineteenth-century elections in the United States. There were many strong issues that the Democrats could have employed—conscription, violation of civil rights, war profiteering, failures on the battlefield, the Legal Tender Act—but all of these issues were secondary to the racial policies of the Republicans. The most ballyhooed of all the attempts to exploit Northern racism in this election turned out to be one of the biggest hoaxes in U.S. political history.[1]

In December 1863, a small book titled *Miscegenation: The Theory of the Blending of the Races, Applied to the American White Man and Negro* was published. No author was listed and, though a few copies appeared on newsstands, most of that first printing had been sent to selected people along with an anonymous letter soliciting the endorsement of the reader. The recipients of these complimentary copies, all prominent antislavery leaders, were asked to respond to a New York post office box.[2]

The introduction pointed out that "miscegenation" was a new word formed from the Latin *miscere*, to mix, and *genus*, race, and "is used to denote the abstract idea of the mixtures of two or more races." Other new terms included "miscegen," a child of parents of different races; "miscegenate," the mingling of persons of different races; and "miscegenetic," the adjective form of the word. The author further suggested that since the issue under discussion was mixing of the black and white races, two more specific words would be appropriate: "melaleukation," from the Greek *melas*, black, and *leukas*, white, and its derivatives "melaleukon" and "melaleuketic"; and "melamigleukation," formed by adding the stem from the Greek *mignumi*, to mix.[3]

The term "miscegenation" has been used since to refer to sexual or marital relations between people of different races. A November 1864 article in the London *Morning Herald* stated, "Whatever good or evil the authors of 'Miscegenation' may have done in a political way, they have achieved a sort of reflected fame on the coining of two or three words— at least one of which is destined to be incorporated into the language. Speakers and writers of English will gladly accept the word 'Miscegenation' in the place of the word amalgamation."[4]

The tract, ostensibly the plea of an Abolitionist for the government-sanctioned mixing of the races, was actually conceived and written by David Goodman Croly and George Wakeman of the virulently anti-Abolitionist New York *World*. Owned principally by Manton Marble, a leading power broker of the Democratic Party, the *World* was generally regarded as the nation's leading Copperhead publication.[5] Born in Ireland, Croly had grown up in New York City and had previously worked for two of the city's leading newspapers, the *Herald* and the *Evening Post*. In 1862, he had become the managing editor of the *World*. There he became friends with Wakeman, a twenty-two-year-old reporter. They conceived a scheme to get leading Abolitionists and Republicans to endorse the principles in the tract and particularly to applaud the concept of miscegenation as a means for improving the state of the nation. They would then circulate the responses widely in the Democratic press. In this way the Republican prospects in 1864, from the courthouse to the White House, would be greatly damaged.[6]

Croly and Wakeman realized that the issue of race was an emotional tinderbox. George Julian, a Midwestern Abolitionist, said it very bluntly: "The American people are emphatically a 'Negro-hating' people." Edward

Dicey, a British correspondent who spent much of 1862 traveling through the Northern states, wrote, "It is hard for a European to quite appreciate the intensity of American feeling about color," and commented that the usual question asked him by an American was "whether you would like your sister to marry a Negro." Also, the strong rejection of Republican candidates in much of the lower North in the 1862 election, coming only weeks after Lincoln issued the preliminary Emancipation Proclamation, had previewed the potential influence that racial prejudice could have on the polling place.[7]

The tract itself was a collage of pseudo-truths purporting to have some credibility by virtue of reference to scholars and philosophers from Aristotle to Wendell Phillips. It was a disorganized, nonsensical piece of work that rambled from one absurd generalization to another, interspersed inferences with rhetorical questions, and eventually arrived at a number of provocative conclusions. Chapters included: "Superiority of Mixed Races," "The Blending of Diverse Bloods Essential to American Progress," "The March of the Dark Races Northward," "Love of the Blonde for the Black," "Present and Future Relations of the Irish and the Negro," "All Our Victorious Battlefields Baptized by the Blood of the Negro," "The Future—No White, No Black," and "Miscegenation in the Presidential Contest."[8]

The second chapter began, "If any fact is well-established in history, it is that the miscegenetic or mixed races are much superior, mentally, physically, and morally, to those pure or unmixed." The argument appeared particularly designed to arouse the racist passions of the Irish-Americans.

> A striking instance of the decay of the races is shown in the history of the Irish. The parts of Ireland that are most habitable, and have the most thrifty population, are those in which Englishmen and Scotchmen have settled. In the north, and other portions of Ireland, the native race, by emigration, and by death, has been steadily decreasing, and will decrease until it blends with a separate people. The Irish, however, transplanted to our soil, become prolific again, because they mix with the American, the German, the Negro, all of whom are brought up under different climatic influences.[9]

The chapter "Present and Future of the Irish and the Negro" states:

> Notwithstanding the apparent antagonism which exists between the Irish and negroes on this continent, there are the

strongest reasons for believing that the first movement towards a melaleuketic union will take place between these two races. Indeed, in very many instances it has already occurred. . . . The white Irishwoman loves the black man, and in the old country, it has been stated that the Negro, is sure of the handsomest among the poor white females. The very bitterness of feeling which exists on the part of the Irish in the large cities towards the negroes is an evidence that they will be the first to mingle. . . .

The fusion, whenever it takes place, will be of infinite service to the Irish. They are a more brutal race and lower in civilization than the negro. The latter is mild, spiritual, fond of melody and song, warm in his attachments, fervid in his passions, but inoffensive and kind, and only apparently brutal when his warmest of emotions are brought into play in his love for the white woman. The Irish are coarse-grained, revengeful, unintellectual, with very few of the finer instincts of humanity. . . .

The blending of the Irish in this country with the negro will be a positive gain to the former. With education and an intermingling with the superior black, the Irish may be lifted up to something like the dignity of their ancestors, the Milesians.[10]

Croly was Irish and knew the effect these words would have on the hundreds of thousands of Irish voters. He had seen the fury of a predominantly Irish mob during the summer rioting. They were not likely to respond well to the assertions of *Miscegenation* that they were inferior to the African, and that they would benefit from the inevitable mingling of the two groups.

Another chapter began, "Nor are the Southern women indifferent to the strange magnetism of association with a tropical race. Far otherwise. The mothers and daughters of the aristocratic slaveholders are thrilled with a strange delight by daily contact with their dusky male servitors." Like the Englishman Dicey, Croly was well aware of how most white men felt about physical contact between white women and black men. Such statements would not be well received by the overwhelming majority of Northerners who would decide the election in November.[11]

Croly also wanted to assure that one of the primary issues that had separated Lincoln from the Radicals, the goal of the government in prosecuting the war, would still divide Republican ranks. The president had asserted repeatedly that his primary purpose as commander in chief was to restore the Union. He defended emancipation as a war measure to bring that about. *Miscegenation* asserted:

It is idle to maintain that this present war is not a war for the negro. It is a war for the negro. Not simply for his personal rights or his physical freedom—it is a war, if you please, of amalgamation, so called—a war of looking, as its final fruit, to the blending of the white and the black. All attempts to end it without a recognition of the political, civil, and social rights of the negro will only lead to still bloodier battles in the future.[12]

In the concluding chapters, Croly arrived at the heart of the matter. No contest in 1864 would be as important as the one waged for the White House. The president had issued the Emancipation Proclamation; he was the only man who could have taken the step that had resulted in the freedom, at least in theory, of millions of slaves. If anyone could undo the proclamation, it was Lincoln. At stake, therefore, was the continued subjugation of those millions of Africans in America, the overwhelming majority of whom had been isolated to one region of the country (and who would continue to be if slavery survived the war). It was an issue of such significance that a political hoax of the dimension of *Miscegenation* had been warranted, at least in the minds of certain Democrats. If *Miscegenation* was to have an impact, then it had to be seen by the voters as a program favored or endorsed by Lincoln or his party.[13]

Chapter XIX began:

The question of miscegenetic reform should enter into the approaching presidential contest. . . . The times are propitious. If the progressive party of this country have courage, have faith in humanity and in their own doctrines, they can solve the problem which has perplexed our Statesmen since the establishment of the Government. That problem is, What to do with the black race.[14]

The pamphlet entreated the Republicans to "rise to the height of the great argument; let them ordain that, as a matter of simple justice, the man whose toil has enriched the Southern plantations should own them."

For three or four generations, the profits of the labor of the slaves of the South have been spent in idleness by a few thousand white families. This great crime against the black man, thanks to the president's proclamation, the confiscation

act, and the growing humanity of public opinion at the North,
is no longer possible. As a matter of justice, the lands of the
South must be divided among the negroes, who are its only
loyal population.[15]

Croly concluded this appeal to the Republican Party with a splash of
spread-eagle patriotism:

Let the Republican party go into the next contest with a
platform worthy of itself; worthy of the events which have
occurred during the last three years; worthy of America, worthy
of the great future. Let the motto then of the great progressive
party of this country be Freedom, Political and Social Equality;
Universal Brotherhood. Let it send a message to all the nations
of the earth, "Come hither with your means, come hither in the
strength of your manhood, come hither with the wealth of your
varied bloods. Let us establish here a nation founded on the
principles of eternal justice, and upon the application of the
doctrine of human brotherhood."[16]

This stirring conclusion to such a dubious document may have disarmed
readers who received advance copies. It reinforced the notion that the author
was a naive but kindred spirit who was overzealous but certainly on the
correct side of the battle line.[17]

Even though the authors never achieved the kind of response they hoped
for, they did receive letters from a few notable Abolitionists. Within several
weeks after advance copies were mailed out, Lucretia Mott, Dr. James
McCune Smith, Sarah and Angelina Grimke, Parker Pillsbury, and Albert
Brisbane replied. Their responses indicated their belief that the author was
earnest in his assertions, and they all professed admiration of his courage.
The replies varied in tone from cautious to enthusiastic. Only Dr. McCune
Smith, however, felt that a policy of governmental encouragement of
miscegenation would fare very well as a political plank. It must have made
these Abolitionists wonder if they had not been duped when on February
17, 1864, Samuel Sullivan Cox delivered a tirade condemning *Miscegenation* to the House of Representatives, listing all of these Abolitionists as
persons who had endorsed the tract.[18]

Croly and Wakeman did not lure into their ambush any of the prominent
Abolitionists they had sought. Still, they drew attention to their new word

and the Abolitionist press helped their cause. By the first week in February, Abolitionist newspapers around the country were advertising it provocatively as available for purchase at newsstands or from the publisher. In the *National Anti-Slavery Standard,* the advertisement for *Miscegenation* shared equal billing with an announcement of the publication of William Wells Brown's *The Black Man.*[19]

The editor of the *Anglo-African Review,* Dr. McCune Smith, publicly extolled the virtues of the tract:

> The word—nay the deed—miscegenation, the same in substance with the word amalgamation, the terror of our abolition friends twenty years ago, and of many of them today . . . "miscegenation," which means the absolute practical brotherhood or social intermingling of blacks and whites, he would have inscribed on the banner of the Republican Party, and held up as the watchword of the next presidential platform.[20]

Shortly thereafter the *National Anti-Slavery Standard* welcomed the tract to the Abolitionist cause, praising the direct and fearless manner in which it addressed the idea of which the American people were "more afraid than any other."

> No accusation has been more effective in stirring up the rancor of editors and the brutality of mobs, than the charge against Abolitionists of advocating "amalgamation." . . . Now the idea thus charged Abolitionists, individually and collectively, of "preference" for black people as partners in marriage, is the very idea seriously advocated and urged in the pamphlet.[21]

The *Standard* boasted that "many will agree with us in finding the pamphlet interesting and instructive, and in thanking the unknown author for it."[22]

Apart from Smith's call for the Republican Party to advocate miscegenation in its platform, no other newspaper or periodical had expressed an opinion. Similarly, most of the Abolitionists who had responded to *Miscegenation* had ignored the question of inclusion in the party's platform or disapproved of the idea. The prospect of linking this controversial idea to some important Republican, to somebody whose endorsement would mean something, began to wane. The authors had wanted a figure who would be regarded as a representative of the party. Then they could condemn Republican candidates in the same way they had berated and lambasted the most radical elements of the Abolitionist movement. This didn't happen.

Croly behaved quite strangely during this period. From the release of *Miscegenation* through January and most of February, the *World* didn't mention the pamphlet and never in the 1864 campaign used "miscegenation" except when mentioning the tract or reprinting an article from another periodical. The *World* always preferred to use "amalgamation," the previous term for racial mixing. Perhaps Croly sought to deflect attention from the true source of the pamphlet. Nevertheless, for the leading Democratic newspaper, which throughout 1862–63 had reveled in racist rhetoric, to suddenly cease its demagoguery was an extraordinary change of editorial tone. Perhaps Croly was embarrassed and wished to avoid attention; the answer will never be known, as he and Wakeman went to their graves without ever having admitted their roles in the controversy.[23]

Still, Croly's trepidation was not so profound as to keep him from trying to get other Democrats to fan the flames. On February 17, 1864, *Miscegenation* made its way to the floor of the House of Representatives. During the debate on establishment of a Freedmen's Bureau, Congressman Samuel Sullivan Cox of Ohio attempted to use the pamphlet as evidence of evil design by the Republicans. "Sunset" Cox began his tirade by referring to letters that prominent Abolitionists had sent to the anonymous author in response. He sneered at the so-called scientific findings in the work: "The physiologist will tell the Gentleman that the mulatto does not live; he does not recreate his kind; he is a monster. Such hybrid races by a law of Providence scarcely survive beyond one generation." Cox eventually came to the point of his tirade.

> There is a doctrine now being advertised and urged by the leading lights of the Abolition party, toward which the Republican party will and must advance.... They used to deny, whenever it was charged, that they favored black citizenship; yet now they are favoring free black suffrage in the District of Columbia, and will favor it wherever in the South they need it for their purposes. . . . The Senate of the United States is discussing African equality in street cars. All these things . . . culminating in this grand plunder scheme of a department of freedmen, ought to convince us that that party is moving

steadily forward to perfect social equality of black and white,
and can only end in this detestable doctrine of Miscegenation![24]

Cox's speech breathed life into his party. He emerged as a Democrat
with an issue that could win widespread national support. He championed
a cause about which most Americans would not be objective. The speech
was reprinted in the Washington office of *The Constitutional Union*, a
"Democratic Conservative Union Newspaper." Thereafter it received wide
circulation in the Democratic press.[25]

In *Black Scare*, historian Forrest Wood asserts Cox knew of the hoax
and the roles of Croly and Wakeman. His evidence was Cox's statement
in *Eight Years in Congress*, written in 1865, that the authors were "two
young men connected with the New York press" and that the pamphlet had
been a fraud. Despite the secrecy of Croly and Wakeman, knowledge of
their roles was not limited to their intimates. The truth was revealed by the
British press even before the election, and by late November, the revelation
had appeared in American newspapers as well.[26]

The best evidence that Cox knew of the hoax when he delivered his tirade
was his knowledge of the contents of the letters mailed by various Abolitionists to the author. These had been sent to an unlisted post office box
in New York City. Cox could have known of the contents of these dispatches
only if the authors or somebody in their confidence had informed him. Cox
had frequent correspondence with S. L. M. Barlow and Manton Marble
between March 1863 and the summer of 1864. Both owned substantial
interests in the *World*. Also, Cox declined an invitation to attend the
dedication of the Gettysburg cemetery on November 19, 1863, in order to
travel to New York, where he met with Marble and won support for the
speakership of the House. Barlow and Marble were power brokers in the
national Democratic Party and Marble was the editor of the newspaper.
Could Croly and Wakeman have pulled off such a hoax without Marble
knowing and approving it? The correspondence between Cox and Marble
was warm and personal. It was also likely that in November 1863, Croly
and Wakeman were at work on their pamphlet. It was completed and
published before Christmas. If Barlow and Marble were aware of the prank,
it means that two of the leading Democrats in the country countenanced
it. The seemingly ambivalent attitude of the *World* toward the issue might
be explained by Marble acquiescing on the conditions that authorship never
be revealed and that the *World* play a low-key role about it.[27]

At least one person who was not an insider knew of the hoax before the election. In mid-October, the New York correspondent of the pro-Confederate London *Morning Herald* sent a dispatch home that appeared on the front page November 1. His cover letter read, "As this letter will not return in printed form to the United States before the presidential election will have taken place, it will do no harm where harm might otherwise possibly be done, to give the history of one of the most extraordinary hoaxes that ever agitated the literary world." Headlines for the article read:

> THE GREAT HOAX OF THE DAY! The Great
> Miscegenation Pamphlet Exposed—The "Moon Hoax" in the
> Shade—Who Wrote the Book—How it Came into Notice—
> Letters of Indorsement from Leading Progressives.[28]

The *Morning Herald* ebulliently described the prank. It revealed that the pamphlet "was written by two young gentlemen connected with the newspaper press of New York, both of whom are obstinate democrats in politics, and was got up solely with the view of committing, if possible, the orators and essayists of the Republican Party to the principle it enunciated, that of the complete social equality, by marriage, of the white and black races." The correspondent seemed delighted that nobody had been aware that *Miscegenation* had been written by "people who abhor the doctrine it sets forth." All of its readers had been "swindled." He pointed out that the authors had "dextrously managed to make it appear that an amalgamation or miscegenation of the two races was not only desirable but inevitable," and had employed Republican arguments to do so. The reporter, obviously well acquainted with the course followed by Croly and Wakeman in carrying out their scheme, wrote that the two "obstinate Democrats" had spent much time preparing for their scheme by cramming at the Astor Library. The article affirmed that the object of the connivers was to bring "the Republican party into conflict with the strong anti-negro prejudice existing in the North."[29]

The unnamed reporter admired the way "the dextrous manipulation of the authors" had succeeded in getting the subject introduced before Congress, where Cox had made "a brilliant and forcible speech against the theory." The hoax surpassed even the "Moon Hoax" which had been perpetrated by J. Locke immediately after the completion of Lord Ross's great telescope. The reporter said that it was "very likely that the writers of the book will never be discovered," which suggests that he not only knew who the authors were, but also their intention never to reveal themselves publicly.[30]

That Croly or Wakeman were on intimate terms with this English reporter seems obvious; his admiration for them became clear in the conclusion of the dispatch:

> Either we must have a war of races, which would inevitably result in the extirpation of the negroes; or we must incorporate them with ourselves, in the succeeding generations by marriage. Either horn of this dilemma is frightful. . . . No sane man supposes that our people will ever marry the negroes out of existence; there remains, then, war to the knife, and the knife to the belt, till every vestige of the African race disappears from the continent.[31]

It was just such violent and irrational hatreds that the authors sought to arouse. It was no surprise that in reprinting the *Herald* article on November 23, the *World* left off the concluding paragraph.[32]

In a *Herald* article on November 9, the same writer said he was awaiting with interest the reaction in the United States when this fraud was exposed, as he knew that his article "will be the first that will have been made regarding the matter." The smugness with which this reporter basked in his "scoop" suggests that he had been in direct contact with the perpetrators and had been assured that nobody else would release the story until it had been published in his newspaper. It might even suggest that the authors had initiated the contact.[33]

Croly and Wakeman reserved to the *World* the honor of printing this startling revelation. Two weeks after the election, it prominently displayed the story of the hoax. Again they avoided any implication of firsthand knowledge by simply reprinting the *Morning Herald* article (minus the concluding paragraph) along with an editorial that stated that the British correspondent had just revealed that the work "was simply a clever Democratic quiz perpetrated upon the owlish leaders of the abolitionists." The authors of the tract seemed to enjoy writing a critical review of their own creation. The "doctrine of miscegenation, conceived as a satire," had been "received as a sermon." It had made its sensational appearance and then "passed into history." In a suitable conclusion to a review of their own stunt, the *World* editorial summed it up thus: "The hoax and the hoaxed, the quiz and the quizzed, will live forever in the grateful midriff of a nation."[34]

One revealing sentence in the editorial read, regarding the authors, "Scared by the sound themselves had made, the wicked wags, its authors, left events to their natural course; and from their anonymous castle of safety watched with delight the almost divine honors paid to their Abbot of Misrule." This sentence was consistent with the mind of a man who does not want to appear innocent so much as he does not want to be noticed at all. The prank took on a dimension far exceeding what Croly and Wakeman had probably ever considered possible. When the election had passed, so too had the immediate danger of incurring the wrath of a nervous government, such as when the *World* was raided in May 1864 and several of its employees arrested.

In mid-March the leading Republican journal, the New York *Tribune*, finally got into the fray when Horace Greeley editorialized, "We notice a tolerably warm discussion going on in the newspapers and elsewhere, concerning what used to be called 'amalgamation,' and is now more sensibly styled 'miscegenation'—a word tolerably accurate, although a little too long for popular and daily use."[35] Greeley wrote that prejudice against blacks was "the result of a cruel and systematic degradation." He likened it to the anti-Semitism of the Middle Ages, when he said a marriage between a Christian and Jew would have been more likely to incite violence than the marriage of a white man to a black woman. "God has made all men of one blood," he wrote, and if a white man wished to marry a black woman then nobody had a right to interfere.

This was the response Croly and Wakeman had sought. The Democratic press attacked the *Tribune* vehemently. The New York *Herald* shrieked, "The fact is—and the *Tribune* cannot disguise it—that the radical party wants a war cry. They tried free love and it failed. Then they tried abolitionism, and it served their purpose for many a long year. But now the war has deprived them of that shibboleth."[36] The *Daily News* exclaimed that the principle of miscegenation had become "doctrine and dogma" of the Republican Party.[37] The New York *Journal of Commerce* was sarcastic. "Pursuing the natural course of radicalism, the editors of several of the abolitionist sheets have recently been seized with a strong desire for the introduction of amalgamation into social and domestic life of their and other radical families." The *New York Times* accused the *Tribune* of advocating miscegenation, which Greeley denied, while the *Herald* published an article, "The Beastly Doctrine of Miscegenation and Its High Priests," which accused the *Times* of being "a bright mulatto on the subject of miscegenation." In the New York *Day-Book*, a poem was published:

> Beautiful word, and more beautiful after thought
> None but the wise have its origin sought, . . .
> Fill with mulattoes and mongrels the nation,
> THIS IS THE MEANING OF MISCEGENATION.[38]

The final proof of *Miscegenation*'s notoriety was when Lincoln's favorite political humorist, Petroleum Vesuvius Nasby, pastor of the "Church uf the Noo Dispensashun," advised a divinity student who was also a Democrat:

> Alluz preach agin the nigger, a youth uv much promise who votid twict for Bookannon. It's soothin' to a ginooine, constooshnel Southern-rites Dimekrat to be constantly told that ther is a race uv men meaner than he is. . . .
> Preach agin amalgamashen at leest 4 Sundays per munth. A man uv straw that set up yerself is the eesiest nockt down, pertikelerly if you set him up with a view uv nockin him down. . . . Lern to spell and pronownce Missenegenegenashun. It's a good word."[39]

The controversy generated by *Miscegenation* peaked in mid-March. The New York press' flurry of comment, criticism, accusation, and response culminated with the *World* finally emerging from its status of semi-hibernation regarding the issue. On March 4, Croly and Wakeman inserted an advertisement for the tract in the *Liberator*, stressing the point that *Miscegenation* was directed toward the subject of "the relations of the Irish and the Negro." On St. Patrick's Day, perhaps by way of pandering to the strong Irish sentiment of New York City, the *World* published a long review of *Miscegenation*. The review, perhaps written by Croly himself, cited many of the same comments of "leading negrophilists" that Cox had cited in his speech in Congress. Again the article carefully avoided any mention of or question regarding authorship of the mysterious tract.[40]

Although the fire's center of the controversy was in New York, its heat reached other Eastern cities. The Philadelphia *Age*, an unabashedly partisan and racist newspaper, went on an editorial tirade denying that "the thing was a hoax." On the contrary, there was "abundant evidence to prove that the views set forth in that pamphlet [were] shared by a large part of the Abolition party." What evidence the *Age* relied on was never revealed. It asked, "Will it be a plank in Mr. Lincoln's next platform?"[41]

The Copperhead press dispensed racist rhetoric throughout the spring of 1864, and like Croly and Wakeman, it had few qualms about committing fraud if it served the purpose. On March 18 the New York *Sunday Mercury* ran two personal notices, one of which read:

> Attention All Ladies—"Hunky Boy," every inch of a soldier and alive and full of fun and miscegenation . . . solicits correspondence of all unmarried ladies between the ages of sixteen and sixty.[42]

The second notice, similar to the first, was followed by the names Albert E. Dunwoodie, sergeant, and Oscar D. Leonard, both of the 55th Massachusetts Colored Volunteers, stationed at Folly Island, South Carolina. The letters were forgeries and the roll of this regiment never carried either name.[43]

In March, the New Hampshire *Patriot* charged that sixty-four teachers from New England, all Abolitionists, "who went to Port Royal [South Carolina] to teach the little niggers how to read and pray," had given birth to mulatto babies. The story was a total fabrication, but other Democratic newspapers across the country reprinted it, causing much of the Republican press to respond defensively. The *National Anti-Slavery Standard* referred to the story as an "atrocious calumny" and a "Copperhead slander."[44]

The frenzied campaign of editorial hyperbole that *Miscegenation* inspired also had a strong salacious quality. Even more moderate Democratic newspapers like the Detroit *Free Press* and Ohio *Statesman* willingly joined in the prurience. On June 4, the *Statesman* reprinted an article from the *Free Press* under the headline "Practical Miscegenation." The sub-headline pointed out in bold type that this was an article about "The Daughter of a Wealthy Farmer" who ran off with a black laborer, an act of "Tender Passion" of which the "Fond Parents" approved. The article described how the two had eloped and, upon their return, "the doting parents will receive them with open arms and establish them in a home of their own, as a living illustration of the beauties of practical miscegenation."[45]

This was mild compared to the tone of most Democratic newspapers.

In April, the *World* ran a story about two society matrons who had married their black lovers and flaunted their actions by promenading down a busy avenue. It added that these were "women of wealth and refinement, and [that] their conduct [was] approved by their acquaintances." The *World* said this was proof that Abolitionism had taken over the Republican Party, and that "the natural repugnance of the white to the negro race" had been replaced by a "sentimental regard" for blacks. Since Democrats would never behave in such a manner, the newspaper concluded, the Republicans were responsible for the whole affair.[46]

The New York *Daily News* wrote that white women did not want any physical contact with black men because "the negro's body is disagreeably unctuous, especially in warm weather, and when under the influence of the strong 'emotional' excitement so certainly produced on his animal nature if permitted to follow her with lascivious glances, and to lay lascivious hands upon her."[47]

The women whose virtue the *Daily News* championed did not include female Abolitionists. Only five days after describing the wanton and lustful qualities of black men, the editor wrote that "we are induced to believe that some American women have gone, and others are going, to this shocking extremity of unnatural, legal prostitution, known as miscegenation." They were doing this for the purpose of "elevating the despised African race to their own social level," and of "preserving the effete Caucasian race in America by mixing its weak and watery blood with the warmer, purer, fresher, thicker, nobler blood of the Ethiopian." Who were these women? They could be found "near to the center of modern civilization, the hub of the universe, Boston itself."[48]

Any charge of the rape of a white woman by a black man was given front-page treatment. On July 8, the Ohio *Daily Statesman* ran an article about a black man who had kidnapped a white widow, kept her confined and drugged, and committed repeated outrages on her. Police finally found the woman, weak and near death, and at the same time found evidence of a recent abortion. They concluded that she had become pregnant by her abductor and had been so traumatized as to be on the verge of insanity.[49]

A Pennsylvania Copperhead publication, the West Chester *Jeffersonian*, referred to the Emancipation Proclamation as "a thoroughgoing program for 'miscegenation,'" a word its editor became obsessed with as he repeatedly wrote about it during that campaign year. The issue of race was also frequently raised by Ohio Democrats. During Ohio gubernatorial campaign rallies in 1863, "a popular feature was a procession of young women bearing placards inscribed, 'Fathers, Save Us From Negro Equality.'" During the spring of 1864, the Cincinnati *Daily Enquirer* wrote, "Boston will, we do not doubt, furnish forth a devoted band of zealous miscegenators. Those reverend clergymen who have given their sanction to the plan, and who see the movings of the divine spirit in the suggestion, will not hesitate to put their hands to the miscegenation plow, and beget seals to their ministry."[50]

In the midst of this, not all of the rhetoric concerned sexual or social relations. A July story in the Dayton *Daily Empire* must have strained the credulity of even the most diehard Democrat. The *Empire* published an article under the headline "Black Republicanism Illustrated" that made an incredible claim.

> The Arlington Estate, the property of Gen. R. E. Lee, is to be made a grand depository of Federal bones—and these are to be surmounted by a free nigger colony. The founding of a nigger colony upon the bones of white soldiers is a perfect and complete illustration of black republican brutality. It is spoken of in abolition prints as a "happy conception of Secretary Stanton." The "conception" is altogether worthy of the origin imputed to it, and whether it be "happy" or not, it has the merit of being suggestive. We may add, in view of another draft for half a million men, that the prospect is flattering that Government will soon have enough of Federal bones to establish several more first class "colonies" of the same sort, and upon the same principle. Soldiers bones and free niggers are the order of the day.[51]

Perhaps the strangest of the racist editors and politicians during the Civil War was Dr. John H. Van Evrie. Though he had a medical degree, Van Evrie devoted his adult life to writing and publishing outrageous and provocative rhetoric on race relations. In midsummer he published, anonymously, a reconstructed edition of one of his old books. He titled it *Subgenation: The Theory of the Normal Relations of the Races*, subtitled *An Answer to Miscegenation*. It was to counter the program described in *Miscegenation*. Van Evrie was probably trying to attract a large following of readers to his publication, because he aped Croly and Wakeman in virtually every possible way. "Subgenation," like "miscegenation," was created out of whole cloth, and *Subgenation* was also a compilation of half-truths, generalizations, and illogical conclusions.[52]

Van Evrie said slavery could only exist between people of the same or equal races. It could not exist as a relationship between a superior and inferior race, such as the white and black in the United States; therefore, there was no slavery in the Southern states. Since "Miscegenation is Monarchy; Subgenation is Democracy. When Lincoln issued his Miscegenation Proclamation he proclaimed a monarchy"; thus, the real question before the country was "Subgenation vs. Miscegenation." Peace Democrats had to "nominate a candidate for President who shall bear upon his banner Peace and Subgenation" and bring about "the adoption by the North of the Confederate Constitution!"[53]

Among other things, Van Evrie also had written that mulattoes became sterile after the fourth generation and that no pure black African had ever attained eminence in anything. In addition to writing ridiculous books, Van Evrie also was co-publisher of the racist New York *Weekly Day-Book*. From October 1861 to October 1863, its official name was *The Caucasian*, and its editorial policy was on the masthead of most of its editorial pages: "White Men Must Rule America."[54]

Van Evrie ardently tried to inject racism into the political campaign and to link the Republicans with miscegenation. The natural targets included Lincoln, Charles Sumner, and Greeley. In July the *Weekly Day-Book* ran an ad for a drawing, titled "Miscegenation, or the Millenium of Abolitionism," which was described in detail.

> Sumner is introducing a strapping "colored lady" to the President. A young woman (white) is being kissed by a big buck nigger, while a lady lecturer supposed to be "The inspired Maid" [Miss Anna Dickinson] sits upon the knee of a sable brother urging him to come to her lectures, while Greeley, in the very height of ecstatic employment, is eating ice-cream with a female African of monstrous physique, declaring that society at last had reached absolute perfection. In the background is a carriage, negroes inside, with white drivers and footmen; a white servant girl drawing a nigger baby, and a newly arrived German surveying the whole scene exclaiming, "Mine Got, vot a guntry! Vot a beeples!"[55]

The advertisement told readers that the caricature could be obtained at twenty-five cents per copy or less if purchased in quantity. "It ought to be circulated far and wide as a campaign document," read the ad.[56]

The most important goal of the Democrats in 1864 was Lincoln's defeat. Since he headed the Union ticket, his defeat by a substantial margin would also hurt other Republican or Union candidates. Since Lincoln had long avoided political speeches and public appearances that would be seen as partisan, he had been an elusive target for Democratic editors and orators.

The Democrats seized upon a reply Lincoln made in March to the New York Workingmen's Democratic Republican Association. It had elected him as an honorary member and asked his views on the address it prepared in recognizing his membership. In a reply, not in Lincoln's hand, he "gratefully accepted" the offer and said the address demonstrated that the organization understood that the rebellion was about more, and had broader implications, "than the perpetuation of African slavery—that it is, in fact, a war upon the rights of all working people." He repeated a passage from his State of the Union message from 1861:

> None are so deeply interested to resist the present rebellion as the working people. Let them beware of prejudice, working division and hostility among themselves. The most notable feature of a disturbance in your city last summer, was the hanging of some working people by other working people. It should never be so. The strongest bond of human sympathy, outside of the family relation, should be one uniting all working people, of all nations, and tongues, and kindreds.[57]

Since that March reply, the Democratic press had sought to twist Lincoln's words in such a way that they were anti-Irish and anti-labor. The *Jeffersonian* reported that Lincoln had insulted working people by classing them with blacks. "In this brief sentence, we have the new doctrine of 'miscegenation' or amalgamation officially announced," it added and it expressed surprise that Lincoln supported the doctrine.

> The most advanced school of Abolitionists now take the position that our citizens of Irish birth are inferior to the negro, and that they could be vastly improved by the intermixture with the negro. The "working people" to whom Mr. Lincoln refers, are, of course, the Irish, for it was upon them the responsibility of the riot was thrown. . . . It is the direct tendency of Aboli-

tionism to reduce the white laboring classes of the country to negro equality and amalgamation.[58]

The New York *Freeman's Journal & Catholic Register* said that the peak of depravity had been achieved, that the "beastly doctrine of the intermarriage of black men with white women" was being "openly and publicly avowed and indorsed and encouraged by the President of the United States." The writer bemoaned that "filthy black niggers . . . now jostle white people and even ladies everywhere, even at the President's levees."[59]

As the summer passed, the amount and intensity of anti-black propaganda declined. The Democratic press had saturated the public with its tirade. Also, the government's lack of military progress, particularly in the East, was clear; Lee had in three months of 1864 inflicted two-thirds as many casualties on the Army of the Potomac as it had suffered in the three years preceding that summer.[60] Nothing would influence the prospects of electoral victory in November more than military events in the months from May through October, and the Democratic press began exploiting this issue more as its importance became apparent.

In addition, the Republicans had gotten a lot of bad press from intra-party battles between Radical and conservative factions. The Chase candidacy, Pomeroy Circular, Frémont nomination, and Niagara Falls peace offensive had all contributed to the growing perception of Republican disharmony. As Republicans such as Greeley presented their differences in public, the Democrats watched delightedly. Under these circumstances, they had good reason to tone down their own campaign and project an image of calm assurance. A primary reason for moving the Democratic convention from July 4 to August 29 was the belief of many party leaders, especially those of the peace wing, that the longer they waited, the greater would be the peace sentiment and disaffection with the present administration.[61]

When the Democrats convened in Chicago, they were positive about their prospects for victory. Most leaders in both parties, including the president, felt that a Democratic victory in November was probable. Under those conditions, Democrats felt no inhibitions about crowing a bit.

Speaker after speaker lashed out at the "flat-nosed, wooly-headed, long-heeled, cursed of God and damned of men descendants of Africa." One berated the "negro-loving, negro-hugging worshippers of old Abe Lincoln." If the racism displayed by so many Democratic editors before the convention had been a matter of individual preference, after the convention, the activities were not just sanctioned but in many instances actually sponsored by the national party.[62]

However, the prospects that appeared so bright as August ended and the jubilant conventioneers left Chicago were short-lived. Before most of the delegates had arrived home from Chicago, Atlanta fell in what may have been the most important military event of the war. Overnight, Democratic optimism turned into desperation. The Georgia campaign had been seen by many people, North and South, as the critical conflict of the war. If Sherman could have been forced to withdraw from Georgia or had even been denied Atlanta until November 8, the incumbent government could have lost. The Democrats would most assuredly have dismantled the machinery of emancipation and regardless of whether the Union prevailed militarily, slavery would have continued in some areas after 1864. The fall of Atlanta improved the government's position immeasurably.

In September, with its hopes suddenly shaken, the Democratic Central Campaign Committee also joined in the miscegenation controversy. It circulated a long leaflet directed particularly at the working class of New York City. Entitled "Miscegenation and the Republican Party," it exploited *Miscegenation* and reprinted the replies of the various Abolitionists.[63] The pamphlet condemned an array of slavery foes, but the primary target was Lincoln, who in acknowledging the honor bestowed upon him by the Workingmen's Democratic Republican Association had taken "especial pains to place working negroes and white men on an equality." As Lincoln's brief reply to the Workingmen's Association had expressed sorrow because "some working people" had been killed by "other working people," the Committee accused him of wanting every white working man to love his black fellow working man who "might possibly, in time, become a relative."[64]

Van Evrie recognized that most people were not going to read "long speeches and pamphlets," and argued that what was "put before the people should be short, pithy and pointed." The *Weekly Day-Book* was devoted entirely to wooing New York's workers to the Copperheads. He said that people in the professions, "banker, lawyer, preacher, or other non-producing classes," had nothing to fear from the abolition of slavery, "but the producing classes, the mechanic, laborer, etc., had better cut the throats of their children at once than hand them to 'impartial' degradation and amalgation with negroes."[65]

In the closing days of the campaign, Van Evrie released "Campaign Broadside No. 1—The Miscegenation Record of the Republican Party."

Van Evrie first reminded the reader about one of *Miscegenation*'s most provocative passages: "The fusion between Negro and Irish will be of infinite service to the Irish. They are a more brutal race and lower in civilization than the Negro. . . . Of course we speak of the laboring Irish." The president, according to the article, had insulted "every white working-man by including him in the category of negroes, or, in other words, calling him a nigger." Van Evrie then made an enormous leap of logic. When Lincoln had ignored "all distinctions of color among the laboring classes," by referring to both blacks and whites as "working people," he had, in effect, recommended "amalgamation of the white working classes with negroes! In other words, white workingmen should love a negro *better than anyone except a relative*." The newspaper urged its readers to action, claiming that "millions of these little documents ought to be distributed at once."[66]

Another Copperhead pamphlet that appeared during this time was *A Voice From the Pit*. Written by George Francis Train, the forty-eight-page tract was a blatant appeal to Irish Catholic workers' racism. The author asked, "What is a Mis-ce-ge-na-tor? . . . He is an Abolitionist (altered Democrat), Black Republican. . . . Sneers at Catholics, and calls naturalized citizens d—d Irishmen." The "campaign cry of Copperhead" was "white Man on the Brain, to distinguish its class from Mis-ce-gen-na-tor, or Nigger on the Brain." According to Train, the platform of the Republicans was: "Subjugation. Emancipation. Confiscation. Domination. Annihilation. Destruction, in order to produce Miscegenation!"[67]

The Lincoln Catechism, a thoroughly racist appeal to the voters, also appeared during the campaign. A long series of political questions with partisan and rhetorical answers, it at one point asked, "Who is Thad Stephens?" and then answered, "An amalgamation from Pennsylvania, who honestly practices what he preaches." (This was in reference to the longstanding and well-known relationship between Stevens and his mulatto housesitter, Lydia Smith.) At another point the catechism set out the Ten Commandments under the Lincoln administration.

> What are the Ten Commandments? Thou shalt have no other God but the negro.
> Thou shalt make an image of a negro, and place it on the Capitol as the type of the new American man.
> Thou shalt swear that the negro shall be the equal of the white man. . . .
> Thou shalt not honor thy father nor thy mother, if they are

Copperheads, but thou shalt serve, honor, and obey Abraham
Lincoln.
Thou shalt commit murder—of slaveholders.
Thou mayest commit adultery—with contrabands.
Thou shalt steal—everything that belongeth to a slave-
holder. . . . [68]

A number of Democratic publications during the campaign sought to
excite common racial prejudices. The Society for the Diffusion of Political
Knowledge, which became a primary Democratic propaganda producer,
turned out a number of circulars that criticized the Emancipation Proclamation and supported slavery while arguing the natural inferiority of blacks.
No. 8 of the society's tracts was *Bible View of Slavery,* basically a
restatement of the argument that had been preached from many antebellum
Southern pulpits. No. 12, written by inventor and artist Samuel F. B. Morse,
who was president of the society and a nationally prominent Democrat, was
*An Argument on the Ethical Position of Slavery in the Social System, and
Its Relation to the Politics of the Day.* Many of the other Democratic
documents were speeches by such luminaries as Governors Horatio Seymour
of New York and Joel Parker of New Jersey, Senator Edgar Cowan of
Pennsylvania, and Representatives George Pendleton (the Democratic
nominee for vice president), James Brooks, and "Sunset" Cox. [69]

Democratic standing with the voters declined considerably after the
convention. For one thing, the Democrats had a flesh-and-blood nominee,
somebody with flaws and foibles who made himself and his party vulnerable
to attack. They also had nominated a war candidate who was to run on a
peace platform, an inconsistency exploited by many Republicans. Above
all, public morale was buoyed by Federal victories at Atlanta and Mobile
Bay, Alabama. As Democratic prospects waned, conspirators Croly and
Wakeman sought to bring the now tepid waters of the *Miscegenation*
controversy back to the boil. [70]

One prominent antislavery Republican who had not been on their mailing
list the previous December was Abraham Lincoln. He was the primary
object of their efforts, the one whose political defeat could do the most to
restore Democratic prosperity, deflate emancipation, and discredit the
Republican Party. On September 29, 1864, Croly and Wakeman anonymously sent Lincoln a copy of *Miscegenation* with a cover letter that asked
whether the author could dedicate to the president his next work, one on

"melaleukation," or the specific blending of white and black races in North America. It said the request was inspired by the Lincoln administration's efforts toward "the recognition of the great doctrine of brotherhood" and Lincoln's reply to the workingmen's society. The author also said, "I am aware that the subject creates prejudice" but that he was sure Lincoln supported the genetic blending of black and white as the only "solution of the negro problem" and concluded that a second Lincoln administration would ensure black rights and full integration of blacks into the future U.S. society.[71]

If Croly and Wakeman honestly expected a response, they badly underestimated Lincoln. If he had done so, the *World* and rest of the Democratic press would have enjoyed an editorial field day at the president's expense. The connivers must have watched breathlessly for a communiqué from the White House as the weeks of October and November passed. But Lincoln was much too wise to risk recording personal impressions on such a controversial topic.

Even if Croly and Wakeman had made some Abolitionists appear ridiculous and fooled their competitors into writing some vituperative columns on the pamphlet, any satisfaction was outweighed by the overwhelming defeat suffered by their candidate. Despite the authors' efforts, they had not diminished Lincoln in the eyes of the voters. Their efforts might even have helped him by diverting attention away from more important issues. Perhaps the racist rhetoric spewed forth for almost a year before the election had desensitized the average voter. Voters may have decided that there was a greater possibility of a rebel army taking their livestock or a Copperhead attacking a government installation than there was of a free black man assaulting their wives or taking their jobs.

The issue of race did not win the election for the Democrats in 1864. In the end, it may well have hurt them. They failed to attract voters as they had in 1862, and in Illinois, Ohio, and Indiana, Lincoln won by greater margins than he had in 1860. As these were all states with strong pro-Southern streaks, the conclusion is unavoidable that the Democrats failed to raise race as an issue. All of these states had returned Democratic majorities in 1862, when, in the public reaction to the preliminary Emancipation Proclamation, voters had been more susceptible to race-baiting tactics. In 1864, they returned to the Republicans—Unionists, to be accurate—with Democratic invective ringing in their ears. No voter in 1864 could have been unaware of the race-dominated campaign waged by the

Democrats. Since postwar events showed that these people had not been transformed into racial egalitarians, the answer lies elsewhere.[72]

Social scientists often grant racial factors a disproportionately large role in influencing voters; race relations have generated tremendous passions in American history. However, having labelled people as racist, the scientists then cast them into an entirely negative mold and struggle to explain why their actions occasionally deviate from it. That most white people in free states in 1864 did not consider blacks to be their social or intellectual equal did not mean they were unwilling to see them released from their shackles. Many white Northerners in 1864 had developed a dislike for white Southerners as well, which would diminish the intensity of their fear and hostility toward black Americans ("The enemy of my enemy is not my enemy").

Lincoln had adeptly defined the Emancipation Proclamation as a war measure designed to weaken the Confederacy. It certainly accomplished that, and many people loyal to the government, particularly Union soldiers, realized it and on that basis supported the measure wholeheartedly. The proclamation had also allowed black men to serve in the military, and by fall 1864 more than 100,000 had done so. Many fought courageously and died. They often fought tenaciously and even desperately, realizing that if they were captured, they would be killed or enslaved. This distressed white troops who saw what happened to black soldiers wounded in battle. Whatever other feelings whites might have had about them, blacks who fought alongside them were their comrades in arms.[73]

The achievement of black soldiers was praised by many high-ranking officers, and the Republican press had passed the information on to the home front. As well, incidents such as the massacre of black troops at Fort Pillow or in the Crater at Petersburg had won them the sympathy of many Northern racists who might never have conceived such feelings.[74]

The draft riot in New York had likewise moved many Northerners. It erupted just before the apotheosis of Colonel Robert Gould Shaw and the all-black 54th Massachusetts Infantry at Fort Wagner, South Carolina, a coincidence Republican newspapers quickly noted: "Black men who fought for the Union deserved more respect than white men who fought against it." Many whites instinctively agreed and were less receptive to Democrats' pandering to racial prejudice.[75]

The importance of the racist campaign of the Democrats in 1864 was not the help or harm it rendered to either party. It distracted voters from more potentially decisive issues. The infringements on civil liberties, the lack of military success, the possibility of a negotiated peace, the printing of paper money and inflation of the economy, and serious infighting in the Republican Party over Reconstruction were all issues to which the incumbents were vulnerable. All of these issues were addressed by Democratic speakers and propaganda, but the arguments were deflected by the race-baiting.

This was true at all levels, but probably national party leaders were most culpable because they set the tone for party loyalists from the statehouse to the precincts and wards. Every time race seemed to be wafting from the public eye, they generated a new campaign of exaggeration and racist rhetoric. Their knowledge of and collusion in the *Miscegenation* hoax was not only undignified; the party leadership had actually carried out a huge fraud on not just its political opponents but ultimately on all the voters. When hundreds of thousands of young men were fighting and dying for their country, such a political trick would not have been well received by the voting public.

The hysteria with which the Democrats raised the race issue really signaled the death of slavery in the United States. For two and a half centuries, it had dominated the economy of Southern colonies and states, and now its probable end was assured by the re-election of Lincoln. Its friends were fighting for its life, and like all death struggles, the fight was desperate. The invective, dirty tricks, and unprincipled methods exceeded anything seen before or since in American politics. When the dust settled, what remained was a shining example of democratic government working best at its moment of greatest peril.

10

"And the Promise Being Made, Must Be Kept"

"The political campaign which ends in the election of the eighth of November decides the most important question in history." *Harper's Weekly* stated a view of the 1864 election commonly held by the Civil War generation. "It has always been the fate of republics to be destroyed by faction. That fear is now about to be confirmed or dissipated forever."[1] Secretary of State William H. Seward observed, "The country is entering on a new and perilous time, a canvass for the presidency in time of civil war."[2] In late August, Francis Lieber, a leading New York citizen and a prominent Union supporter, wrote Charles Sumner, "If we come triumphantly out of this war, with a presidential election in the midst of it, . . . I shall call it the greatest miracle in all the historic course of events."[3]

When the Republican National Convention ended in early June, the appearance of a party united behind a president and a platform belied the truth. Tensions within the party were intense. Legislation pending in Congress differed greatly from Lincoln's plan of Reconstruction, so a showdown appeared imminent. But in the meantime, another fissure in Lincoln's political family appeared.[4]

In late June, Treasury Secretary Salmon P. Chase requested the appointment of a protégé, Maunsell B. Field, to the New York Customs House. Lincoln declined because of opposition by Senator Edwin D. Morgan of New York.[5] For the fifth time during Lincoln's presidency, an angry Chase tendered his resignation. This time, Lincoln took him up on it.

Your resignation of the office of Secretary of the Treasury, sent me yesterday, is accepted. Of all I have said in commendation of your ability and fidelity, I have nothing to unsay; and yet you and I have reached a point of mutual embarrassment in our official relation which it seems can not be overcome, or longer sustained, consistently with the public service.[6]

Though Lincoln was losing an able Treasury secretary, he also was ridding himself of the one Cabinet member who had continuously undermined him with the Radicals. His sudden unemployment allowed Chase to once again seek the presidency. He had earlier been approached by several Democratic senators who asked if he would consider accepting their nomination; he expressed interest if they would "only cut loose from slavery and go for freedom and the protection of labor by a national currency."[7]

Lincoln also had to contend with a third-party faction calling itself the Radical Democracy, which met in Cleveland on May 31 and nominated John C. Frémont. A group of Germans were primarily responsible for this convention, as they had been for a meeting in Cleveland the previous October. At the earlier meeting, the conferees had adopted a strongly Abolitionist platform that denounced states' rights, called for the aggressive prosecution of the war, the abolition of slavery, and urged the revision of the Constitution so that it would conform to "the spirit of the Declaration of Independence." The platform had also called for a Reconstruction policy that would view the South as conquered territories, where plantations were to be given to former slaves and a national militia was to be established based upon the system in Switzerland, where militias were under local control. Not forgetting what had led them to immigrate to the United States, the drafters also demanded support for all revolutionary movements in Europe.[8]

Only 158 people attended the Cleveland convention in May; none was a well-known political figure. Some who helped arrange it were conspicuously absent, including Wendell Phillips, Horace Greeley, and Frederick Douglass. The convention basically consisted of the same radical Germans who had convened the previous October, and some Eastern Abolitionists who were determined not to support Lincoln under any circumstances.[9]

The convention adopted a platform very similar to the one from the previous October. The platform criticized violations of the rights of free speech, free press, and the habeas corpus, and called for a constitutional amendment making all men equal before the law. The platform also called for recognition of the right of asylum, a one-term presidency, congressional control over Reconstruction, and a foreign policy that prohibited the establishment of an anti-Republican government in North America.[10]

Any doubt about the political character of the platform was answered when its introduction was followed by the reading of a letter from Wendell Phillips. The letter was primarily an indictment of the Lincoln administration. It charged that the incumbent "has not done half that it should and could have done toward" crushing the rebellion. "The Administration, therefore, I regard as a civil and military failure, and its avowed policy ruinous to the North in every point of view." Despite Phillips' rhetoric, he did not attend the convention.[11]

The Detroit *Tribune* derisively asked, "Were the immortal 158 the masses? Truly answers Echo—Them Asses!" When the convention nominated John Cochrane of New York as the vice-presidential candidate, the press derided the convention for committing the incredible blunder of nominating two men from the same state. Even if Frémont had won the popular count, the electors from New York probably would not have been allowed to cast their votes for him because of a constitutional proscription.[12]

In his acceptance letter, Frémont castigated Lincoln's conduct of the war and held him accountable for the division in the party and the disloyalty in the country.

> If the Convention at Baltimore will nominate any man whose past life justifies a well-grounded confidence in his fidelity to our cardinal principles, there is no reason why there should be any division among the really patriotic men of the country. To any such I shall be most happy to give a cordial and active support.[13]

Frémont said that he preferred not to be a candidate, but if Lincoln were nominated, "it would be fatal to the country to indorse a policy and renew a power which has cost us the lives of thousands of men, and needlessly put the country on the road to bankruptcy." In that case, Frémont would be left no alternative but to "organize against him every element of conscientious opposition with the view to prevent the misfortune of his reelection." Perhaps the "Pathfinder" had no prospect of being elected president, but he would actively seek to prevent Lincoln from gaining a second term. The bitter dispute of 1861 still held powerful sway with the vengeful Frémont.[14]

Most of the pro-war press treated the meeting with disdain. *Harper's*

Weekly claimed the delegates were motivated by a feeling of vengeance toward Lincoln. The *New York Times* referred to the meeting as a "form of mental hallucination" and called those who attended "Quixotic individuals in the Union party who had gotten their fancies strangely set on John C. Frémont. For what reason, they could not intelligibly tell." According to the Philadelphia *Evening Bulletin,* the delegates were "broken-down politicians" who were angry at Lincoln because he had not given them "a fine fat office or a high military position."[15]

Even most of the Radicals were troubled by the gathering in Cleveland. Zachariah Chandler attempted to put the best interpretation on it by viewing it as a rallying point in the case of the development of significant anti-Lincoln sentiment. George Julian referred to it as a sad mistake. Several Westerners wrote to Lyman Trumbull that even in their section, support for Frémont was slight at best. And William Lloyd Garrison could not remember a more abortive or ludicrous gathering.[16]

Lincoln supporters feared that even though the Radical Democrats could not possibly win the election, they might take enough votes away from Lincoln in several large states to throw them into the Democratic column. Any vote cast for Frémont would have been a Union vote or one simply not cast for Lincoln. He would take no votes from the Democratic candidate. The Republicans' greatest fear was that if the war went too badly, large numbers of dispirited Abolitionists and Radicals might bolt the party and vote for Frémont.[17]

The Frémont factor could have been significant because he could have attracted uncompromised Abolitionists who could never rationalize voting for Lincoln. And as the events of the summer made administration prospects gloomier, the presence of a viable (and radical) third-party candidate could have kept the incumbent from working out a compromise without permanently alienating a substantial part of one or the other wing of the party. The loss of a significant portion of either could have guaranteed Republican defeat in November.[18]

Lincoln's most serious problem, however, was his disagreement with Congress over Reconstruction. After his 1863 Reconstruction Proclamation, Lincoln organized new state governments in Louisiana and in Arkansas.[19] Some Radicals had suspected Lincoln for some time of trying to create a new conservative party by fusing Republican moderates and War Democrats with any other groups hostile to the Radical program. As part of this plan, they thought he was trying to create "pseudo" states from among those in secession that were partially under Union control, so that he could control congressional votes from those states. They would be valuable to him in the battle over Reconstruction.[20]

The result was the Wade-Davis Bill, sponsored by two congressional Radicals, Representative Henry Winter Davis of Maryland and Senator Benjamin Wade of Ohio. It said that when a majority of white men in a Confederate state took an oath of allegiance to the United States, a constitutional convention could be called. The bill excluded all men who held high civil office under the Confederacy or military rank above the rank of colonel from voting for a legislator or governor or serving in those offices; no one could take the oath who had held office or voluntarily borne arms against the United States. The legislation forbade those who did not take the oath from voting for the constitutional convention. Lastly, state constitutions had to abolish slavery.[21]

According to historian T. Harry Williams, the purpose of the Wade-Davis Bill was not to hammer out a final formula for Reconstruction but rather to prepare the best bill for the moment, in order to forestall Lincoln's attempt to bring back the rebellious states unpunished and unrepentant.[22] Congressman James G. Blaine said of the proposal: "It was commonly regarded as a rebuke to the course of the President in proceeding with the grave and momentous task of reconstruction without awaiting the action or invoking the council of Congress."[23] Wade claimed that Lincoln, driven by a lust for power, was usurping Congress' authority.[24] The bill was passed by both Houses on July 4, one hour before final adjournment.

Lincoln was at the Capitol signing bills from the last-minute rush when Wade-Davis was placed before him. He laid it aside. Chandler, who was standing nearby, asked the president whether he meant to approve it. Lincoln replied that he could not, to which Chandler said, "If it is vetoed, it will damage us fearfully in the Northwest. The important point is that one prohibiting slavery in the reconstructed states." Lincoln responded, "That is the point on which I doubt the authority of Congress to act." "It is no more than you have done yourself," Chandler replied. "I conceive that I may in an emergency," Lincoln stated, "do things on military grounds which cannot be done constitutionally by Congress."[25]

As Lincoln prepared to leave, someone said that Radical threats were unfounded and that they would not bolt the ticket. Lincoln answered:

> If they choose to make a point upon this, I do not doubt that

they can do harm. They have never been friendly to me. At all events, I must keep some consciousness of being somewhere near right. I must keep some standard or principle fixed within myself.[26]

On July 8, Lincoln, aware of Radical unhappiness at his pocket veto, released a Reconstruction proclamation that elaborated his views on that thorny issue. First, he was unprepared to commit himself to any single plan of restoration or to set aside the constitutions and governments already established in Louisiana and Arkansas. He was unwilling to declare constitutional authority to abolish slavery in the states. He hoped that Congress would propose a constitutional amendment abolishing slavery throughout the nation. Finally, Lincoln said the Wade-Davis plan was proper for any state choosing to adopt it.[27]

The proclamation only provoked the Radicals further. Adam Gurowski recorded in his diary, "Wait, wait, Mr. Lincoln! You have not yet heard the last on account of this escamotage."[28] Thaddeus Stevens thundered, "What an infamous proclamation! The President is determined to have the electoral votes of the seceded states. The idea of pocketing a bill and then issuing a proclamation as to how far he will conform to it."[29] Chase wrote in his diary:

> The President pocketed the great bill providing for the reorganization of the rebel States as loyal States. He did not venture to veto, and so put it in his pocket. It was a condemnation of his amnesty proclamation and of his general policy of reconstruction, rejecting the idea of possible reconstruction with slavery, which neither the President nor his chief advisers have, in my opinion, abandoned.[30]

The most stinging criticism of the president's action came from the authors of the legislation. Davis prepared, and Wade also signed, a manifesto that, according to Nicolay and Hay, was "the most vigorous in attack that was ever directed against the President from his own party during his term."[31] On August 5, the New York *Tribune* published the manifesto, titled "To the Supporters of the Government":

> We have read without surprise, but not without indignation, the proclamation of the President of the 8th of July, 1864. The

supporters of the administration are responsible to the country for its conduct; and it is their right and duty to check the encroachments of the Executive on the authority of Congress, and to require it to confine itself to its proper sphere.[32]

Wade and Davis said that the president's pocket veto "indicated a persistent though unavowed purpose of the President to defeat the will of the people by the Executive perversion of the Constitution."[33] According to the manifesto, Lincoln must have had the lowest personal motives in taking this action:

The President, by preventing this bill from becoming a law, holds the electoral votes of the rebel States at the dictation of his personal ambition. . . . If electors for President be allowed to be chosen in either of those States, a sinister light will be cast on the motives which induced the President to 'hold for naught' the will of Congress rather than his government in Louisiana and Arkansas.[34]

The authors concluded, "A more studied outrage on the legislative authority of the people has never been perpetrated." Lincoln "must understand that our support is of a cause and not of a man; that the authority of Congress is paramount and must be respected." If he wished their continued support, he would have to "confine himself to his executive duties" and "not make the laws." Here were Republican members of Congress dictating an ultimatum to the president. Nothing the Democrats of Chicago did during the war so damaged the standing and prestige of the presidency as this act by members of Lincoln's own political family.[35]

Much of the party leadership and press condemned the manifesto, and it "rallied his friends to his support with that same intense form of energy which springs from the instinct of self-preservation."[36] The Wade-Davis Manifesto probably did more harm to its authors than to Lincoln. Davis was not returned to Congress.[37] The War Democrats and moderate Republicans found the president's approach eminently more practical and humane than the Wade-Davis Bill. Though the War Democrats opposed Lincoln on many other constitutional issues, they were willing to stand beside him in battling the Radicals on this.[38]

Most Republican newspapers supported the president in this squabble. *Harper's Weekly* had said of Lincoln's acceptance letter of the Union Party nomination several weeks earlier that "like all he says and does 'it would appeal' to the heart of the people whom he serves so faithfully and well."[39] Now its new editor, George Tichenor Curtis, bared his editorial fangs at the Radical wing of the party, and particularly the authors of the Manifesto:

> We have read with pain the manifesto of Messrs. Wade and Winter Davis, not because of its envenomed hostility to the President, but because of its ill-tempered spirit, which proves conclusively the unfitness of either of the gentlemen for grave counselors in a time of national peril.[40]

Despite the support Lincoln received on the Wade-Davis issue, he still had problems. The need of manpower for the Army was reaching a crisis, and despite pleas from his campaign managers, Lincoln issued a draft call. He knew it would not be well received, particularly in the Midwest, but he could not neglect military needs for political expediency. On July 18 he called for 500,000 volunteers; all deficiencies in each state's quota were to be filled by a draft in September. Since the draft would come on the eve of the all-important state elections in Ohio, Indiana, and Pennsylvania, it was the greatest blow yet against the prospects of Union victory. Many Republicans feared electoral defeat because the administration had said that earlier draft calls would be the last. This announcement began a month of virtually uninterrupted bad news for the Lincoln presidency. It was the low point of his political career.[41]

The Democrats were delighted at the draft call. They charged that Lincoln recklessly sent soldiers to their death at Cold Harbor and then blandly called for another half-million. At a Democratic mass meeting in Springfield, Illinois, on August 18, banners read, "Let the draft be confined to Abolitionists." An investigation of the murder of enrollment officer Eli McCarthy revealed that no fewer than sixteen men had conspired to post themselves along every route he could take. They had done so with the understanding that he would be shot by whoever saw him first. Afterward, his body was weighted with a rock and thrown into the White River. In the late summer and fall, threats of violence and resistance in the Old Northwest often led to acts of outright terrorism and intimidation against government officials.[42]

There was much pressure on Lincoln to renounce emancipation during the summer before the election.[43] As usual, the war in the East was going poorly. By August, Lincoln had sunk to the depths of despair. Some prominent Republicans had concluded that he would be defeated and their only hope was to nominate a different candidate. Major General Benjamin F. Butler was being seriously considered. Following a two-hour conversation with prominent New York politico Thurlow Weed, an admirer of Butler wrote to the general that Weed felt Lincoln could be persuaded to withdraw. Also around this time, Weed told Lincoln candidly that his reelection was impossible. Several days later, writing to Seward from a meeting of Republican state chairmen, he said of Lincoln's imminent defeat: "Nobody here doubts it; nor do I see anybody from other states who authorizes the slightest hope of success." Also, "the people are wild for peace. They are told that the president will only listen to terms of peace on condition slavery be 'abandoned.'" Leonard Swett, longtime friend and political ally of the president, had tested public opinion and apparently agreed with Weed's assessment.[44] Then Lincoln received a letter from his campaign manager, Henry Raymond, that demonstrated just how dismal the picture was.

> I am in active correspondence with your staunchest friends in every state and from them all I hear but one report. The Tide is setting strongly against us. Hon. E. B. Washburne writes that "were an election to be held now in Illinois we should be beaten." Mr. Cameron writes that Pennsylvania is against us. Gov. Morton writes that nothing but the most strenuous efforts can carry Indiana. This State (New York), according to the best information I can get, would go 50,000 against us to-morrow. And so of the rest. . . .
>
> Two special causes are assigned for this great reaction in public sentiment—the want of military successes, and the impression in some minds, the fear and suspicion in others, that we are not to have peace *in any event* under this administration until Slavery is abandoned. In some way or other the suspicion is widely diffused that we *can* have peace with Union if we would.[45]

Raymond suggested that Lincoln appoint a special commission "to make [a] distinct proffer of peace to Davis, as the head of the rebel armies, on the sole condition of acknowledging the supremacy of the Constitution, all other questions to be settled in a convention of the states." He was suggesting that Lincoln withdraw his second condition for peace: abolition. But Raymond pointed out that it would not really be abandoning the issue, for "if it should be rejected, (as it would be), it would plant seeds of disaffection in the South, dispel all the delusions about peace that prevail in the North," and thus would "unite the North as nothing since the firing on Fort Sumter" had done. "Even your Radical friends could not fail to applaud it when they should see the practical strength it would bring to the common cause."[46]

It is difficult to imagine what Lincoln was going through at this stage. He had led the nation for three-and-a-half years through its most trying ordeal and had successfully brought it to the brink of victory over a massive rebellion. He had also struck against slavery, that terrible blemish on American democracy. Yet having led the nation to the threshold of victory, he was in danger of being turned out of office because the greater triumph of freedom and democracy no longer burned as a vision for a war-weary population. The sacrifice and misery were in jeopardy of being rendered meaningless. And not only was he going to be defeated while victory was so near; he was going to lose to George McClellan, the man who had repeatedly displayed contempt and ingratitude in his relations with his commander in chief.

For the first time in his political life, Lincoln sought election for reasons other than his driving political ambition. At the September 1862 Cabinet meeting at which he read his preliminary Emancipation Proclamation, Lincoln had said:

> I know very well that many others might . . . do better than I can; and if I was satisfied that the public confidence was more fully possessed by anyone of them than by me, and knew of any constitutional way in which he could be put in my place, he should have it. I would gladly yield it to him. But though I believe that I have not so much of the confidence of the people as I had some time since, I do not know that . . . any other person has more; and . . . there is no way in which I can have any other man put where I am. I am here. I must do the best I can and bear the responsibility of taking the course which I feel I ought to take.[47]

On that occasion, just as in 1864, there were questions of such importance that personal gain and achievement paled. The future of the United States was in question, as was that of millions of people born into slavery and then given the hope of freedom. For such stakes, even a man of Lincoln's integrity and character had to be tempted by political chicanery. And he was. The president gave serious consideration to Raymond's proposed peace commission.

On August 23, Lincoln attended a Cabinet meeting and passed around the famous blind memorandum, sight unseen, requesting each of the secretaries to sign on the outside of the sealed document. Inside was a message he had composed that morning after receiving the Raymond telegram regarding his election prospects.

> This morning, as for some days past, it seems exceedingly probable that this Administration will not be re-elected. Then it will be my duty to so co-operate with the President elect, as to save the Union between the election and the inauguration; as he will have secured his election on such ground that he cannot possibly save it afterwards.[48]

Clearly, Lincoln accepted the likelihood of defeat. He also knew he was right in not recanting on his two conditions for peace, restoration of the Union and abandonment of slavery. Yet lesser men than he had been right and stood on principle only to lose election or be turned out. Was he truly doing what was best for his nation and people in refusing to participate in a political ploy that might still achieve all those noble goals?

On August 7, Charles D. Robinson, editor of the Green Bay (Wisconsin) *Advocate*, wrote to Lincoln, "I am a War Democrat, and . . . have sustained your Administration . . . because it is the legally constituted government. I have sustained its war policy, not because I endorsed it entirely, but because it presented the only available method of putting down the rebellion." Robinson wrote that he and others like him had been accused of becoming "abolitionized" but they had supported freeing the slaves anyway because it was undertaken to weaken the rebellion. He had been able to do so as a Democrat because of the assurance Lincoln had given in 1862 "that if you could save the Union without freeing any slave, you would do it; if you could save it by freeing the slaves, you would do it; and if you could do it by freeing some, and leaving others alone, you would also do that."

> The Niagara Falls "Peace" movement was of no importance whatever, except that it resulted in bringing out your declaration . . . that no steps can be taken towards peace . . . unless

accompanied with an abandonment of slavery. This puts the whole war question on a new basis, and takes us War Democrats clear off our feet, leaving us no ground to stand upon. If we sustain the war and war policy, does it not demand the changing of our party politics?[49]

Robinson urged Lincoln to give War Democrats something to help them continue supporting the war while not abandoning their political affiliation. On August 17, the president wrote this response:

> On this point, nearly a year ago, in a letter to Mr. Conkling, made public at once, I wrote as follows: "But negroes, like other people, act upon motives. Why should they do anything for us if we will do nothing for them? If they stake their lives for us they must be prompted by the strongest motive—even the promise of freedom. And the promise, being made, must be kept." I am sure you will not, on due reflection, say that the promise being made, must be *broken* at the first opportunity. I am sure you would not desire me to say or to leave an inference, that I am ready, whenever convenient, to join in re-enslaving those who shall have served us in consideration of our promise.[50]

Lincoln never sent the letter. However, in an August 19 meeting with a judge and former governor of Wisconsin, Lincoln addressed the issue Robinson had raised. "There have been those who have proposed to me to return to slavery the black warriors of Port Hudson & Olustee to their masters to conciliate the South. I should be damned in time & in eternity for so doing. The world shall know that I will keep my faith to friends & enemies come what will."[51] It was a statement of the stand Lincoln had taken time and again, but in August 1864, these words must have begun to ring hollow to him. He contemplated that having assumed the responsibility for freeing the slaves, he was about to lose control of the office that had allowed him to do so.

After receipt of Raymond's letter, Lincoln wavered. He composed the peace commission authorization that, if it became an official document, would render meaningless all of those marvelous defenses of his policy raised repeatedly over the previous twenty months.

To Henry J. Raymond

Washington, August 24, 1864

Sir:

You will proceed forthwith and obtain, if possible, a conference for peace with Hon. Jefferson Davis, or any person by him authorized for that purpose.

You will address him in entirely respectful terms, at all events, and in any way that may be indispensable to secure the conference.

At said conference you will propose, on behalf of this government, that upon the restoration of the Union and the national authority, the war shall cease at once, all remaining questions to be left for adjustment by peaceful modes. If this be accepted hostilities to cease at once.

If it be not accepted, you will then request to be informed what terms, if any embracing the restoration of the Union, would be accepted. If any such be presented you in answer, you will forthwith report the same to this government, and await further instructions.

If the presentation of any terms embracing the restoration of the Union be declined, you will then request to be informed what terms of peace would be accepted; and on receiving any answer, report the same to this government, and await further instructions.[52]

On that day, Lincoln considered reneging on the demand for emancipation. He was as certain as Raymond was that the proposal would be rejected and that this would hurt the Confederate government with its constituents, while the Federal government would probably benefit politically. However, much of what was good and decent about the government, about the act of the president in issuing the Emancipation Proclamation, about the course of a nation seeking to achieve a better kind of democracy, one based on freedom and equality, would have been lost. The Emancipation Proclamation would simply fade back among other political acts, a pawn to be maneuvered on a chessboard of compromise. The most noble and unselfish act ever undertaken by an American statesman would lose its luster.

If ever there was a time when Lincoln would have withdrawn emancipation as a condition of peace, it would have been during that last week of August 1864. However, the Raymond commission was never formed because by August 25, when Raymond arrived at the White House, Lincoln had finally rejected the plan. The president had discussed the proposition with Seward, Stanton, and William Pitt Fessenden of Maine, Chase's newly appointed successor. They had decided that to send a peace commission to Richmond would be worse than losing the presidential contest; it would amount to an ignominious surrender.[53]

We will never know how seriously Lincoln considered the idea. In their history of the Lincoln presidency, Nicolay and Hay claimed that he wrote the draft of instructions solely to facilitate examination and discussion of the question.[54] Lincoln was well aware of Raymond's importance and would have given his suggestion serious consideration. Or, the draft written on August 24 may simply have been Lincoln again playing devil's advocate with himself regarding a difficult question. He had always applied Euclidean logic and argument as he made a case for every side of an issue, eliminating the least meritorious as the best position emerged. Possibly, he intended on August 24 when he drafted the commission actually to assign Raymond to follow through. If so, it was a tenuous commitment, because twenty-four hours later, he had changed his mind.

As Lincoln's prospects for re-election descended to their lowest point in late August, the first Republicans to consider abandoning him were the Radicals. Correspondence from late June through August indicated a growing belief that a more radical candidate could be substituted.[55] Congressman James Ashley of Ohio spearheaded an effort to hold a convention at Cooper Union in New York on August 17. The focus was Butler, who was a more-than-willing candidate. Butler's chief of staff, James Shaffer, wrote the general from Washington, "If the War Democracy will go to Chicago . . . and split off from the balance of their party and nominate you *on your own platform* . . . the way is clear." He reported that Henry Winter Davis was writing a protest against Lincoln (the Wade-Davis Manifesto) and suggested that this protest should not be released until after August 9, when the War Democrats would have given Butler their endorsement. "Then have Davis come out with his paper, and have other leading Republicans come out and call a mass meeting at New York, or elsewhere, to endorse the action of the War Democracy, and I think it will settle the matter."[56]

Newspaper editor Edgar Conkling of Cincinnati was scheming to join War Democrats and supporters of Frémont behind Butler. He informed

Butler, "Prompt action on the part of your friends will set the ball in motion, and all of Lincoln's office-holders can't stop it."[57] Conkling claimed that most Republicans were Lincoln men only "from pure necessity" and actually wanted "a competent, loyal President, in the place of our present imbecile incumbent."[58]

In Washington, the administration was disconsolate and reconciled to defeat. Gideon Welles wrote of "the factious and discontented spirit manifested by Wade, Winter Davis, and others" that had "generated a feeling of despondency. . . . Wide discouragement prevails."[59] The despair was reflected in a letter written in mid-August by Lincoln's good friend Leonard Swett to his wife.

> The malicious foes of Lincoln are calling or getting up a Buffalo convention to supplant him. They are Sumner, Wade, Henry Winter Davis, Chase, Fremont, Wilson, etc.
>
> The Democrats are conspiring to resist the draft. We seized this morning three thousand pistols going to Indiana for distribution. The war Democrats are trying to make the Chicago nominee a loyal man. The peace Democrats are trying to get control of the Government, and through alliance with Jefferson Davis, to get control of both armies and make universal revolution necessary.
>
> The most fearful things are probable.
>
> I am acting with Thurlow Weed, Raymond, etc., to try to avert. There is not much hope.
>
> Unless material changes can be wrought, *Lincoln's election is beyond any possible hope. It is probably clean gone now* [italics added].[60]

Lincoln himself was so disconsolate that he acknowledged to an Army officer, "You think I don't know I am going to be beaten, *but I do,* and unless some great change takes place, *badly* beaten."[61]

A group of Radicals met in Hamilton, Ohio, in early August and called for a new convention to be held in Buffalo, New York, on September 22. When they did not receive the desired response they sent out a second call on September 3, to no avail. Additional stirrings for a new convention did begin to arise in New York. Active among this group were Horace Greeley; James Shaffer, General Butler's chief of staff; George Wilkes, editor of *Wilkes' Spirit of the Times*; Parke Godwin, editor of the New York *Evening*

Post; Theodore Tilton; Benjamin Wade; Henry Winter Davis; Governor John A. Andrew of Massachusetts; Charles Sumner; and David Dudley Field. These men met at the home of New York Mayor George Opdyke on August 18 and decided to call for a convention for September 28 in Cincinnati. Each of the two dozen men present was given a stack of possible delegates to the Cincinnati convention and told to contact these prominent men throughout the country. They were to respond to John Austin Stevens, Jr. Then a second meeting of the Radicals would be held on August 30.[62]

When the group met again, they "came to the conclusion that it was useless and inexpedient to attempt to run Mr. Lincoln in the hope of victory against the blind infatuation of the masses in favor of McClellan." A committee was appointed to urge the president to obtain his approval of the Cincinnati convention, and they decided to meet even if Lincoln did not approve of the action. It was also decided that joint letters would be sent out to all the loyal governors asking whether Lincoln could be re-elected, whether their states could be carried for him, and whether there should be another candidate. By September 1, Lincoln's standing within his own party had sunk so low that diarist Adam Gurowski recorded, "'Out Lincoln'. . . is to be the war cry." There was no chance that he could be re-elected. Even his own party stood poised on the threshold of dumping him, an unprecedented act in the history of American political parties. But within a week things changed remarkably. Lincoln, at the ebb tide of his political career, was about to experience a reversal of fortune as dramatic as any in American history—one that would save both the country and the freedom of black Americans.[63]

11

"The Fiery Trial through Which We Pass"

On April 21, 1864, the Augusta (Georgia) *Constitutionalist* reprinted a New York *Herald* editorial that focused cogently on an event still seven months away: "First in order and importance is the grand struggle of the war upon which we are about to enter, for upon its results the Presidential contest will be shaped and determined." Lincoln agreed. Late in the war, he spoke of "the progress of our arms, upon which all else chiefly depends."[1]

As 1863 ended, Lincoln had reason for optimism about the progress of the war and the eventual triumph of Union arms. The Union had won two important battles at Gettysburg and Vicksburg. The Mississippi again flowed unvexed to the sea, the last rebel had been driven from Tennessee, and the prospect of a reconstructed government there looked promising. The naval blockade was tightening and Confederate manpower was being inexorably drained by casualties. The rebel government was no longer able to replace troops lost to casualties, illness, and desertion, so the Confederate Congress had extended the limits of conscription to include all males from ages seventeen through fifty and required that those whose three-year enlistments were ending remain in the service. One Richmonder, writing about 1864 springtime social events, said, "There seemed to lurk a foreshadowing, as in the Greek plays where the gloomy end is ever kept in sight."[2]

The South enjoyed certain advantages, however. If it could hold out until November, perhaps the Republican administration might be replaced. Moreover, the U.S. Congress did not follow the Confederate example of extending age limits for conscription and time of enlistment. Historian Bruce Catton wrote that Congress regarded the three-year term as an inviolable contract and therefore depended on persuasion and inducements. Veterans who re-enlisted were provided a special chevron to wear on their sleeves, a thirty-day furlough, a $400 federal bounty plus local and state bounties, and "the spread-eagle praise of politicians back home." Though more than half of the veterans whose terms were expiring did re-enlist, another 100,000 or so others chose to go home.[3] The North had to rely upon conscripts, substitutes, and bounty men. In September 1864, Grant complained, "The men we have been getting in this way nearly all desert, and out of five reported North as having enlisted, we don't get more than one effective soldier."[4]

The South hoped to exploit Union problems in order to influence the 1864 election. People believed that Confederate victories on the battlefield would allow for electoral success for the Northern peace party. The editor of the Augusta *Constitutionalist* wrote on January 22, 1864:

> Every bullet we can send . . . is the best ballot that can be deposited against his (Lincoln's) election. The battlefields of 1864 will hold the polls of this momentous decision. If the tyrant at Washington be defeated, his infamous policy will be defeated with him, and when his party sinks no other war party will rise in the United States.[5]

Another Confederate newspaper unwittingly registered a remarkably prophetic comment in May 1864:

> A serious disaster to our armies in Georgia and Virginia would promptly revive the enemy. It would secure the re-election of the present incumbent, would silence the voices of our friends, and would stimulate new efforts to effect our subjugation.[6]

This assessment would become painfully accurate in August and September of that year.

Robert E. Lee was certainly aware of the influence that battlefield events would have on the election prospects of the incumbent. "The importance of this military campaign to the administration of Mr. Lincoln . . . leaves no doubt that every effort will be made to secure its success." Lee therefore girded himself to "resist manfully" the southward thrusts of Grant.[7] The man Lee called his "Old War Horse," James Longstreet, wrote, "If we can break up the enemy's arrangements early, and throw him back, he will not be able to recover his position or his morale until the Presidential election is over, and then we shall have a new President to treat with."[8]

In 1864 the Confederate leadership was fully cognizant of the upcoming election, its ramifications upon their quest for independence, and the war-weariness that daily grew more widespread in the North. Despite seemingly decisive setbacks at Gettysburg, Vicksburg, and Chattanooga in 1863, the new year brought renewed hope and determination in the rebel ranks. A primary reason why the war dragged on until spring 1865 was the Confederate belief that the presidential election would improve the South's prospects. Lee expressed on the eve of the 1864 military campaign, "If victorious, we have everything to hope for in the future. If defeated, nothing will be left for us to live for."[9] Thus, every time Lee or General Joseph E. Johnston (opposing Sherman in Georgia) engaged Union armies, it was with the knowledge that the higher the casualties and the longer the Union armies were denied their principle objectives, the greater the possibility of a Republican defeat in the election and of a peace acceptable to the Confederacy.

Lincoln, in the meantime, had found a commander who would press the rebels so relentlessly that they would not have the luxury of a protracted recovery after every battle. Lieutenant General Ulysses S. Grant would push Lee's army to the limit, which was exactly what Lincoln wanted.

For the moment, early in 1864, Grant wanted to return to the West. He had a strategy for ending the war that year and he needed to confer with Sherman, who would command the Western armies. He traveled to Chattanooga, Tennessee, staying only long enough to gather up topographical maps of the South as well as Sherman. They traveled to Cincinnati, checked into a hotel, and spread out their maps.[10]

The plan was simple. Grant in the East and Sherman in the West would simultaneously lead armies into the Confederacy, their destinations being Richmond and Atlanta, the most important cities remaining to the rebels. Their primary purpose would be the destruction of the Confederate armies defending those cities. As long as rebel armies could fight, the war would go on. Grant proposed a war of attrition, a war against all who supported the insurrection. He was declaring total war, grim, ugly, destructive, and relentless.[11]

Simultaneously, the Navy was to apply pressure, particularly at Mobile Bay, Alabama, to prevent the Confederacy from stripping its coastal defenses to reinforce its two principle armies. The two main armies would press the rebels constantly, never allowing them to move units from East to West, parrying uncoordinated Union advances. The plan also sought to avoid the prospect of an administration having to stand for re-election while the nation was engaged in a civil war. It was brilliant in its simplicity; it was the formula for victory.[12]

On the Eastern front, Grant's plan involved a three-pronged assault toward Richmond. The Army of the Potomac would remain under the nominal command of Major General Gordon Wade. For the sixth time in the war, it would move on the Confederate capital from the north, engaging the main rebel army somewhere along the east-west courses of the Rappahannock and Rapidan rivers. This was the primary thrust and it was with this force that Grant would travel. An army under Major General Franz Sigel would strike south through the Shenandoah Valley and then move toward the capital from the west. Simultaneously, Major General Benjamin F. Butler would land his Army of the James at City Point, Virginia, at the confluence of the James and Appomattox rivers. From there, he could strike directly at the Petersburg and Weldon Railroad, which carried most of Richmond's reinforcements and provisions from the south. Though the Sigel and Butler offensives were intended to be diversions, the Army of the James had real opportunities, as it would be much closer to Richmond than Grant and it would not have to go through the Army of Northern Virginia. If Butler acted aggressively and intelligently, he might win the prize for capturing the rebel capital.[13]

The great offensive began with the Army of the Potomac crossing the Rapidan and plunging into the Wilderness on May 5. There Lee's army struck them and in two days of savage fighting inflicted a tactical defeat on the new commander as decisive as any in the war. Having suffered 18,000 casualties in the confused fighting, the men of the Army of the Potomac saw familiar signs on May 7 as the wagons, filled with wounded, departed to the north, followed by the artillery, a sure sign that the army again was going to retreat after having ventured into Lee's neighborhood. However, when the troops were ordered from their entrenchments, they turned toward Richmond. The men began to sing and cheer as they realized their new commander would not accept the ignominious retreat, like the ones that had invariably followed their battles in Virginia. They were still on the offensive. This new commander was cut from different cloth.[14]

From the Wilderness, the armies sprinted south and east toward the crossroads at Spotsylvania Courthouse, where battle ensued for eleven days. On May 12, at a place called Bloody Angle, tens of thousands of Union and Confederate soldiers engaged for twenty hours in the most horrific fighting of the war. It was one of the few times in the war when large numbers of the men engaged in hand-to-hand combat. It was aptly described as "concentrated terror."[15]

In just two weeks, Grant's army had suffered more than 34,000 casualties, and the situation only got worse. He was convinced that if he could get Lee on open ground, without the protection of forests or entrenchments, he could inflict casualties that Lee couldn't replace. That, Grant knew, was the North's great advantage.[16]

The day before the fighting at the Bloody Angle, Grant had informed Washington, "I propose to fight it out on this line if it takes all summer." Northern newspapers picked up on this phrase and made it as famous as his "unconditional surrender" proclamation of two years earlier. Many hoped he was pushing a campaign that would decide the war once and for all. On May 15, diarist George Templeton Strong recorded, "All the prospect of this campaign is splendid beyond our hopes. But will it last?" On May 17, Navy Secretary Gideon Welles noted in his diary, "We know it cannot be long before one or more bloody battles will take place in which . . . probably the Civil War will be decided as to its continuance, or termination. My faith is firm in Union success, but I shall be glad when faith is fact."[17] Even the usually understated Grant wrote to the chief of staff, Major General Henry W. Halleck, on May 26:

> Lee's army is really whipped. The prisoners we now take show it, and the action of his army shows it unmistakably. A battle with them outside of entrenchments cannot be had. Our men feel that they have gained the morale over the enemy and attack with confidence. I may be mistaken but I feel that our success over Lee's army is already assured.[18]

Grant was wrong. Lee's army was not whipped. After Spotsylvania, Grant again turned east and south. The armies side-slipped each other until they met at Cold Harbor, just a few miles northeast of Richmond and near where McClellan's Peninsula campaign had come to grief in 1862. Another flanking movement at this point would simply drive Lee into his Richmond defenses and incur the siege Grant wanted to avoid, so he decided to attack.

Furthermore, a number of Union regiments were to be mustered out of the service when their enlistments ran out in July, and the commander knew that the green troops which would replace them would hardly compensate for their loss. The army was suffering from mental and physical exhaustion. Nobody had experienced this kind of warfare previously, where both armies were in constant contact with each other for a month, every day engaged in either fighting or marching and digging new entrenchments.[19] Captain Oliver Wendell Holmes, Jr., a future justice of the Supreme Court, wrote, "Many a man has gone crazy since this campaign began from the terrible pressure on mind and body."[20]

This was one time Grant grossly misjudged the mood and capabilities of his army. In the main frontal attack, he hit the entrenched Confederates with three army corps. As the blue lines emerged from the woods, they were met by a sheet of flame from the Confederate earthworks. The closer the attackers came to the entrenched defenders the worse the carnage. The rebel lines had been constructed in zigzag fashion, which subjected the Federals not just to fire from the front, but also to enfilade fire from both sides. It was a preview of the warfare to be waged in France and Belgium a half-century later. The initial attack lasted less than ten minutes, during which nearly 7,000 Union soldiers were killed or wounded. These were the most concentrated minutes of killing in the entire war. For the remainder of the nine hours before Grant called off the attack, the soldiers simply hugged the ground, digging in as best they could, many using the bodies of fallen comrades for protection. Despite repeated orders to renew the assault, the soldiers simply increased their rate of fire and refused to budge from the limited protection they had.[21]

Grant's army had been pushed to the limits of its endurance. A court-martial was preferable to attacking those trenches. When the order came down to suspend the attack, those who could crawled back to the Union lines or dug new trenches wherever they were. Later Grant admitted, "I regret this assault more than any one I have ever ordered."[22] Lincoln came to share those sentiments as well.

For three days following the battle, Grant made no attempt to propose a truce or to otherwise help the wounded Union soldiers between the battle lines. Tradition held that the first commander who asked to bring in wounded is the loser. Just as Grant would not admit losing at the Wilderness by retreating, he would not propose a truce at Cold Harbor.[23]

On June 5, Grant finally opened a correspondence with Lee. By the time agreement was reached on June 7, "all but two of the wounded had died," as Grant noted in his memoirs.[24]

For the first time during Grant's summer campaign, the Democratic press failed to exploit a bloody Federal setback or to report the horror of the battlefield in the aftermath. It was the most lopsided defeat suffered by a Union army in the war. In a matter of minutes, the corps of Hancock, Wright, and Smith had suffered more casualties than those experienced during twenty hours of terrible fighting at the Bloody Angle of Spotsylvania. The scene in the no-man's land between the armies for three days following the battle was one of unspeakable horror. Yet, for a week following June 3, the Democratic press hardly mentioned Cold Harbor, except to parrot War Department releases. Those reports did not even mention the suffering at Cold Harbor from June 3–7. After the similar defeat at Fredericksburg in 1862, the news had been reported immediately and the nation plunged into its deepest despair. It was more than a week before newspapers such as the *World* and the *Age* published anything approaching the true dimension of what had taken place at Cold Harbor. By then, it was old news—the Republicans had nominated Lincoln and Grant was preparing another promising flanking maneuver.[25]

There were several reasons for the failure to exploit this defeat. The three correspondents of the *World* who reported the movements and activities of the Army of the Potomac were all unavailable to file reports during this time. The principal reporter had been captured by Confederates and the other two were out sick. They had to rely on the report filed by the *New York Times* reporter.[26] As well, there were some weather-related telegraphic problems in the area at the time. A War Department release dated June 3 at 10:00 P.M. stated, "Nothing has been heard from General Grant since his dispatch dated at 7 o'clock yesterday morning." The purported reason for this silence, according to Edwin Stanton, was that "telegraphic communication has been delayed by a violent storm on the peninsula yesterday evening and last night and cannot be re-established before sometime tomorrow."[27] June 3 was the same day that Grant's army entered the "slaughter pen" in the Chickahominy bottomland near Cold Harbor. Perhaps the breakdown of the telegraph at the same time as the Cold Harbor defeat was coincidental, but it helped spare the administration a major setback in public opinion.

Other Democratic correspondents may have left the battlefield to attend the Republican, or Union, nominating convention in Baltimore. Though the convention did not begin until four days after the battle, it is likely that they were already in transit on June 3. For whatever reason, the only immediate press coverage of the event was based on Grant's report to the War Department.

Southern newspapers knew the extent of Grant's defeat, and when they saw the innocuous descriptions of the battle in the Northern press, they assumed that Grant was telegraphing false accounts in order to enhance Lincoln's prospects for renomination. This is the only message he ever sent the War Department about Cold Harbor:

> We assaulted at 4:30 this a.m., driving the enemy within his entrenchments at all points, but without gaining a decided advantage. We now occupy a position close to the enemy and in some places within fifty yards. Our loss was not severe, nor do I suppose the enemy lost heavily. We captured over three hundred prisoners mostly from Breckinridge's command.[28]

If Grant was hesitant to report the extent of the defeat, he probably had Stanton's formidable support. The secretary of war had issued a release dated June 4 that served to upgrade the seriousness of the fighting, but it hardly depicted the extent of the defeat. On June 6 the *World* reported as to the fighting at Cold Harbor, "Another official report, not from Grant estimates our killed and wounded at 3,000." In fact, that was less than a third of the army's total loss from May 31 to June 3, and less than half of those who fell in one ten-minute period. Grant's initial release, if not an outright fabrication, was a serious distortion of the truth.

On June 9, the Philadelphia *Age*, seemingly more aware of the lost opportunity than the *World*, published the following editorial:

> We think Mr. Stanton might be a little more explicit in his telegrams about the condition of affairs in Virginia. He has of late been very meagre in giving intelligence. From his dispatches we can scarcely find out that there was fought one of the bloodiest battles of the war, yet, until yesterday, no one knew its result. If Mr. Stanton knew the public anxiety there is in the public mind to hear the truth about Virginia, he would be a little more explicit in his dispatches . . . they have lost all significance as candid reports of military operations.[29]

Stanton probably did know the public's anxiety, and that was why his dispatches were vague, weather notwithstanding. Stanton straddled the role of civilian administrator over the Army and member of the incumbent political family with all the subtlety of a pit bull. Perhaps nobody knew better the impact that news of Cold Harbor would have on the public if revealed on the eve of the Republican convention. Nobody else was in a better position to screen the information coming from the battlefield.

In *The Passing of the Armies*, Joshua Lawrence Chamberlain wrote about the movement of the Army as it emerged from the Wilderness in 1864:

> Then the rushing, forced flank-movements, known and overmatched by the ever-alert; followed by reckless front attacks, where highest valor was deepest loss; buffetings on bloody angles; butcherings in slaughter pens,—all the way down to the fateful Chickahominy once more—a campaign under fire for twenty-seven days and nights together; *morning reports at last not called for and when we asked explanation our superiors answered,—confidentially, lest it seem disloyal; "Because the country would not stand it, if they knew"* [italics added].[30]

It was not an official policy of the Army of the Potomac's command structure to release officers from the writing of official reports because the truth would be too damaging. However, a certain casualness prevailed that spring when it came to writing after-action reports which would help to preserve the vividly horrible picture of a bloody defeat. Veteran officers certainly understood that complete disclosure of some facts would jeopardize the Army's campaign and its leadership. Nobody was going to report them for not recording battlefield incidents that would further the image of Grant as a "butcher" and fuel the campaign of the peace advocates. Chamberlain went a step further in a speech he gave before the Society of the Army of the Potomac in 1889.

> I desire to say here to-day that in this Army of the Potomac whose suffering and losses were such in that same year of 1864 that we were not called upon or permitted to report our casualties during that whole campaign from the Rapidan Rappahannock to the James and Appomattox, for fear the country could not stand the disclosure.[31]

The occurrence on June 3 should have given rise to banner headlines and severe condemnation by the peace press, yet it was more than a week before the Democratic press began reporting the actual events. By the time the enormity of the disaster began to seep through to the Democratic newspapers, the Republicans had renominated Lincoln and adopted a platform calling for a constitutional amendment permanently prohibiting slavery. The potentially devastating news of Cold Harbor had, by fortuitous circumstances and a cover-up by the army high command, been kept from the public until it was overtaken by other events. It was not by accident that the full extent of Cold Harbor was not officially acknowledged by the government until after the war.

Grant had officially done nothing for which he could be disciplined. His distorted communication to the War Department may have been influenced by conflicting reports from the battlefield, faulty intelligence, or any number of other circumstances. His subsequent messages did little to correct the initial error and, for the rest of his life, on the few occasions when Grant did mention Cold Harbor, he was clearly embarrassed and shamed by it.[32]

Occurring when it did, the Battle of Cold Harbor could have resulted in Republican disharmony in Baltimore, threatening the renomination of Lincoln, or at least diminished the appearance of almost universal Union support for the president's second term. It would certainly have triggered a tremendous outcry from the Democratic press. There would probably have been an increase in the activities of the Sons of Liberty, Confederate agents in Canada, and enhanced support for the already substantial peace movement in the North. These did not occur, or not to the extent they should have, because most people would not learn about what happened at Cold Harbor until long after the event.

The Army of the Potomac was not the same after the Bloody Angle and Cold Harbor. The average soldier was less willing to accept the competence of the officer corps, and many began remembering when McClellan had commanded the army. He would never have ordered such needless slaughter. It was the low point of the summer campaign and, less than a month after Cold Harbor, the memory of that event would haunt the army when it lost a chance to take Petersburg. That opportunity was lost partly because of soldiers' unwillingness to attack as they had in May and early June.[33]

In a June 24 letter to his parents, Captain Oliver Wendell Holmes wrote, "The feeling for McClellan has grown this campaign." On June 11 diarist Adam Gurowski had recorded, "Ambulances cross the city [Washington, D.C.] in all directions; crippled, lame, wounded in all the streets; thousands and thousands under the sod in the cursed Virginia soil, and all this sacrifice seems to have been made for the glory of the politicians." On June 9, U.S. Sanitary Commission member George Templeton Strong had written in his diary, "People are blue. They have found out somehow that Grant will never get into Richmond after all. . . . Snooks says he knows Grant's losses have been per-fect-ly tremendous."[34] On June 2, even before Cold Harbor, Welles had recorded in his diary, "There is intense anxiety in relation to the Army of the Potomac. Great confidence is felt in Grant, but the immense slaughter of our brave men chills and sickens us all." Two days later, he wrote, "Still there is heavy loss, but we are becoming accustomed to the sacrifice. Grant has not great regard for human life."[35] Ever greater numbers of people, military and civilian, were beginning to share this assessment of the new commander.

In the West, events at least as important were unfolding. Armies roughly comparable to those in the East were contending for strategic advantage in North Georgia. Much of the Northern press treated this as secondary, but the issues resolved in Georgia that summer were more decisive than what happened around Richmond. It was in the West in September and October 1864 that the presidential election, and the war, were won.[36]

One reason Sherman and Johnston received less attention, at least before September, was that they spent most of that spring maneuvering. Also, North Georgia was very different from Virginia and it provided for a different sort of military operation. Historian James McPherson noted that "steep, rugged mountains interlaced by swift rivers dominated the landscape between Chattanooga and Atlanta."[37] Natural defensive barriers would allow an outnumbered force to hold out almost indefinitely against greatly superior numbers. The terrain discouraged using the tactic of frontal assault.

Commanding the Confederate Army of Tennessee was General Joseph E. Johnston. Before the war Johnston and McClellan had been friends, and they shared a common reluctance to commit troops to all-out combat. Like his friend, Johnston was idolized by his men and was a genius on the defense.[38] Jefferson Davis suffered the same frustration in getting Johnston to attack as Lincoln had with McClellan. A wartime story made the rounds about Johnston's unwillingness to fire his gun even during an antebellum duck-hunting excursion.

> Never in his life could he make up his mind that everything
> was exactly right, that the time to act had come. There was

always something to fit that would not fit. Joe Johnston is that way, too. Wade Hampton brought him here to hunt . . . but as to hunting he made a dead failure. He was a capital shot. . . . But then with Colonel Johnston . . . the birds flew too high or too low—the dogs were too far or too near—things never did suit exactly. He was too fussy, too hard to please, too cautious, too afraid to miss and risk his fine reputation for a crack shot. . . . Unless his ways are changed, he'll never fight a battle— you'll see.[39]

Opposing Johnston was Major General William Tecumseh Sherman, known to his men as "Uncle Billy." Despite his ferocious reputation, Sherman was reluctant to engage in frontal assaults. The eccentric Ohioan had once remarked about combat that, "Its glory is all moonshine; even success the most brilliant is over dead and mangled bodies, with the anguish and lamentation of distant families."[40]

There were no major engagements until the armies reached Dallas, Georgia, twenty miles from Atlanta. There was sharp fighting on May 25 and 27 near New Hope Church before both armies settled in for weeks of skirmishing and sniping.[41] Sherman began stretching his lines eastward, attempting to get back to the railroad supplying his forces, until both armies were astride the Western and Atlantic Railroad just north of Marietta. Here the Confederates entrenched atop Kennesaw Mountain and its spurs.[42]

Sherman became increasingly anxious about the impasse. He was concerned about not only the rebels in his front, but also those in the rear, particularly the peerless Confederate cavalryman, Major General Nathan Bedford Forrest. The Federals were dependent on the 300 miles of railroad track that led back to Nashville, and the line was vulnerable with Forrest on the loose. Forrest's most recent exploit had been the destruction of the Union garrison at Fort Pillow on the Mississippi River. Some of Forrest's men had murdered several dozen Union soldiers, mostly black, after they had surrendered. They had also killed the commander, Major William F. Bradford, who was shot "while attempting to escape."[43]

As Sherman had begun his movement into Georgia, Johnston had urged that Forrest be moved into Middle Tennessee to cut the rail line. Sherman responded by ordering the garrison commander in Memphis to send out 8,000 men to track Forrest down.[44] He did, and on June 10, the Federals were routed by him at Brices Cross Roads, Mississippi, one of the most humiliating Union defeats in the Western theater.[45] An angry Sherman ordered that a larger expedition be sent out of Memphis to "follow Forrest to the death, if it cost 10,000 lives and breaks the Treasury. There never will be peace in Tennessee until Forrest is dead."[46] This time, on July 14, the Union force defeated Forrest at Tupelo, Mississippi, wounding the rebel cavalryman. Sherman's lifeline was safe.[47]

Meanwhile, the main rebel force at Kennesaw Mountain had Sherman stymied just as Lee had Grant in a like situation outside of Petersburg. He feared that the constant maneuvering and entrenching were dulling his army's fighting edge. Since Johnston would probably expect another flanking movement, Sherman proposed to feint on both flanks and assault the center. The Battle of Kennesaw Mountain proved to be the Cold Harbor of the Western theater, a totally one-sided engagement in which the Union casualties were in the thousands and Confederate losses in the hundreds.[48]

By the end of June, Sherman's losses, though only a fourth of those suffered by Grant, still totaled 17,000. The combined losses from all Union operations during May and June had been 90,000. All they had to show for it was that the country's two principal armies sat stalemated opposite their rebel adversaries in Virginia and Georgia. The Democratic New York *World* asked on July 12, "Who shall revive the withered hopes that bloomed at the opening of Grant's campaign?"[49] Even most Republicans had become discouraged about the progress of the war. As noted on July 23 by diarist George Templeton Strong:

> Today's atmosphere unwholesome. People seem discouraged, weary, and faint-hearted. They ask plaintively, "Why don't Grant and Sherman do something?" . . . Such is the talk of not only Copperhead malignants, but of truly loyal men with weak backbones. . . . To be sure, a stiff upper lip can be maintained in these days only by the liveliest faith, such as removes mountains.[50]

Things would appear even worse before they began to look better. In late June, Lieutenant General Jubal A. Early was dispatched by Lee to drive the Federals out of the Shenandoah Valley. He did so and then, discovering there was no other Union force in the area to oppose him, marched North and crossed the Potomac on July 6. After pushing aside a hastily assembled militia force on the Monocacy River in Maryland, Early put men in front of Washington's fortifications on July 11, five miles north of the White House.[51] Since Grant had stripped the Washington garrison in order to add to his army in Virginia, there were only convalescents, militia men, and individual units on leave or official business in the capital available to defend the city. Fortunately, Grant sent the Sixth Corps under Major General Horatio C. Wright in response to frantic appeals from the War Department. After a skirmish, Early withdrew.[52] Strong's diary on this occasion said, "I see no bright spots anywhere. . . . I fear the blood and treasure spent on this summer's campaign have done little for the country."[53]

Several things happened in July and August that set the stage for the battlefield successes of September and October that had such a dramatic effect on Northern voters. Johnston's reluctance to engage Sherman had frustrated Confederate authorities, especially Davis. When the Union Army forded the Chattahoochee River on July 9 without a fight, the last great natural defensive barrier north of the city had been crossed. Atlantans panicked and Davis sent his military adviser, General Braxton Bragg, to investigate. While in Georgia, Bragg conferred primarily with Lieutenant General John Bell Hood, the former division commander in Lee's army who was clearly angling for the command in the West.[54] "We should attack," declared Hood. "I regard it as a great misfortune to our country that we failed to engage the enemy many miles north of our present position."[55] Bragg recommended that Hood replace Johnston, though Lee cautioned against it, suggesting, "It is a bad time to release the commander of an army situated as that of Tenne. We may lose Atlanta and the army too. Hood is a bold fighter. I am doubtful as to other qualities necessary."[56]

Davis disregarded the advice and replaced Johnston. Attack was Hood's forte; caution and defense were unfamiliar to him. Within a day of his appointment to command, he decided to strike the Federals. The attack at Peachtree Creek was defeated soundly. Two days later, Hood again attacked Federal forces then closing on Atlanta from the east. This came to be known as the Battle of Atlanta, and though it appeared for a time that the rebels would succeed, by day's end, Hood again had lost. The Confederates fell back into the city's outer defenses.[57]

Nevertheless, Hood's instincts remained intact. Having failed to score a decisive victory in separate attacks north and northeast of Atlanta, he launched an attack on July 28 west of the city near a rural chapel known as Ezra Church. By day's end, the Confederates had sustained 3,000 casualties, compared with fewer than 700 suffered by the defenders and the Union troops were still in place.[58]

Though these were clearly tactical defeats for the Confederates, at the time they were seen by many Southerners as victories or at least draws. They did, at least temporarily, help to bring the Federal campaign to a halt. In conjunction with the movement that led to the fighting at Ezra Church, Sherman had also sent the bulk of his cavalry forces on an ill-advised raid south of Atlanta. The raid had several purposes, including the freeing of Federal prisoners at Macon and Andersonville, Georgia. More than six hundred of the raiders did reach the compound at Andersonville—as prisoners. The failed raid reduced Sherman's effective cavalry strength by nearly one-fifth.

After Ezra Church the weakened Confederates had no choice but to go on the defensive, and the siege of Atlanta began.[59] As it continued, another event that had a telling consequence on the war and the election occurred on August 5. Mobile, Alabama, was the last Confederate port on the Gulf of Mexico open to blockade runners. It had long been a prized object of Union military plans. The approaches to Mobile Bay were defended by barrier islands, coastal batteries, and minefields. If Union forces could pass the forts and mines—or torpedoes, as they were called—they would face a Confederate flotilla that included the ponderous ironclad ram *Tennessee*.[60]

Early on August 5, Rear Admiral David A. Farragut embarked on one of the spectacular naval engagements of the war. Farragut's flotilla, with four monitors leading fourteen ships, headed directly between the two barrier islands at the entrance to the bay. The lead monitor, the *Tecumseh*, struck a torpedo and sank, taking down all but a score of its 114 men. The remainder of the flotilla, particularly the wooden ships, absorbed a deadly fire from nearby Fort Morgan. Unable to see what was going on because of the smoke, the sixty-one-year-old admiral was tied to the rigging of his flagship, the *Hartford*, "lest a collision or a chance shot might bring him crashing to the deck some twenty feet below." This became an unforgettable image in Navy traditions. Farragut soon landed a memorable phrase as well. When he demanded why the ship immediately ahead of the *Hartford* had stopped, the reply was: "Torpedoes ahead." "Damn the torpedoes!" he cried. "Full speed ahead!"[61]

Once through the minefield, Farragut subdued the small Confederate flotilla, including the *Tennessee*, the last formidable ironclad in the Confederate Navy. Three weeks of combined operations by the Army and Navy resulted in the capture of the three forts that protected the harbor. Farragut's colorful operation effectively closed the port. Though this action received little notice at the time, with so much bad news coming from Virginia and

Georgia, in September the Mobile Bay victory, plus the fall of Atlanta, caused a marked upswing in the Northern public mood.[62]

A third event had a significant impact on Northern morale before the election. Actually, it was a series of events that began with an appointment on August 1. Grant had been annoyed by Early's exploits in the Shenandoah Valley in June and his threatening move on Washington in July. It particularly piqued Grant that he had to dispatch his best corps, the Sixth, to the capital because of the raid. When Early departed from Washington and meandered through Western Maryland and Southern Pennsylvania, terrorizing people and extorting money from towns, Grant's ire escalated. The fact that Union armies under the respective commands of Major Generals David Hunter and Franz Sigel could have stopped Early while he was still in the Shenandoah Valley had further exasperated Grant. Grant had run out of patience with timid and ineffectual commanders, so on August 1, he put Major General Philip H. Sheridan in charge. "Unless General Hunter is in the field in person, I want Sheridan put in command of all the troops in the field, with instructions to put himself south of the enemy and follow him to the death. Wherever the enemy goes let our troops go also," Grant wired the War Department.[63]

He could have found no better soldier in the Union Army for this job. The previous May, Sheridan had led a cavalry expedition toward Richmond to draw Major General J. E. B. Stuart and his cavalry into battle. Sheridan intended to destroy Stuart's force and eliminate a major source of harassment to Union communication lines in Virginia. He failed, but Stuart was mortally wounded at Yellow Tavern near Richmond. Sheridan was as ferocious, cold-blooded, and aggressive a leader as the North produced during the war.[64]

On August 6, Sheridan took command of the new Army of the Shenandoah, which outnumbered Early's Army of the Valley by more than two to one. Lee had to weaken his lines around Petersburg to reinforce Early and protect the valley, the breadbasket of the Army of Northern Virginia. Later, Lee again thinned his Petersburg lines to send men to Early. The stage was set for a dramatic reversal of Union fortunes of war, and the timing was almost perfect.[65]

The Democratic convention concluded on August 31. Delegates celebrated in the streets of Chicago, confident that in November they would gain control not only of the White House and Congress but of most statehouses in the Northwest as well. Unknown to them, as they were adopting a platform calling for a cease-fire and nominating a war supporter to run on it, dramatic events had transpired in Georgia.

On August 10, Hood sent half of his cavalry on a raid designed to break the Union rail line in North Georgia and Tennessee. The destruction of two Federal cavalry divisions several weeks earlier had apparently led Hood to conclude that he could dispatch a major portion of his own cavalry contingent. It was the last hope of the Western Confederacy to force Sherman to withdraw from Atlanta. It also was a serious risk, for it so reduced Hood's cavalry strength that the remainder had to patrol the army's rear and flanks to protect it from a surprise attack. After August 10, Hood was without effective eyes and ears when it came to discerning enemy movement.[66]

On August 26, Sherman pulled all but one of his corps out of their trenches and began a massive counterclockwise movement.[67] Hood, due in large part to the absence of an effective cavalry force, was unaware of what Sherman was up to. He remained in the dark for three full days as Sherman's men destroyed one of the two railroad lines leading into the city, turning rails into "Sherman neckties."[68] On August 30, as Sherman's army was moving toward the last rebel-controlled railroad into Atlanta, Hood finally discerned his enemy's intentions. He immediately ordered two-thirds of his army south of the city to Jonesboro, where on August 31 he attacked the Federals for the fourth time. The brief, disjointed battle was the last Confederate attempt to save Atlanta. On September 1, Hood blew up all his supplies and munitions that could not be moved, and began evacuating the city. On September 2, Sherman's troops marched into Atlanta.[69]

On September 3, Sherman's message—"Atlanta is ours, and fairly won"[70]—reached Washington, and Northerners celebrated. George Templeton Strong recorded, "Glorious news this morning—Atlanta taken at last!!! . . . If it be true, it is . . . the greatest event of the war."[71] Adam Gurowski wrote, "Atlanta taken by Sherman. Sherman is 'the' general of this war."[72] Farragut's victory took on new significance. "Sherman and Farragut have knocked the bottom out of the Chicago platform," said an ebullient Seward. The despondency in the South rivaled the jubilation in the North. "The disaster at Atlanta," wrote the Richmond *Examiner*, came "in the very nick of time [to] save the party of Lincoln from irretrievable ruin . . . . It obscures the prospect of peace, late so bright. It will also diffuse gloom over the South."[73] Diarist Mary Chesnut recorded, "Since Atlanta I have felt as if all were dead within me, forever."[74] On September 22, she wrote, "The end has come. No doubt of the fact. . . . We are going to be wiped off the face of the earth."[75] A Georgian wrote his brother of his feelings upon hearing the news of Atlanta: "I shall never forget last Sunday. A load seemed to weigh down the spirits of the old and young. Friends passed and offered no word of greeting, while many shut themselves out from the world and tried to forget the gloom overhanging our late cheerful prospects."[76]

The editor of the Richmond *Examiner* was well aware of the impact the fall of Atlanta would have on the Northern election. On September 6, he wrote, "The Democratick party would have been forever obliged to General Hood if he had managed to hold Atlanta for another fortnight."[77] Southerners watched as the North celebrated Sherman's victory. "The fickle and besotted multitude but recently clamoring for peace, now elated by a single success after a multitude of defeats, is shouting with mad enthusiasm for the subjugation of the South," wrote the editor of one Southern newspaper.[78] The Richmond *Sentinel* reported on September 16: "All Yankeedoodledom is clapping hands, and huzzaing and flinging up caps, as though there was no longer a 'live rebel' in all America."[79] A Georgia newspaper wrote, "We have suffered a great disaster. We cannot conceal from ourselves the magnitude of the loss we have sustained in the fall of Atlanta."[80] The attitude of many Confederate soldiers was reflected in the letter of one man in the trenches at Petersburg: "I am afraid that the fall of Atlanta will secure Lincoln's re-election and do much to prolong the war."[81] Like a scale that had simply tilted from one extreme to the other, the North now rejoiced in celebrations that often turned into Union Party rallies favoring the re-election of Lincoln and the continued prosecution of the war. At the same time in the South, a public that had genuinely believed that the election would bring peace and independence to its region was now staggered by the realization that the war would go on and that they would not win.[82]

While the Northern press and public were still enjoying the news from Atlanta and Mobile Bay, Sheridan had been sparring with Early. After a September 19 clash at Winchester, Early retreated twenty miles south to a strong defensive position on Fisher's Hill. On September 22, Sheridan struck again and sent Early staggering southward sixty miles to a pass in the Blue Ridge.[83]

Sheridan's victories caused the value of gold to fall below $200 for the first time since May. As a New York Republican wrote, "General Sheridan has knocked down gold and G. B. McClellan together. The former is below 200, and the latter is nowhere."[84] The higher the price of gold, the worse was the government's credit. The dramatic drop in September signaled new confidence in the government and prosecution of the war.[85]

Sheridan now carried out the other part of Grant's orders, to turn "the Shenandoah Valley into a barren waste . . . so that crows flying over it for the balance of this season will have to carry their provender with them."[86] In less than two weeks, Sheridan's men "destroyed over 2,000 barns filled with wheat, hay, and farming implements; over seventy mills filled with flour and wheat; have driven in front of the army over 4,000 head of stock; and have killed and issued to the troops not less than 3,000 sheep."[87] Sheridan was not through, for he promised that by the time he was finished "the valley, from Winchester up [south] to Staunton, ninety-two miles, will have little in it for man or beast."[88]

Early was down but not out. On October 19, reinforced with an infantry division and a cavalry brigade, he attacked two of Sheridan's divisions encamped at Cedar Creek near the Fisher's Hill battlefield. The surprise was complete and the blue-clad soldiers fell back in panic, piling on top of other Union divisions and causing them to flee as well. The panic spread and within a short time it seemed that the entire Army of the Shenandoah was in full-scale retreat northward.[89] Early and his men, thinking they had won a great victory, began celebrating prematurely. Rather than pursuing their routed enemy, the hungry rebels broke ranks to forage in the Union camps. They soon learned that not all of Sheridan's army had been routed.[90]

On October 16, Sheridan had taken the train to Washington for a strategy conference. He returned to Winchester on the evening of the 18th. The next morning, he was eating breakfast ten miles from Cedar Creek when he heard the rumble of artillery to the south. Promptly, he mounted his horse "Rienzi" and rode off into legend. As he approached the battlefield, retreating soldiers recognized him and began cheering. Sheridan shouted at them, "God damn you, don't cheer me! If you love your country, come up to the front! . . . There's lots of fight in you men yet! Come up, God damn you! Come up!"[91] In small knots, then in larger groups, regiments, and finally whole brigades, soldiers stopped running, shamed by their commander's apparent willingness to attack the whole Confederate force by himself. This display inspired them to follow him back toward the battlefield. When he got there, Sheridan found the Sixth Corps, which had not been routed, and the cavalry, formed in line of battle. The soldiers who returned with Sheridan began re-forming their divisions in the rear as Sheridan prepared to strike. Not only did Sheridan's men rout the rebels, recapturing all eighteen cannon lost that morning plus twenty-three more, but they also pursued Early's army until it virtually disintegrated. "Within a few hours Sheridan had converted the Battle of Cedar Creek from a humiliating defeat into one of the more decisive Union victories of the war."[92] Sheridan's action was probably the most outstanding example of personal battlefield leadership in the war.

One of the most effective Republican campaign documents in the three weeks between the battle and the election was a poem written by Thomas B. Read titled "Sheridan's Ride":

> Up from the South at the break of day,
> Bringing to Winchester fresh dismay. . .
> But there is a road from Winchester town,
> A good, broad highway leading down. . . .
>
> Still sprang from these swift hoofs, thundering south,
> The dust like smoke from the cannon's mouth,
> Or the tail of a comet, sweeping faster and faster,
> Foreboding to traitors the doom of disaster. . . .
>
> Hurrah! Hurrah for Sher-i-dan!
> Hurrah! Hurrah for horse and man!
> I have brought you Sheridan,
> all the way from Winchester, down to save the day.[93]

In Charleston, South Carolina, Mary Chesnut wrote, "These stories of our defeats in the Valley fall like blows upon a dead body."[94] She spoke for many Southerners in the fall of 1864. The end was near. In November, the final official and symbolic act of Northern victory took place in thousands of polling places. On battlefields in North Georgia and the Shenandoah Valley, and in the deep waters of Mobile Bay, soldiers and sailors in blue had written the final scene for this great American tragedy. On November 8, their loyal countrymen would ratify and ennoble their sacrifices.

They Played Roles

Stephen Douglas, who defeated Lincoln for the Senate in 1858, then lost the presidential race to him in 1860. *National Portrait Gallery, Smithsonian Institution/ Art Resource, New York.*

Thurlow Weed, who was firmly convinced that Lincoln could not win re-election. *National Portrait Gallery, Smithsonian Institution/Art Resource, New York.*

Ulric Dahlgren, whose death changed many attitudes about the nature of the war. *Massachusetts Commandery Military Order of the Loyal Legion and the U.S. Army Military History Institute.*

Carl Schurz' support of Lincoln in 1864 was important among German-Americans. *National Portrait Gallery, Smithsonian Institution/Art Resource, New York.*

Lincoln Meets his Adversary

The president and the general confer inside McClellan's headquarters tent on October 2, 1862. *Massachusetts Commandery Military Order of the Loyal Legion and the U.S. Army Military History Institute.*

Lincoln is surrounded by members of McClellan's staff. *The Frank and Virginia Williams Collection of Lincolniana.*

The President

Abraham Lincoln in October 1859, a year after he lost the Senate race to Stephen Douglas and a year before he was elected president. The youthful qualities of the fifty-year-old rising politician would be gone shortly after the war began as the responsibility for leadership took its toll on him. *Massachusetts Commandery Military Order of the Loyal Legion and the U.S. Army Military History Institute.*

The Challenger

Major General George B. McClellan was young, handsome, graceful, intelligent, and immensely popular among his troops. *The Frank and Virginia Williams Collection of Lincolniana.*

Secretary of State William Seward (*left*) and Postmaster General Montgomery Blair (*right*), the two Cabinet members most despised by Republican Radicals. *The Frank and Virginia Williams Collection of Lincolniana.*

Would-be Challengers

Salmon Portland Chase, the very effective Treasury secretary whose belief that he should be president led him to repeatedly undermine the administration. *National Portrait Gallery, Smithsonian Institution/ Art Resource, New York.*

Benjamin Butler, the political general whose unsympathetic treatment of Confederate civilians had made him a darling of the Radicals. *Massachusetts Commandery Military Order of the Loyal Legion and the U.S. Army Military History Institute.*

The Toll of Power

The last photograph taken of Lincoln, the famous broken-glass plate negative made April 10, 1865. The toll taken by the war shows on his face. *National Portrait Gallery, Smithsonian Institution/Art Resource, New York.*

Two Pivotal Campaigns

Lieutenant General Ulysses S. Grant (in front of the two trees) and his staff confer during the Wilderness-Spotsylvania Campaign in the spring of 1864, the bloodiest sustained period of fighting in the war. *The Frank and Virginia Williams Collection of Lincolniana.*

The failure of Grant's campaign to capture Richmond in the East meant that unless Major General William T. Sherman could succeed against the formidable defenses of Atlanta, Lincoln's prospects of re-election were bleak. *The Frank and Virginia Williams Collection of Lincolniana.*

Difficult Friends

Lincoln's stoic but ultimately successful secretary of war, Edwin M. Stanton. *The Frank and Virginia Williams Collection of Lincolniana.*

Major General Ambrose E. Burnside caused Lincoln repeated embarrassment. *The Frank and Virginia Williams Collection of Lincolniana.*

Dangerous Foes

John Charles Frémont was willing to form a coalition with McClellan in order to defeat Lincoln in 1864. *The Frank and Virginia Williams Collection of Lincolniana.*

Clement Vallandigham, the only political leader to be banished to the Confederacy. *The Frank and Virginia Williams Collection of Lincolniana.*

"I KNEW HIM, HORATIO; A FELLOW OF INFINITE JEST. * * * WHERE BE YOUR GIBES NOW?—*Hamlet, Act IV., Scene 1.*

Parodying a scene from *Hamlet*, this political caricature shows McClellan about to bury the head of Lincoln in a grave dug by an Irish worker. *Library of Congress.*

Fernando Wood, the mayor of New York, threatened to declare the nation's largest metropolis a free city. *The Frank and Virginia Williams Collection of Lincolniana.*

James Gordon Bennett, editor of the *New York Herald*, a frequent critic of Lincoln and the Republicans until offered an ambassadorship in 1863. *The Frank and Virginia Williams Collection of Lincolniana.*

Men Who Changed the Odds

Lieutenant General Ulysses S. Grant unqualifiedly endorsed Lincoln's re-election as necessary to Union success. *The Frank and Virginia Williams Collection of Lincolniana.*

Major General William T. Sherman, whose capture of Atlanta influenced the popular verdict in the election. *The Frank and Virginia Williams Collection of Lincolniana.*

Rear Admiral David Farragut won the first important Union victory of the summer at Mobile Bay. *The Frank and Virginia Williams Collection of Lincolniana.*

Major General Philip H. Sheridan's victories in the Shenandoah Valley provided campaign fodder for Union candidates. *The Frank and Virginia Williams Collection of Lincolniana.*

Balancing the Ticket

Lincoln's two vice presidents, Hannibal Hamlin (*left*) of Maine and Andrew Johnson (*right*) of Tennessee. The decision to replace Hamlin on the ticket with Johnson, a Southern Democrat, was made in order to strengthen the Union coalition. Lincoln's role in that decision remains disputed. *The Frank and Virginia Williams Collection of Lincolniana.*

Indiana's two leading Republicans, Governor Oliver Morton (*left*) and House Speaker Schuyler Colfax (*right*). Both appealed to Lincoln in the summer of 1864 to suspend the draft or face the prospect of losing Indiana, one of the crucial October States. *The Frank and Virginia Williams Collection of Lincolniana.*

Radicals and Abolitionists

William Lloyd Garrison, founder and spiritual leader of the abolition movement. *The Frank and Virginia Williams Collection of Lincolniana.*

Charles Sumner of Massachusetts, the first abolitionist senator. *The Frank and Virginia Williams Collection of Lincolniana.*

Thaddeus Stevens of Pennsylvania, Republican leader in the House of Representatives. *The Frank and Virginia Williams Collection of Lincolniana.*

Senator Benjamin Wade of Ohio, whose contempt for Lincoln almost caused him to sit out the 1864 campaign. *The Frank and Virginia Williams Collection of Lincolniana.*

Documents for Freedom

The Francis Carpenter rendering of the famous September 22, 1862, Cabinet meeting at which Lincoln announced his preliminary Emancipation Proclamation. *Left to right*: Edwin Stanton, Salmon Chase, Lincoln, Gideon Welles, Caleb Smith, William Seward, Montgomery Blair, and Edward Bates. *Massachusetts Commandery Military Order of the Loyal Legion and the U.S. Army Military History Institute.*

Alfred R. Waud's sketch of soldiers voting in camp appeared in *Harper's Weekly. Library of Congress.*

Parodies Fair and Foul

An appeal to the racist instinct of voters, this political cartoon shows an oafish and inarticulate black man cloaked in Union garb denying a mutilated veteran the right to vote for McClellan. *Library of Congress.*

A political cartoon showing the two leading Confederate figures brought to bay by the four Union officers who made the greatest contributions to Federal victory during the summer and fall of 1864. *Library of Congress.*

Dirty Tricks

One of a number of political caricatures that attempted to exploit the miscegenation controversy. This appeared in the *New York World* on September 23, 1864, claiming to be a "perfect facsimile" of what had occurred there the day before. *Library of Congress.*

One story during the campaign accused Lincoln of asking Ward Hill Lamon to sing a humorous song on an inspection of the Antietam battlefield in 1862 while bodies remained on the field. It was untrue. *Library of Congress.*

12

"The Brave Men, Living and Dead"

The United States by 1860 had developed a unique military tradition. The concept of the citizen-soldier, the minuteman of Revolutionary lore, had become revered. The Union military was composed almost entirely of civilians responding to the crisis. These men did not sacrifice their basic democratic principles in order to wear their uniforms. The Union army was perhaps the most democratic military organization in history. This sometimes worked to its detriment as a fighting force, since allowing the election of company and regimental officers by the troops did not necessarily encourage promotion based on merit. Often officers simply bought their commissions by paying for votes. Elected officers and non-coms also often did not apply the strict discipline and military regimen necessary to create an effective fighting force.[1]

However, certain characteristics of this citizen army encouraged the fighting qualities and esprit de corps of individual units. Since most of the volunteer units were raised locally, many men served with neighbors and friends. Thus, local officials and men of distinction and education were often elected to lead, just as they had in their communities. Men tended to be more comfortable training and fighting with their friends and neighbors, and likewise tended to have greater confidence in their comrades in arms.[2]

The Union armies were also probably the best-educated military force in history. Most men could read and write, leading to the world's first military postal service. Blue-clad soldiers maintained close communications with their families and friends at home, and their many letters included uncensored political comments of all sorts, including ones on the conduct of the war, the abilities of government officials and military commanders, secession, and emancipation. Politicians were thus peculiarly well informed of the attitudes and aspirations of these citizen-soldiers and, as more and more states allowed absentee voting, state and national legislators became even more responsive to their soldier constituents.[3]

The soldiers were unstained heroes in the eyes of their families and neighbors back home, and what they said in their correspondence was widely accepted. To vote or act inconsistently with what the boys in the field called for was to undermine them and the war effort. They were "thinking bayonets," a phrase Lincoln liked. His ability to serve as commander in chief thus depended on his ability to earn and keep the support of citizens in the ranks. If his or his party's program exceeded what these soldiers accepted, then their willingness to continue fighting would be seriously compromised. Likewise, if the government could not define and give purpose to their sacrifices, it would lose the support necessary to prosecute the war.

Lincoln was greatly concerned about the effects of the Emancipation Proclamation and permitting blacks in the army. Would these actions increase or decrease whites' willingness to fight?[4] In 1864, the continued support of Union soldiers was indispensible to the administration's successful prosecution of the war. Would the soldiers continue to support their present leaders? Or would the enormous sacrifice demanded of them, plus their disgust with bungled combat initiated by their commanding officers, cause them to break with the Republicans? This consideration became even more compelling when the Democrats nominated the highly popular McClellan.

The 1864 election was the first time that many states allowed soldiers in the field to cast absentee ballots. There were nearly a million men in uniform, most of whom were serving outside their home states, usually in rebel states. The soldier vote was extremely important. Never before had such a large number of eligible voters been away from home. Thus absentee balloting became a major legislative issue in Northern states.[5]

Up to the Civil War, voter registration and holding elections had been almost solely functions of state government. In the previous wars in which Americans were away from home, the greatest military strength had been during the Mexican War in 1846–47, at 105,454. The period of service for most was brief and no national election had been held. Even if there had been one, the number of voters affected would have been fewer than a tenth of those affected in the Civil War.[6]

Most state constitutions allowed that no one would lose his residence because of absence for official service for his state or country. However, most courts had construed this to mean that servicemen would have to vote in the district where they resided at the time they entered the armed forces. For Union soldiers serving in Virginia, Georgia, or Louisiana during the Civil War, this would present a problem. If they were to vote, either large numbers of men would have to be furloughed home at the same time (though the dates of state elections might vary, national elections were always held at the same time) or the laws would have to be changed to permit voting in the field.[7]

Nobody expected the war to last as long or involve as many men as it did. Most states approached the midterm elections in 1862 without having addressed the problem. Wisconsin and Minnesota were the first to allow absentee voting by soldiers in the field. In Wisconsin, the constitution was interpreted to permit soldiers to vote outside state borders, and the state legislature enacted a law that directed officers to conduct the balloting in their camps, to permit all qualified "white" voters to cast their ballots, and then to forward those ballots to the governor and secretary of state for final tabulation.[8]

In Minnesota, legislation authorized anyone who had been mustered into service ten or more days prior to the election to cast his ballot wherever he might be by mailing his ballot to the election judges in his home district. Both states later supplemented the rather rudimentary initial enactments.[9] Connecticut and New Hampshire attempted to enact soldier voting laws in 1862, but the respective state supreme courts ruled the laws unconstitutional.[10]

Republican electoral reverses in 1862, particularly in the five most populous states, brought swift action by party leaders everywhere. After 1862, the Republicans and many War Democrats supported the legislation while the Regular and Peace Democrats opposed it. In the five key states the Democrats polled a majority of the votes cast in 1862. However, only in Illinois was their margin of victory more than 11,000 votes, and in Pennsylvania they won by 3,524 votes out of more than 430,000 ballots cast. In Ohio, New York, and Pennsylvania, a 2 percent swing among the voters would have meant Republican victories. Lincoln was determined not to let the Emancipation Proclamation become the scapegoat of the defeat. He pointed out that in all of those states, the margin of defeat could more than be explained by the absence of many Republican voters at the front.[11]

Since most of those voters could be expected to support the government, it would greatly behoove those Republicans who wanted to be elected in 1864 to assure that soldiers could vote. Ohio and Vermont successfully enacted soldier voting laws in 1863, and the constitution of the new state of West Virginia provided for soldier suffrage. Other states amended their constitutions to sanction soldier voting. In 1864, in time for the November election, these states allowed soldiers in the field to vote: Michigan, Missouri, Kentucky, Iowa, Kansas, Maryland, Maine, California, Massachusetts, New York, Connecticut, Pennsylvania, and New Hampshire.[12]

The two very important states that did not were Indiana and Illinois.[13] Illinois eventually approved a law, but not until February 16, 1865. Indiana was governed without a legislature from January 1863 to 1865, so it had no opportunity to allow soldiers to vote in 1864.[14]

F. T. Frelinghuysen, the attorney general of New Jersey, issued an opinion in 1864 declaring that the state constitution, adopted twenty years earlier, sanctioned absentee voting. Because the legislature was dominated by Democrats and the governor was a Democrat, however, New Jersey did not enact absentee balloting for soldiers until 1875.[15]

Maryland held a constitutional convention in 1864 for the primary purpose of abolishing slavery. However, the new constitution also provided for camp elections. But its approval was delayed, preventing the legislature from enacting a soldier-voting law until March 25, 1865. Many Marylanders in the army voted in camp in accordance with the constitutional provision, however, and their votes were tabulated in the general election.[16]

Oregon and Nevada did nothing about soldier suffrage, but there were few Oregonians in the army, and Nevada's first legislature didn't convene until December 17, 1864.[17]

New York's state constitution, like most other states, did not specifically disenfranchise its men serving in the army. However, state law required them to cast ballots in their respective home election districts, which would have permitted very few soldiers and sailors to vote in 1864. Because New York was the most populous state of the Union, the issue of soldier voting there was of great interest nationally. Democratic Governor Horatio Seymour in 1863 had vetoed the state legislature's attempt to enact a statute for soldier voting, holding that it violated the state constitution. In a special message to the legislature, Seymour proposed that the constitution be amended to permit soldiers to vote in the field. Although this led to a clash between Seymour and members of his own party in the legislature, state lawmakers proposed a constitutional amendment that was approved in March 1864, clearing the way for the legislature to enact laws enabling soldier voting.[18]

A New York soldier had to execute affidavits as to age, residence, and identity as a member of the armed services to accompany his ballot. That information was then placed in a sealed envelope, which was inserted into another envelope marked "Soldier's Vote." (The ballot was actually more of a proxy or power of attorney, whereby the soldier designated an elector from his voting district.) The package was delivered to the elector, who on election day would deliver the sealed envelope containing the soldier's ballot to his voting district. The envelope had to be opened at the polling place in public and the name on the affidavit compared with the election register before the ballot was deposited in the appropriate box. Thus the votes of servicemen and civilians would be mixed together in the ballot boxes, making it impossible to discern for which candidates the military had voted.[19]

This rather cumbersome procedure required the ballot to be in the custody of two different sets of people between the time the soldier cast his ballot and it was recorded. This invited the possibility of fraud, and in October 1864 fraudulent ballots were often substituted in place of those submitted by New York troops. One case of alleged fraud was detected in Washington, D.C., resulting in the arrest and imprisonment of Colonel Samuel North and others. Although these defendants were later acquitted, the stories of the voter scandals made front-page news across the country. The Republican press excoriated the Democrats, and the *New York Times* attacked Governor Horatio Seymour in particular. Seymour was up for re-election, and he was branded with the misdeeds of his agents in collecting the votes of soldiers.[20]

> The discovery of the conspiracy to falsify the suffrage of the soldiers, puts the last brand of infamy on the brow of Horatio Seymour.... His plotting to reverse, by fraud, the votes of living soldiers, and forget the votes of dead soldiers, affixes the supreme stigma.[21]

Connecticut, Massachusetts, Missouri, and West Virginia also permitted their troops to vote in the field. But like New York, their ballots remained unopened until they arrived in the soldiers' home districts, where they were deposited in regular ballot boxes. Ohio, Vermont, New Hampshire, Michigan, Maine, Kentucky, Iowa, Kansas, California, and Pennsylvania all permitted their soldiers to vote in the field, and the vote totals were determined independently of civilian totals.[22]

In some states the soldier vote was of little consequence. Massachusetts, where Lincoln received more than 70 percent of the vote, was an example; so was Kentucky, where McClellan won by nearly the same percentage. However, in states where the popular vote was close, the overwhelmingly pro-administration vote of the soldiers was important. In several of these states, the margin of victory for Union candidates was provided by that state's soldiers. The states extending west and south from New York to Illinois contained the greatest concentrations of people in the mid-nineteenth century. Several states were of an even greater significance in 1864 than simply the numbers of electoral votes they would cast; in Pennsylvania, Ohio, and Indiana, elections for state and local offices were held in October, less than a month before the presidential canvass. The results from these "October States" were considered an accurate barometer of what would happen in the general election and helped influence many undecided voters.[23]

The largest of the October States and the second-largest in the Union was Pennsylvania. The legislature had a difficult time proposing an amendment to the state constitution before the 1864 election, but finally set up a referendum in August in which absentee soldier voting was approved two to one. However, few Pennsylvania soldiers had voted in October, primarily because of the lack of time to implement the legislation (which partly explains the huge difference between the vote totals from October to November), and Lincoln was skeptical about how many would vote for president.[24] When he wrote out his prediction for the November election on October 13, Pennsylvania was listed in the McClellan column.[25]

There were probably more than the usual number of uncommitted or tenuously committed voters before this November election. Primarily because of the stigma attached to the Democratic Party by Clement Vallandigham, Ohio was regarded as the safest Union state outside of New England. However, close balloting was expected in Indiana and Pennsylvania. Democrats had done well there in 1862, and both had been among only five free states that had gone for President James Buchanan in 1856.

The tens of thousands of soldiers from these two states might mean the difference between victory or defeat for the administration in 1864.[26]

Indiana Congressman Schuyler Colfax stated the significance of the soldier vote in these states. On July 25, 1864, he wrote Lincoln:

> I have been in various counties in Northern Indiana the past ten days and have everywhere been told that I must write you if the State is to be saved this fall, the soldiers of Indiana must be allowed to come home to vote. All the Northern States, save the hopeless one of New Jersey, seem to be either safe politically; or their soldiers are allowed to vote in the field, *except Indiana & Illinois.* As in 1856 & 1860, the October elections may decide the Presidential election, by deciding such states as New York. Pennsylvania & Indiana are the two doubtful states that vote in October. *Both carried then, the contest ends.* The soldiers of Pennsylvania can vote in the field. *Indiana's cannot.* And, if you desire to strengthen the Army, what better means than to allow the Indiana Regiments to return home *to recruit?* They can do it more successfully than all other agencies; & their moral fervor for the Right will be very great, in addition to their votes.[27]

Colfax mentioned another factor that would influence the Indiana electorate and in particular the soldier voters. On July 18, 1864, Lincoln had issued a call for 500,000 volunteers. If the number had not been met by September 5, he would order a draft to fill the rest of the call.[28]

This was probably the most unpopular act undertaken by Lincoln in 1864, but it was well received by soldiers. To them, some of whom had served since the spring of 1861, this act confirmed that Lincoln was a friend of the soldier. One New Jersey officer wrote to his wife:

> Tell them all that we in the army are delighted with the President's Proclamation calling for 500,000 more men. That is a move in the right direction. Had it been don months since, the Rebellion would have been pute down.[29]

Even if it meant personal defeat at the ballot box, Lincoln would assure that those who were fighting to save their country would never be left shorthanded or vulnerable.

Colfax felt that ordering the draft call in September might be disastrous. He suggested that if "it happens to be *pending* at the October election, that fact will keep from the polls thousands of hostile Southern refugees, or unnaturalized foreigners, who will fear . . . that their illegal voting will add their names to those in the wheel." Colfax was subtly prodding Lincoln to suspend action on his draft proclamation for an additional month, presumably to allow additional time to fill the quota stated, but he actually was trying to avoid the impact the call would have on civilian voters.[30]

Colfax was not the only Hoosier who warned Lincoln about the negative impact of going forward with the draft call in September. Governor Oliver Morton and leading Indiana Republicans joined in, pleading with Stanton on September 12 to delay the draft.

> We express it as our profound conviction that upon the issue of the election that occurs within a month from this date may depend the question as to whether the secession element shall be effectually crushed or whether it shall acquire strength enough . . . to sever her (Indiana) from the general government, so far as future military aid is concerned.
>
> We further express the gravest doubts as to whether it will be possible for us to secure success at the polls on the 11th of October unless we can receive aid—1. By delay of the draft until the election has passed. 2. By the return, before election day, of fifteen thousand Indiana soldiers.[31]

On September 17, Sherman telegraphed Stanton: "If the President modifies it [the draft call] to the extent of one man, or wavers in its execution, he is gone. Even the Army would vote against him."[32] Stanton then told the anxious Hoosiers: "You can judge from this what effect the recall of troops and delaying the draft is likely to have on your election."[33]

Lincoln knew that the draft call would be unpopular. Yet he also knew that in reaching a solution to a problem where the troops were involved, the soldiers' safety and well-being would always be the priority. He would not suspend or postpone the draft call, but Colfax's advice did influence Lincoln. On September 19, he told Sherman:

> The state election of Indiana occurs on the 11th of October, and the loss of it to the friends of the Government would go far toward losing the whole Union cause. The bad effect upon the November election, and especially the giving the State

Government to those who will oppose the war in every possible way, are too much to risk, if it can possibly be avoided. The draft proceeds notwithstanding its strong tendency to lose us the State. Indiana is the only important State, voting in November, whose soldiers cannot vote in the field. Any thing you can safely do to let her soldiers, or any part of them, go home and vote at the State election, will be greatly in point. They need not remain for the Presidential election, but may return to you at once. This is, in no sense, an order, but is merely intended to impress you with the importance, to the army itself, of your doing all you safely can, yourself being the judge of what you can safely do.[34]

Sherman was well known for his aversion to politics and his support for a draft. He was impressed by Lincoln's unswerving adherence to his July proclamation and, though he would not release many of his able-bodied troops in October, he did furlough several thousand Indiana soldiers, plus all convalescents in military hospitals, so that they could return home and vote.[35]

The pressure on the administration to send troops home to influence the balloting rose as the election neared. Particularly active in arranging furloughs were Stanton and his troubleshooter, Charles A. Dana. In his *Recollections of the Civil War*, Dana wrote:

During the presidential campaign of 1864, ... we were busy in the department arranging for soldiers to go home to vote, and also for the taking of ballots in the army. There was a constant succession of telegrams from all parts of the country requesting that leave of absence be extended to this or that officer, in order that his district at home might have the benefit of his vote and political influence. Furloughs were asked for private soldiers whose presence in close districts was deemed of especial importance, and there was a widespread demand that men on detached service and convalescents in hospitals be sent home.[36]

It was not just from the crucial states of the Middle Atlantic and Middle West that such demands were made. On October 27, 1864, William Cannon, the governor of Delaware, wrote Stanton that, "Without the vote of our troops in the field it will be utterly impossible to carry our State, and the election of U.S. Senator, Representative to Congress and Emancipation in

Delaware, depend on the result." Colonel Robert McCallister, who took an active interest in the campaign and election, wrote, "We are getting all our soldiers home to vote that will not be fit for duty in fifteen days. This will help to swell the vote for Lincoln. We are sending all such to hospitals." McCallister was from New Jersey, where Democratic control of the statehouse prevented the enactment of soldier-voting legislation.[37]

The sentiments of the soldiers were influenced by several factors. Army of the Potomac veterans from 1862 felt a profound loyalty to McClellan. He had given them pride and had led them during such battlefield successes as they had enjoyed during the first two years of the war. They regarded him almost as a friend, yet felt similar sentiments toward Lincoln.[38] Though the average soldier in the Western armies may not have felt so attached to McClellan, in early August there was significant support for him among them as well. The Democratic convention at the end of August did more than any other event to undermine the soldiers' confidence in McClellan, particularly its peace platform. A soldier in Sherman's army wrote on September 30, "There were in the Western Army many McClellan men at the time of his nomination, but since the platform has been read and then to know that the nomination of McClellan was made unanimous on the motion of that Traitor Valindlingham is more than the admirers of little 'Mac' could stand and I can assure that 'Mac' has lost thousands of votes within three weeks."[39] Another soldier wrote from just outside Atlanta that the president had to be re-elected. "Every one that is against him is against the union" because "numerically there will be but two ways to vote, one will be for seceshion, one for union." After the city fell, the same soldier wrote his parents that a vote for the Democrats would place one "hand in hand with the vilest traitors that America ever knew."[40] In October, Chauncey Welton, having conversed with Southern citizens and rebel prisoners and deserters, wrote:

> Their opinion is, as a rebel prisoner (said) when we told him we was a going to elect Old Abe again. Says he if you do that we are gone up but says if you elect McC[lellan]D we are all right yet and will whip you yet. this as nigh as I can find out is the universal opinion of the Rebel Army. So I tell you if you hope vote for some man besides our union candidate, If you wish to crush every hope of the rebel army and by so doing cause a steady restoration of the union vote for A. Lincoln.[41]

The Chicago *Tribune* on September 13 ran an editorial saying that

McClellan's acceptance of the Democratic platform had killed his popularity with soldiers. On September 29, it denounced a Democratic editor who had faulted Sherman for his harsh methods of waging war. The newspaper took several remarks of McClellan's and, referring to them entirely out of context, suggested that the Democratic candidate had contempt for the military.

Major Thaddeus H. Capron of the 59th Illinois Regiment shared the views of so many contemporaries. "There was much anxiety while the Chicago convention was in session, as to who its nominee would be, and what kind of platform it would adopt." However, "the army now understands the party and the principles they advocate," and as a result, stood solidly behind Lincoln. Capron noted two weeks later that of those soldiers who were allowed to cast absentee ballots the choice "will be overwhelmingly for 'Old Abe.' A large proportion feel that he can put down this rebellion much better than any other man, and none are for peace with armed rebels."[42]

Dr. Edwin Hutchinson, a surgeon in the XX Army Corps under Sherman, wrote that the idea of an "honorable peace" short of military victory was absurd. The rebels were not fighting for "state rights under the *old Union*, but for *Independence*," and "the moment you begin to propose terms to these men short of absolute submission, you acknowledge yourself either whipped or fighting for a bad cause." Regarding the Democrats:

> I would hide my head with shame sooner than vote for any man nominated under the Chicago banner. Should McClellan be elected, I think that the question of 'Union' is at an end. However, he may talk in his letter [accepting the nomination], still I have no confidence in the man, and think he would do the wishes of his weak kneed party, sooner than act up to his own notions of right.[43]

The most important soldier in the Union's Western armies, whose influence extended far beyond the single vote he cast, was Sherman. He probably came as close as any other Union commander to earning the affection and loyalty from troops that McClellan had achieved with the Army of the Potomac in 1862. Any opinion of Sherman regarding the presidential election would have a tremendous influence. But even more so than Grant, Sherman avoided politics and politicians. It was known that Sherman did not share the negative feelings toward McClellan that much of the rest of the officer corps in the Western armies held. One Boston cotton broker wrote to McClellan in late September asking whether they could outflank the Republicans "by getting a letter from Gen. Sherman (who it is very generally believed here advocates your election) endorsing the Chicago nominations?"[44] But Sherman could not be enticed from his neutral position. The *New York Times*, whose editor was Lincoln's campaign manager, expanded on a statement reported to have been made by Sherman, that "I believe Mr. Lincoln has done the best he could." "What higher commendation is possible?" the *Times* asked. Though this was hardly a ringing endorsement, Sherman's correspondence did make it apparent that he preferred Lincoln's re-election. McClellan, he said, was unjustly accused of weakness, though he lacked the "simple courage and manliness" of an effective leader. "I believe McClellan to be an honest man as to money, of good habits, descent, and of far more than average intelligence, and therefore I never have joined in the hue and cry against him." Nevertheless, "of the two . . . I would prefer Lincoln."[45]

Sherman's opinions were more subtle and restrained than those of his friend who directed Union military activities in the Eastern theater. Grant was rare among Civil War generals in that he had no aspirations for postwar political office. The highest-ranking U.S. soldier since George Washington, Grant did not feel Sherman's aversion to politicians. The general in chief recognized the political realities of 1864 and the effect of battlefield fortunes. Although he attempted to keep his army's attention on the task at hand, as fall approached, he demonstrated an acute and intelligent understanding of the electoral process and the role of the soldiers. In correspondence with Stanton, he set forth a plan for voting in the field. This was sent to Stanton September 27:

> The exerise of the right of suffrage by the officers and soldiers of armies in the field is a novel thing. It has, I believe, generally been considered dangerous to constitutional liberty and subversive of military discipline. But our circumstances are novel and exceptional. A very large proportion of the legal voters of the United States are now either under arms in the field, or in hospitals, or otherwise engaged in the military service of the United States. Most of these men are not regular soldiers in the strict sense of that term, still less are they mercenaries who give their services to the government simply for its pay, having little understanding of political questions,

or feeling little or no interest in them. On the contrary, they are American citizens, having still their homes and social and political ties binding them to the States and districts from which they come and to which they expect to return. They have left their homes temporarily, to sustain the cause of their country in the hour of its trial. In performing this sacred duty, they should not be deprived of a most precious privilege. They have as much right to demand that their votes shall be counted in the choice of their rulers as those citizens who remain at home—nay, more; for they have sacrificed more for their country.[46]

Feeling that he was simply a soldier, Grant took no active part in the political campaign, although he never failed to let it be known that he ardently desired a Republican triumph. When his name was mentioned as a potential candidate of the War Democrats, he responded to the Chairman of the Democratic Central Committee:

> The question astonishes me. I do not know of anything I have ever done or said which would indicate that I could be a candidate for any office whatever within the gift of the people. I shall continue . . . supporting what ever Administration may be in power, in their endeavor to suppress the rebellion and maintain National unity, and never desert it.
>
> Nothing likely to happen would pain me so much as to see my name used in connection with a political office. I am not a candidate for any office nor for favors from any party. . . . I wish to avoid notoriety as far as possible, and above all things desire to be spaired the pain of seeing my name mixed with politics.[47]

Grant concluded the letter with the admonition "wherever . . . you hear my name mentioned in connection with the candidacy for any office, say that you know from me direct that I am not 'in the field,' and cannot allow my name to be used before any convention."[48]

Certainly Grant had a preference in this election. The war and Lincoln had raised him from an insignificant officer to the highest rank and the most successful battlefield leader in U.S. history. He wrote Congressman Elihu B. Washburne on September 21, "I have no objection to the President using any thing I have ever written to him as he sees fit—I think however for him to attempt to answer all the charges the opposition will bring against him will be like setting a maiden to work to prove her chastity." Grant's policy toward the election was to maintain a free and orderly polling place and to permit both parties to circulate their newspapers and campaign documents to the soldiers. As early as August 1863, when some states held off-year elections, Grant received letters from Democrats claiming that their newspapers and pamphlets were being destroyed by postmasters, provost marshals, and others screening what reached the soldiers. In responding to one such letter Grant wrote, "If such a thing has ever been done in any one instance it has been without authority and has never been reported to me. . . . This Army is composed of intelligent, reading, thinking men, capable of forming their own judgement, and acting accordingly." Documents and papers "of all pursuasions, political and religious, are received and freely read," including "those from Mobile & Selma." The commander insisted that "no effort is made to keep them out of the hands of soldiers." Grant concluded:

> I will state however that whilst the troops in this command are left free to vote the ticket of their choice no electioneering or circulation of speeches of a disloyal character, or those calculated to create dissentions, will be tolerated if it can be avoided. Disloyalty in the North should not be tolerated whilst such an expenditure of blood and treasure is going on to punish it in the South.[49]

The president's call for troops that summer must have impressed Grant. On July 19, he wrote to Lincoln, "In my opinion there ought to be an immediate call for say 300,000 men to be put in the field in the shortest time." He informed Lincoln that the rebels had exhausted their human resources and could not replace their losses—"They have robbed the cradle and the grave equally to get their present force." Recognizing that the end was near, he said the only hope left to the Confederacy was "a divided North. . . . With the draft quietly enforced the enemy would become dispondent and would make but little resistance." An addition of large numbers of Union troops at this stage would strike a blow against the rebel army, increasing their rate of desertion and shortening the war.[50]

Grant later learned that the day before his dispatch, Lincoln had issued a proclamation calling not for 300,000, but for 500,000 volunteers and decreed that if that number had not been achieved within fifty days a draft would be conducted. Grant knew of the political implications of a draft call.

> I have no doubt but the enemy are exceedingly anxious to hold out until after the Presidential election. They have many hopes from its effects. They hope a counter revolution. They hope the election of the peace candidate. In fact, like McCawber, they hope *something* to turn up.[51]

He also understood the consequences of Confederate victory.

> Our peace friends, if they expect peace from separation, are much mistaken. It would be but the beginning of the war with thousands of Northern men joining the South because of our disgrace allowing seperation. To have peace "on any terms" the South would demand restoration of their slaves already freed. They would demand indemnity for losses sustained, and they would demand a treaty which would make the North slave hunters for the South. They would demand pay or the restoration of every slave escaping to the North.[52]

Lincoln's issuance of the call for troops reinforced Grant's estimation of his chief when he discovered that the president had acted before receiving the general's request and that the number called for had exceeded Grant's by 200,000.

Grant did not vote in the election. Being from Illinois, he had to return home to vote. He did do all he could to assure that camp balloting was fair and orderly. In his September 27 letter to Stanton, he pointed out that newspapers and campaign literature were freely circulated, but "beyond this, nothing whatsoever should be allowed—no political meetings, no harangues from soldiers or citizens, and no canvassing of camps or regiments for votes." Grant said soldiers should be able to vote "according to their own convictions of right, unmolested and unrestricted."[53]

Grant was an interested spectator on November 8, strolling through camps during the balloting, "and watched with interest how quietly and effectively the system for depositing the ballots worked." According to Grant's biographer and wartime aide, Horace Porter, "Every soldier was allowed absolute freedom in the choice of candidates and perhaps no election had ever been conducted with greater fairness." When the outcome was learned at headquarters on November 10, Grant telegraphed Halleck, the chief of staff: "Congratulate the President for me for the double victory. The election having passed off quietly, no bloodshed or riot throughout the land, is a victory worth more to the country than a battle won."[54]

That Grant allowed campaign literature at all is surprising; officers generally restrained activities and influences not directly related to their military task. There had also never been an election in which soldiers could vote in the field. This lack of precedent may have made Grant uneasy as he contemplated just how distracting a hotly contested election might be for soldiers. Yet, just as he had relied on his instincts to make battlefield decisions, so he acted on his perception of how political events influenced the Union cause. Like Lincoln, Grant recognized that any overt efforts to restrict the opposition party among troops would only diminish the government's credibility. So far as he could do so without compromising military goals, Grant permitted newspapers and pamphlets to circulate.[55]

A particular Republican strategy employed in the closing months of the campaign seemed to influence many Democratic or independent soldiers. This was to accuse the opposition of domestic treason and to associate all non-Union candidates with the worst Copperhead elements. The party that had been largely immune from attack before the 1864 campaign made itself vulnerable in late August by adopting a peace platform and nominating a Peace Democrat for vice president. With the Union military successes that coincided with the Democratic convention, much of the public began to regard the Copperheads, not the administration, as the real threat. Republicans exploited this at every opportunity in September and October. Almost every Democratic candidate in the country was hurt to some degree by the Chicago convention.[56]

The "war failure" plank of the Democratic platform was especially exploited among the soldiers of the Army of the Potomac. Campaign literature carefully treated the former general in chief with respect and sympathy while lamenting that he had fallen under the spell of Vallandigham, Fernando Wood, and other Copperheads. One tract suggested that the Democrats were trying to beguile the soldiers by exploiting "the blind affection which the soldier feels for his chief" and that in courting the Army, the opposition was "concealing its principles, and asking you to vote for the General whom you once loved and trusted." The authors disowned any ability to assess McClellan's military capacity and achievements, "but we may reasonably claim to know more of the objects and designs of political parties," and though "we once honored and trusted McClellan," as the soldiers may still, "we know the man to whom he has surrendered himself, and we can judge better than you what must be necessarily his course under such guidance, in the new and untried field of politics to which he has suffered himself to be led."[57]

The war failure plank was said to contain "the only allusion to the war in which you have played so glorious a part, and to the strife which is imperilling our national existence." The tract said that the Democracy "recognizes that war only to pronounce it a failure" and chastised the party for adopting a platform that did not criticize the rebellion, while reserving "its indigntion for those acts of the Administration by which you have been protected against the machinations at home."[58]

> And to crown it all, it proposes that you should lay down your arms, abandon your conquests, and leave to a set of designing and knavish politicians the settlement of terms of peace! We all want peace—a peace conquered by your bayonets, a lasting peace in which the Union, cemented by the blood of countless heroes, shall endure for us. . . .
>
> Are you prepared to see the reward of your struggles thus snatched away from you, and are you ready to bequeath to your children the long succession of deadly strife which must continue between the dissevered States?[59]

The Democrats had formed "secret armed organizations in the North" and had thereby attempted to provoke the national authorities to divert attention and resources to the home front. This would "allow you to be sacrificed, unsupported by the North." One of the party's "most influential managers . . . was Vallandigham, a convicted traitor, returned from exile in defiance of the authorities of the country." Democrats had "vainly endeavored to deny to you" the right to vote. "You are no longer disfranchised; you can vote, and the Democracy is at last willing to pat you on the head and to try if your suffrages can be secured by a few honeyed words and hollow promises of protection." This was an "exquisite mockery," since it came from men "who discourage enlistments . . . who resist the draft . . . who got up the Copperhead riots in New York last year when Governor Seymour called the anti-draft mob 'his noble-hearted friends,' and pledged himself to have the draft postponed."[60]

The summation suggested an alternative to a defeatist agenda. In doing so, the clearly partisan document stated some truths that were probably not as apparent in 1864 as they have become. Speaking of the Confederacy, the authors asserted, "Well may they believe that the North has grown tired of the war, and that if they can resist until the fourth of next March, their independence will be secured. . . . The crushing defeat of McClellan and Pendleton, will dash the hopes of rebeldom. The re-election of Abraham Lincoln, will show . . . that the determination of the North is unconquerable."[61]

This was strong stuff. Though there is no evidence that the Democrats ever commanded a majority among the troops, among Eastern soldiers McClellan probably enjoyed considerably more support before accepting the nomination than he did afterward. Letters and diaries of soldiers indicated that many were influenced by Unionist campaign literature or came to the independent conclusion that the Democratic platform was flawed. An officer in the Army of the Cumberland wrote his wife:

> You ask me what I think of McClellan's letter of acceptance. I like it very much for the reason that he don't whine about *peace* in it, he talks *war*, he thinks he means war himself—as a soldier he would not dare think anything else, but the trouble with him is that he is not Major General McClellan who fought stubbornly before Richmond, but is "a man of straw" set up by Wood, Richmond, Seymour, Cox, *et id omne genus*, to enable them to steal into the Capitol and the Cabinet, . . . patch up a dishonorable peace and pocket the spoils. He is like a verdant spooney whom old gamesters have inveigled into their snares. . . . I couldn't vote for McClellan either on a *peace* platform or on a *war platform*.[62]

A New York officer in the Army of the Potomac wrote, "Indeed, Pendleton being on the same ticket with McClellan almost deterred me from voting at all, and I know has taken hundreds of votes from him in the army." A colonel from New Jersey wrote home, "The former friends of George B. McClellan have abandoned him because he has got in *such bad company*."[63] The eloquent defender of the extreme left flank at Gettysburg, Joshua Lawrence Chamberlain, wrote of the election:

> The men in the field were authorized to vote in the general election of President of the United States, and so to participate directly in the administration of the government and the determination of public policy. The result of this vote showed how much stronger was their allegiance to principle than even

their attachment to McClellan, whose personal popularity in the army was something marvelous. The men voted overwhelmingly for Lincoln. They were unwilling that their long fight should be set down as a failure, even though thus far it seemed so.[64]

Throughout September and October, similar letters were sent by many Union men in uniform. The strong pro-administration sentiment, or perhaps anti-Democratic feeling, was confirmed on election day. More than a quarter-million Union soldiers voted in camp. Thousands of others were furloughed home to vote in Indiana, Illinois, New Jersey, Rhode Island, and Delaware. The results in the eleven states that published soldier voting separately revealed that more than 77 percent supported Lincoln. In none of those states was the soldier vote decisive.[65]

However, those states accounted for less than 45 percent of the total popular vote. In two states where soldier and civilian ballots were combined, New York and Connecticut, the popular vote was close. The Empire State cast more than 730,000 votes; Lincoln's margin of victory was less than 7,000. If New York soldiers voted for the president by the same percentage as the soldiers of the eleven states whose soldier results were published, then he carried the military vote by more than forty thousand. Without those votes, he probably would have lost New York decisively. In Connecticut, where Lincoln won by 2,405 votes, if the soldiers had voted like their comrades from other New England states, then again the military probably supplied the margin of victory.[66]

On the other hand, in two of the states McClellan won, the vote was close. Neither New Jersey nor Delaware had enacted soldier balloting laws. In New Jersey, where McClellan won by 7,391 votes, the soldier vote would probably have been in favor of Lincoln by more than twice that number.[67]

Historian Harold M. Hyman described the balloting in states that did not allow absentee voting. Since Grant in particular felt strongly about soldiers participating in the election, he allowed thousands of bluecoats furloughs to return home. Hyman wrote of the election:

> On election days there was the extraordinary spectacle not of expected military dominations of elections but of soldiers transforming themselves into citizens; of the sword sustaining rather than suppressing the ballot box. In a century when usurpers-on-horseback were common, the citizen-soldier voting

was a measure of the strength the nation had amassed since the Sumter shame.[68]

A Union soldier from Connecticut offered a sage evaluation of the election in the immediate aftermath of the voting. William Grosvenor wrote that since mid-1863, "the apprehensions of the wisest loyalists and the shrewdest rebels were alike turned to the political contests at the North, as affording to the rebellion a second chance of the victory which it could no longer hope to attain by triumphs in battle." He continued:

> The trial by ballot reached its crisis in the presidential election. In that most exciting canvass, conducted with the utmost license of speech and of the press even in the face of a great civil war, all the influences which could pervert the judgment, sap the loyalty, or shake the purpose of the people, culminated in a final appeal against the war and the administration. . . . It would not have been strange if a few thousand votes had changed the result. But though. as at Gettysburg, the victory was won only when the last brigade of reserve had been called to the front of the battle, it was complete and overwhelming; and the nation was saved in the trial of patriotism on the 8th of November, 1864, as decisively as on the 4th of July, 1863, it was assured of final victory in the trial of arms.[69]

The soldier vote in 1864 was most remarkable in the fact that it was cast and counted during the national plebiscite. Amid the longest and most destructive war in the Western world in the nineteenth century, the United States allowed ballots, many cast by soldiers, to determine basic civil and military policies and the destiny of millions of slaves.[70] The military vote was not decisive in the outcome, for even if several states might have yielded a different result without the soldier ballot, this would have increased or diminished the mandate of the victorious party. What was remarkable was that for the first time in history, soldiers in combat zones far from their homes cast ballots in a free and fair election that would determine the course of the nation they had been fighting to preserve. And they did it in a peaceful and orderly fashion that was so uneventful that it did not result in even a small interruption of the war effort. Their example would set a model for future generations of Americans during wartime.

13

"I Want to Finish This Job"

It was a fortnight that has had no equal in the political history of the American republic. The last week of August and first week of September 1864 brought a remarkable shift in voter mood as a divided Republican Party closed ranks behind the nominee while the Democrats descended into bickering and strife that nearly split the party on the eve of the election. Zachariah Chandler wrote his wife on September 8, "There has been the most extraordinary change in publick opinion here that ever was known within a week."[1]

Leonard Swett, an important Republican politician and friend of Lincoln, whose letter to his wife on August 22 had sounded of doom and gloom, wrote to her again on September 8. "There has never been an instance in which Providence has kindly interposed in our behalf in our national struggles in so marked and essential manner as in the recent Union victories." He reminded her that he had been fearful before leaving home and that upon arriving in New York, "I found the most alarming depression possessing the minds of all the Republicans, Greeley, Beecher, Raymond, Weed; and all the small politicians without exception utterly gave up in despair." He described the mood of the Republican leadership.

> Raymond, the chairman of the National Committee, not only gave up, but would do nothing. Nobody would do anything. There was not a man doing anything except mischief.
>
> A movement was organizing to make Mr. Lincoln withdraw or call a convention and supplant him.

> I felt it my duty to see if some action could not be inaugurated. I got Raymond, after great labor, to call the committee at Washington three days after I would arrive here, and came first to see if Mr. Lincoln understood his danger and would help to set things in motion. He understood fully the danger of his position, and for once seemed anxious I should try to stem the tide bearing him down. When the committee met, they showed entire want of organization and had not a dollar of money.[2]

Then Swett changed tone in a transition that paralleled the shift in voter mood.

> The first gleam of hope was in the Chicago convention. The evident depression of the public caused the peace men to control that convention, and then, just as the public began to shrink from accepting it, God gave us the victory at Atlanta, which made the ship right itself, as a ship in a storm does after a great wave has nearly capsized it.[3]

Historian William Zornow has identified the fall of Atlanta as "the turning point of the canvass of 1864."[4] So has almost every other historian of the Civil War era. This focus has resulted in concentrating so much attention on military victory that other factors influencing the shift in voter attitudes have been largely ignored or understated. The Democratic National Convention and the platform it adopted also played a major part in this phenomenon. The convention gave credence to the Republican accusation of domestic treason that became the dominant theme of the closing months of the campaign.[5]

The Democratic platform and victory at Atlanta were the primary causes of a shift in voter sentiment, but the change in popular perception was but one of the results. Chicago and Atlanta also inspired a fusion of the feuding elements of the Republican Party. Zornow wrote, "The Chicago platform put the quietus on the proposed new convention that had been planned at the Opdyke and Field meetings." And even though there "was still some talk on the subject," the Democratic convention "had made such a move unlikely." It necessitated the mending of fences within the Union camp and the return of many prodigals.[6]

Immediately after learning of the victory at Atlanta, John Murray Forbes, one of those most enthusiastic about holding a new convention, now suggested that a meeting of selected Westerners be held. These men would organize Lincoln's campaign for re-election and advise the president as it continued. He feared that Lincoln might be induced by Raymond to enter into negotiations with the South. This became more likely after Hood's defeat at Atlanta, because Jefferson Davis had to be more amenable to reunion after the fall of the critical city.[7]

Governor John A. Andrew of Massachusetts had dropped out of the "dump Lincoln" movement in late August after learning that the president had stood firm on emancipation as a condition of peace during the Jaquess/ Gilmore peace mission. Now he too felt that Lincoln's re-election prospects had brightened considerably and that it was important that "men of motive and ideas [should] get into the lead." In that way, they could gain control of the party "machine and 'run it' themselves." He shared Forbes' concern that Lincoln might yield to those who wished for peace even if it were obtained at the cost of emancipation. He proposed a meeting in New York that would include the governors of Ohio, Indiana, and Illinois, so that they could "rescue" the president from "those who for want of political and moral courage" would tempt him to accept "an unworthy and disgraceful offer to compromise with the leaders of the rebellion."[8]

The meeting was never held, but a great deal of Republican dialogue followed Atlanta's fall. Those who still opposed Lincoln's re-election suddenly found themselves a small and isolated faction in a party that had virtually overnight restored its unity and common purpose. George Wilkes wrote to Benjamin Butler, "If we could only get a convention together we could make it the master of the situation, in spite of the Lincoln influences. . . . I confess, however, the prospect now looks very slim." As a face-saving gesture, Wilkes suggested that the proponents of a new convention could encourage Republican voters to write their preferences for the new government on their ballots, which would "enable us . . . to get gracefully out of the failure of the . . . Convention."[9]

Thurlow Weed wrote to Secretary of State William H. Seward on September 20, 1864.

> The conspiracy against Mr. Lincoln collapsed on Monday last [September 12]. It was equally formidable and vicious, embracing a larger number of leading men than I supposed possible. Knowing that I was not satisfied with the President, they came to me for cooperation, but my objection to Mr.

Lincoln is that he has done too much for those who now seek
to drive him out of the field.[10]

As the Radicals gathered about Lincoln, they sought to control his
direction during a second term. Andrew, Forbes, and others who had sought
a new convention now went to Washington to persuade Lincoln to stay the
course and to give no more consideration to peace negotiations while the
rebellion was dying. They brought with them letters from Governors Yates
and Brough of Illinois and Ohio.[11]

Some moderates sought to help Lincoln in a way that did not ameliorate
the Radicals. Speaking to a crowd in his hometown of Auburn, New York,
Seward said, "While the rebels continue to wage war against the government
of the United States, the military measures affecting slavery, which have
been adopted from necessity to bring the war to a speedy and successful
end, will be continued." However, Seward also told his listeners that once
the war had ended, "all the war measures then existing, including those
which affect slavery, will cease also." In the same speech, referring to the
Democratic platform's call for an immediate cessation of hostilities, Seward
said, "Who can vouch for the safety of the country against the rebels during
the interval which must elapse before the new administration can constitutionally come into power?" Seward's ill-advised words, though undoubtedly well intentioned, subjected Lincoln to attacks from Radicals and the
press. Some Radicals felt Seward had promised that in Lincoln's second
term, the emancipation edict would end. The opposition press seized upon
his remarks about "the safety of the country . . . during the interval" as a
threat that the administration intended to keep itself in power "whatever
might be the verdict of the people."[12]

The clamor created by Seward continued until the eve of the election.
Lincoln, who remained aloof throughout the spring and summer, addressed
the matter in late October. It had been his friendship with Seward, plus the
importance of the office of secretary of state, that led people to believe that
he must have spoken with Lincoln's blessing. According to his secretaries,
he felt "the distorted and unjust conclusions which had been drawn from
Seward's remarks had gone far enough, and that the time had come to put
an end to them." The occasion he chose was a serenade by a group of loyal
Marylanders who had come to Washington to celebrate the Republican
victory in the state elections.

A word upon another subject. Something said by the Secretary of State, in his recent speech at Auburn, has been construed by some into a threat that if I shall be beaten at the election I will, between then and the end of my constitutional term, do what I may be able to ruin the Government. Others regard the fact that the Chicago Convention adjourned, not *sine die*, but to meet again, if called to do so by a particular individual, as the intimation of a purpose that if their nominee shall be elected he will at once seize control of the Government. I hope the good people will permit themselves to suffer no uneasiness on either point.[13]

Lincoln explained that he was "struggling to maintain government, not to overthrow it." He was "struggling especially to prevent others from overthrowing it." In an eerily prophetic statement, he said, "If I shall live, I shall remain president until the fourth of next March; and that whoever shall be constitutionally elected therefore, in November, shall be duly installed as president on the fourth of March." Lincoln assured them that in the interim, he would do his "utmost that whoever is to hold the helm for the next voyage shall start with the best possible chance to save the ship."[14]

Perhaps the most significant act of party loyalty in the 1864 campaign came from one of the most vocal Radicals. Zachariah Chandler was the senior senator from Michigan, a Radical Republican whose closest friend in the Senate was Ben Wade of Ohio. Wade "possessed Henry Winter Davis' confidence, and had long been Frémont's political associate." However, unlike other Radicals, Chandler enjoyed relatively amicable relations with Lincoln. Toward the end of August 1864, he set out to heal some party wounds.[15]

The major question about the Radicals in 1864 was whether they would support Lincoln, support the futile third-party candidacy of John Charles Frémont, or merely sit on the sidelines. Chandler first visited Wade, knowing his friend was a key to winning Radical support of Lincoln's candidacy. If he could not convince the man who had been his closest ally during many hard-fought battles in the Senate, then the effort was probably useless. A witness to the meeting described it as "titanic." Chandler prevailed on Wade to support the national ticket, but only on the condition that Lincoln would drop Postmaster General Montgomery Blair from the Cabinet. Apparently no definite understanding was reached as to what Wade would do to induce Frémont to withdraw, although Chandler would later claim otherwise. According to Wade, Chandler suggested that he (Wade) had some influence with Frémont and might be able to get him to pull out. Wade later claimed that it was not essential to the bargain and he believed that Chandler regarded the matter as unimportant. The Michigan senator always believed Frémont's withdrawal was an essential part of the bargain.[16]

From his meeting with Wade in Ohio, Chandler proceeded to Harrisburg to meet with Simon Cameron, the powerful Republican boss in Pennsylvania. After gaining the former secretary of war's collaboration in his plan, he traveled to Washington for the crucial meeting with Lincoln. His letter to his wife upon arriving reflected Chandler's sense of urgency. "I am more and more of the opinion that the election of Mr. Lincoln & the salvation of the country depends on my mission. . . . You see my whole heart is set upon success & I must win or leave the country. If traitors rule this land it is no place for me, nor do I believe I *could* live here if I would."[17]

Chandler first met with Lincoln's friends and advisers. Knowing that his proposal was the kind of political deal Lincoln disliked, Chandler cultivated those in whom the president had confidence. While the senator was in Washington waiting to meet with Lincoln, the Democrats nominated McClellan and adopted a peace platform. This made Chandler's goals all the more compelling. His meetings with the president's friends had yielded nothing, and on August 30 he hurried off to Philadelphia to meet with the Republican State Central Committee, from which he hoped to enlist support for his project.[18]

He met with Cameron and Henry Raymond and apparently was received coolly. He braved an uncomfortable train ride back to Washington, "sitting up all night" but buoyed by the knowledge that "I am trying to do my duty & save the country." He was driven even though "I may accomplish nothing, but I would certainly prefer the traitor Jef Davis to the equal traitor McLelland for President."

> I am disgusted beyond the power of language to express & yet here I am. . . . I *won't* stay much longer *any how*. If it was only Abe Lincoln I would say, go to ____ in your own way, I will not stop a second to save you but it is this great nation with all its hopes for the present & future I cannot abandon the effort now.[19]

Chandler, accompanied by Congressman Elihu Washburne, Senator James Harlan of Iowa, and President James Edmunds of the Union League, finally met with Lincoln on September 3 and made his proposal. The president wished to think it over and agreed to meet with Chandler the following day. In the interim, word of the fall of Atlanta was received. On September 4, Lincoln promised that if Frémont could be persuaded to withdraw in return for Blair's separation from the Cabinet, then an accommodation could be worked out. Chandler promptly departed for New York, expecting to meet Wade there and then approach Frémont. Wade failed to show, and even after Chandler wired him that he was urgently needed, the Ohioan would not come. The frustrated senator wrote, "The President was most reluctant to come to terms *but came* & now to be euchered is hard." He had seen Frémont on September 7 and was going to see him again the following day, "when the matter will be decided one way or another."[20]

Chandler had enlisted two important Radicals, David Dudley Field and George Wilkes. But they underestimated the animus Frémont felt toward Lincoln. The New York *Herald*, reporting on the negotiations, said on September 7, "It is asserted . . . that General Frémont will withdraw his name from the Presidential contest within ten days. It is also stated that the Hon. B. F. Wade is shortly to take the stump for the Baltimore nominees." But the *Herald*'s analysis was premature. The Pathfinder had not yet been persuaded to withdraw.[21]

While Frémont procrastinated, other Radicals, who thoroughly despised Lincoln, finally boarded the re-election bandwagon. In addition to Wade, Henry Winter Davis and Salmon P. Chase announced their support. Frémont found himself increasingly isolated in his candidacy. Unbeknownst to Chandler, an agent of Frémont had negotiations going on with McClellan at the same time that these efforts were underway.[22]

Chandler seemed convinced that so long as Frémont remained in the race, Lincoln would lose. He seemed equally convinced that unless he was successful, the country would suffer a terrible loss. On September 18, he wrote, "Harlan told me this morning that if I succeeded I should accomplish more to save the campaign & the country than any ten men could do upon the stump or in any other way." He also told his wife, "They all seem to rely wholly upon me in this matter & say no one else can do it." Chandler was unaware that Frémont had made up his mind on September 17 to pull out and had announced such in a letter that day to supporters. Several days later in New York, he told Chandler of his decision. The senator then became concerned that Frémont's unconditional withdrawal would remove the leverage the Radicals had against Lincoln to dismiss Blair. It was too late,

Frémont said, because the letter announcing his decision had been turned over to the press. Chandler rushed back to Washington to make sure the president kept his end of the bargain. Lincoln, who had not yet seen Frémont's withdrawal, was willing to dismiss Blair, but said he had to proceed in his own time and manner in order to soften the blow. Chandler was confident that Lincoln would follow through.[23]

When Chandler returned to see the president on September 22, Lincoln was in a foul mood. He had received Frémont's letter "and it was a document as offensive as it was tactless." Though he assured Lincoln that he would support the party ticket "in order to assure the permanence of the Union and the emancipation of the slaves," his attitude toward the administration had not changed. "I consider that this administration has been politically, militarily, and financially a failure, and that its necessary continuance is a cause of regret to the country." The letter was not consistent with the spirit of the agreement, but Chandler argued that there had been no stated condition as to the form of the withdrawal. Finally Lincoln relented, and on September 23 addressed a letter to Blair: "You have generously said to me more than once, that whenever your resignation could be a relief to me, it was at my disposal. The time has come."[24]

Lincoln's secretaries did not mention Chandler or these negotiations in their account of his presidency. They did record that there was a lot of rancor among Radicals regarding several members of the Cabinet and that Blair in particular was an irritant. Part of the reason was undoubtedly because of his brother's speech on the floor of the House that had done so much to derail Chase's presidential hopes. Because they could not get at Frank Blair, Jr., they directed their fury at his brother, Montgomery. There also were moderate Republicans who had suggested the dismissal of Blair simply because he caused so much friction between the administration and the Radicals.[25]

A strange episode occurred in September at the same time Chandler was attempting to broker Frémont's withdrawal. It revolved around initiatives made by Frémont to McClellan's campaign strategists the previous spring. Before Frémont's nomination by the Radical Democrats, one of his handlers had approached a former McClellan staff officer, proposing an alliance. If the two of them became the respective nominees of the two major parties, the winner would name the loser general in chief of the Army. Later, Frémont's political aide attended the Democratic convention apparently bearing Frémont's commitment to an armistice if it would make his nomination at Chicago more likely. In mid-September, McClellan's father-in-law, Randolph Marcy, was approached by Justin McKinstry, a Frémont supporter, who offered to swing the votes of the Radical Democrats to McClellan. When Marcy reported back to his candidate, he also suggested making an accommodation with the Pathfinder. "I think a good office would command his influence." On both of these occasions, McClellan considered the actions of Frémont's promoters strange and made no response to the initiatives. Finally, on September 20, at the same time Chandler was pleading with Frémont to withdraw, McKinstry approached Marcy again, claiming he was authorized by Frémont "to make any arrangement which the Democrats determined to be best in regard to running or withdrawing from the Presidential contest."[26]

McClellan despised Frémont as much as Frémont despised Lincoln and would make no political accommodation with him. Frustrated in his efforts to salvage something from his third-party candidacy, on September 22 Frémont indignantly withdrew, claiming his support of the administration was due solely to his belief in "the permanence of the Union and the emancipation of the slaves." One can only wonder how he thought an alliance with McClellan would have furthered emancipation.[27]

Frémont's withdrawal removed the last impediment to a Lincoln-McClellan preference in the election. Though Frémont could not have won, his candidacy might have taken enough votes away from Lincoln in states such as New York and Connecticut that a mandate would have been less clear. With Lincoln against McClellan, the voters had a clear choice. Whether McClellan would have ordered an immediate and unconditional cease-fire has been much debated. The candidate, as cautious in politics as he had been on the battlefield, did not know how to proceed with the party platform and the notorious "war failure" plank. James McPherson pointed out that if McClellan endorsed the platform or ignored it, he would by implication commit himself to an armistice and negotiations. There was much pressure on him from Peace Democrats to do just that. Chief among them was Vallandigham, who urged the candidate, "Do not listen to your Eastern friends, who, in an evil hour, may advise you to *insinuate* even a little war into your letter of acceptance." Vallandigham warned anything that implied continued war would lose him two hundred thousand votes in the West.[28]

In the initial drafts of his acceptance, McClellan did endorse an armistice qualified by the condition that the fighting would be renewed if reunion were not achieved. However, August Belmont and S. L. M. Barlow, two very important Democratic figures, convinced him to repudiate the peace plank, arguing that if the war were ever stopped, it would not be started again. Thus, his final acceptance stated, "The Union is the one condition of peace—we ask no more." Though this infuriated the Copperheads, it was a smart tactic. It would fare well among many Northerners when contrasted with Lincoln's "two conditions for peace—Union and emancipation." It also distanced McClellan from the peace-at-any-price faction and the domestic treason issue.[29]

The country focused on the October States. If the Democrats were to oust the administration, they needed to win Pennsylvania and Indiana. Ohio was clearly beyond hope of Democratic victory. However, Republican victory required at least one of the other October States as well as Ohio. If Lincoln were to obtain the mandate he needed in order aggressively to prosecute the war, the Unionists needed all three. Indiana appeared the most likely to desert. The intensely partisan situation had resulted in herculean Democratic efforts to unseat Republican Governor Oliver P. Morton, who had denied the party the benefits of its 1862 election victory.[30]

Doubts about the outcome in Indiana plus the lack of a soldier-voting law made Hoosier Republicans particularly eager to form a broad-based Union coalition that would appeal to as many War Democrats as possible. The strategy worked well. The Union state campaign chairman in 1864 was War Democrat Joseph A. Wright. Union candidates for state auditor, treasurer, attorney general, and Supreme Court judge were all War Democrats. All had been Douglas supporters in 1860. Three Lincoln electors in Indiana were War Democrats, as were two Union candidates for Congress.[31]

The seizure of the weapons cache in Indianapolis convinced many people who had been skeptical about the Sanderson and Carrington reports and made treason a viable and powerful campaign issue for Unionists in the closing months. As the prospects for Republican victory improved, party regulars and generals were imported to canvass the state. Several thousand Indiana soldiers were sent home to vote.[32]

Morton's request that Lincoln delay the draft call for September had been refused. He even made an unsuccessful visit to Washington to emphasize his request. When the state election took place on October 13, Morton's concern proved unfounded. The 9,000 disabled and wounded soldiers who were rounded up and returned home only swelled the margin of victory. Morton polled nearly 20,000 votes more than his Democratic opponent.[33]

Morton fared best in the most populous counties. In Marion County, by far the largest county and the site of the state capital, Morton ran three to one over McDonald. The ten most populous counties of the state gave Morton half of his twenty thousand vote margin, even though those counties totalled less than 22 percent of the votes cast statewide. In only two of those ten did McDonald win, and Allen County (Fort Wayne) was the only one of the nine most populous counties where the Democrat outpolled his opponent. In the ten least populous counties, the result was a dead heat. Both candidates received 4,883 votes in those counties.[34]

Eleven thousand more voters participated in the October election in Indiana than in the 1860 presidential poll, when Lincoln won with 51.5 percent of the votes. This suggests that the Union ticket not only kept the voters from 1860, but also gained some who had not voted Republican previously. In the 1862 midterm election, 37,000 fewer votes were cast and the Democrats had won by about 9,500.[35]

Pennsylvania was the second most populous state of the Union. Though the Democratic candidate for governor there in 1863, Copperhead George Woodward, had enjoyed McClellan's endorsement, he had been defeated by a fairly comfortable 15,000-vote margin. However, in 1863, Union prospects had been very bright in the aftermath of Gettysburg and Vicksburg, and Woodward had suffered from the taint of Copperheadism and the anti-Vallandigham backlash. Pennsylvanians had cast more than 56 percent of their votes for Lincoln in 1860, but in 1862 the Keystone State had cast more Democratic than Republican votes. Pennsylvania was important in 1864 also because demographically it more closely approximated New York than either of the other states that held October elections. If New York went for McClellan in November, the Unionists needed Pennsylvania to offset the loss. New York was at best only a possible Republican victory in November, even after the fall of Atlanta. Before that, Unionists had considered it impossible to carry the Empire State.[36]

In 1860, Pennsylvania had sent Republicans to the House of Representatives from twenty of its twenty-five congressional districts. In 1862, the state had been reduced by one seat in the House of Representatives, but Democrats still gained seven seats. The passage of soldier-voting legislation improved Republican prospects greatly. In the 1862 midterm election, 58,000 fewer Pennsylvanians cast votes than had gone to the polls the year before, because of the absence of tens of thousands of young men in the Union army and navy. In October 1861, when large-scale recruiting was still in its infancy, the votes of Union soldiers still in the state (thus able to cast their votes) were distributed as follows: 11,351 voted for the Republican candidate while 3,173 favored the Democrat. By October 1862, when more Pennsylvanians were in the service than the year before, only fourteen regiments remained in the state, and their votes were 1,867 for Republicans and 251 for Democrats. Seven times as many soldiers were within the state and thus eligible to vote in 1861 as were in 1862, despite at least as many citizens of the state being in the military in the latter year. Therefore, it is probable that at least six out of every seven of Pennsylvania's soldiers who would have voted in 1862 were unable to cast ballots. Since the wartime voting record of Union soldiers was nearly 80 percent for Republican or Union candidates, Lincoln's belief that the primary reason for Republican setbacks in 1862 is borne out by the numbers.[37]

In 1863, almost 90,000 more Pennsylvanians voted than had the year before, in spite of the absence of nearly all Pennsylvania regiments. The only explanations for this are the population increase and a heightened participation by the electorate. George Woodward's defeat in 1863 by 15,000 votes would have been by a much larger margin had the soldiers voted in that election. A straw poll taken of five Pennsylvania regiments stationed at Knoxville, Tennessee, in 1863 resulted in 1,392 votes for Curtin and 53 for Woodward.[38]

Of the five most populous states in 1864, only Ohio was more supportive of the war than Pennsylvania. However, most Pennsylvanians in the military were in the Army of the Potomac, and many had served under McClellan. Affection toward the general ran deep in that command. Potentially their votes might help rather than hurt McClellan in Pennsylvania.[39]

There was an extraordinarily large turnout in Pennsylvania in October. Nearly 64,000 more ballots were cast in 1864 than two years earlier. The Republican/Union margin of victory overall was less than 12,000, smaller than had been expected. However, of that margin, more than 9,000 came from the ten most populous counties. In the three largest counties— Philadelphia, Allegheny, and Lancaster—the Republican vote exceeded the Democratic total by more than 20,000. If the heavily Republican counties, which included the cities of Philadelphia and Lancaster plus Chester County, were eliminated, in the other populous counties of southeastern Pennsylvania the Democrats ran more than 16,000 votes ahead of their opponents. McClellan's state campaign manager wrote him, "You are

30,000 stronger in Pennsylvania than our congressional vote will be." Pennsylvania remained in doubt up until the day of the national election.[40]

No state underwent such a major swing in voter attitude toward the war and administration from 1860–64 as did Ohio. The lowest participation in any wartime election occurred during the 1861 gubernatorial contest, when 358,791 voters cast ballots. In the 1863 election for governor, more than 476,000 votes were registered. Less than half of this increase can be accounted for by soldier ballots, which were first permitted in 1863. In 1861, while support for the war was still white hot after Fort Sumter and Bull Run, Ohio had given Republican David Tod a 55,000 vote margin over Democrat H. J. Jewett. Jewett outpolled Tod in only twenty-six of Ohio's eighty-eight counties.[41]

In 1862, when many more Ohioans were away at war and thus unable to vote, the turnout increased by more than 4,000. The Democrats increased their vote by more than 33,000 and garnered a majority of the votes cast in twenty-one counties where they had been the minority party the year before. In the twenty-one counties, Democrats outpolled Republicans by more than 11,000 votes; in 1861, they had lost those counties by 8,000 votes.[42] Similar shifts were reflected in every county. Ohio was the best barometer of popular dissatisfaction with the administration in 1862, particularly regarding emancipation and conscription.[43]

The Democrats sensed this and underwent a major shift in attitude toward the war. Their success in 1862 plus the arrest, trial, and banishment of Vallandigham led to an explosion of peace sentiment among party leaders and members. Racist rhetoric and resistance to the draft became basic to the Ohio Democratic Party. Even "Sunset" Cox, a supporter of the war effort during the Thirty-Eighth Congress, aligned with the peace wing. As home to one of the strongest and most virulent Copperhead populations, Ohio became a battleground between the supporters of the war and the peace-at-any-price men during the last two years of the war. This was accentuated by the nomination of Vallandigham as the Democratic candidate for governor in 1863. No Republican energy or resource was spared to defeat the leading Copperhead. In 1863, the Union vote increased by more than 110,000. Even though Vallandigham increased the Democratic vote by nearly 3,000 over the previous year, it was insignificant compared to the additional Union votes.[44]

Ohio had returned to the Union column and would remain there in 1864.

Though its people had been shaken by emancipation and conscription issues in 1862 and the arrest of one of the state's leading Democrats in 1863, most were offended by the Copperheads' campaign of racist rhetoric. It was certain the Unionists would win in 1864; the question was by how much. Lincoln wanted a mandate to complete the war and follow through on the changes he had undertaken. He needed to win convincingly in the state where the Unionist candidate had compiled a more than 100,000-vote margin the previous year. The October election result was promising as the Union candidates piled up a 60,000-vote margin of victory.[45]

Even the results in the October States did not resolve the question of victory or defeat in November. Democrats were encouraged by the closeness of the vote in Pennsylvania and believed that McClellan's popularity in the Army would make the difference in the final poll. William Prime, editor of the New York *Journal of Commerce* and close adviser to McClellan, predicted that the Democrats would carry New York, Pennsylvania, New Jersey, Kentucky, California, Oregon, Maryland, and Delaware, and had a good chance in Illinois, Connecticut, Missouri, Michigan, New Hampshire, and Indiana. If he carried all of these, it would give him 154 electoral votes, more than thirty over what was needed to win.[46]

A week earlier, as he received the results from the October States, Lincoln had written his own estimate of what would happen in November. Perhaps he was imagining the worst possible result, but his note had McClellan winning Pennsylvania, New Jersey, New York, Kentucky, Maryland, Delaware, Missouri, and Illinois. He would win the rest. The result would be a narrow Unionist victory, 120 to 114 electoral votes. That evening, he may have felt more hopeful than he had on August 24, but he was by no means certain yet that the nation was going to survive the crisis.[47]

14

"Of the People, by the People, for the People"

The shifting sands of political fortune were probably never so active as they were in the summer and fall of 1864. Between late August and mid-October, the prospects of the political parties had virtually reversed themselves. The results in the October States presaged a Union victory in November. Salmon P. Chase wrote to Senator John Sherman of Ohio, "There is not now the slightest uncertainty about the re-election of Mr. Lincoln. The only question is by what popular and what electoral majorities." The letter was written a week and a half before the election in the October states. Certainly those results did nothing to dampen Chase's balmy projection.[1]

Even Lincoln seemed to look more favorably upon his prospects in the final weeks before the election than he had October 13, when he saw himself winning by the narrowest of electoral margins. But he still was not certain beyond doubt. An election as partisan and divisive as this one, with the potential for election-day violence orchestrated by Confederate agents, could harm the war effort and might even yet be lost.

Some curious tales arose in those final weeks before the election. William Frank Zornow, who has written the only historical monograph on the 1864 election, claimed that late in October, Lincoln summoned Francis P. Blair, Sr., and suggested that he might use his influence to induce McClellan to withdraw, since his defeat now appeared inevitable. Zornow's information was based upon an account by Lincoln's bodyguard, Ward Hill Lamon, published more than thirty years after the war. Lincoln historians have generally discounted the reliability of many of Lamon's recollections, and this was one of them.[2]

According to Lamon, Blair took the proposal to McClellan in New York, along with an offer to make the general commander of the armies and to promote his father-in-law to the rank of major general. It is possible that Lincoln, fearing for the nation's future and the freedom of the slaves, could have considered such a deal. He did more backroom dealing at this time than at any other in his political career—witness the Zachariah Chandler effort and the Jaquess/Gilmore mission. However, it would have been out of character for Lincoln to have originated such a scheme, and without corroboration independent of Lamon's suspect memory, it is difficult to believe this account.[3]

What Lamon probably remembered years after the fact was an independent mission undertaken by Blair in July. McClellan and Blair met at Astor House in New York on July 21. He told McClellan he was not acting on instructions from the president, but he was confident that if McClellan would refuse the Democratic nomination, the general could again be appointed to a command appropriate to his rank. The elder politician appealed to McClellan's patriotism, suggesting it was his duty to ensure national unity while the war continued. Apparently McClellan gave serious consideration to Blair's proposal but remained noncommittal. It was still nearly six weeks till the convention.[4]

Blair returned to Washington and told Lincoln what he had done and that he might soon hear from McClellan. Blair said Lincoln "neither expressed approval nor disapprobation of what I had done." It was probably this meeting that Lamon remembered years later. Regardless, the initiative failed, as the Democrat took advantage of the occasion to draft a political statement lamenting the perversion of war by the president. "I think the original object of the war, as declared by the Gov't., viz: the preservation of the Union, its Constitution & its laws, has been lost sight of, . . . & that other issues have been brought into the foreground which either should be entirely secondary, or are wrong or impossible of attainment." McClellan never sent the letter, apparently distrusting Blair and most certainly the president, and therefore probably cost himself the opportunity to return to a prestigious command, perhaps overall command of the upper Potomac. Several weeks later, that command was given to Sheridan.[5]

McClellan and Lincoln respected the traditional role of the presidential candidate during the campaign, making few public appearances and refusing to descend into the mudslinging that characterized nineteenth-century political campaigns. Still, in the midst of a civil war, Lincoln had to have some contact with the public. On the few occasions when he did, he demonstrated the character that had always made him more popular with the people than with other politicians. On August 31, he spoke to the 148th Ohio Regiment as it was about to be mustered out after temporary service.

> Whenever I appear before a body of soldiers, I feel tempted to talk to them of the nature of the struggle in which we are engaged. I look upon it as an attempt on the one hand to overwhelm and destroy the national existence, while, on our part, we are striving to maintain the governments and institutions of our fathers, to enjoy them ourselves, and transmit them to our children and our children's children forever.[6]

"To do this," according to Lincoln, "the constitutional administration of our government must be sustained." He said that it was necessary to impose "all necessary measures for that purpose" and that they must be vigilant to avoid falling prey "to miserable picayune arguments addressed to your pockets, or inflammatory appeals made to your passions or your prejudices."

> This government must be preserved in spite of the acts of any man or set of men. It is worthy your every effort. Nowhere in the world is presented a government of so much liberty and equality. To the humblest and poorest amongst us are held out the highest privileges and positions. The present moment finds me at the White House, yet there is as good a chance for your children as there was for my father's.[7]

Campaigning was organized and funded by the political parties, plus a number of support groups. There had been hotly contested presidential elections before 1864, but none had involved the outpouring of political leaflets and money seen in the closing months of this one. People knew that current issues were weightier than any they or any other generation of Americans had voted on previously. Questions of the permanent destruction or the continuation of human bondage, whether there was to be one or more than one nation between Canada and the Rio Grande, whether the experiment in government "of the people, by the people, for the people," should or should not perish from the earth; these were matters to be decided by them, and the decisions they made would influence the nation and world long after they were gone. They did not have to be prophets to realize there was something different about this election.

Union support organizations included the Union League of America, founded in Tazewell County, Illinois, in 1862. It spread rapidly to become the primary extraparty group aiding pro-administration candidates. Others included the Loyal League, National Union Association, National League, and the Union Club. Membership probably totaled one million and in 1863–64, millions of pieces of literature were distributed in support of Union candidates. Corollary organizations supplied the troops with political literature and worked to offset the "disloyal" Democratic propaganda. The New England Loyal Publication Society grew out of the idea of creating regional organizations to perform the same function as the Loyal Publication Society. The Union Executive Congressional Committee was the most active of the Union publishing organizations, sending out nearly six million pieces of literature during the war. Most efficient was the Union League Board of Union Publications in Philadelphia, which, in 1864, wrote to the Republican committee chairmen of every school district in Pennsylvania, instructing them to identify doubtful voters. The league then concentrated "a stream of ideas in print" on each such voter. Postmasters, teachers, and other respected figures in the community were enlisted as distributors.[8]

Newspapers such as the Chicago *Tribune* printed and distributed documents at their own expense. Also, the Union League mailed out 560,000 copies of its *Union League Gazette* during the 1864 campaign. Zornow hazarded that the Union Party and support organizations sent out more than ten million copies of pamphlets and circulars during 1863–64. In the spring of 1864 Samuel F. B. Morse, active campaigner for Democratic candidates, received a letter from an acquaintance bemoaning the quantity of Union propaganda:

> I have been aware for a long time that the elections have been carried against us by opinions formed by reading the *Tribune* and kindred prints. At this time immense supplies of reading matter in the shape of speeches and Loyal League documents are flooding the country. You can hardly go into a public office or store but you will see such documents on the table, counters, and even posted up in the shape of handbills. . . . The Loyal Leagues are really affecting public opinion

seriously with their meetings, documents, etc., and I am confident that it needs immediate action on our part.[9]

The Democrats had support organizations as well—the Sons of Liberty, the Order of American Knights, and the McClellan Guards. The effectiveness and reputations of the first two groups were hurt by the treasonous activities attributed to some members, and the McClellan Guards foolishly adopted a flag that resembled the Confederate banner. However, the Society for the Diffusion of Political Knowledge actively prepared and dispersed campaign pamphlets. Headed by Morse and funded by a group of wealthy New York Democrats, it reproduced the words of various Democratic speakers. The society had a penchant for speeches against emancipation or ones that warned of miscegenation. The New York *World* also was a major publisher and distributor of campaign literature.

The Union campaign focused on the domestic treason issue but struck a strongly positive note as well, appealing to voters to consider the simple decency and compassion of Lincoln and what his first term had meant to the nation. An impressive cadre of speakers trekked the Northern countryside speaking on behalf of Union candidates. In addition to leading political figures, the cause boasted such luminaries as Anna Dickinson, Frederick Douglass, Henry Ward Beecher, and, in an attempt to reach the German population, Major General Carl Schurz and Gustave Koerner.[10]

The Democrats also had an array of stump speakers. Because they had fewer politicians of national prominence, Governors Horatio Seymour and Joel Parker, plus former Governor Thomas Seymour, were called frequently to the hustings. Other Democratic luminaries included Morse, Judge Jeremiah Black, and James Gallatin. To offset the impression that the soldiers were going to vote Union overwhelmingly, as many Army officers as possible were enlisted to speak on behalf of Democratic candidates. The Democrats attacked most heavily on emancipation and black equality, though the tone probably offended many voters. Democratic speakers gave more attention in the closing stages to civil liberties, arbitrary arrest, usurpation and abuse of power, an inflated economy, and mismanagement of the war. There was little they could say or do in late October and early November to offset the recent image of a government successfully prosecuting the war and approaching every day closer to the total victory that Republicans had been talking about since the beginning.[11]

November 8 was an ugly day. In Washington, the sun never appeared, the rain and drizzle were continuous, and the streets were turned into lakes of mud. Diarist George Templeton Strong described it: "So this momentous day is over, and the battle lost and won. We shall know more of the result tomorrow. Present signs are not unfavorable. Wet weather, which did not prevent a heavy vote."[12] He made other observations regarding election day in New York City. "This election has been quiet beyond precedent. Few arrests, if any, have been made for disorderly conduct. There has been no military force visible." Strong found that surprising, because he knew that thousands of troops were poised nearby in anticipation of the rumored trouble and because of the numerous Confederate agents in the city that day. "No one could have guessed from the appearance of the streets that such a momentous issue was *sub judice.*"[13]

Few voters, Republican or Democrat, stayed at home on November 8, and in terms of significance to the Civil War, the day brought a Union victory that made Gettysburg, Antietam, and Atlanta pale by comparison.

By the time the last polling place had closed, the people had guaranteed that millions of people born into slavery would live out their lives as free men and women. About three and a half million people who had legally been property in 1860 would soon become citizens of a country that had declared at its beginning that freedom and equality were the birthright of all people. Though the full realization was far off, the United States was finally taking a great step toward that ideal. The election ratified Lincoln's signature on the Emancipation Proclamation. On January 1, 1863, he had said, "If history remembers me for anything, it will be for this."[14] The voters of the country affirmed on November 8, 1864, that his prediction of two years earlier would be true.

Perhaps the greatest victory achieved on that date was that the government conducted an orderly and peaceful election during a civil war. On November 9 the entry in the diary of George Templeton Strong spoke the feelings of many Republicans on that date:

> *Laus Deo!* The crisis has been past, and the most momentous popular election ever held since ballots were invented has decided against treason and disunion. My contempt for democracy and extended suffrage is mitigated. The American people can be trusted to take care of the national honor. Lincoln is re-elected by an overwhelming vote. The only states that seem to have McClellanized are Missouri, Kentucky, Delaware, and New Jersey. New York, about which we have been uneasy

all day, is reported safe at the Club tonight. The Copperheads are routed.[15]

The election was perhaps the greatest act of faith since independence was declared. Even at the hour of its greatest crisis, democratic government worked.

It was a day when Confederate agents were present in a number of the largest Northern cities to disrupt the election. However, Federal troops were sent into cities where problems were expected, and though they remained out of sight, their well-publicized presence was sufficient to discourage most of the planned activities of rebel infiltrators. The assignment of General Benjamin Butler in New York City was announced conspicuously and apparently dissuaded the fifty or so Confederate agents in that city from doing their intended damage. The result was, as Butler telegraphed to Lincoln at noon on election day, "the quietest city ever seen."[16] Similar precautions taken in Chicago and Indianapolis had similar results. Although there were some reports of voter intimidation and ballot box stuffing by Federal soldiers, the reports were nothing out of the ordinary, and the possible effects on the outcome were negligible. Lincoln was re-elected in a landslide, losing only three states, two of those closely. Kentucky, the state of his birth and the one place where the presence of Federal troops was a factor in the voting, went decisively against Lincoln. There, the suspension of habeas corpus and the presence of troops, who made many arrests, had been onerous in the months before the election. The results of the balloting reflected that.[17]

In most states, the margin exceeded the Republicans' most optimistic predictions. Lincoln won comfortably even where his state chairmen had been certain in August he would lose decisively. With the exception of New Jersey, whose electoral votes he divided with Stephen Douglas in 1860, he carried every state he had won in 1860. He carried each of the October States by margins about the same as or greater than those the Republicans had achieved a month earlier, even though Indiana soldiers who had been furloughed to vote in October did not get to vote in November. He carried New York, where McClellan had been expected to win, by more than 7,000 votes. There, the soldier vote almost certainly gave Lincoln the margin of victory.[18]

Nearly four of every five soldiers who voted supported Lincoln. In the Army of the Potomac, whose soldiers had loved and cheered McClellan when he was their commander, seven of ten soldiers voted for Lincoln, while in the Western armies the percentage was nearly nine out of ten. The soldier vote had provided the margin of victory, however, in probably only two states, New York and Connecticut.[19] If not a single man in uniform had voted, Lincoln would still have easily won the election.

On election day, Lincoln, always slow to change his mind, still had doubts about the outcome in spite of battlefield victories and results in the October States. "I am just enough of a politician to know that there was not much doubt about the result of the Baltimore Convention, but about this thing I am far from certain. I wish I were certain,"[20] he told Noah Brooks, the young correspondent to whom he had grown so close during the last couple of years. Earlier in the day, as he mused on the campaign just ended with its angry epithets of "race mongrelization" and "domestic treason," he told his young secretary, John Hay:

> It is always singular that I, who am not a vindictive man, should always, except once, have been before the people for election in canvasses marked for their bitterness. When I came to Congress it was a quiet time; but always, except that, the contests in which I have been prominent have been marked with great rancor.[21]

That evening, Lincoln went with Hay and Brooks to the telegraph office to watch the returns come in. The assistant navy secretary, Gustavus Fox, reported that Henry Winter Davis had been defeated in Maryland. "It served him right," Fox declared. Lincoln responded, "You have more of that feeling of personal resentment than I. Perhaps I have too little of it; but I never thought it paid. A man has no time to spend half his life in quarrels. If any man ceases to attack me, I never remember the past against him."[22] It was perhaps this quality more than anything else that appealed to voters on November 8, that inexplicable calm in the midst of so much anger and animosity.

Lincoln was apprehensive most of the election day but by evening his anxiety was relieved. The early returns showed he was not only doing better than he had in 1860, but he was improving on the Republican numbers a month earlier in the October States. The Republicans had lost eastern Pennsylvania in October, but now Philadelphia, population center of that region, reported a 10,000-vote majority for Lincoln. In Maryland, where he had received only 2,000 votes in 1860, he compiled a 15,000-vote margin in Baltimore alone.[23]

In his home state, Illinois, where the Democrats had won by 16,500 votes in 1862, Lincoln carried the state by more than 30,000 votes. In 1860, he had only outpolled the opposition by 12,000. Lincoln received more votes than McClellan in every one of the thirty northernmost counties of the state. In the fourteen counties closest to Lake Michigan Lincoln won by a margin of nearly 27,000 votes. In the remaining eighty-seven counties only 4,070 votes separated the candidates. McClellan won in fifty-four of the seventy-one counties south of Peoria County (including Lincoln's home county, Sangamon). Curiously, of the seventeen counties south of Peoria which Lincoln won, four of them were on the Ohio River and three others were situated in the heart of the area known as Egypt. In the eight national elections since Andrew Jackson in which Illinoisans had voted (through 1864), the only times they had not gone Democratic were 1860 and 1864.[24]

The Empire State was probably the most pleasant surprise for the Unionists in 1864. Though it had voted Republican in 1860 by more than 48,000, the tremendous influx of Irish immigrants had added a sizable Democratic voting bloc by 1864. Lincoln fared poorest in the largest cities. New York City went against him two to one, and in Kings, Albany, and Erie counties, he trailed McClellan by 8,000. The soldier ballots from New York were not tabulated separately, but with more than 70,000 soldiers casting absentee ballots, they had to give him well in excess of his 6,750-vote margin of victory. Lincoln's coattails proved long in New York as Union candidates won every state office.[25]

Pennsylvania had voted with the winning candidate in every presidential election since Jackson. It did not break the tradition in 1864, giving Lincoln a victory by several thousand votes more than Union candidates had won by in October. In Indiana, the voting remained consistent with the October election. Northern Indiana went strongly for the Union candidates, while the southern part of the state was predominantly Democratic. Lincoln won in twelve of the fourteen northernmost counties, while McClellan carried fifteen of the twenty southernmost. In the ten most populous counties of Indiana, Lincoln outpolled his opponent by eleven thousand votes, and received 59 percent of the ballots cast.

Considering just the five most populous counties, he won by 9,000 and garnered 62 percent of the votes.[26] In Ohio, Lincoln ran 5,000 votes ahead of the October candidates and won in nine of the ten most populous counties.[27]

Lincoln generally fared well in the cities. Outside of New York State, where McClellan outpolled him in every major city except Rochester, the only Northern cities where the president did not poll a majority were Detroit and Milwaukee. Milwaukee, where he received the lowest percentage of votes of any Northern city, contained a large number of German Catholics. Lincoln did poorly with Catholic immigrants, among whom support for the war was weakest. They felt little attachment to a war being waged for the freedom of blacks. Almost universally he lost the Irish vote. Pundits viewing the election went to great lengths to establish that the source of Lincoln's support was in the soil, the rural areas where hard-working, honest, Protestant farmers lived the same life that young Lincoln had. The facts do not necessarily bear that out. In very few places did the president do better than he did in Cook County, Illinois, where he won more than 81 percent of the vote. In Boston, Providence, Pittsburgh, Cleveland, and St. Louis, he received more than three of every five ballots. In Cincinnati, he won 56 percent; Philadelphia, 55 percent; and Rochester, 53 percent. Also, before going too far in pursuit of the idea that Lincoln's strength was with "men of the soil," it should be remembered that most Confederate soldiers were yeoman farmers.[28]

More than four million Americans voted in 1864, 55 percent of them for Lincoln. His total had increased by more than 350,000 over 1860. On November 10, in response to a serenading crowd, Lincoln delivered what John Hay later characterized as "one of the weightiest and wisest of all his discourses. He read it at the window that opened on the north portico of the Executive Mansion, a secretary standing beside him lighting the page with a candle. 'Not very graceful,' he said, 'but I am growing old enough not to care much for the manner of doing things.'"

> It has long been a grave question whether any Government not too strong for the liberties of its people can be strong enough to maintain its own existence in great emergencies. On this point the present rebellion brought our republic to a severe test, and a Presidential election occurring in regular course during the rebellion added not a little to the strain. If the loyal people united were put to the utmost of their strength by the rebellion, must they not fail when divided and partially paralyzed by a

political war among themselves? But the election was a necessity. We can not have free Government without elections; and if the rebellion could force us to forego or postpone a national election, it might fairly claim to have already conquered and ruined us. . . . But the election, along with its incidental and undesirable strife, has done good, too. It has demonstrated that a people's Government can sustain a national election in the midst of a great civil war. Until now, it has not been known to the world that this was a possibility. It shows, also, how sound and how strong we still are. . . . But the rebellion continues; and, now that the election is over, may not all having a common interest reunite in a common effort to save our common country? For my own part, I have striven and shall strive to avoid placing any obstacle in the way. So long as I have been here, I have not willingly placed a thorn in any man's bosom. While I am deeply sensible to the high compliment of a re-election, and duly grateful, as I trust, to Almighty God for having directed my countrymen to a right conclusion, as I think, for their own good, it adds nothing to my satisfaction that any other man may be disappointed by the result.[29]

15

"Shall Not Perish from the Earth"

On Good Friday, April 14, 1865, Lincoln was shot by actor John Wilkes Booth as he watched the comedy "Our American Cousin" at Ford's Theater in Washington. It was one of the final incidents of a war that had claimed the lives of more than 620,000 Americans. When Lincoln died nine hours later, he passed into legend.

He had lived six weeks into his second term and less than a week earlier had seen the Union victory completed by Lee's surrender to Grant at Appomattox Court House, Virginia. On the day of the assassination, distinguished military officers and dignitaries had gathered at Fort Sumter in Charleston Harbor, where it had all begun four years earlier. With bands playing and Navy guns firing, brevet Major General Robert Anderson seized the halyards and hoisted the same banner that he had lowered there in 1861.[1] It was the final symbolic act of victory for the government.

The North was wrenched from its victory celebration into deep mourning at the insane act that had struck down the leader at the moment of his triumph, and national grief quickly turned into anger. George Templeton Strong's diary entry for April 15 read:

> Nine o'clock this morning. *Lincoln and Seward assassinated last night!!!!* The South has nearly filled up the measure of her iniquities at last! Lincoln's death not yet certainly announced, but the one o'clock dispatch states that he was then dying . . .

Ellie brought me this news two hours ago, but I can hardly take it in yet. I have been expecting this. I predicted an attempt would be made on Lincoln's life when he went into Richmond; but just now, after his generous dealings with Lee, I should have said the danger was past. But the ferocious malignity of Southerners is infinite and inexhaustible. I am stunned, as by a fearful personal calamity.[2]

Strong predicted that "we shall appreciate him at last," and called for *"the Black Flag now!"* He went to the Custom House where a large meeting was taking place and the mood "would compare with that of the first session of the Jacobins after Murat's death." The diarist recorded, "It was the first great patriotic meeting since the war began at which there was no talk of concession and conciliation."[3]

Even the Radicals were struck by the tragedy of the event. Adam Gurowski wrote on April 15:

The immense majority of the population horrified, dumbstruck; only some few ultra-secesh and slaveocrats satisfied. Of course. The pilot of the government welters in his blood. . . . This murder, this oozing blood, almost sanctifies Lincoln. His end atones for all the short-comings for which he was blamed and condemned by earnest and unyielding patriots. Grand and noble will Lincoln stand in the world's history. . . . His hand and his blood sealed the terrific struggle.[4]

Congressional Radicals who had maligned and chastised the president throughout his term would now learn how good a friend he had actually been. Andrew Johnson's obstinacy and independence eventually led to an open break and his impeachment in the House.

Johnson obstructed the attempts to gain justice and protection for freedmen in the postwar South. He encouraged people who had been defeated and demoralized in 1865 to initiate a counterrevolution to defeat the gains that had been achieved before the fighting ended. The result was thousands of murdered freedmen, burned-out homes, the rise of the Ku Klux Klan and other terrorist organizations, and the passage of laws seeking to reimpose as much as possible the antebellum Southern social system. The noble sentiments of Lincoln's inaugural address, that the postwar period might be spent in "binding up the nation's wounds," and in doing what was necessary to "achieve a just and lasting peace,"[5] descended into an era during which the country developed a tradition of racial violence and bitterness that would not change significantly until a century after the war.

Nevertheless, the major obstacles to permanent emancipation had been removed with the passage of the Thirteenth Amendment by the lame-duck Thirty-Eighth Congress. This was achieved primarily through Lincoln's influence.[6]

Lincoln had always been concerned about the efficacy of the Emancipation Proclamation. The Supreme Court that had issued the *Dred Scott* decision might take a dim view of Lincoln's invocation of the war power to free the slaves. The fragility of that policy had been tested in 1864 when Lincoln was re-elected against a firm foe of emancipation. Also, the proclamation had not freed the slaves in the border states or in portions of Virginia, Louisiana, and Tennessee that had been under Union control on January 1, 1863. The only way that nationwide emancipation would be assured was by a constitutional amendment.[7]

In his last State of the Union message, Lincoln spoke of the proposed amendment, which had been introduced at the last session of Congress. "Although the present is the same Congress, and nearly the same members, and without questioning the wisdom or patriotism of those who stood in opposition, I venture to recommend the reconsideration and passage of the measure at the present session."[8] He pointed out that although the issue was the same, the recent election had resulted in a Congress that would almost certainly pass the measure if this one did not.

> Hence there is only a question of *time* as to when the proposed amendment will go to the States for their action. And as it is to so go, at all events, may we not agree that the sooner the better? It is not claimed that the election has imposed a duty on members to change their views or their votes, any further than, as an additional element to be considered, their judgment may be affected by it. It is the voice of the people now, for the first time, heard upon the question. In a great national crisis, like ours, unanimity of action among those seeking a common end is very desirable—almost indispensable. And yet no approach to such unanimity is attainable, unless some deference shall be paid to the will of the majority, simply because it is the will of the majority. In this case the common end is the maintenance of the Union; and, among the means to secure that

end, such will, through the election, is most clearly declared in favor of such constitutional amendment.[9]

Lincoln had analyzed the election in a manner that historians for the next century would be reluctant to affirm; that it was "the voice of the people now, for the first time, heard upon the question."[10] No previous nominee of a major party had allowed the population to register a position on slavery. In 1864, that issue was before the voters, and they overwhelmingly rejected the institution. Lincoln's unbending resolve on this point had been clear to the voters and the Democrats had attempted in every way to exploit it by pandering to their most deep-seated racial fears.

Toward the end of his message, Lincoln attempted to present the olive branch to the Confederacy so that the war might be ended without further cost of lives, yet he reaffirmed his stance on the future of slavery:

> In presenting the abandonment of armed resistance to the national authority on the part of the insurgents, as the only indispensable condition to ending the war on the part of the government, I retract nothing heretofore said as to slavery. I repeat the declaration made a year ago, that 'while I remain in my present position I shall not attempt to retract or modify the emancipation proclamation, nor shall I return to slavery any person who is free by the terms of that proclamation, or by any of the acts of Congress.' If the people should, by whatever mode or means, make it an Executive duty to re-enslave such persons, another, and not I, must be their instrument to perform it.[11]

The House approved the proposed Thirteenth Amendment on January 31. Though Lincoln generally avoided pressuring Congress on legislation, this time he used his powers of persuasion and patronage extensively. He invited conservative Republicans and recalcitrant Democrats to the White House and buttonholed former Whigs and exhorted them in the name of Henry Clay to support the amendment.[12] Thirteen Democrats joined the four Democrats who had previously voted for the proposal, while every House Republican voted in favor. The final vote was 119–58, with eight members not present. When the result was announced, cheers broke out among the Republicans. The same celebrating erupted in the galleries, turning the chamber into a spontaneous festival of rejoicing. Representative George Julian of Indiana remarked that he felt as though he were in a new country.[13]

Poet Walt Whitman analyzed the election after the event.

> What we have seen here is not, towering above all talk and argument, the . . . last-needed proof of democracy. . . . That our national democratic experiment, principle, and machinery could triumphantly sustain such a shock, and that the Constitution could weather it, like a ship in a storm, and come out of it as sound and whole as before, is by far the most signal proof yet of the stability of that experiment—Democracy—and of those principles and that Constitution.[14]

The 1864 election was the most important one in history. If McClellan had won, it would have changed the course of history. Two questions were of surpassing importance in 1864, and both were resolved by Lincoln's re-election. First, would the Union have been restored had McClellan won? Stated otherwise, would McClellan have prosecuted the war to a successful conclusion? Or, alternatively, would Lincoln have gained the unconditional surrender of the Confederacy during his lame-duck period from November 8, 1864, to March 4, 1865? Second, would emancipation have survived Lincoln's defeat? Would slavery have ended permanently in the United States within a year of the end of the war had McClellan been elected?

What would McClellan have done differently had he won in 1864, and what would it have done to change the course of history? Historians have generally regarded McClellan as a War Democrat, albeit one who did not join ranks with the Republicans in a Union coalition and one who certainly opposed the wartime emancipation and conscription measures. Thus, by definition, he would have to be regarded as a Regular Democrat. Most Regular Democrats had before 1864 ceased to support the war because it was being prosecuted by a Republican administration and Congress that considered emancipation and conscription necessary to secure unconditional surrender. Would they have supported the war again under McClellan? Clearly McClellan opposed both policies at all times. Could he have overturned them as president? It would have been difficult for McClellan to have withdrawn the Emancipation Proclamation without also discharging all black soldiers. By November 1864, nearly one-fifth of the Union soldiers and sailors were black. Of those, more than three-fourths had been slaves when the war began. Even if he had discharged only the former slaves, more than 100,000 men in uniform would have been lost. At a time when Lincoln had to issue draft calls for a half-million men each, first in July and again in December, the loss of 100,000 men would probably have dealt a fatal blow to McClellan's prospects of battlefield victory.[15]

Even if he could have retained the support of most Regular Democrats in prosecuting the war after his inauguration, the only way McClellan could have compensated for such a loss of men would have been with a draft call. This would have been difficult, since conscription was as unacceptable to Democrats as emancipation. He could not have made a draft call without alienating many of those who had voted for him in the election. Also, disarming the blacks in uniform would have created problems within the military as great as any the rebels could have caused in 1865. Would this sizable number of former slaves agree to lay down their arms, knowing they were being returned to slavery? It is inconceivable that such a process could have occurred without bloodshed and disruption. If there were resistance and white troops had to be ordered to disarm them, how many would actually do so? How many would join with black units in resisting any attempt at disarmament? Though most soldiers were committed to remain for the term of their enlistment, thousands of officers whose service was inspired by the sense that they were warriors in the cause of human freedom would probably resign their commissions. Desertion and straggling, serious problems for the Union during the best of times, would not improve during the administration of a man for whom less than one-quarter of the soldiers had voted.

The Confederate soldier had counted on the defeat of Lincoln as the best hope of Southern independence. How many of the more than 150,000 rebel soldiers who were absent without leave would have availed themselves of the opportunity to return to their armies without facing punishment? As the difficulties of the Union army increased, the prospects of the Confederacy cheating defeat improved reciprocally.[16]

It also was improbable that the Radicals, whether politicians or military officers, would participate or cooperate in any way with a McClellan-led effort. There would also probably have been some moderate Republicans who despised McClellan enough to seek almost any alternative to collusion with his administration. And if there had been any Peace Democrats who did not jump ship when he took office without calling for a cease-fire, they and some Regular Democrats would spurn him the moment he attempted to form a coalition with any member of the despised party of conscription, confiscation, and emancipation.

McClellan would have suffered political gridlock as to any wartime policy that required the cooperation of Congress. Though a Democratic victory would certainly have meant increased Democratic representation in the Thirty-Ninth Congress, the new representatives would not take their seats until December 1865, more than a year after the election. In the meantime, Republicans would continue to maintain a comfortable majority. In the Senate, where only one-third of the seats came up for election in 1864, the more than three-to-one Republican majority would continue to hold a veto-proof advantage under even the most favorable Democratic scenario. Given the depth of the animosity that influenced relations in the Thirty-Eighth Congress, the Republican majority could have attempted impeachment, even if high crimes or misdemeanors had to be contrived.

If the Union had not won the war before March 4, 1865, McClellan could not have done so afterward. Had he attempted to continue the war without disturbing Lincoln's policies, he would have lost the support of all Peace Democrats and most Regulars. If he had kept faith with his and his party's opposition to emancipation, he would not have been able to maintain a military force sufficient to continue the war.

Could Lincoln have won the war between the election and the inauguration? When he had his Cabinet members sign the blind memorandum on August 23, 1864, it would appear that he sought a total effort by his administration and the military. That is the only reasonable interpretation. Lincoln was not given to meaningless acts. Though no historian has so interpreted this strange act, made at the nadir of Lincoln's political career, there is no other sensible explanation. He intended to call upon all the supporters of his government for a total commitment to end the war before he left office. An absolute dedication to bring about the speedy defeat of a now-rejuvenated Confederacy would have necessitated a new draft call, probably for substantially more than the half-million men he called for in December. Having just won the office they had coveted since 1860, and already concerned that the Republicans might attempt to hold power by military force, the oft-referred to Northwest Confederacy probably would have become a reality. At the least, previous violence against conscription would have increased exponentially during any post-election efforts to enforce the draft.

Also, to carry out what appeared to be Lincoln's intention if he were defeated would have necessitated a winter offensive. Only Burnside in the East and Rosecrans in the West had attempted such an operation. It had been in 1862, and both Federal armies had suffered terrible losses. Burnside's Fredericksburg campaign and Mud March had been two of the worst Union setbacks of the war, and though Rosecrans had achieved a qualified strategic victory at Stone's River, in Tennessee, it was six months before the Army of the Cumberland was in shape to undertake another offensive operation. When Grant undertook winter operations against Vicksburg in late 1862, he suffered greater casualties from the weather than he had suffered in military campaigns against the river forts in Tennessee and at Shiloh. The prospect of a forced offensive during the 1864–65 winter that would compel unconditional Confederate surrender was highly unlikely.[17]

A negotiated peace during the lame-duck period also would have been unlikely. If Lincoln had been unwilling to surrender emancipation in order to save the Union in late August, when his defeat appeared imminent, there would have been no reason to do so after the election. In August, there was potentially something to be gained from offering such a sacrifice; he might have saved his re-election. After the voter verdict, no such justification existed. Even more certain, if the Confederates had been able to influence the election, they would have been even less likely to accept a compromise peace that included reunion. Jefferson Davis and other Confederate leaders would never agree to return to the old Union, even if the only alternative was destruction and devastation of the South. The closing months of the war proved that.

Thus no compromise peace acceptable to the Confederacy could have been reached by a lame duck Lincoln administration without sacrificing every significant principle the government had been fighting for since 1861. Unable to prosecute the war to a successful conclusion or achieve a compromise peace that would save some fundamental principle of the Union cause, the Unionists would have to trust to the McClellan administration the attainment of anything positive that could be salvaged after the election.

Would McClellan have continued to prosecute the war? There is conflicting evidence. The nominee's principal political adviser, Samuel L. M. Barlow, informed Manton Marble on August 24 that McClellan "is for peace, not war. . . . If he is nominated, he would prefer to restore the Union by peaceful means, rather than by war." On September 3, Barlow wrote to McClellan that he needed to drop phrases such as "cessation of hostilities" and "we have fought enough to satisfy the military honor of both sections." A St. Louis businessman wrote on August 24 that McClellan had that day told him, "If I am elected, I will recommend an immediate armistice and a call for a convention of all the states and insist upon exhausting all and every means to secure peace without further blood shed."[18] Yet, August Belmont, chairman of the Democratic National Convention, wrote to him on September 3:

> It is absolutely necessary that in your letter of acceptance you place yourself squarely and unequivocally on the ground that you will never surrender one foot of soil and that peace can only be based upon the reconstruction of the Union.[19]

Who knows whether this was simply a campaign tactic or a policy that McClellan would be bound to pursue if elected? Obviously, if elected, McClellan would make his own choice. The path he followed would lose him a following and inspire a significant, perhaps violent, opposition. McClellan would have been unable to save the Union and preserve emancipation. He probably could not have preserved the Union under any circumstances, but if he could have, it would have been at the expense of emancipation. The minimum result of a McClellan victory would have been the continuation of slavery in some form for some time. Thus the most important and benevolent act performed by a president would have been voided.

Although Confederate independence would not have been inevitable, how could Union victory still have been possible? What would Confederate independence have meant? The American experiment in democratic government would have failed. In the words of Lincoln, those who could not win with the ballot would have succeeded with the bullet. The nobility and dignity extended to the common man by the Founding Fathers would have been irrelevant. Lincoln and the Radicals would have been reduced to the fate of Robespierre and the Committee for Public Safety, an interesting but momentary quirk of history—a failed revolution.

A divided United States would have been fraught with bitterness for years after peace was negotiated. What would have happened to Missouri and Kentucky? The bloody strife that characterized the antebellum, the wartime, and postwar periods could only have been intensified by a contest whether those states joined an independent Confederate States of America or remained a part of the United States. The tensions in these areas, plus the distrust each section would have harbored, would have required a strong military presence for years. With a continued emphasis on national security, the unrestrained growth of American business and economic power could not have occurred the way it did. Trade and transportation would have been encumbered by national borders.

And there may have been more than two sections. Would the breakaway of the South have set a precedent for the final break of the Northwest from New England? If the Pacific states were to remain a part of a nation more than 1,000 miles away, which nation would that be? As the American West was settled late in the century, what conflicts would the extension of slavery cause? Would the South be willing to respect a Missouri Compromise line that had been rendered non-existent by the Kansas-Nebraska Act and the *Dred Scott* decision?

Without a strong Western Hemisphere democracy, would the European and Asian monarchs and despots have deferred to growing demands for more responsive and responsible government? Would the United States have been able during World War I and World War II to save the Western European democracies from defeat by a central European power that would have imposed anti-democratic rule? Would the United States as a world power in the mid-twentieth century have been able to assume the lead in combatting and finally defeating an aggressive international communist movement?

All of these questions remain hypothetical. The re-election of Lincoln and the Union victory ratified the Emancipation Proclamation and Thirteenth Amendment and assured the end of slavery in the Western world. They guaranteed participation in governance (even if not immediately realized) as a birthright of all Americans. They assured the existence of a haven and access for people escaping religious or political persecution overseas. They ratified the principle of the Declaration of Independence that all men are created equal as a basis for defining relations between the government and the people, and among the people in their relations with one another.

The election established that democratic government prevails over all other rights of the nation or individual, that elections were so fundamental that even a great civil war could not suspend or postpone them. If one could be held in 1864, it is difficult to imagine how a future election might be cancelled. That the right to vote was retained by all Americans, particularly those away from home in the service, became a powerful example. The election ratified that constitutional union was perpetual and secession impossible.

For all of these reasons, the 1864 election was the most important electoral event in history. Its impact is still felt and will be for many years. It was, in the words of Lincoln, a "people's contest," one in which the voters ratified that a "government not too strong for the liberties of its own people can be strong enough to maintain its own existence in great emergencies." The election was a necessity, Lincoln said, and he was right. The nation passed the test and faced the future stronger and more confident.[20]

Lincoln had borne the mantle of leadership during the nation's most difficult hour. He had done so with grace, intelligence, and integrity that in retrospect is difficult to comprehend. At the same time, he made what was preserved worth preserving. Every generation since the Civil War has owed a debt to this remarkable man. That he has been accused of racism and tyranny is a testament to the historical ingratitude of mankind.

Abraham Lincoln's reward in his lifetime was an assassin's bullet delivered less than a week after the effective end of the war. His oft-repeated prophecy that "when this war ends, I will end," had come true. But in one sense, John Wilkes Booth made many contemporary ingrates of Lincoln aware of the loss they and the nation had suffered. Some came to the realization even before the assassination. On February 4, 1865, William Lloyd Garrison, who had for much of the war raised his voice and his pen against Lincoln, spoke of the importance of Abraham Lincoln and his re-election in 1864 in ending slavery:

> And to whom is the country more immediately indebted for this vital and saving amendment of the Constitution than, perhaps, to any other man? I believe I may confidently answer—to the humble railsplitter of Illinois—to the Presidential chainbreaker for millions of the oppressed—to Abraham Lincoln! (Immense and long continued applause, ending with three cheers for the President.) I understand that it was by his wish and influence that that plank was made part of the Baltimore platform; and taking his position unflinchingly upon that platform, the people have overwhelmingly sustained both him and it, in ushering in the year of jubilee.[21]

Just as his life had been so extraordinary, his death seemed to exceed the boundaries defining most mortals. Early on April 2, 1865, the day Lee evacuated the Richmond-Petersburg lines, Lincoln had an ominous dream. He later described it to his wife and a few close friends, on what was very near the last day of his life.

About ten days ago, I retired very late. I had been up waiting for important dispatches from the front. I could not have been long in bed when I fell into a slumber, for I was weary. I soon began to dream. There seemed to be a death-like stillness about me.[22]

Lincoln described hearing sobs, leading him to search the White House for the source of the "mournful sounds of distress" made by "people who were grieving as if their hearts would break." He finally found the source—the East Room, where he would lie in state several days later.

There I met with a sickening surprise. Before me was a catafalque, on which rested a corpse wrapped in funeral vestments. Around it were stationed soldiers who were acting as guards; and there was a throng of people, some gazing mournfully at the corpse, whose face was covered, others weeping pitifully. "Who is dead in the White House?" I demanded of one of the soldiers. "The President," was his answer; "he was killed by an assassin!" Then came a loud burst of grief from the crowd, which awoke me from my dream. I slept no more that night; and although it was only a dream, I have been strangely annoyed by it ever since.[23]

At the moment of triumph, the man who had led the nation was cruelly snatched from a people still intoxicated with the realization that the horrible war was over. The celebration was muted by the loss of that life that had best symbolized what was good and decent about the nation; the life that had touched so many and helped to sustain the weary through the difficult times. But despite the rejection of Lincoln as a primary source for their freedom by many twentieth century African-Americans, to those who were his contemporaries, his loss was everything. He had been the living symbol of freedom, a larger-than-life deliverer from the bondage that had been the permanent lot of their parents and grandparents, and of themselves until Lincoln had signed the magical document. To them, his loss meant something much more than it did to white Americans; it shook the fragile foundation of their freedom, their hope for the future that had been as secure as the promise of the president. The last year of his life demonstrated that the fragile security of their freedom had been safe in the strong but gentle hands that had subscribed the Emancipation Proclamation. But now those hands had gone stiff and cold, and somehow the promise again seemed in doubt. Gideon Welles recorded the scene outside the White House on the morning of April 15, shortly after Lincoln died.

> I went after breakfast to the Executive Mansion. There was a cheerless cold-rain and everything seemed gloomy. On the Avenue in front of the White House were several hundred colored people, mostly women and children, weeping and wailing their loss. This crowd did not appear to diminish through the whole of that cold, wet day; they seemed not to know what was to be their fate since their great benefactor was dead, and their hopeless grief affected me more than almost anything else, though strong and brave men wept when I met them.[24]

One of the most poignant eulogies was penned by one of his most frequent and malignant detractors during his lifetime. It was only Lincoln's death that caused Tom Taylor, the editor of *Punch*, to realize not only what Lincoln had meant to democracy and freedom in the United States, but the quality of his character and what his life had stood for. *Punch*, through Taylor, had been one of the most constant British critics of the North and of Lincoln. Upon learning of the assassination, Taylor published the following *mea culpa*.

> You lay a wreath on murdered Lincoln's bier,
> You, who with mocking pencil wont to trace
> Broad for the self-complacent British sneer
> His length of shambling limb, his furrowed face,
>
> His gaunt, gnarled hands, his unkempt, bristling hair,
> His garb uncouth, his bearing ill at ease;
> His lack of all we prize as debonair,
> Of power or will to shine, of art to please.
>
> You, whose smart pen backed up the pencil's laugh,
> Judging each step, as though the way were plain;
> Reckless, so it could point its paragraph
> Of chief's perplexity or people's pain.
>
> Beside this corps, that beats for winding sheet
> The Stars and Stripes he lived to rear anew,

Between the mourners at his head and feet,
Say, scurril-jester, is there room for you?

Yes, he had lived to shame me from my sneer,
To lame my pencil, and confute my pen—
To make me own this hind of princes peer,
This rail-splitter a true-born king of men.[25]

However, probably the most eloquent and simplest eulogy was spoken moments after the president died by a man not known for displays of tenderness. Secretary of War Edwin Stanton's voice quivered with emotion as he bade farewell to this man he had come to know so well, while never really knowing at all—"Now he belongs to the ages."[26]

APPENDIX A

McCLELLAN'S ACCEPTANCE LETTER

To the Democratic Nomination Committee Orange, New Jersey Sept 8, 1864[1]

Gentlemen:

I have the honor to acknowledge the receipt of your letter informing me of my nomination by the Democratic National Convention, recently assembled at Chicago, as their candidate, at the next election, for President of the United States.

It is unnecessary for me to say to you that this nomination comes to me unsought. [Crossed out: Since the record of my public life has been open to the world, I assume that that record was kept in view.] I am happy to know that when the nomination was made the record of my public life was kept in view. The effect of long and varied service in the Army, during war and peace, has been to strengthen and make indelible in my mind and heart the love and reverence for the Union, Constitution, Laws and Flag of our country impressed upon me in early youth.

---

[1] This sixth and final draft of McClellan's acceptance letter was the product of intensive revisions on September 7–8 in company with Samuel L. M. Barlow, and perhaps other advisers, in New York. It is a copy of the much-altered fifth draft, with the additional final revisions indicated.

These feelings have thus far guided the course of my life, and must continue to do so to its end.

The existence of more than one Government over the region which once owned our flag is incompatible with the peace, the power, and the happiness of the people.

The preservation of our Union was the sole avowed object for which the war was commenced.

It should have been conducted for that object only, and in accordance with those principles which I took occasion to declare when in [crossed out: command of armies, and especially in my letter to the President from Harrison's Landing.] active service. Thus conducted, the work of reconciliation would have been easy, and we might have reaped the benefits of our many victories on land and sea.

The Union was originally formed by the exercise of a spirit of conciliation and compromise.

To restore and preserve it the same spirit must prevail in our Councils, and in the hearts of the people. The reestablishment of the Union in all its integrity is, and must continue to be, the indispensable condition in any settlement [crossed out: of the questions at issue in this war]. So soon as it is clear, or even possible, that our present adversaries are ready for peace upon the basis of the Union, we should exhaust all the resources of statesmanship practiced by civilized nations, and taught by the traditions of the American people, consistent with the honor and interests of the country, to secure such peace, reestablish the Union, and guarantee for the future the Constitutional rights of every State. The Union is [crossed out: our only] the one condition of peace. We ask no more.[2]

Let me add what I doubt not was, although unexpressed, the sentiment of the Convention, as it is of the people they represent, that when any one State is willing to return to the Union, it should be received at once, with a full guarantee of all its Constitutional rights.

But if a frank, earnest and persistent effort to achieve these objects should fail, [crossed out: it will be necessary to insist upon the preservation of the Union at all hazards, and] the responsibility for ulterior consequences will fall upon those who remain in arms against the Union. But the Union must be preserved at all hazards. I could not look in the face of my gallant comrades of the Army and Navy, who have survived so many bloody battles,

---

[2]These last two sentences are in Barlow's hand.

and tell them that their labors, and the sacrifice of so many of our slain and wounded brethren had been in vain—that we had abandoned that Union for which we have so often perilled our lives.

A vast majority of our people, whether in the Army and Navy or at home, would, as I would, hail with unbounded joy the permanent restoration of peace, on the basis of the Union under the Constitution, without the effusion of another drop of blood. But no peace can be permanent without Union.

As to the other subjects presented in the resolutions of the Convention, I need only say that I should seek in the Constitution of the United States, and the laws framed in accordance therewith, the rule of my duty and the limitations of executive power,—endeavor to restore economy in public expenditure, reestablish the supremacy of law, [crossed out: and assert for our country and people that commanding position to which our history & our principles entitle us among the nations of the world.] & by the assertion of a more vigorous nationality reserve our commanding position among the nations of the Earth.[3] The condition of our finances, the depreciation of the paper currency, and the burdens thus imposed on labor, [crossed out: industry] & capital show the necessity of a return to a sound financial system; while the rights of citizens and the rights of States, and the binding authority of law over President, Army and people are subjects of not less vital importance in war than in peace. Believing that the views here expressed are those of the Convention and the people you represent, I accept the nomination.

I realize the weight of the responsibility to be borne should the people ratify your choice.

Conscious of my own weakness, I can only seek fervently the guidance of the Ruler of the Universe, and, relying on His all-powerful aid, do my best to restore Union and Peace to a suffering people, and to establish and guard their liberties and rights.

> *I am, Gentlemen, very respectfully your obedient servant*
> *Geo B McClellan*

Hon Horatio Seymour
and others, Committee etc.
ALS, Barlow Papers, Huntington Library

---

[3] The phrasing replacing the crossed-out section is by Barlow.

APPENDIX B

THE REPUBLICAN PLATFORM RESOLVES

RESOLVED. That it is the highest duty of every American citizen to maintain against all their enemies the integrity of the Union, and the permanent authority of the Constitution and the laws of the United States; and that, laying aside all differences of political opinion, we pledge ourselves as Union men, animated by a common sentiment and aiming at a common object, to do everything in our power to aid the government in quelling by force of arms the rebellion now raging against its authority, and in bringing to the punishment due to their crimes the rebels and traitors arrayed against it.

RESOLVED. That we approve the determination of the government of the United States not to compromise with rebels, or to offer them any terms of peace except such as may be based upon an unconditional surrender of their hostility and a return to their just allegiance to the Constitution and laws of the United States; and that we call upon the government to maintain this position, and to prosecute the war with the utmost possible vigor to the complete suppression of the rebellion, in full reliance upon the self-sacrificing patriotism, the heroic valor, and the undying devotion of the American people and its free institutions.

RESOLVED. That, as slavery was the cause and now constitutes the strength of this rebellion, and as it must be, always and everywhere, hostile to the principles of republican government, justice and the national safety demand its utter and complete extirpation from the soil of the republic; and that, while we uphold and maintain the acts and proclamations by which the government, in its own defense, had aimed a deathblow at this gigantic evil, we are in favor, furthermore, of such amendment to the Constitution, to be made by the people in conformity with its provisions, as shall terminate and forever prohibit the existence of slavery within the limits of the jurisdiction of the United States.

RESOLVED. That the thanks of the American people are due to the soldiers and sailors of the army and navy who have periled their lives in defense of their country and in vindication of the honor of its flag; that the nation owes to them some permanent recognition of their patriotism and their valor, and ample and permanent provision for those of their survivors who have received disabling and honorable wounds in the service of the country; and that the memories of those who have fallen in its defense shall be held in grateful and everlasting remembrance.

RESOLVED. That we approve and applaud the practical wisdom, and unselfish patriotism and the unswerving fidelity with which Abraham Lincoln has discharged, under circumstances of unparalleled difficulty, the great duties and responsibilities of the presidential office; that we approve and indorse [sic], as demanded by the emergency and essential to the preservation of the nation and as within the provisions of the Constitution, the measures and acts which he has adopted to defend the nation against its open and secret foes; that we approve, especially, the proclamation of emancipation and the employment as Union soldiers of men heretofore held in slavery; and that we have full confidence in his determination to carry these and all other constitutional measures essential to the salvation of the country into full and complete effect.

RESOLVED. That we deem it essential to the general welfare that harmony should prevail in the national councils, and we regard as worth of public confidence and official trust those only who cordially indorse [sic] the principles proclaimed in these resolutions, and which should characterize the administration of the government.

RESOLVED. That the government owes to all men employed in its armies, without regard to distinction of color, the full protection of the laws of war; and that any violation of these laws, or of the usage of civilized nations in time of war, by the rebels now in arms, should be made the subject of prompt and full redress.

RESOLVED. That foreign immigration, which in the past has added so much to the wealth, development of resources, and increase of power to this nation,—the asylum of the oppressed of all nations,—should be fostered and encouraged by a liberal and just policy.

RESOLVED. That we are in favor of a speedy construction of the railroad to the Pacific coast.

RESOLVED. That the national faith, pledged for the redemption of the public debt, must be kept inviolate, and that for this purpose we recommend economy and rigid responsibility in the public expenditures, and a vigorous and just system of taxation; and that it is the duty of every loyal State to sustain the credit and promote the use of the national currency.

RESOLVED. That we approve the position taken by the government, that the people of the United States can never regard with indifference the attempt of any European power to overthrow by force, or to supplant by fraud, the institutions of any republican government on the Western Continent; and that they will view with extreme jealousy, as menacing to the peace and independence of their own country, the efforts of any such power to maintain new footholds for monarchial governments, sustained by foreign military force, in near proximity to the United States.

APPENDIX C

THE DEMOCRATIC PLATFORM RESOLVES

RESOLVED. That in the future, as in the past, we will adhere with unswerving fidelity to the Union under the Constitution as the only solid foundation of our strength, security, and happiness as a people, and as a framework of government equally conducive to the prosperity of all the States, both Northern and Southern.

RESOLVED. That this convention does explicitly declare, as the sense of the American people that after four years of failure to restore the Union by the experiment of war, during which, under the pretense of a military necessity of war-power higher than the Constitution itself has been disregarded in every part, and public liberty and private right alike trodden down, and the material prosperity of the country essentially impaired, justice, humanity, liberty, and public welfare demand that immediate efforts be made for a cessation of hostilities, with a view of an ultimate convention of the States, or other peaceable means, to the end that, at the earliest practicable moment, peace may be restored on the basis of the Federal Union of the States.

RESOLVED. That the direct interference of the military authorities of the United States in the recent elections held in Kentucky, Maryland, Missouri, and Delaware was a shameful violation of the Constitution, and a repetition of such acts in the approaching election will be held as revolutionary, and resisted with all the means and power under our control.

RESOLVED. That the aim and object of the Democratic party is to preserve the Federal Union and the rights of the States unimpaired, and they hereby declare that they consider that the administrative usurpation of extraordinary and dangerous powers not granted by the Constitution—the subversion of the civil by military law in States not in insurrection; the arbitrary military arrest, imprisonment, trial, and sentence of American citizens in States where civil law exists in full force; the suppression of freedom of speech and of the press; the denial of the right of asylum; the open and avowed disregard of State rights; the employment of unusual test-oaths; and the interference with and denial of the right of the people to bear arms in their defense in calculated to prevent a restoration of the Union and the perpetuation of a Government deriving its just powers from the consent of the governed.

RESOLVED. That the shameful disregard of the Administration to its duty in respect to our fellow citizens who now are and long have been prisoners of war and in a suffering condition, deserves the severest repro-bation on the score alike of public policy and common humanity.

RESOLVED. That the sympathy of the Democratic party is heartily and earnestly extended to the soldiery of our army and sailors of our navy, who are and have been in the field and on the sea under the flag of our country, and in the events of its attaining power, they will receive all the care, protection, and regard that the brave soldiers and sailors of the republic have so nobly deserved.

APPENDIX D

RESULTS OF THE PRESIDENTIAL ELECTION OF NOVEMBER 8, 1864

(in those states where the soldier and sailor votes were tabulated separately, the absentee ballots are in parentheses)

State	Popular Vote		Electoral Vote	
	Lincoln	McClellan	Lincoln	McClellan
Connecticut	44,693	42,288	5	
Delaware	8,155	8,767		3
Illinois	189,487	158,349	16	
Indiana	150,422	130,233	13	
Iowa	90,017 (17,252)	49,484 (1,920)	8	
Kansas	12,387 (2,191)	8,448 (608)	3	
Kentucky	27,786 (1,194)	64,301 (2,823)		11
Maine	72,227 (4,174)	47,736 (741)	7	
Maryland	40,153 (2,800)	32,730 (321)	7	
Massachusetts	126,742	48,745	12	
Michigan	91,521	74,604	8	
Minnesota	25,060	17,375	4	
Missouri	72,991	31,026	11	
Nevada	9,826	6,594	2	
New Hampshire	36,595 (2,066)	33,034 (690)	5	
New Jersey	60,723	68,014		7
New York	368,726	361,986	33	
Ohio	265,154 (41,146)	205,568 (9,764)	21	
Oregon	9,888	8,457	3	
Pennsylvania	296,391 (26,712)	276,316 (12,349)	28	
Rhode Island	13,343	8,718	4	
Vermont	42,716 (243)	13,276 (49)	5	
West Virginia	23,223	10,457	5	
Wisconsin	79,564 (11,372)	68,875 (2,458)	8	
California	62,134 (2,600)	43,841 (237)	4	
TOTAL	**2,219,924**	**1,814,228**	**212**	**21**
Soldier Vote	**121,152**	**34,922**		
Home Vote	**2,098,772**	**1,779,306**		

Appendix D

RESULTS OF THE STATE ELECTIONS
IN THE OCTOBER STATES

State	Unionist	Democratic	Unionist Margin	Lincoln Margin
Indiana	152,084	131,201	20,883	20,189
Ohio	237,210	182,439	54,771	59,586
Pennsyl-vania	249,959	236,061	13,898	20,075

Notes

CHAPTER ONE
"In Giving Freedom to the Slave"

1. William E. Baringer, *Lincoln's Rise to Power* (Boston, 1937), chapters 1–4; James M. McPherson, *Battle Cry of Freedom* (New York, 1988), 219.

2. Erik W. Austin, *Political Facts of the United States Since 1789* (New York, 1986), 139.

3. James G. Randall, *Lincoln the President*, 4 vols. (New York, 1945–1955), I: 362.

4. New York *Evening Post*, April 23, 1861; Winfield Scott's daily reports to Abraham Lincoln, Abraham Lincoln Papers, Robert Todd Lincoln Collection, Library of Congress; John G. Nicolay to Mrs. Nicolay, April 26, 1861, John G. Nicolay Papers, Library of Congress.

5. E. B. Long and Barbara Long, *The Civil War Day by Day: An Almanac 1861–1865* (New York, 1960), 62.

6. Lincoln to Albert G. Hodges, April 4, 1864, *The Collected Works of Abraham Lincoln*, edited by Roy P. Basler, 9 vols. (New Brunswick, NJ, 1953), VII: 281–82 (hereafter cited as *CWL* with volume and page number[s] following immediately thereafter and separated by a colon); *The War of the Rebellion: A Compilation of the Official Records of the Union and Confederate Armies* (Washington, DC, 1890–1901), Ser. II, Vol. 1, 567–68 (hereafter cited as *O.R.*); Allan Nevins, *The War for the Union: War Becomes Revolution 1862–1863* (New York, 1960), 309–10.

7. Jean H. Baker, *The Politics of Continuity: Maryland Political Parties from 1858 to 1870* (Baltimore, MD, 1973), 58.

8. *CWL*, VII: 281.

9. McPherson, *Battle Cry of Freedom*, 287–89.

10. Clement L. Vallandigham, "The Great Civil War in America" (New York, 1863), published in *Union Pamphlets of the Civil War*, edited by Frank Freidel, 2 vols. (Cambridge, MA, 1967), II: 697–738.

11. Orville Hickman Browning, *The Diary of Orville Hickman Browning*, edited by James G. Randall, 2 vols. (Springfield, IL, 1933), I: 455; John G. Nicolay and John Hay, *Abraham Lincoln: A History*, 10 vols. (New York, 1890), III: 327–43; New York *Herald*, March 5, 1861; Allan Nevins, *The Emergence of Lincoln: Prologue to Civil War 1859–1861* (New York, 1950), 455–60.

12. Don E. Fehrenbacher, ed. *Abraham Lincoln: Speeches and Writings 1859–1865: Speeches, Letters, and Miscellaneous Writings, Presidential Messages and Proclamations* (hereafter referred to as *Speeches and Writings*), 2 vols. (New York, 1989), II: 266–70; Stephen B. Oates, *With Malice Toward None: The Life of Abraham Lincoln* (New York, 1977), 280–84.

13. *CWL*, IV: 506.

14. Ibid., IV: 512–13.

15. Ibid., IV: 512–15.

16. Ibid., IV: 517–19; David Donald, *Charles Sumner and the Rights of Man* (New York, 1961), 26; Hans L. Trefousse, *The Radical Republicans: Lincoln's Vanguard for Racial Justice* (New York, 1969), 177.

17. Charles Sumner, *The Works of Charles Sumner*, 8 vols. (Boston, 1870–73), VI: 152.

18. Trefousse, *Radical Republicans*, 173.

19. Benjamin F. Butler, *Private and Official Correspondence of General Benjamin F. Butler During the Period of the Civil War*, 5 vols. (Norwood, MA, 1917), I: 105–6, 116–17.

20. Speech of Congressman George P. Fisher in House of Representatives, March 11, 1862, *Congressional Globe*, 37th Congress, 2d Session, 1175–76; H. C. Conrad, *History of the State of Delaware*, 3 vols. (Wilmington, DE, 1908), I: 205; Nevins, *War Becomes Revolution*, 8.

21. Lincoln to Albert G. Hodges, April 4, 1864, *CWL*, VII: 282.

22. Oates, *Our Fiery Trial*, 73–75.

23. Ibid., 75.

24. *Speeches and Writings*, 295–97.

25. Ibid., 282.

26. Ibid., 292–93.

27. Ibid., 293; James G. Randall, *Constitutional Problems under Lincoln* (University of Illinois Press, 1951; reprinted Gloucester, MA, 1963), 279–80.

28. *Speeches and Writings*, 307.

29. Donald, *Sumner and the Rights of Man*, 50; New York *Tribune*, March 7, 1862; Oates, *With Malice Toward None*, 323.

30. New York *Tribune*, March 7, 1862.

31. Oates, *Our Fiery Trial*, 76; Nevins, *War Becomes Revolution*, 114.

32. McPherson, *Battle Cry of Freedom*, 413.

33. T. Harry Williams, *Lincoln and His Generals* (New York, 1952), 24–35; Noah Brooks, *Washington, D.C., in Lincoln's Time*, edited by Herbert Mitgang

(New York, 1895; edited and republished Athens, GA, 1958, 1962, 1971, 1989), 25–26; William Starr Myers, *A Study in Personality: General George Brinton McClellan* (New York, 1934), 212–14.

34. Warren W. Hassler, Jr., *Commanders of the Army of the Potomac* (Baton Rouge, LA, 1962), 26–31; George B. McClellan, *McClellan's Own Story* (New York, 1887), 82–85, 229.

35. Benjamin Wade to Zachariah Chandler, October 8, 1861, Zachariah Chandler Papers, Library of Congress; Wade to Mrs. Wade, October 25, 1861, Benjamin Wade Papers, Library of Congress; Chandler to Mrs. Chandler, October 27, 1861, Chandler Papers, Library of Congress; as cited in Trefousse, *Radical Republicans*, 178–80, 186.

36. *Cong. Globe*, 37th Congress, 2d Session, 94; as cited in Trefousse, *Radical Republicans*, 184.

37. *Cong. Globe*, 37th Congress, 2d Session, March 12, 1862, 1199–1200.

38. McClellan to Mary Ellen McClellan, November 17, 1861, *The Civil War Papers of George B. McClellan: Selected Correspondence*, edited by Stephen B. Sears (New York, 1989), 135.

39. Joseph E. Johnston, *Narrative of Military Operations* (New York, 1874), 98–106; Nevins, *War Becomes Revolution*, 46–47.

40. McClellan, *McClellan's Own Story*, 149–62.

41. Nicolay and Hay, *Lincoln*, V: 169; *Lincoln Day by Day: A Chronology 1809–1865*, edited by Earl Schenck Miers, 3 vols. (Washington, DC, 1960), III: 98–99; as cited in Oates, *With Malice Toward None*, 318–19.

42. President's General War Order No. 3, March 8, 1862, *CWL*, V: 151.

43. James Longstreet, "Our March Against Pope," in *Battles and Leaders of the Civil War*, originally published as part of "The Century War Series," of *Century* magazine, edited by Robert Underwood Johnson and Clarence Clough Buel, 4 vols. (New York, 1884–87; reproduced Secaucus, NJ, 1989), II: 512–28; Allen C. Redwood, "Jackson's 'Foot-Cavalry' at the Second Bull Run," in *Battles and Leaders*, II: 530–38; *O.R.*, Ser. I, Vol. 12, Pt. 2, 644; G. F. R. Henderson, *Stonewall Jackson and the American Civil War*, 2 vols. (New York, 1898), II: 148.

44. Shelby Foote, *The Civil War: A Narrative*, 3 vols. (New York, 1963), I: 666.

45. New York *Tribune*, July 5, 1862; *New York Times*, July 3, 1862; New York *Herald*, July 4, 1862; Chicago *Tribune*, July 5, 1862.

46. Randall, *Lincoln the President*, II: 87.

47. Ibid., II: 213.

48. *CWL*, V: 222–23.

49. Ibid.

50. *U.S. Statutes at Large*, Vol. XII, 627; Lincoln's objection to the legislation was based upon its violation of the Constitution. Article I, Section 9 prohibits the passage of a bill of attainder, a device historically used to "attaint" the family of a criminal, usually one who had been convicted of treason, by extinguishing their civil rights. It had once been common in England to take the real estate of a traitor, thereby extinguishing his family's future interest in that property. Lincoln also objected because the proceeding would be *in rem*, or based upon jurisdiction over

the property rather than the person of the defendant. Thus the proceeding would forfeit the property of the accused "without a conviction of the supposed criminal, or a personal hearing given him in any proceeding." This would violate the Fifth Amendment due process guarantee plus other fundamental Fourth, Fifth, and Sixth amendment rights. Randall, *Constitutional Problems Under Lincoln*, 280; Donald, *Sumner and the Rights of Man*, 62–67; Trefousse, *Radical Republicans*, 215; *CWL*, V: 318.

51. *CWL*, V: 317–19.

52. Gideon Welles, "History of Emancipation," *Galaxy* (December 1872), 842–43; Welles, *Diary of Gideon Welles*, edited by Howard K. Beale, 3 vols. (New York, 1960), I: 70–71.

53. Charles Eugene Hamlin, *The Life and Times of Hannibal Hamlin* (Cambridge, MA, 1899), 428–29.

54. *CWL*, V: 336–37; Salmon P. Chase, *Inside Lincoln's Cabinet: The Civil War Diaries of Salmon P. Chase*, edited by David H. Donald (New York, 1954), 98–99.

55. Chase, *Inside Lincoln's Cabinet*, Donald, ed., 98–99; F. B. Carpenter, *Six Months in the White House with Abraham Lincoln* (New York, 1867), 24; Nicolay and Hay, *Lincoln*, VI: 127; Glyndon G. Van Deusen, *William Henry Seward* (New York, 1967), 331; Oates, *With Malice Toward None*, 336–37.

56. *CWL*, V: 370–75; *Speeches and Writings,* II: 353–57.

57. *Speeches and Writings*, II: 353–57.

58. Oates, *With Malice Toward None*, 344; Welles, *Diary,* Beale, ed., I: 143; Chase, *Inside Lincoln's Cabinet*, Donald, ed., 150.

59. *CWL*, V: 419–25; *Speeches and Writings*, II: 361–67.

60. *CWL*, V: 419–21.

61. Ibid., V: 425.

62. Chase, *Inside Lincoln's Cabinet,* Donald, ed., 149–50; Welles, *Diary,* Beale, ed., I: 143.

63. Welles, *Diary*, Beale, ed., I: 143–49; Chase, *Inside Lincoln's Cabinet*, Donald, ed., 149–53.

64. Chase, *Inside Lincoln's Cabinet*, Donald, ed., 149–53; Oates, *With Malice Toward None*, 346.

65. *CWL*, V: 433–36.

CHAPTER TWO
"We Assure Freedom to the Free"

1. T. Harry Williams, *Lincoln and the Radicals* (Madison, WI, 1969), 2; John Hay, *Lincoln and the Civil War in the Diaries and Letters of John Hay,* edited by Tyler Dennett (New York, 1939), 31–32; Trefousse, *Radical Republicans*, 20; James G. Randall, *Lincoln the Liberal Statesman* (New York, 1973); Zornow, *Lincoln & the Party Divided*, 15; Oates, *With Malice Toward None*, 197.

2. Williams, *Lincoln and the Radicals*, 5; Oates, *With Malice Toward None*, 197; Zornow, *Lincoln & the Party Divided*, 16.

3. Joshua Leavitt to Salmon P. Chase, November 7, 1860; John Bingham to Chase, November 6, 1860, Salmon P. Chase Papers, Library of Congress; Thaddeus Stevens to Edward McPherson, December 19, 1860, Thaddeus Stevens Papers, Library of Congress; *CWL*, IV: 156, 158; Trefousse, *Radical Republicans*, 161–62.

4. Trefousse, *Radical Republicans*, 14.

5. Oates, *With Malice Toward None*, 197–98.

6. Hay, *Diaries and Letters*, Dennett, ed., 119, 135.

7. *CWL*, V: 318.

8 Trefousse, *Radical Republicans*, 181–99.

9. *Congressional Globe*, 37th Congress, 2d Session, 658; *A Compilation of the Messages and Papers of the Presidents, 1789–1897*, edited by James D. Richardson, 10 vols. (Washington, DC, 1896–99), 6: 68–69; T. Harry Williams, *Lincoln and the Radicals* (Madison, WI, 1941, 1965; renewed 1969), 156–68.

10. William E. Baringer, *Lincoln's Rise to Power* (Boston, 1937), 48–88; David M. Potter, *Lincoln and His Party in the Secession Crisis* (New Haven, CT, 1942), 23–24; Glyndon G. Van Deusen, *William Henry Seward* (New York, 1942), 162–219; as cited in Oates, *With Malice Toward None*, 191–92.

11. Joseph P. Medill to Salmon P. Chase, September 15, 1861, Salmon P. Chase Papers, Historical Society of Pennsylvania; O. Brown to Alexander Ramsay, September 19, 1861, Alexander Ramsay Papers, Minnesota Historical Society; Charles Sumner to Lieber, September 17, 1861, Charles Sumner Papers, Huntington Library; George Headley to Chase, September 18, 1861, Chase Papers, Library of Congress; as cited in Trefousse, *Radical Republicans*, 177.

12. New York *Herald*, November 23, 1861; Zachariah Chandler to Mrs. Chandler, October 12, 1861, Zachariah Chandler Papers, Library of Congress; *CWL*, IV: 562, and V: 1–2; as cited in Trefousse, *Radical Republicans*, 177.

13. Nicolay and Hay, *Lincoln*, V: 125; Alexander McClure, *Lincoln and Men of War Times* (Philadelphia, 1892), 192–93.

14. Benjamin P. Thomas and Harold M. Hyman, *Stanton: The Life and Times of Lincoln's Secretary of War* (New York, 1962), 135–42.

15. McDowell had commanded the Union army at the First Battle of Bull Run, July 21, 1861. Pope had commanded the Army of Virginia at the Second Battle of Bull Run, August 28–30, 1862. Hooker had led the Army of the Potomac at the Battle of Chancellorsville, May 1–4, 1863.

16. Hay, *Diaries and Letters*, Dennett ed., 50; Wade to George Julian, September 29, 1862, Julian/Giddings Papers, Library of Congress; Hannibal Hamlin to Lincoln, September 25, 1862, Lincoln Papers: Robert Todd Lincoln Collection, Library of Congress; Carl Schurz, *The Reminiscences of Carl Schurz*, 3 vols. (New York, 1907–8), II: 317; McClure, *Lincoln and Men of War Times*, 262; Trefousse, *Radical Republicans*, 228–30.

17. New York *Herald*, August 27, 1861; Lyman Trumbull to Mrs. Trumbull, July 28, 1861, Lyman Trumbull Papers, Illinois State Historical Library; Salmon

Chase to John Sherman, September 20, 1862, Chase Papers, Historical Society of Pennsylvania, Philadelphia; Chase to Horace Greeley, September 7, 1862, Greeley Papers, Library of Congress; Trefousse, *Radical Republicans*, 240.

18. Chase, *Inside Lincoln's Cabinet*, 11, 16–17, 22–23, 94, 136; as cited in Oates, *With Malice Toward None*, 354.

19. Edward Bates, *The Diary of Edward Bates,* edited by Howard K. Beale (Washington, DC, 1859–66), 269–71; Orville H. Browning, *The Diary of Orville H. Browning,* edited by Theodore Calvin Pearse and James G. Randall, 2 vols. (Springfield, IL, 1927), I: 596–603; Welles, *Diary*, I: 194–206; Trefousse, *Radical Republicans*, 241.

20. Browning, *Diary*, I: 602–4; Hay, *Diaries and Letters*, Dennett ed., 111–12; Bates, *Diary*, Beale ed., 268–69; as cited in Oates, *With Malice Toward None*, 357.

21. Francis Fessenden, *Life and Public Services of William Pitt Fessenden,* 2 vols. (Boston, 1907), I: 243–46; Bates, *Diary*, 270.

22. Chandler to Austin Blair, December 22, 1862, Austin Blair Papers, Detroit Public Library; as cited in Trefousse, *Radical Republicans*, 241.

23. O. Brown to Alexander Ramsay, September 19, 1861, Alexander Ramsay Papers, Minnesota Historical Society; Charles Sumner to Francis Lieber, September 17, 1861, Charles Sumner Papers, Library of Congress; Benjamin Wade to Zachariah Chandler, September 23, 1861, Zachariah Chandler Papers, Detroit Public Library; Chase to Lincoln, May 16, 1862, Abraham Lincoln Papers, Robert Todd Lincoln Collection, Library of Congress; T. Harry Williams, *Lincoln and the Radicals* (Madison, WI, 1941), 164–66; William Hesseltine, *Lincoln and the War Governors* (New York, 1963), 241–43.

24. *The American Annual Cyclopaedia 1862*, 703–5, 654–56, 527–29, 518–19; George H. Porter, *Ohio Politics During the Civil War Era* (New York, 1911), 88–89; A. K. McClure, *Old Time Notes of Pennsylvania* (Philadelphia, 1905); Charles A. Church, *History of the Republican Party in Illinois, 1854–1912* (Rockford, IL, 1912), 89; Blaine, *Twenty Years of Congress*, I: 499–502.

25. Christopher Dell, *Lincoln and the War Democrats* (Cranbury, New Jersey, 1975), 146, 201, 294.

26. George Meade, *The Life and Letters of George Gordon Meade*, 2 vols. (New York, 1913), II: chaps. 2–4; *Report of the Joint Congressional Committee on the Conduct of the War*, 38th Congress, 2d Session, Sen. Rep. No. 142 (Washington, DC, 1865), I; New York *Tribune*, March 6, 8, 1864.

27. Helen Nicolay, *Lincoln's Secretary: A Biography of John G. Nicolay* (New York, 1949), 149; Randall, *Lincoln the President*, II: 87.

28. Nevins, *War Becomes Revolution*, 304.

29. Stewart Mitchell, *Horatio Seymour of New York* (Cambridge, MA, 1938), 146–47.

30. Ibid., 245.

31. *Tribune Almanac for 1863* (New York, 1863), 51.

32. *CWL*, V: 536–37.

33. Frederick W. Seward, *Seward at Washington as Senator and Secretary of State*, 3 vols. (New York, 1891), III: 166; Charles Eliot Norton to Frederick Law

Olmstead, May 20, 1863, Frederick Law Olmstead Papers, Library of Congress; New York *World*, May 8, 1863.

34. *O.R.*, Ser. I, Vol. 23, Pt. 2, 518; Foote, *Civil War*, II: 467–69; *O.R.*, Ser. I, Vol. 27, Pt. 3, 539; Foote, *Civil War*, II: 567–68, 575; Clifford Dowdey, *Death of a Nation: The Story of Lee and His Men at Gettysburg* (New York, 1958), 341; *O.R.*, Ser. I, Vol. 24, Pt. 1, 227–28; Samuel Carter III, *The Final Fortress: The Campaign for Vicksburg, 1862–1863* (New York, 1980), 155, 182, 207–8; Ulysses S. Grant, *The Personal Memoirs of U. S. Grant*, 2 vols. (New York, 1885), I: 531, 542–43; Bruce Catton, *Never Call Retreat* (New York, 1967), 195–96; New York *Tribune*, September 8, 1865; *Atlantic Monthly*, quoted in McPherson, *Battle Cry of Freedom*, 686–87.

35. Laurence Lader, *The Bold Brahmins* (New York, 1961), 290.

36. McPherson, *Battle Cry of Freedom*, 687.

37. *CWL*, V: 462–63.

38. Charles H. McCarthy, *Lincoln's Plan of Reconstruction* (New York, 1901), 190–217; Herman Belz, *Reconstructing the Union: Theory and Policy during the Civil War* (Ithaca, NY, 1969), 7–13; McPherson, *Battle Cry of Freedom*, 699.

39. *CWL*, VIII: 402–3.

40. James A. Hamilton, *Reminiscences of James A. Hamilton or Men and Events, at Home and Abroad During Three Quarters of a Century* (New York, 1869), 455.

41. *CWL*, VII: 54.

42. Hay, *Diaries and Letters*, Dennett ed., 131.

43. New York *Tribune*, December 10, 1863.

44. *New York Times*, December 11, 1863.

45. *Atlantic Monthly*, October 1863, Vol. XII, No. LXXII, 507–29.

46. Ibid., 507.

47. Ibid.; Nicolay and Hay, *Lincoln*.

48. Nicolay and Hay, *Lincoln*, X, 84–85.

49. Salmon P. Chase, *Inside Lincoln's Cabinet: The Civil War Diaries of Salmon P. Chase*, edited by David H. Donald (New York, 1954), 5ff.

50. Bates, *Diary*, 310.

51. Welles, *Diary*, I: 525.

52. Chase to James A. Stevens, July 23, 1863, Chase Papers, Library of Congress; Chase to Daniel A. Dickinson, November 18, 1863; Chase to William Sprague, November 18, 1863, Chase Papers, Historical Society of Pennsylvania; Zornow, *Lincoln & the Party Divided*, 26.

53. Andrew Johnson, *The Papers of Andrew Johnson*, 9 vols., edited by Leroy P. Graf (Knoxville, Tennessee, 1986), VI: 477.

54. Donnal V. Smith, *Chase and Civil War Politics* (Columbus, Ohio, 1931), 76–77.

55. Salmon P. Chase, *Diary and Correspondence of Salmon P. Chase*, Annual Report of the American Historical Association, 1902 (Washington, DC, 1903), XX: 433.

56. Ellis P. Oberholtzer, *Jay Cooke: Financier of the Civil War*, 2 vols.

(Philadelphia, 1907), I: 360; Clinton Rice to Chase, October 29, 1863, Chase Papers, Historical Society of Pennsylvania; Zornow, *Lincoln & the Party Divided*, 34.

57. C. H. Ray to Chase, November 14, 1863; Ray to Chase, November 28, 1863; Chase to John Austin Stevens, July 23, 1863; Stevens to Chase, June 11, 1863; William P. Smith to Chase, October 20, 1863, Chase Papers, Historical Society of Pennsylvania.

58. Chase to the Rev. J. Leavitt, cited in Robert B. Warden, *Account of the Private Life and Public Services of Salmon Portland Chase* (Cincinnati, OH, 1874), 562; Nicolay and Hay, *Lincoln*, VIII: 312.

59. Chase to William Dickson, January 27, 1864, in Warden, *Life of Chase*, 564; Nicolay and Hay, *Lincoln*, VIII: 312–13.

60. Chase to F. Ball, February 2, 1864, in Warden, *Life of Chase*, 564; Nicolay and Hay, *Lincoln*, VIII: 313.

61. Hay, *Diaries and Letters*, Dennett, ed., 100–101.

62. Ibid.

63. Zornow, *Lincoln & the Party Divided*, 33.

64. Lincoln to Samuel C. Pomeroy, May 12, 1864, demonstrating something of the strained nature of the relationship between the two, found at *CWL*, VIII: 338; Nicolay and Hay, *Lincoln*, VIII: 318–20.

65. Washington *National Intelligencer*, February 22, 1864.

66. The text of Chase's letter to Lincoln is reprinted in the notes to Lincoln's February 23, 1864, response to Chase, along with the following commentary: "Chase's statement that he had no knowledge of the circular before it appeared in print is contradicted by a statement of James M. Winchell, author-in-fact of the circular, who wrote in reply to Jacob W. Schuckers' *Life and Public Services of Salmon Portland Chase* (1874) a detailed account of the Pomeroy Committee which included the following: *Mr. Chase was informed of this proposed action and approved it fully. He told me himself that the arraignment of the Administration . . . was one which he thoroughly endorsed and would sustain. The circular was, therefore, sent out.*" (J. M. Winchell to editor, September 14, 1864, *New York Times*, September 15, 1874. Italics are in the source.); Nicolay and Hay, *Lincoln*, VIII: 321–21.

67. Lincoln to Chase, February 29, 1864; *CWL*, VII: 212–13; Nicolay and Hay, *Lincoln*, VIII: 322.

68. Thomas Graham Belden, *So Fell the Angels* (Boston, 1956), 108–17; James G. Randall and Richard N. Current, *Lincoln the President: Last Full Measure* (New York, 1955), 95–110; Zornow, *Lincoln & the Party Divided*, 23–56; McPherson, *Battle Cry of Freedom*, 714–15.

69. McPherson, *Battle Cry of Freedom*, 715.

70. G. W. Gordon to John Sherman, February 26, 1864, John Sherman Papers, Library of Congress.

71. Cincinnati *Daily Gazette*, March 3, 1864.

72. Nicolay and Hay, *Lincoln*, VIII: 325; Schuckers, *Life of Chase*, 502–3.

73. New York *Tribune*, February 22, 1864.

74. Ibid., February 23, 1864; Greeley to Beman Brockway, February 28, 1864,

Horace Greeley Papers, Library of Congress; New York *Evening Post*, February 23, 1864; Zornow, *Lincoln & the Party Divided*, 61; Whitelaw Reid to Anna Dickinson, April 10, 1864, Anna Dickinson Papers, Library of Congress.

75. Albert D. Richardson, *A Personal History of Ulysses S. Grant* (Hartford, CT, 1868), 407, 434.

76. Edgar Conkling to Benjamin Butler, July 18, 1864, in Benjamin F. Butler, *Private and Official Correspondence of General Benjamin F. Butler during the Period of the Civil War*, 5 vols., edited by Jessie A Marshall (Norwood, MA, 1917), IV: 512; Carl Schurz, *Speeches, Correspondence, and Political Papers of Carl Schurz*, edited by Frederic Bancroft, 3 vols. (New York, 1907–8), III: 102–4.

77. F. B. Carpenter, *Six Months at the White House with Abraham Lincoln* (New York, 1866), 168.

78. Nicolay and Hay, *Lincoln*, IX: 70.

79. Ibid.; "The incident at Fort Pillow involved the massacre of a number of Union troops, most of them black, after surrendering to a Confederate force under the command of Nathan Bedford Forrest. The extent of this killing is disputed; however, at the time a Congressional investigation done by Senator Benjamin Wade and Representative Daniel W. Gooch claimed that nearly all of the 230 or so dead Union soldiers were killed after resistance had ceased." Robert Selph Henry, *"First With the Most" Forrest* (Wilmington, NC, 1987), 248–69.

80. Harold M. Dudley, "The Election of 1864," *The Mississippi Valley Historical Review* XVIII (March 1932), 509; Alexander McClure, *Our Presidents and How We Make Them* (New York, 1900), 184–85; James H. Glonck, "Lincoln, Johnson and the Baltimore Ticket," *Abraham Lincoln Quarterly* 6 (March 1951), 255–71; Zornow, *Lincoln & the Party Divided*, 717.

CHAPTER THREE
"And the Niggers Where They Are"

1. Richard P. McCormick, *The Second American Party System: Formation in the Jacksonian Era* (Chapel Hill, NC, 1966); John Ashworth, "Agrarians and Aristocrats," *Party Political Ideology in the United States, 1837–1846* (London, England, 1983); Samuel Eliot Morrison, *The Oxford History of the American People* (New York, 1965), 421–26; Roy F. Nichols, *The Disruption of the American Democracy* (New York, 1948).

2. Leon Friedman, "The Democratic Party 1860–1884," *History of U.S. Political Parties*, edited by Arthur M. Schlesinger, Jr., 4 vols. (New York, 1973), II: 885–88.

3. Thomas M. Eddy, "The Patriotism of Illinois," quoted in Christopher Dell, *Lincoln and the War Democrats: the Grand Erosion of Conservative Tradition* (Cranbury, NJ, 1975), 75; *Northern Editorials on Secession*, edited by Harvard C. Perkins (New York, 1942), I: 645; George H. Porter, *Ohio Politics during the Civil War* (New York, 1911), 87.

4. Edward Stanswood, *A History of the Presidency* (Boston, 1975), I: 298;

Alexander McClure, *Lincoln and Men of War Times* (Philadelphia, 1892), 73; Christopher Dell, *Lincoln and the War Democrats*, 59.

5. Friedman, "Democratic Party," II: 888.

6. Dell, *Lincoln and the War Democrats*, 117.

7. Frank L. Klement, *The Copperheads in the Middle West* (Chicago, 1960), 2.

8. Henry Claude Hubbart, "Pro-Southern Influences in the Free West," *Mississippi Valley Historical Review* XX (September 1933), 45–62.

9. *Dictionary of American Biography*, III: 46; Wood Gray, *The Hidden Civil War: The Story of the Copperheads* (New York, 1942; republished 1964), 138–42.

10. Frank L. Klement, *The Limits of Dissent: Clement Vallandigham and the Civil War* (Lexington, KY, 1970), 106.

11. Allan Nevins, *The War for the Union: The Improvised War 1861–1862* (New York, 1959), 429.

12. Ibid., 429–30; La Crosse (Wis.) *Weekly Democrat*, November 21, 24, 1864; two other Copperhead newspapers of note in the Buckeye State were Clement L. Vallandigham's Dayton *Empire* and the Cincinnati *Enquirer*. In Illinois, the Chicago *Times,* Joliet *Signal,* and Bloomington *Times* were consistent organs of the Peace Democrats, while in Indiana the Indianapolis *Sentinel*, Evansville *Gazette*, and Terre Haute *Journal* spread the Copperhead message. In Iowa, the Dubuque *Herald*; in New Hampshire, the Concord *Patriot*; in Rhode Island, the *Providence Post*; and in New Jersey, the Newark *Journal* and Paterson *Register* were all newspapers of note that propounded Copperhead propaganda.

13. *The Tribune Almanac for 1863* (New York, 1863), 56–58; Peter J. Parrish, *The American Civil War* (New York, 1975), 208–9; Joel H. Silbey, *A Respectable Minority: The Democratic Party in the Civil War Era 1860–1868* (New York, 1977), 144; William B. Hesseltine, *Lincoln and the War Governors* (New York, 1948), 165.

14. Cincinatti *Gazette*, October 17, 1862.

15. William E. Chandler, "The Soldier's Right to Vote," (Washington, DC, 1864); William F. Zornow, "Lincoln Voters Among the Boys in Blue," *Lincoln Herald* 54, no. 3 (Fall 1952), 22–25.

16. *Tribune Almanac for 1863*, 50–64; Oscar O. Winther, "The Soldier Vote in the Election of 1864," *New York History* 25 (1944), 440–58; McPherson, *Battle Cry of Freedom*, 562; Lincoln to Carl Schurz, November 10, 1862, in *CWL*, V: 494.

17. *New York Times*, November 5, 1862; Providence *Journal*, November 17, 1862; Horace Greeley, *The American Conflict: A History of The Great Rebellion in the United States of America, 1860–65* (Hartford, CT, 1867), II: 254.

18. Stewart Mitchell, *Horatio Seymour of New York* (Cambridge, MA, 1938), 245.

19. Philadelphia *Inquirer*, September 20, 1862; Cleveland *Leader*, January 16, 1862; David Lindsey, *"Sunset Cox," Irrepressible Democrat* (Detroit, MI, 1959), 62–65; Cleveland *Leader*, July 19, 1862; Allan Nevins, *The War for the Union: War Becomes Revolution 1862–1863* (New York, 1960), 308.

20. *Speeches and Writings*, II: 439–40.

21. Nevins, *War for the Union*, II: 302–3.

22. *O.R.*, Ser. I, Vol. 27, Pt. 2, 878–81; *American Annual Cyclopaedia, 1863,* 811–17; New York *Herald,* July 14, 1863; New York *Tribune,* July 14, 1863.

23. New York *Herald,* July 14, 1863; Allan Nevins, *The War for the Union: The Organized War 1863–1864* (New York, 1971), 121–23.

24. Greeley, *The American Conflict,* 506.

25. New York *World,* July 13, 1863.

26. New York *Daily News,* July 13, 1863.

27. *CWL,* VI: 370; *O.R.,* Ser. III, Vol. 3, 612–19.

28. *CWL,* VI: 369–70.

29. Ibid., 369–70, 381–82, 389–91.

30. Albert G. Riddle, *Recollections of War Times* (New York, 1895), chap. XX, as cited in Nevins, *War Becomes Revolution,* 191.

31. Edward L. Pierce, *Memoirs and Letters of Charles Sumner* (Boston, 1877–93), IV: 114.

32. Clement L. Vallandigham, *The Great Civil War in America* (New York, 1863), reprinted in *Union Pamphlets of the Civil War,* edited by Frank Freidel, 2 vols. (Cambridge, MA, 1967), II: 697–738.

33. Ibid.

34. Ibid., II: 706.

35. Ibid., II: 719.

36. *O.R.*, Ser. I, Vol. 23, Pt. 2, 237.

37. Columbus *Crisis,* May 13, 1863; James G. Randall, *Lincoln the President* (New York, 1945–55), III: 218.

38. Ibid.

39. George H. Porter, *Ohio Politics During the Civil War Period* (New York, 1911; reprinted 1968), 181–99.

40. *The Tribune Almanac for 1864,* 60–61.

41. Union League of Philadelphia, *Record of Harister Clymer and Historical Parallel between Him and Major General John W. Geary. Also Official Returns on Elections on Constitutional Amendments Allowing Soldiers the Right to Vote* (Philadelphia, 1864), 7–8.

42. Nevins, *War for the Union,* III: 450–51.

43. Stephen W. Sears, *George B. McClellan: The Young Napoleon* (New York, 1988), 47–49.

44. Ibid., 78.

45. *O.R.*, Ser. I, Vol. 2, 197, 236; Jacob D. Cox, "McClellan in West Virginia," *Battles and Leaders,* I: 137; Winfield Scott to McClellan, July 13, 1861; *O.R.*, Ser. I, Vol. 2, 204; New York *Herald,* July 15, 1861; New York *Tribune,* July 16, 1861; *New York Times,* July 20, 1861; Sears, *Young Napoleon,* 93.

46. McClellan to Thomas A. Morris, July 12, 1861, Civil War Collection, Huntington Library; McClellan to Mary Ellen McClellan, July 3, 1861, McClellan Papers, Library of Congress; McClellan to Mary Ellen McClellan, July 2, 1861, McClellan Papers, Library of Congress.

47. Charles Winslow Elliott, Winfield Scott: *The Soldier and the Man* (New York, 1937), 698; *O.R.,* Ser. I, Vol. 51, Pt. 1, 387; McPherson, *Battle Cry of*

Freedom, 334, 359–60; McClellan to Ellen Marcy McClellan, August, 8, 9, 1861, McClellan Papers, Library of Congress.

48. McClellan to Mary Ellen McClellan, August 2, 1861, McClellan Papers, Library of Congress.

49. Ibid., August 4, 1861.

50. McClellan to Winfield Scott, August 8, 1861; *O.R., Ser.* I, Vol. 11, Pt. 3, 3–4.

51. McClellan to Mary Ellen McClellan, August 8, 1861, McClellan Papers, Library of Congress.

52. Ibid., August 15, 1861.

53. Ibid., August 16, 1861.

54. George B. McClellan, *The Civil War Papers of George B. McClellan: Selected Correspondence 1860–1865,* edited by Stephen W. Sears (New York, 1989), 69–71, 75–76, 81–82, 85–86, 89, 98, 106–7, 112.

55. McClellan to Mary Ellen McClellan, August 9, 1861, McClellan Papers, Library of Congress.

56. Jacob D. Cox, *Military Reminiscences of the Civil War* (New York, 1900), I: 360.

57. McClellan to Mary Ellen McClellan, September 25, 1862, McClellan Papers, Library of Congress.

58. Ibid., October 5, 1862, quoted in Sears, *Young Napoleon,* 327.

59. McClellan to Abraham Lincoln, July 7, 1862; *O.R.,* Ser. I, Vol. 11, Pt. 1, 73–74.

60. McClellan to Mary Ellen McClellan, October 5, 1862, McClellan Papers, Library of Congress.

61. *O.R.,* Ser. I, Vol. 19, Pt. 2, 549.

62. McClellan, *Papers and Selected Correspondence,* Sears, ed., 523.

63. Ibid., 524.

64. New York *Express,* November 16, 1862; Sears, *Young Napoleon,* 345; Edward H. Eldredge to John H. B. McClellan, November 28, 1862, McClellan Papers, Library of Congress; T. J. Barnett to S. L. M. Barlow, May 15, 1863, S. L. M. Barlow Papers, Henry E. Huntington Library; William Dennison to McClellan, August 4, 1863, McClellan Papers, Library of Congress; as cited in Sears, *Young Napoleon,* 345–46.

65. Sears, *Young Napoleon,* 346; Darius Starr to his brother, June 18, 1863, Starr Papers, William H. Perkins Library, Duke University; *Illustrated History of the Civil War,* edited by Henry Steele Commager (New York, 1976), 180.

66. McClellan to Mary Ellen McClellan, September 20, 1862; Samuel S. Cox to McClellan, May 31, 1863; McClellan to Cox, June 8, 1863, McClellan Papers, Library of Congress; Sears, *Young Napoleon,* 345–50.

67. William B. Hesseltine, *Lincoln and the War Governors* (New York, 1948), 328; Philadelphia *Press,* October 13, 1863.

68. Manton Marble to McClellan, October 11, 1863, McClellan Papers, New Jersey Historical Society, quoted in Sears, *Young Napoleon,* 357–58.

69. McClellan to Elizabeth B. McClellan, December 6, 1863, in response to Mrs. McClellan's letter of December 3, McClellan Papers, Library of Congress.

70. Montgomery Blair to S. L. M. Barlow, May 1, 1864, Barlow Papers, Huntington Library.

71. Francis P. Blair to editor, printed in *National Intelligencer*, October 8, 1864.

72. McClellan to Francis P. Blair, July 22, 1864, McClellan Papers, Library of Congress.

73. *CWL*, VII: 517–18.

74. S. L. M. Barlow to Manton Marble, August 24, 1864, Barlow Papers, Huntington Library; James Harrison to Louis V. Bogy, August 24, 1864, Clement C. Clay Papers, National Archives, quoted in Kinchen, *Confederate Operations in Canada*, 93; also cited in McPherson, *Battle Cry of Freedom*, 771–72.

75. McClellan to W. C. Prime, August 10, 1864, McClellan Papers, Library of Congress.

76. Marble to McClellan, August 10, 1864, McClellan Papers, Library of Congress; Barlow to Marble, August 21, 1864, Manton Marble Papers, Library of Congress.

77. Barlow to McClellan, August 28, 1864, McClellan Papers, Library of Congress; August Belmont to Barlow, August 29, 1864, Barlow Papers, Huntington Library; H. S. Lansing to McClellan, August 28, 1864, McClellan Papers, Library of Congress.

78. Marble to Barlow, August 27, 1864, Barlow Papers, Huntington Library; Vallandigham to editor, New York *Daily News*, October 22, 1864, published in Dayton *Daily Empire,* October 29, 1864; *Missouri Republican,* August 29–31, September 2, 1864.

79. William Cassidy to Barlow, September 5, 1864, Barlow Papers, Huntington Library.

80. Ibid.; Sears, *Young Napoleon*, 372–73.

81. Vallandigham to McClellan, September 4, 1864, McClellan Papers, Library of Congress.

82. E. B. Long with Barbara Long, *The Civil War Day by Day: An Almanac 1861–1865* (New York, 1971), 563; Noah Brooks, "Two War-Time Conventions," *The Century* 49 (March 1895), 733–34.

83. Thomas Key to McClellan, September 4, 1864, McClellan Papers, Library of Congress.

CHAPTER FOUR
"You Say You Will Not Fight to Free Negroes"

1. Dean Sprague, *Freedom Under Lincoln* (Boston, 1965), 31–32; Opinion of Attorney General Edward Bates, July 5, 1861, in *O.R.*, Ser. II, Vol. 2, 20–30; Reverdy Johnson, *Power of the President to Suspend the Habeas Corpus Writ* (New York, 1861); Wood Gray, *The Hidden Civil War: The Story of the Copperheads* (New York, 1942; republished 1964), 51–77; *CWL*, VI: 372, 428–32; Ibid., VI: 263–64.

2. Henry B. Hubbart, *The Older Middle West, 1840–1880* (New York, 1936);

Richard Lyle Power, *Planting Corn Belt Culture: The Impress of the Upland Southerner and Yankee in the Old Northwest* (Indianapolis, IN, 1953); G. R. Treadway, *Democratic Opposition to the Lincoln Administration in Indiana* (Indianapolis, IN, 1973), 1–6.

3. *CWL*, V: 436–37; Robert E. Sterling, *Civil War Draft Resistance in the Middle West*, Ph.D. dissertation, Northern Illinois University, 1974, chaps. 3–4; as quoted in McPherson, *Battle Cry of Freedom*, 493.

4. Treadway, *Democratic Opposition in Indiana*, 8–17, 41–44; McPherson, *Battle Cry of Freedom*, 493; Albert Matthews, "Origin of Butternut and Copperhead and Butternut," *Proceedings of the Colonial Society of Massachusetts* (Boston, 1918), 205–37.

5. Frank L. Klement, "Economic Aspects of Middle Western Copperheadism," *Historian* 14 (1951), 27–44; McPherson, *Battle Cry of Freedom*, 593; Columbus *Crisis*, January 21, 1863.

6. Rockport *Democrat*, July 27, November 30, 1861; Evansville *Gazette*, September 7, 1861; Indianapolis *Daily Sentinel*, December 31, 1861; Sullivan *Democrat*, August 22, 1861; Vincennes *Western Sun*, June 14, 1862; Cincinnati *Commercial*, July 11, 1862; Dayton *Daily Empire*, July 24, 1862.

7. White River *Gazette*, February 19, 1863; Vincennes *Western Sun*, October 25, 1862; Huntington *Democrat*, September 25, 1862; Goshen *Democrat*, November 5, December 31, 1862; Indianapolis *Daily Sentinel*, September 24, 1862; Lawrenceburg *Democratic Register*, October 24, 1862.

8. Samuel and Charlotte McMannas to John McMannas, January 11, 1863, as printed in Indianapolis *Daily Journal*, February 28, 1863.

9. Frank Smith Bogardus, "Daniel W. Voorhees," *Indiana Magazine of History* XXXVII (1931), 98; Indianapolis *Daily Sentinel*, September 24, 1862.

10. Illinois *Daily State Register*, January 5, 1863 (hereafter cited as *Register*); Chicago *Daily Tribune*, January 6, 1863.

11. Camilla A. Quinn, *Lincoln's Springfield in the Civil War* (Macomb, IL, 1991), 41; Illinois *Daily State Journal* (hereafter cited as *Journal*), January 7, 1863; Chicago *Daily Tribune*, January 6, 1863; *Journal*, January 7, 1863.

12. *Register*, January 6, 1863.

13. Ibid.; Quinn, *Lincoln's Springfield*, 42.

14. *Journal*, January 9, 1863; *Register*, January 9, 1863; Quinn, *Lincoln's Springfield*.

15. *O.R.*, Ser. 3, Vol. 5, 232–35, 757–58; W. H. H. Terrell (comp.), *Indiana and the War*, 5 vols. (Indianapolis, IN, 1889), I: 277.

16. S. F. Horrall, *History of the Forty-Second Indiana Volunteer Infantry* (Chicago, 1892), 183–84; Lewis and Richard Collins, *History of Kentucky*, 2 vols. (Louisville, 1924), I: 134; Oscar O. Winther, ed., *With Sherman to the Sea: The Civil War Letters and Diaries of Theodore F. Upson* (Baton Rouge, 1943), 55–56; as reported in G. R. Tredway, *Democratic Opposition to the Lincoln Administration in Indiana* (Indianapolis, IN, 1973), 102.

17. *Congressional Globe*, 37th Congress, 2d session, 1735, 1829; George H. Porter, *Ohio Politics During the Civil War Period* (New York, 1968), 138–39; Columbus *Crisis*, May 14, 1862.

18. August Belmont, *Letters, Speeches and Addresses of August Belmont* (New York, 1890), 134: John Van Buren to Samuel J. Tilden, September 4, 1863, in *Letters and Literary Memorial of Samuel J. Tilden*, edited by John Bigelow, 2 vols. (New York, 1908), I: 34; McPherson, *Battle Cry of Freedom*, 506.

19. Edmund Ruffin, *The Diary of Edmund Ruffin: The Years of Hope, April, 1862–June, 1863* (Baton Rouge, LA, 1976), 34: McPherson, *Battle Cry of Freedom*, 506.

20. Foote, *Civil War*, I: 708; McPherson, *Battle Cry of Freedom*, 559–60.

21. George H. Porter, *Ohio Politics During the Civil War Period* (New York, 1911; reprinted 1968), 144–58; Resolution of the Pennsylvania Democratic Convention, July 4, 1862, quoted in William Lofton, Jr., "Northern Labor and the Negro During the Civil War," *Journal of Negro History* 34 (1949), 254; Forrest G. Wood, *Black Scare: The Racist Response to Emancipation and Reconstruction* (Berkeley, CA, 1968), 35; Congressman Samuel S. Cox in House of Representatives, *Congressional Globe*, 37th Congress, 2d Session, Appendix, 242–49; Senator Lyman Trumbull in Senate, *Congressional Globe*, 37th Congress, 2d Session, 1780.

22. *CWL*, V: 436–37; Robert E. Sterling, "Civil War Draft Resistance in the Middle West," Ph.D. dissertation, Northern Illinois University (1974), chaps. 3–4; McPherson, *Battle Cry of Freedom*, 492–94; Peter Levine, "Draft Evasion in the North During the Civil War, 1863–1865" in *Journal of American History* 67, no. 4 (March 1981), 816–34; "Final Report Made to the Secretary of War, by the Provost Marshal General," *House Executive Documents*, 39th Congress, 1st Session (Washington, DC, 1866), 165–213.

23. Sullivan *Democrat*, June 25, 1863; July 2, 1863.

24. Oliver P. Morton MSS, W. R. Holloway to Morton, July 18, 1863; Sullivan *Democrat*, June 25, 1863; Vincennes *Gazette*, July 11, 1863; Indianapolis *Daily Sentinel*, June 29, 1863.

25. Huntington *Democrat*, September 25, 1862; Goshen *Democrat*, October 1, 1862; New Albany *Weekly Ledger*, October 1, 1862; as cited in Tredway, *Democratic Opposition in Indiana*.

26. *Congressional Globe*, 37th Congress, 3rd Session, 1293, 1389; Robert E. Sterling, *Civil War Draft Resistance in the Midwest*, Ph.D. dissertation, Northern Illinois University, 1974, 150.

27. Wood Gray, *The Hidden Civil War: The Story of the Copperheads* (New York, 1942; reprinted 1964), 122.

28. Ibid.

29. McPherson, *Battle Cry of Freedom*, 605–9.

30. Joseph Fried, ". . . The Draft Riots," in *Civil War Times Illustrated* 4, no. 5 (August 1965): 4–10, 28–31.

31. Ibid., 8–9.

32. Lt. Col. Arthur J. L. Fremantle, *Three Months in the Southern States* (New York, 1864; reprinted 1991, Lincoln, NE), 300.

33. Fried, "Draft Riots," 29; McPherson, *Battle Cry of Freedom*, 610.

34. Gray, *Hidden Civil War*, 215–16.

35. Detroit *Free Press*, March 6–8, 1863; Illinois *State Register*, March 9, 1863.

36. William Dudley Foulke, *Life of Oliver P. Morton* (Indianapolis, 1898), 229–39.

37. *Illinois State Journal*, June 15, 1863; Illinois Senate, *Journal of the Senate of the Twenty-Third General Assembly of the State of Illinois, at Their Regular Session, Begun and Held at Springfield, January 5, 1863* (Springfield, IL, 1865), 297–98; Illinois House of Representatives, *Journal of the House of Representatives of the Twenty-Third General Assembly of the State of Illinois, at Their Regular Session, Begun and Held at Springfield, January 5, 1863* (Springfield, IL, 1865), 78, 280; Nevins, *War Becomes Revolution*, 392; Chicago *Tribune*, June 11, 1863.

38. Among the prominent War Democrats were Ulysses S. Grant, Edwin Stanton, George Meade, Andrew Johnson, John Brough, John Schofield, William Sprague, Benjamin Butler, David Tod, John A. Dix, John A. McClernand, Lew Wallace, John A. Logan, Irvin McDowell, Henry Halleck, Joseph Holt, George Thomas, William Cannon, and John A. Rawlins.

39. Christopher Dell, *Lincoln and the War Democrats: The Grand Erosion of Conservative Tradition* (Rutherford, NJ, 1975), 236–37, 242, 244–45, 247, 252–53, 255, 258, 276, 280.

40. Ruffin, *Diary: Years of Hope*, Scarborough, ed., 34; Joel H. Silbey, *A Respectable Minority: The Democratic Party in the Civil War Era, 1860–1868* (New York, 1977), chaps. 4–6.

41. Union League of Philadelphia, *Addresses and Resolutions* (n.p., n.d.), September 16, 1863; Harrisburg (PA) *Patriot and Union*, June 25, 1863; Whitelaw Reid, *Ohio in the Civil War*, 2 vols. (Columbus, OH, 1893), I: 168; John P. Pritchett, "Michigan Democracy in the Civil War," in *Michigan History Magazine* XI, no. 1 (January 1927), 92–109; Dell, *Lincoln and the War Democrats*, 231–61.

42. Ibid.

CHAPTER FIVE
"Must I Shoot a Simple-Minded Soldier Boy?"

1. Robert E. Sterling, "Civil War Draft Resistance in the Middle West," Ph.D. Dissertation, Northern Illinois University, 1974, 129, 248, 545; as cited in McPherson, *Battle Cry of Freedom*, 493.

2. Dayton *Daily Ledger*, May 27, 1863, as reported in Frank L. Klement, *The Limits of Dissent: Clement L. Vallandigham & the Civil War* (Lexington, KY, 1970), 202–4; Gray, *Hidden Civil War*, 124.

3. Braxton Bragg to Samuel Cooper, June 1, 1863, *O.R.*, Ser. II, Vol. 5, 965–68; Jefferson Davis to Bragg, June 7, 1863, Vallandigham Papers, as cited in Klement's *Limits of Dissent*.

4. Seddon to Ould, *O.R.*, Ser. II, Vol. 5, 968; Jones, *A Rebel War Clerk's Diary* (Philadelphia, 1866), II: 729–30.

5. Seddon to Ould, *O.R.*, Ser. II, Vol. 5, 968; Jones, *A Rebel War Clerk's Diary*, II: 729–30.

6. Richmond *Sentinel*, June 25, 1863, as cited in Klement, *Limits of Dissent*, 211–12.

7. *O.R.*, Ser. II, Vol. 6, 48–53, 56–59, 64–68; Columbus *Crisis*, June 17, 1863.

8. Vallandigham to Manton Marble, May 12, 15, 1863, Manton Marble Papers, Library of Congress.

9. Detroit *Free Press*, August 26, 1863.

10. *Harper's Weekly*, May 30, 1863.

11. Cox to Manton Marble, June 1, 1863; Klement, *Limits of Dissent*, 183–84.

12. Entry of May 5, 1863, Daniel Read Larned, "Journal," Daniel Read Larned Papers, Library of Congress; Vallandigham spoke at a Democratic rally on October 10, 1867, where he related what happened during his arrest in 1863; the speech was reported in the Dayton *Daily Ledger*, October 30, 1867; Cincinnati *Daily Enquirer*, May 6, 1863; cited in Klement, *Limits of Dissent*, 157–59.

13. Dayton *Daily Empire*, May 5, 1863; Dayton *Daily Journal*, May 6, 1863; Burnside, "Special Orders, No. 164," published in the Dayton *Daily Journal*, May 7, 1863; Klement, *Limits of Dissent*, 160–61.

14. Klement, *Limits of Dissent*.

15. CWL, VI: 451–52.

16. Ibid.

17. *Historical Times Illustrated Encyclopedia of the Civil War*, edited by Patricia L. Faust (New York, 1986), 96–97. As a young officer, Burnside had established a reputation that would stick for the rest of his career when his betrothed left him standing alone at the altar.

18. *O.R.*, Ser. I, Vol. 23, Pt. 2, 381; Richard Yates to Secretary of War Edwin Stanton, August 7, 1862, *O.R.*, Ser. III, Vol. 2, 316; *Diary of Gideon Welles*, I: 321; *O.R.*, Ser II, Vol. 5, 724; as cited in J. G. Randall, *Constitutional Problems Under Lincoln* (Gloucester, MA, 1963), 494–95.

19. *O.R.*, Ser. II, Vol. 5, 724.

20. *CWL*, VI: 300–2.

21. Ibid.

22. Ibid., 303–4.

23. Ibid.

24. Ibid., 304–5.

25. Ibid., 305

26. Strong, *Diary*, 330; CWL, VI: 319–20; Henry Adams to Charles Francis Adams, Jr., July 23, 1863, in *A Cycle of Adams Letters,* edited by Worthington C. Ford, 2 vols. (Boston, 1920), II: 59–60; McPherson, *Battle Cry of Freedom*, 664.

27. *CWL*, VI: 406–7.

28. Ibid., 407.

29. Ibid., 407–8.

30. Ibid., 408–9.

31. Ibid., 409.

32. Ibid.

33. Ibid., 410.

34. Ibid.

35. Abraham Lincoln during his first debate with Stephen Douglas at Ottawa, Illinois, August 21, 1858, in *Lincoln on Black and White: A Documentary History*, edited by Arthur Zilversmit (original edition 1971, reprint edition 1983 at Malabar, FL), 42.

CHAPTER SIX
"With Malice toward None, with Charity for All"

1. Jesse M. Fell to Trumbull, August 11, 1863, Lyman Trumbull MSS, Library of Congress.

2. *O.R.*, Ser. II, Vol. 4, 857, 916, 940–41, 945–46, 954; Colonel Frank Powers to Colonel Jonathan L. Logan, September 2, 1863, in *Freedom: A Documentary History of Emancipation*, Series II, *The Black Military Experience*, edited by Ira Berlin et al. (Cambridge, MA, 1982), 585; Jefferson Davis to Robert E. Lee, Braxton Bragg, and Edmund Kirby Smith, September 7, 1862, in Jefferson Davis, *Jefferson Davis: Constitutionalist, His Letters, Papers, and Speeches,* edited by Dunbar Rowland (New York, 1923), V: 338–39; Richmond *Examiner*, March 4, 1864; Richmond *Dispatch*, March 5, 1864; Richmond *Sentinel*, March 5, 1864.

3. Ibid.; Richmond *Whig*, March 7, 1864; Richmond *Dispatch*, March 5, 1864; John W. Headley, *Confederate Operations in Canada and New York* (New York, 1906), 175.

4. Davis, *Letters, Papers, and Speeches*, V: 409.

5. *O.R.*, Ser. II, Vol. 4, 916; James D. Richardson (comp.), *A Compilation of the Messages and Papers of the Confederacy Including the Diplomatic Correspondence 1861–1865* (Nashville, TN, 1906), I: 290–91; Richmond *Enquirer*, December 17, 1863.

6. William Hanchett, *The Lincoln Murder Conspiracies* (Urbana, IL, 1983), 7–34.

7. William A. Tidwell with James O. Hall and David Winfred Gaddy, *Come Retribution: The Confederate Secret Service and the Assassination of Lincoln* (Jackson, MS, 1988), 241–45.

8. Headley, *Confederate Operations in Canada and New York*, 176.

9. Richmond *Examiner*, March 4, 1864.

10. The dispute centered on Dahlgren's signature, which appeared to be misspelled. The Confederates photographed the documents, and it did appear that the signature was "Dahlgren." Of course, the writer of the document would have known how to spell his own name, and this constituted the strongest evidence presented by Northern skeptics that the papers were forgeries. However, in 1955, historian V. C. Jones, assisted by Elmer O. Parker, supervisory archivist in the Army and Air Corps Branch of the National Archives, studied the only remaining photocopy of the original orders (the original had apparently been destroyed in the Richmond fires in April 1865), and under special lighting they were able to determine that the "ink forming the tail of the 'y' in the word 'destroying' had

soaked through the sheet at the exact spot to make the 'h' in Dahlgren's name appear to be an 'l,' thus causing what had been taken to be a transposition."

11. Emory M. Thomas, "The Kilpatrick-Dahlgren Raid," *Civil War Times Illustrated* 17 (April 1978), 32.

12. Headley, *Confederate Operations in Canada and New York*, 176.

13. Richmond *Dispatch*, March 5, 1864.

14. Richmond *Sentinel*, March 5, 1864.

15. Richmond *Whig*, March 7, 1864.

16. Tidwell, Hall and Gaddy, *Come Retribution*, 247; Nelson, *Bullets, Ballots, and Rhetoric*, 20–25, 30–33.

17. Bruce Catton, *A Stillness at Appomattox* (New York, 1953), 22–24.

18. Welles, *Diary*, II: 24; *CWL*, VII: 329, 345–46; Nicolay and Hay, *Lincoln*, VI: 478–84.

19. Nicolay and Hay, *Lincoln*, VI: 478–84.

20. Welles, *Diary*, II: 24; *CWL*, VII: 329, 345–46; McPherson, *Battle Cry of Freedom*, 794.

21. Dunbar Rowland, ed., *Jefferson Davis, Constitutionalist, His Letters, Papers, and Speeches*, 10 vols. (Jackson, MS, 1923), V: 409; *O.R.*, Ser. II, Vol. 4, 857, 945–46, 954.

22. Larry E. Nelson, *Bullets, Ballots, and Rhetoric: Confederate Policy for the United States Presidential Contest in 1864* (University, AL, 1980), 18–19.

23. Ibid.; Jefferson Davis, *Rise and Fall of the Confederate Government* (London, England, 1881), II: 611.

24. Jefferson Davis to Robert E. Lee, Braxton Bragg, and Edmund Kirby Smith, September 7, 1862, in Davis, *Letters, Papers, and Speeches*, Rowland, ed., V: 338–39.

25. Nelson, *Bullets, Ballots, and Rhetoric*, 18–19, 26; McPherson, *Battle Cry of Freedom*, 561–62.

26. Oscar A. Kinchen, *Confederate Operations in Canada and the North* (North Quincy, MA, 1970), 29; R. A. Alston letter to War Department in Jones, *Diary*, II: 155; J. W. Tucker to Jefferson Davis, March 14, 1864, in Davis, *Letters, Papers, and Speeches,* Rowland, ed., VI: 206; Frank L. Klement, *Dark Lanterns: Secret Political Societies, Conspiracies, and Treason Trials in the Civil War* (Baton Rouge, LA, 1984).

27. John Hunt Morgan to James A. Seddon, January 27, 1864, in *O.R.*, Ser. I, Vol. 32, Pt. 2, 621–22; Stephen R. Mallory to James D. McCulloch, March 21, 1864, in *Official Records of the Union and Confederate Navies in the War of the Rebellion,* hereafter referred to as *O.R., Navies* (Washington, DC, 1894–1927), Ser. II, Vol. 2, 613.

28. Benjamin H. Hill, speech at LaGrange, Georgia, March 1, 1864, reported in Augusta *Chronicle & Sentinel*, March 18, 1864.

29. Ibid.

30. Morgan to James A. Seddon, January 27, 1864, in Ibid., Pt. II, 621–22.

31. Chicago *Tribune*, reprinted in Augusta *Constitutionalist,* May 1, 1864.

32. Augusta *Chronicle & Sentinel*, March 29, 1864; Richmond *Sentinel*, April

29, 1864; Mobile *Daily Advertiser and Register*, April 23 and 30, 1864; Jones, *Diary*, II: 187; Galveston *Tri-Weekly News*, May 1, 1864; Richmond *Examiner*, January 25, 1864.

33. New York *Daily News*, reprinted in Richmond *Sentinel*, April 15, 1864.

34. Jones, *Diary*, II: 229.

35. *O.R.*, Ser. I, Vol. 32, Pt. II, 172; Nelson, *Bullets, Ballots, and Rhetoric*, 44.

36. Augustus R. Wright, "Resolution," U.S. Congress, Senate, *Journal of the Congress of the Confederate States of America,* S. Doc. 234, 58th Congress, 2d session, 1904, VI, 738.

37. Jones, *Diary*, II: 143; Selma *Daily Reporter*, February 10, 1864; as cited in Nelson, *Bullets, Ballots, and Rhetoric*, 33.

38. Congress to the People of the Confederacy (February 17, 1864), *O.R.*, Ser. IV, Vol. 3, 129–37; as cited in Nelson, *Bullets, Ballots, and Rhetoric*, 34.

39. Alexander H. Stephens to Jefferson Davis, April 9, 1864, in Georgia Portfolio, II, 50, Duke University; Jefferson Davis to Alexander H. Stephens, April 19, 1864, in Davis, *Letters, Papers, and Speeches*, Rowland, ed., VI: 231.

40. Nelson, *Bullets, Ballots, and Rhetoric*, 45.

41. Thomas H. Hines, "The Northwestern Conspiracy," *Southern Bivouac*, New Series II (1886), 443; James D. Horan, *Confederate Agent: Discovery in History* (New York, 1954).

42. Kinchen, *Confederate Operations in Canada*, 55; *O.R.*, Ser. 1, Vol. 43, Pt. 2, 930–36.

43. Ibid.

44. Indianapolis *Daily Sentinel*, January 9, 1864; Joseph J. Bingham, testimony, October 28, 1864, in Proceedings of the Military Commission Convened in Indianapolis, General Courts Martial Records, Records of the Office of the Judge Advocate General, National Archives; Klement, *Dark Lanterns*, 91–135.

45. Nicolay and Hay, *Lincoln*, VIII: 13.

46. Headley, *Confederate Operations in Canada and New York*, 222–23; Klement, *Dark Lanterns*, 214.

47. Thompson to John Slidell and James M. Mason, August 23, 1864, in Hines, "Northwest Conspiracy," 502, 505–6.

48. Ibid.; Headley, *Confederate Operations in Canada and New York*, 222–23.

49. Ibid.; Castelman, *Active Service*; Headley, *Confederate Operations in Canada and New York*; Klement, *Dark Lanterns*, 214–15.

50. Frank L. Klement, *The Copperheads in the Middle West* (Chicago, 1960); Klement, *Dark Lanterns*; Klement, *The Limits of Dissent*; Robert Rutland, "The Copperheads of Iowa: A re-examination," in *Iowa Journal of History* LII (1954), 1–54; David Lindsey, *"Sunset" Cox: Irrepressible Democrat* (Detroit, MI, 1959); Justin E. Walsh, "Radically and Thoroughly Democratic: Wilbur F. Storey and the Detroit *Free Press*," *Michigan History* XLVII (1963), 193–225; John D. Bankhart, "The Impact of the Civil War in Indiana," *Indiana Magazine of History* LVII (1961), 185–224.

51. McPherson, *Battle Cry of Freedom*, 76; Gray, *Hidden Civil War*, 185.

52. Richmond *Sentinel*, July 15, 1864.

53. Horan, *Confederate Agent*, 134–35.

54. Note regarding James C. Robinson in Hines's signature, Hines Papers, University of Kentucky.

55. Castelman, *Active Service*, 168–71.

56. Horan, *Confederate Agent*, 135.

57. Hines's accounting of money expended in support of Northwest Confederacy, Hines Papers, University of Kentucky; Thompson to Judah P. Benjamin, December 3, 1864, *O.R.,* Ser. I, Vol. 43, 930–36.

58. Headley, *Confederate Operations in Canada and New York*, 231–36

59. Nelson, *Bullets, Ballots, and Rhetoric*, 62; Clement Clay and James Holcombe to Jefferson Davis, July 25, 1864, in Clement C. Clay Papers, Duke University; Clement Clay to Judah P. Benjamin, August 11, 1864, in *Southern Historical Society Papers*, VII: 335–36.

60. Ibid., 335; Herschel V. Johnson to Alexander H. Stephens, September 28, 1864, Herschel V. Johnson Papers, Duke University; *New York Times*, July 21, 1864; Lincoln memorandum "To Whom It May Concern," in *CWL*, VII: 451; John R. Brumgardt, "Presidential Duel at Midsummer: The 'Peace' Missions to Canada and Richmond, 1864," *Lincoln Herald* 78, no. 4 (Fall 1975), 97; Clay to Benjamin, August 11, 1864, in *O.R.*, Ser. IV, Vol. 3, 585–86.

61. Stephen R. Mallory to Mrs. Clement C. Clay, August 1, 1864, Clement C. Clay Papers, Duke University, as cited in Brumgardt, "Presidential Duel at Midsummer," 98.

62. Clay to Benjamin, August 11, 1864, in *O.R.*, Ser. IV, Vol. 3, 585–86; McPherson, *Battle Cry of Freedom*, 767.

63. Columbus *Crisis*, August 3, 1864.

64. Nicolay and Hay, *Lincoln*, IX: 193–94.

65. Stephen R. Mallory to Mrs. Clement C. Clay, August 1, 1864, in Clement C. Clay Papers, Duke University; Richmond *Dispatch*, July 27, 1864; Richmond *Examiner*, July 27, 1864; Charleston *Mercury*, August 1, 1864; Nelson, *Bullets, Ballots, and Rhetoric*, 80–81.

66. Clay to Benjamin, August 11, 1864, in *O.R.*, Ser. IV, Vol. 3, 585.

67. Headley, *Confederate Operations in Canada and New York*, 234–39, 248–54.

68. Ibid., 231–55; William Frank Zornow, "Confederate Raiders on Lake Erie: Their Propaganda Value in 1864," in two parts, *Inland Seas* V (Spring 1949), 42–47, 101–5; Allan Keller, "Canada and the Civil War," in *Civil War Times Illustrated* III (November 1964), 45.

69. Headley, *Confederate Operations in Canada and New York*, 256–63; Horan, *Confederate Agent*, 166–80.

70. Thompson to Benjamin, December 3, 1864, in *O.R.*, Ser. I, Vol. 43, Pt. 2, 930–36; Horan, *Confederate Agent*, 208–11; Headley, *Confederate Operations in Canada and New York*, 263–67.

71. Horan, *Confederate Agent*, 181–84; Headley, *Confederate Operations in Canada and New York*, 284; Hines, "The Northwestern Conspiracy."

72. Horan, *Confederate Agent*, 181–83.

73. Headley, *Confederate Operations in Canada and New York*, 267.

74. Ibid., 284–87.

75. *New York Times*, November 6, 1864.

76. Headley, *Confederate Operations in Canada and New York* , 284–87.

77. Ibid., 274–79.

CHAPTER SEVEN
"We Shall Nobly Save or Meanly Lose"

1. Horace Greeley, *The American Conflict: A History of the Great Rebellion in the United States of America, 1860–'65*, 2 vols. (Hartford, CT, 1867), II: 665; Henry Luther Stoddard, *Horace Greeley: Printer, Editor, Crusader* (New York, 1946), 163–206.

2. Stoddard, *Horace Greeley*, 207–28.

3. W. C. Jewett, *The Friendly American Mediation Move of the Emperor of France* (Portland, ME, 1862), 4–7; W. C. Jewett, *Mediation Address to England* (London, 1863?), 5; W. C. Jewett, *Mediation Position of France in Connection with the Congress of Nations* (London, 1863?), 5–8, 18–20; W. C. Jewett, *National Appeal in Connection with the Independent Peace Mission of William Cornell Jewett* (London, 1863?); W. C. Jewett, *A National Appeal to the American People and the Church Universal* (New York, 1864), as cited in Edward Chase Kirkland, *The Peacemakers of 1864* (New York, 1927), 68–71.

4. Castelman, *Active Service*, 135–36; *O.R.*, Ser. II, Vol. II, 220–23.

5. New York *Tribune*, January 15 and March 19, 1864, as cited in Kirkland, *Peacemakers of 1864*, 71.

6. *CWL*, VII: 436.

7. Horace Greeley to Lincoln, July 7, 1864, *CWL*, VII: 435nn.

8. Ibid.

9. *WL*, VII: 435; Nicolay and Hay, *Lincoln*, VII: 187–88.

10. Nicolay and Hay, *Lincoln*, IX: 186.

11. Lincoln to Horace Greeley, July 9, 1864, *CWL*, VII: 435.

12. *CWL*, VII: 440–41.

13. Greeley to Lincoln, July 13, 1864, *CWL*, VII: 441n.

14. Ibid.

15. George N. Sanders, July 12, 1864, in McPherson, *A Political History of the United States During the Great Rebellion,* 301.

16. Ibid.

17. Lincoln telegram to Greeley, July 15, 1864, *CWL*, VII: 440.

18. Lincoln to Greeley, July 15, 1864, *CWL*, VII: 441–42.

19. Lincoln telegram to John Hay, *CWL*, VII: 443.

20. Greeley to commissioners, July 17, 1864, in McPherson, *A Political History of the United States During the Great Rebellion,* 301.

21. C. C. Clay, Jr. and J. P. Holcombe to Greeley, July 18, 1864, in McPherson, *A Political History of the United States During the Great Rebellion,* 301.

22. Nicolay and Hay, *Lincoln*, IX: 191–92.

23. Ibid.

24. Lincoln proclamation, July 18, 1864, in *CWL*, VII: 451.

25. Allan Nevins, *The War for the Union: The Organized War to Victory 1864–1865* (New York, 1971), 88–89.

26. Frank E. Vandiver, *Jubal's Raid* (New York, 1960), 122–79; London *Times*, quoted in Shelby Foote, *The Civil War: A Narrative*, 3 vols. (New York, 1974), III: 461; Charles Medary to Samuel Medary, July 20, 1864, Samuel Medary Papers, Ohio Historical Society; New York *World*, July 12, 1864.

27. Nicolay and Hay, *Lincoln*, IX; John Hay, *Letters of John Hay and Extracts From Diary*, 3 vols. (Washington, DC, 1908), I: 216–17.

28. Nicolay and Hay, *Lincoln*, IX: 195–96; Hay, *Letters and Extracts From Diaries*, 217–18; McPherson, *A Political History of the United States During the Great Rebellion*, 301–2.

29. McPherson, *A Political History of the United States During the Great Rebellion*, 301–2.

30. Ibid.

31. Nicolay and Hay, *Lincoln*, IX: 195–97; Zornow, *Lincoln & the Party Divided*, 109.

32. Henry J. Raymond, *The Life and Public Services of Abraham Lincoln* (New York, 1865), 195–96.

33. Raymond, *Life, Services, and Papers of Lincoln*, 586; Welles, *Diary*, II: 111–12.

34. Nicolay and Hay, *Lincoln*, IX: 199; Donnal V. Smith, *Chase and Civil War Politics*, 148–49; John Shaffer to Benjamin Butler, August 17, 1864, in Marshall, ed., *Butler Correspondence*, V: 67–69; Henry L. Stoddard, *Horace Greeley, Printer, Editor, Crusader* (New York, 1946), 227; Zornow, *Lincoln & the Party Divided*, 114.

35. John R. Brumgardt, "Presidential Duel at Midsummer: The 'Peace' Missions to Canada and Richmond, 1864," *Lincoln Herald* 77, no. 2 (Summer 1975), 98.

36. Col. James F. Jaquess to Gen. James A. Garfield, May 19, 1863, cited in Nicolay and Hay, *Lincoln*, IX: 202.

37. William Rosecrans to Lincoln, May 21, 1863, in *CWL*, VI: 225f.

38. Lincoln to William Rosecrans, May 28, 1863, in *CWL*, VI: 236.

39. Nicolay and Hay, *Lincoln*, IX: 205–6.

40. James R. Gilmore, *Personal Recollections of Abraham Lincoln and the Civil War* (Boston, 1898), 66–102.

41. Ibid., 141–49; 156–64.

42. James R. Gilmore, "Our Last Day in Dixie," *Atlantic Monthly* XIV (December 1864), 725; Kirkland, *Peacemakers of 1864*, 92; Brumgardt, "Presidential Duel at Midsummer," 99.

43. New York *Tribune*, September 5, 1864; James R. Gilmore, "Our Visit to Richmond," *Atlantic Monthly* XIV (September 1964), 372–73.

44. Nicolay and Hay, *Lincoln*, IX: 206.

45. James G. Randall, *Constitutional Problems Under Lincoln* (Gloucester, MA, 1963), 59–73; *Prize Cases*, 67 U.S. 635, 666, 670; *Ford vs. Surget*, 97 U.S.

605, 612; *Miller vs. United States,* 78 U.S. 306–7; *Congressional Globe,* 37th Congress, 2d session, 1717, 2189–90, 2234–35, 2299; J. G. Randall and David Donald, *The Civil War and Reconstruction* (Lexington, MA, 1969), 293–95.

46. Gilmore, *Personal Recollections,* 243–46; Gilmore, *Suppressed Chapter,* 444–45; Kirkland, *Peacemakers of 1864,* 92.

47. Gilmore, *Personal Recollections,* 238–59; *O.R., Navies,* Ser. II, Vol. 3, 1191.

48. Boston *Evening Transcript,* July 22, 1864.

49. Ibid.

50. Strong, *Diary of the Civil War,* 474.

51. McPherson, *Battle Cry of Freedom,* 768–71.

CHAPTER EIGHT
"With Malignant Heart and Deceitful Speech"

1. Nicolay and Hay, *Lincoln,* VIII: 1.

2. Ibid.

3. Jacob Thompson to Judah P. Benjamin, in *O.R.,* Ser. I, Vol. 43, pt. 2, 930–36; Frank Klement, *Dark Lanterns: Secret Political Societies, Conspiracies, and Treason Trials in the Civil War* (Baton Rouge, 1984), 33, 154–77.

4. Nicolay and Hay, *Lincoln,* VIII: 6

5. Beaver Dam (Wisconsin) *Argus,* n.d. 1864; La Crosse (Wisconsin) *Democrat.*

6. Benn Pitman, *Assassination of President Lincoln, 1865* (Cincinnati, 1865) 39, 45, 49, 125, 127, 174.

7. Oscar A. Kinchen, *Confederate Operations in Canada and the North* (North Quincy, MA, 1970), 29–30; James D. Horan, *Confederate Agent: A Discovery in History,* (New York, 1954), 72–73; William A. Tidwell, with James O. Hall and David Winfred Galby, *Come Retribution: The Confederate Secret Service and the Assassination of Lincoln* (Jackson, MS, 1988), 20, 24, 66.

8. Klement, *Dark Lanterns*; Wood Gray, *The Hidden Civil War: The Story of the Copperheads* (New York, 1942, 1964); Frank L. Klement, *Limits of Dissent: Clement L. Vallandigham and the Civil War* (Lexington, KY, 1970); Frank L. Klement, *The Copperheads in the Middle West* (Lexington, KY, 1960); G. R. Tredway, *Opposition to the Lincoln Administration in Indiana* (Indianapolis, IN, 1973); George Fort Milton, *Abraham Lincoln and the Fifth Column* (New York, 1952).

9. Horan, *Confederate Agent,* xiv–xviii, 286–88.

10. Ibid.

11. Ibid., 286.

12. Ibid.

13. Ibid., 287.

14. Ibid

15. Ibid., 287–88.

16. Ibid.

17. Castelman, *Active Service,* 157–91.

18. Headley, *Confederate Operations,* 267; Castelman, *Active Service,* 168–71; Thomas H. Hines, "The Northwestern Conspiracy," *The Southern Bivouac: A Monthly Literary and Historical Magazine,* new series, II (1887), 437–45, 500–10; Gray, *The Hidden Civil War,* 166–69.

19. Gray, *The Hidden Civil War,* 172–88.

20. Ibid.

21. "The Chicago Conspiracy," *Atlantic Monthly* XVI (July 1865), 108–20.

22. Columbus *Crisis,* June 22, June 15, July 20, 1864.

23. Ibid., July 13, 1864.

24. Ibid., March 30, April 6, 1864; Cincinnati *Daily Enquirer,* March 24, 1864; Gray, *Hidden Civil War,* 173.

25. Alexander H. Long address before the House, April 8, 1864, *Congressional Globe,* 38th Congress, 1st session, 1499–1503.

26. *Crisis,* July 13, July 27, August 3, August 17, September 7, 1864; Rockford (Illinois) *Register,* April 30, 1864; *Crisis,* July 6, 1864, reprinted from the Indianapolis *Sentinel; Crisis,* August 3, 1864.

27. Chicago *Times,* August 1, 1864.

28. *CWL,* VII: 448–49, 451; *O.R.,* Ser. III, Vol. IV, 515–16.

29. La Crosse *Democrat,* August 2, 1864; Gray, *Hidden Civil War,* 175.

30. Ibid.; Cairo *City Democrat,* July 23, 1864.

31. *O.R.,* Ser. III, Vol. 4, 632–33; Ibid., 569; S. P. Heintzelman to Henry W. Halleck, August 9, 1864, in *O.R.,* Ser. III, Vol. 4, 1286–87; Ibid., 682–84.

32. *Crisis,* August 17, 1864, Chicago *Times;* Gray, *Hidden Civil War,* 181.

33. Detroit *Advertiser and Tribune,* August 18, 1864.

34. Ibid.

35. Gray, *Hidden Civil War,* 179.

36. Dayton *Daily Empire,* June 16, 1864; Cincinnati *Daily Commercial,* June 16, 1864; Vallandigham, *Vallandigham,* 352–53; Klement, *Limits of Dissent,* 271–72.

37. Ibid.

38. Dayton *Daily Empire,* June 16, 1864; Klement, *Limits of Dissent,* 274.

39. Report of William Taylor, June 18, 1864, in John P. Sanderson Papers, Ohio Historical Society; Samuel P. Heintzelman Papers, Library of Congress.

40. Murat Halstead to William Henry Smith, June 21, 1864, William Henry Smith Papers, Indiana State Historical Society Library, Indianapolis, IN; New York *Tribune,* June 17, 1864; *CWL,* VII: 402; Detroit *Free Press,* July 17, 1864; Klement, *Limits of Dissent,* 276–77.

41. Thompson to Benjamin, July 7, 1864, cited in Hines, "Northwestern Conspiracy," 507; J. P. Holcombe to Clement C. Clay, July 10, 1864, quoted in Kinchen, *Confederate Operations in Canada,* 55; Thompson to Benjamin, December 3, 1864, in *O.R.,* Ser. I, Vol. 43, Pt. 2, 931; Nelson, *Bullets, Ballots, and Rhetoric,* 87–88; McPherson, *Battle Cry of Freedom,* 765.

42. Thompson to Benjamin, December 3, 1864, in *O.R.,* Ser. I, Vol. 43, Pt. 2,

931; Thompson to John Slidell and James M. Mason, August 23, 1864; McPherson, *Battle Cry of Freedom*, 765.

43. Thompson to Benjamin, December 3, 1864.

44. Gray, *Hidden Civil War*, 179.

45. Kinchen, *Confederate Operations in Canada*, 55; Thompson to Benjamin, December 3, 1864, in *O.R.*, Ser. I, Vol. 43, Pt. II, 931–32; Horan, *Confederate Agent*, 121–28; Castelman, *Active Service*, 148, 157–59; Report of Capt. John B. Castelman to Secretary of War James A. Seddon, September 7, 1864, in *O.R.*, Ser. I, Vol. 45, Pt. I, 1077–78; Headley, *Confederate Operations in Canada and New York*, 225–28; Kirkland, *Peacemakers of 1864*, 125–26.

46. Hines, "The Northwestern Conspiracy," 567–74; Castelman, *Active Service*, 157–59.

47. William E. Larners, *The Edge of Glory: A Biography of General William S. Rosecrans, U.S.A.* (New York, 1961), as cited in Stewart Sifakis, *Who Was Who in the Union* (New York, 1988), 342–43; Missouri *Democrat*, July 28, 1864; Chicago *Daily Tribune*, July 31, 1864; Cincinnati *Daily Gazette*, July 30, 1864; Illinois *State Journal*, July 30, August 1, 1864; New York *Tribune*, July 29, 1864.

48. George Fort Milton, *Abraham Lincoln and the Fifth Column* (New York, 1952), 73–74; *Tribune Almanac for 1860*, 57–58; Indianapolis *Daily Sentinel*, May 25, 1871; Foulke, *Life of Morton*, 1: 374, 405, 407; Carrington to General Lorenzo Thomas, February 18, 1863, JAGO NN3409, box 1165; Felix G. Stidger, *Treason History of the Sons of Liberty, Formerly Circle of Honor, Succeeded by Knights of the Golden Circle, Afterward Order of American Knights*, hereafter referred to as *Treason History* (Chicago, 1903), 55–57; Tredway, *Democratic Opposition in Indiana*, 215–16.

49. Carrington to Henry S. Lane, January 12, 1863, in Henry S. Lane Papers, Lilly Library, Indiana University; Morton to Stanton, January 2, 1863, in Letter Press Books of Governor Oliver P. Morton, 9 vols., Archives Division, Indiana State Library; Morton to Carrington, July 7, 1863, in Departmental and General Telegrams (hereafter referred to as Telegrams), 18 vols., Archives Division, Indiana State Library, 11: 128; Carrington to W. R. Holloway, July 9, 1863, in Ibid., 1: 143; G. R. Tredway, *Democratic Opposition to the Lincoln Administration in Indiana* (Indianapolis, IN, 1973), 209–10.

50. Carrington to Stanton, December 22, 1862, Records of the Judge Advocate General's Office (hereafter referred to as JAGO), General Courts-Martial, 1812–1939, NN3409, box 1165; Carrington to Stanton and Lincoln, March 19, 1863, *O.R.*, Ser. II, Vol. 5, 363–67; Carrington to Stanton, February 17, 1863, in JAGO, NN 3409, box 1165; Carrington to General Lorenzo Thomas, January 24, February 18, 1863, Ibid.; Indianapolis *Daily Sentinel*, March 27, 1863.

51. Terrell, *Report of the Adjutant General*, I: appendix, 107; *O.R.*, Ser. I, Vol. 23, Pt. 2, 168; Halleck to Burnside, March 30, 1863, Ibid., 193–94; Thomas to Carrington, March 20, 1863, in Carrington Papers, Archives Division, Indiana State Library; Burnside to Stanton and Stanton to Burnside, April 6, 1863, *O.R.*, Ser. I, Vol. 23, Pt. 2, 216–17; Tredway, *Democratic Opposition in Indiana*, 212.

52. Indianapolis *Daily Sentinel*, August 29, September 7, 1864; Burnside to Carrington, April 23, 1863, in Carrington Papers; Burnside to Morton, April 22, 1863, in Telegrams, 16: 179; Carrington to Morton at Madison, IN, April 22, 1863, in Carrington Papers; Morton to Carrington, April 22, 1863, Ibid.; Burnside to Morton, April 22, 25, 27, May 2, 1863, in Telegrams, 16: 179, 181, 183, 185; Morton to Burnside, April 25, May 2, 1863, in Telegrams, 16: 180, 182, 184; Indianapolis *Daily Journal*, April 23, 1863; Carrington to Morton, June 5, 1863, in "Civil War Letters and Dispatches," edited by Harvey Wish, *Indiana Magazine of History* 33 (1937), 69–70; Tredway, *Democratic Opposition in Indiana*, 213–14.

53. Indianapolis *Daily Sentinel*, May 25, 1871; Morton to James Speed, Louisville, KY, July 9, 1862, in Telegrams, 4: 72; Colonel J. M. Shackelford, Henderson, KY, to Morton, October 8, 1862, in Telegrams, 9: 55; Foulke, *Life of Morton*, 1: 374, 405, 407; Carrington to General Lorenzo Thomas, February 18, 1863, JAGO, NN3409, box 1165; Felix G. Stidger, *Treason History of the Order of Sons of Liberty, Formerly Circle of Honor, Succeeded by Knights of the Golden Circle, Afterward Order of American Knights*, hereafter referred to as *Treason History* (Chicago, 1903), 55–57; Tredway, *Democratic Opposition in Indiana*, 215–16.

54. Indianapolis *State Sentinel*, January 16, 1863; Indianapolis *Daily Journal*, January 9, 15, 17, March 4, 1863; Kenneth M. Stampp, *Indiana Politics during the Civil War* (Indianapolis, IN, 1949), 158–85; Tredway, *Democratic Opposition in Indiana*, 74–107.

55. H. H. Dodd's acceptance speech upon being elected President of the Indianapolis Democratic Club, as reported in Indianapolis *State Sentinel*, January 28, 1863.

56. Sullivan *Democrat*, August 27, 1863.

57. Indianapolis *Daily Journal*, July 30, 1864; Missouri *Democrat*, July 28, 1864; Indianapolis *Daily Sentinel*, August 22, September 5, 1864; Lawrenceburg *Democratic Register*, November 4, 1864; Tredway, *Democratic Opposition in Indiana*, 221–22.

58. Sullivan *Democrat*, August 4, 1864; New Albany *Weekly Ledger*, August 10, 1864; Stampp, *Indiana Politics during the Civil War*, 176–85; Indianapolis *Daily Journal*, January 9, 15, 17, March 4, 1863; Stampp, *Indiana Politics during the Civil War*, 82–83, 137–38, 226–27, 158–85; Indianapolis *Daily Sentinel*, May 21, 1863; Sullivan *Democrat*, May 28, 1863; Tredway, *Democratic Opposition in Indiana*, 30–31, 45, 48.

59. Thompson to Benjamin, December 3, 1864, in *O.R.*, Ser. I, Vol. 43, Pt. 2, 931; testimony of Joseph J. Bingham, JAGO, NN3409, no. 7: 176–77, 193–94; testimony of James B. Wilson in *The Trials for Treason at Indianapolis*, edited by Benn Pitman (Cincinnati, OH, 1865), 144–46; Hines, "The Northwestern Conspiracy," in *Southern Bivouac*, 2: 507; Tredway, *Democratic Opposition in Indiana*, 189; McPherson, *Battle Cry of Freedom*, 787–88, 809–13.

60. Testimony of Bingham, JAGO, no. 7: 176–93; testimony of Felix Stidger, Ibid., 7: 241–43; testimony of James B. Wilson and William M. Harrison, *Trials*

for Treason, Pitman, ed., 90–91, 148; "Hoosier Justice: The Journal of David McDonald, 1864–1868," Donald O. Dewey, ed. *Indiana Magazine of History* 62 (1966), 187; Tredway, *Democratic Opposition in Indiana,* 191–93.

61. Testimony of William M. Harrison, in *Trials for Treason,* Pitman, ed., 92; E. Merton Coulter, *The Civil War and Readjustment in Kentucky* (Durham, NC, 1926), 185.

62. Stidger, *Treason History,* 102–7; Foulke, *Life of Morton,* 404n.

63. Carrington to Potter, June 5, 1864, in *O.R.,* Ser. II, Vol. 7, 339–40; Carrington to Potter, August 16, 1864, Ibid., Ser. I, Vol. 39, Pt. 2, 259–60; Heintzelman to Halleck, Ibid., Ser. III, Vol. 4, 1286–87; Foulke, *Life of Morton,* 1: 408–9.

64. Foulke, *Life of Morton,* 1: 402n.

65. Ibid., 409–10.

66. Ibid.

67. Ibid.

68. Indianapolis *Sentinel,* quoted in Foulke, *Life of Morton,* 1: 409.

69. Tredway, *Democratic Opposition in Indiana,* 218–19; testimony of Joseph J. Bingham, *House Executive Documents,* 39th Congress, 2d session, Doc. No. 50: 269; Indianapolis *Daily Journal,* October 7, 10, 11, 22, December 3, 1864; Berry R. Sulgrove, *History of Indianapolis and Marion County, Indiana* (Philadelphia, 1884), 295.

70. Foulke, *Life of Morton,* 412n.

71. The explanations of these events by revisionist historians have minimized the importance of the weapons seizure, the taking of money from Confederate agents, and the meeting on repeated occasions with representatives of a power at war with the United States, as merely the activities of a loyal opposition trying to protect its civil liberties from infringement by what they perceived to be a wicked and oppressive administration. And whereas their judgment may have sometimes been suspect, their loyalty had never been disproved. In assessing the actions of government and military officials regarding the members of the secret society in Indiana, Frank Klement berated Morton, Carrington, and Stidger, General Alvin P. Hovey (who replaced Carrington in August 1864), General Stephen Burbridge (commanding the District of Kentucky), General Joseph Hooker (who replaced Heintzelman as commander of the Northern Department), Major Henry L. Burnett (judge advocate assigned to hear the case of the Indiana conspirators), Judge Advocate General Joseph P. Holt, Governor Richard Yates, and anybody else who had any part in the arrest and prosecution of members of the Sons of Liberty, or the review of the process, as partisan participants in a conspiracy to silence opposition to the administration and its war effort. Only Heintzelman, who was reluctant to approve the arrests that Morton and others had been lobbying for before August 1864, escaped the acerbic pen of Klement. And yet Heintzelman's reason for not approving arrests was the fear that any such move would precipitate an outbreak of violence. This was hardly tantamount to a denial of the potential for rebellion in the Northwest. To the contrary, Heintzelman, acting in accordance with the wishes of his superiors Stanton and Lincoln, chose to act prudently so that the government

would not provoke the violence and thereby require the recall of thousands of troops from the front where they were needed.

Klement's information regarding the Indiana Sons of Liberty is often errant or the product of a selective and biased reading of the evidence. One example would be his repeated reference to the publication of the so-called "Carrington exposé" by the Republican Indianapolis *Journal*. In *The Copperheads in the Middle West*, Klement wrote that the report appeared in the *Journal* on June 29, 1864. In *Dark Lanterns*, Klement wrote of the same item: "Carrington's revelations, presented as a report to Governor Morton and dated June 28, 1864, appeared two days later in the Indianapolis *Journal*." The footnote citation at the bottom of the page reads "Indianapolis *Daily Journal*, June 30, 1864." Later in the same monograph on page 158, Klement wrote: "Elated, Carrington hurriedly made a copy of each item, and these became the chief source of information for his exposé of late June 1864." The footnote citation immediately following this text reads, "The Carrington exposé of June 28, 1864, was published in the Indianapolis *Daily Journal*, June 29, 1864." In fact, the Carrington exposé did not appear on either June 29 or 30; it first appeared on July 30, 1864, *after* the Sanderson Report was published on July 28, 1864.

72. Testimony of Bingham, in *Trials for Treason*, Pitman, ed., 97–105; Indianapolis *Daily Journal*, October 29, 31, 1864; also see the letter of Congressman Michael Kerr relative to the conspiracy, Indianapolis *Daily Journal*, November 2, 1864; Indianapolis *Daily Sentinel*, August 22, September 5, 1864; Lawrenceburg *Democratic Register*, November 4, 1864; Foulke, *Life of Morton*, 1: 414–16.

73. Randall, *Civil War and Reconstruction*, 393–98; Stidger, *Treason History*, 144, 152; *Ex Parte Vallandigham*, 68 U.S. 251; Tredway, *Democratic Opposition in Indiana*, 224–26. Indianapolis *Daily Journal*, October 8, 1864; Richmond (Indiana) *Palladium*, November 4, 1864.

74. *O.R.*, Ser. II, Vol. 7, 930–53, quotation on 953; as cited in McPherson, *Battle Cry of Freedom*, 782.

75. Klement, *Copperheads in the Middle West*, 201–5; Klement, *The Limits of Dissent*, 293–94; McPherson, *Battle Cry of Freedom*, 782–83.

76. Hay, *Diaries and Letters*, Dennett, ed., 192; Nicolay and Hay, VIII: 13; Klement, *Limits of Dissent*, 2; Klement, *The Copperheads in the Middle West*, 176–205; Klement, *Dark Lanterns*.

77. McPherson, *Battle Cry of Freedom*, 785; Stephen Z. Starr, "Was There a Northwest Conspiracy?" *The Filson Club Historical Quarterly* 38 (1964), 323–41; Thompson to Benjamin, December 3, 1864, *O.R.*, Ser. I, Vol. 43, Pt. 1, 935.

CHAPTER NINE
"I Am Aware That the Subject Creates Prejudice"

1. Forrest G. Wood, *Black Scare: The Response to Emancipation and Reconstruction* (Berkeley, CA, 1968), 53.

2. David Goodman Croly and George Wakeman, *Miscegenation: The Theory*

of the Blending of the Races, Applied to the American White Man and Negro (New York, 1864).

3. Ibid., ii.

4. Ibid.; London *Morning Herald*, November 1, 1864; James Ford Rhodes, *History of the United States* (New York, 1906), IV: 471.

5. *Dictionary of American Biography*, IV: 560; London *Morning Herald*, November 1, 1864; Sidney Kaplan, "The Miscegenation Issue in the Election of 1864," *Journal of Negro History* 34 (July, 1949), 326–27.

6. Kaplan, "The Miscegenation Issue in the Election of 1864," 326–27.

7. Julian to Convention of Colored Citizens of Illinois, September 17, 1853, George W. Julian Papers, Indiana State Library; Edward Dicey, *Spectator of America* (Athens, GA, 1971), 124 (originally published in 1863 under the title *Six Months in the Federal States* by Macmillan and Company, London).

8. Croly and Wakeman, *Miscegenation,* i.

9. Ibid., 8, 15–16.

10. Ibid., 29–31.

11. Ibid., 42.

12. Ibid., 61.

13. Ibid., 61–63.

14. Ibid., 63.

15. Ibid., 61–63.

16. Ibid.

17. Ibid.

18. Samuel S. Cox, *Eight Years in Congress, from 1857 to 1865* (New York, 1865), 354.

19. *Independent*, January 28, February 4, 1864; *Liberator*, February 5, 1864; *National Anti-Slavery Standard*, January 30, 1864.

20. *Anglo-African Review*, January 28, 1864.

21. *National Anti-Slavery Standard*, January 30, 1864.

22. Ibid.

23. In an obituary to Wakeman appearing in the March 21, 1870, edition of the New York *World*, the following language appears: "His humor on paper was conspicuous in the celebrated *Miscegenation* hoax, of which he was part author." Sidney Kaplan asked the question whether Croly, who remained at the *World* as managing editor until 1872, might not have written the obituary. "The Miscegenation Issue in the Election of 1864," 336; Boston *Athenian*, December 15, 1900 (MS letter from Jane Cunningham Croly).

24. Cox, *Eight Years in Congress*, 354.

25. *Congressional Globe,* 37th Congress, 1st session, 4–5, 35–37; *Miscegenation or Amalgamation. Fate of the Freeman. Speech of Samuel S. Cox of Ohio delivered in the House of Representatives,* February 17, 1864 (Washington, DC, 1864), 5, 10; Kaplan, "The Miscegenation Issue in the Election of 1864," 297–98.

26. Wood, *Black Scare*, 56–58; London *Morning Herald,* November 1, 1864; New York *World*, November 23, 1864.

27. Cox engaged in frequent correspondence with Barlow and Marble between

April 1863 and September 1864. He apprised them of the situation in Congress, provided copies of speeches he delivered in the House, and evaluated the prospects of support for the candidacy of George B. McClellan among the Peace Democrats. He was clearly fulfilling the role of minority leader in the House, maintaining regular communications with the party leaders. Samuel L. M. Barlow Papers, Huntington Library; Manton Marble Papers, Library of Congress.

28. London *Morning Herald*, November 1864.

29. Ibid.

30. Ibid.

31. Ibid.

32. New York *World*, November 23, 1864.

33. London *Morning Herald*, November 9, 1864.

34. New York *World*, November 23, 1864.

35. New York *Tribune*, March 16, 1864.

36. Ibid.; New York *Herald*, March 26, 1864.

37. New York *Daily News*, March 17, 1864.

38. New York *Journal of Commerce,* reprinted in *Liberator*, April 8, 1864; *New York Times*, March 19, 1864; New York *Herald*, March 18, 1864; New York *Day-Book*, April 16, 1864.

39. *Divers Views, Opinions, and Prophecies of Yours Truly Petroleum V. Nasby* (Cincinnati, OH, 1867), 182–86.

40. New York *World*, February 20, March 4, March 17, 1864.

41. Wood, *Black Scare*, 59; Philadelphia *Age*, March 14, 17, 26, April 9, May 4, June 25, 1864.

42. New York *Sunday Mercury*, March 18, 1864.

43. Ibid.; *Record of the Service of the Fifty-Fifth Regiment of Massachusetts Volunteer Infantry* (Cambridge, MA, 1968).

44. *National Anti-Slavery Standard*, March 26, 1864.

45. Ohio *Daily Statesman,* June 4, 1864.

46. New York *World*, April 4, 1864; Wood, *Black Scare*, 63.

47. New York *Daily News*, April 4, 1864.

48. New York *Daily News*, April 9, 1864.

49. Ohio *Daily Statesman*, July 8, 1864.

50. Roy H. Abrams, "'The Jeffersonian,' Copperhead Newspaper," *Pennsylvania Magazine of History and Biography* LVII (July 1933), 260-83; Columbus *Crisis*, September 2, 16, 23, 1863; Cincinnati *Daily Enquirer*, September 19, 25, 26, October 3, 10, 12, 13, 1863; reprinted in New York *Freeman's Journal and Catholic Register*, April 9, 1864; Kaplan, "The Miscegenation Issue in the Election of 1864," 312.

51. Dayton *Daily Empire*, July 7, 1864.

52. Kaplan, 313–15, 316n; Wood, 58.

53. John H. Van Evrie, *Subgenation: The Theory of the Normal Relation of the Races: An Answer to "Miscegenaton"* (New York, 1864), 51, 56, 65.

54. Wood, 34.

55. New York *Weekly Day-Book*, July 9, 1864.

56. Ibid.; Kaplan, 317.

57. *The Collected Works of Abraham Lincoln* (Springfield, IL, 1953), VII: 259–60.

58. *Jeffersonian*, quoted in New York *Freeman's Journal & Catholic Register*, April 23, 30, 1864, under title of "Abe's Philanthropy."

59. New York *Freeman's Journal & Catholic Register*, May 21, April 23, 30, 1864.

60. Charles A. Dana, *Recollections of the Civil War* (New York, 1898), 188–89.

61. S. S. Cox to Marble, June 20, 1864; McClellan to Marble, June 25, 1864; Dean Richmond to Marble, June 16, 1864; William Cassidy to Marble, June 11, 1864; J. M. Baldwin to Marble, September 5, 1864, Marble Papers, Library of Congress.

62. *The Real Chicago Platform, as Expounded by the Democratic Orators at Chicago,* Leaflet (Chicago?, 1864)

63. New York *Weekly World*, September 29, October 27, 1864. When later reprinted as "Campaign Document No. 11," the title was altered to "Miscegenation Indorsed by the Republican Party." It was sold at all Democratic Newspaper Offices at $1 per 1,000 pages.

64. "Miscegenation Indorsed by the Republican Party." Campaign Document No. 11 (New York, 1864).

65. New York *Weekly Day-Book*, October 8, 1864.

66. *Campaign Broadside No. 1—The Miscegenation Record of the Republican Party* (New York, 1864).

67. Anon., (George Francis Train), *A Voice From the Pit* (Washington, DC, 1864), 3–5.

68. The Lincoln Catechism, *Wherein the Eccentricities & Beauties of Despotism are Fully Set Forth*, pamphlet (New York, 1864).

69. *Emancipation and its Results*, pamphlet (New York, 1864); *Bible View of Slavery*, pamphlet (New York, 1864); *An Argument on the Ethical Position of Slavery in the Social System, and its Relation to the Politics of the Day*, pamphlet (New York, 1864).

70. Greeley, *The American Conflict*, II: 666–69; Noan Brooks, *Washington, D.C., in Lincoln's Time*, edited by Herbert Mitgang (first published in New York in 1895 under the title *Washington in Lincoln's Time,* republished in 1958 and 1962; Mitgang edition published in Chicago, 1971, and republished in Athens, GA, 1989), 172; *CWL*, VII: 532–33, VIII: 12; Vallandigham to McClellan, September 4, 1864, McClellan Papers, Library of Congress; Bruce Catton, *Never Call Retreat* (New York, 1965), 387.

71. Letter taped to the inside of the front cover of the copy of *Miscegenation* sent to Abraham Lincoln, now on file at the Rare Books and Documents Room at the Library of Congress, Washington, DC.

72. In the 37th Congress elected in 1860, the Republicans had held a 106 to 42 majority over the Democrats in the House; the 38th Congress was composed of 103 Republicans and 80 Democrats. In 1864, the voters sent 145 Republicans (Unionists)

and 46 Democrats to the House in the 39th Congress. In the five most populous states (New York, Pennsylvania, Ohio, Illinois, and Indiana) in 1860, the Republicans led Democrats in the House 67 to 32, in 1862 they trailed them 40 to 59, and in 1864 led them again 74 to 25.

73. *O.R.*, Ser. I, Vol. 24, 2, 466, 459; *Atlantic Monthly*, quoted in Laurence Lader, *The Bold Brahmins* (New York, 1961), 290; Henry Goddard Thomas, "The Colored Troops at Petersburg," *Battles and Leaders*, IV: 563–67.

74. Dana, *Recollections*, 93; Grant, *Memoirs and Selected Letters*, I: 366; Robert Selph Henry, *First With the Most: Forrest* (Wilmington, NC, 1987), 248–69; Albert Castel, "The Fort Pillow Massacre: A Fresh Examination of the Evidence," *Civil War History* 4 (1958), 37–50; John Cimprich and Robert C. Manfort, Jr., "Fort Pillow Revisited: New Evidence about an Old Controversy," *Civil War History* 28 (1962), 293–306; Lewis F. Emilio, *A Brave Black Regiment: History of the Fifty-Fourth Regiment of Massachusetts Volunteer Infantry, 1863–1865* (Boston, 1894), 102–3; New York *Tribune*, September 8, 1864; *O.R.*, Ser. I, Vol. 40, Pt. 1, 17.

75. Adrian Cook, *Armies of the Streets: The New York City Draft Riots of 1863* (Lexington, KY, 1974), 53, 117, 193–96, 310n; McPherson, *Battle Cry of Freedom*, 687.

CHAPTER TEN
"And the Promise Being Made, Must Be Kept"

1. *Harper's Weekly*, November 12, 1864.

2. Stefan Lorant, *The Glorious Burden: The American Presidency* (New York, 1968), 262.

3. Frank Freidel, *Francis Lieber: Nineteenth-Century Liberal* (Baton Rouge, LA, 1947), 351.

4. Gurowski, *Diary*, III: 253; Bates, *Diary*, Beale, ed., 374–75; J. B. Bingham to Andrew Johnson, June 26, 1864, Andrew Johnson Papers, Library of Congress; Zornow, *Lincoln & the Party Divided*, 104.

5. *CWL*, VII: 412–13.

6. Ibid., 419.

7. Robert B. Warden, *An Account of the Private Life and Public Services of Salmon P. Chase* (Cincinnati, OH, 1874), 627.

8. Carl Wittke, *Against the Current: The Life of Karl Heinzen, 1809–80* (Chicago, 1945), 192; Zornow, *Lincoln & the Party Divided*, 73n.

9. James G. Blaine, *Twenty Years of Congress: From Lincoln to Garfield*, 2 vols. (Norwich, CT, 1884), I: 516; Nicolay and Hay, *Lincoln*, IX: 41; Zornow, *Lincoln & the Party Divided*, 78.

10. McPherson, *Political History of the United States*, 413.

11. Ibid.

12. Detroit *Tribune*, June 6, 11, 1864; DeAlva S. Alexander, *A Political History*

of the State of New York, 3 vols. (New York, 1909), III: 92; Zornow, *Lincoln & the Party Divided,* 83.

13. General John Charles Frémont's letter of acceptance to the convention of the Radical Democratic Party, June 4, 1864, in McPherson, *Political History of the United States,* 413–14.

14. Ibid.

15. Chicago *Times,* June 2, 1864; *Harper's Weekly,* June 18, 1864; *New York Times,* June 2, 1864; Philadelphia *Evening Bulletin,* June 1, 1864.

16. Wilmer C. Harris, *Public Life of Zachariah Chandler, 1851–1875* (Lansing, MI, 1917), 79–80; Grace Clarke, *George Julian* (Indianapolis, IN, 1932); John Palmer to Lyman Trumbull, June 8, 1864; James Conkling to Trumbull, June 29, 1864, Lyman Trumbull Papers, Library of Congress; Lindsay Swift, *William Lloyd Garrison* (Philadelphia, 1911), 337; Zornow, *Lincoln & the Party Divided,* 84.

17. Wilmer C. Harris, *Public Life of Zachariah Chandler, 1851–1875* (Lansing, MI, 1917), 79–80; Zornow, *Lincoln & the Party Divided,* 84; Oates, *With Malice Toward None,* 424.

18. Ibid.

19. Nicolay and Hay, *Lincoln,* VIII: 408–37; *O.R.,* Ser. I, Vol. 22, Pt. 1, 14; Lincoln to E. E. Malhiot, Bradish Johnson, and Thomas Cottman, June 19, 1863, *CWL,* VI: 287–89; Lincoln to Nathaniel P. Banks, August 5, 1863, *CWL,* VI: 364–66; Lincoln to Banks, November 5, 1863, *CWL,* VII: 1–2; Lincoln to Benjamin F. Flanders, November 9, 1863, *CWL,* VII: 6–7; Lincoln to Cottman, December 15, 1863, *CWL,* VII: 66–67; Lincoln to Banks, December 24, 1863, January 13, 1864, *CWL,* VII: 89–91, 123–25; Henry J. Raymond, *Life and Public Services of Abraham Lincoln* (New York, 1865), 489; Lincoln to Stephen A. Hurlbut, July 31, 1863, *CWL,* VI: 358–59; Lincoln to Frederick Steele, January 5, 1864, *CWL,* VII: 108–9; Lincoln to Steele, January 20, 1864, *CWL,* VII: 141–42; Lincoln to Alpheus Lewis, January 23, 1864, *CWL,* VII: 145–46.

20. Hay, *Lincoln and the Civil War,* Dennett, ed., 204–6; *Congressional Globe,* 38th Congress, 1st Session, 2906, 3362–63; Wendell Phillips to George Julian, March 27, 1864, Joshua Giddings–George Julian Correspondence, Library of Congress; James A. Woodburn, *Life of Thaddeus Stevens* (Indianapolis, IN, 1913), 316–17; Blaine, *Twenty Years of Congress,* II: 42; George W. Julian, *Political Recollections, 1840–1872* (Chicago, 1884), 247–48.

21. McPherson, *Political History of the United States,* 317–18.

22. Williams, *Lincoln and the Radicals,* 319.

23. Blaine, *Twenty Years of Congress,* II: 42–43.

24. *Congressional Globe,* 38th Congress, 1st Session, 3450, 3491, 3518.

25. Nicolay and Hay, *Lincoln,* IX: 120.

26. Ibid., 122.

27. Proclamation Concerning Reconstruction by the President of the United States, July 8, 1864, *CWL,* VII: 433–34.

28. Adam Gurowski, *Diary, 1863–1864–1865* (Washington, DC, 1866), 274.

29. Thaddeus Stevens to Edward McPherson, July 10, 1864, Thaddeus Stevens Papers, Library of Congress; Williams, *Lincoln and the Radicals,* 321.

30. Warden, *Life of Salmon P. Chase*, 623.

31. Nicolay and Hay, *Lincoln*, IX: 125.

32. New York *Tribune*, August 5, 1864.

33. Ibid.; Nicolay and Hay, IX: 125.

34. New York *Tribune*, August 5, 1864.

35. Ibid.

36. Blaine, *Twenty Years of Congress*, II: 44; *Harper's Weekly*, July 9, 30, August 20, 1864; Nevins, *The Organized War to Victory 1864–1865*, 87–88.

37. Welles, *Diary*, II: 122; Albert G. Riddle, *Recollections of War Times* (New York, 1895), 305; Theodore C. Smith, *The Life and Letters of James Abram Garfield*, 2 vols. (New Haven, CT, 1925), I: 378–79; Zornow, *Lincoln & the Party Divided*, 112.

38. James W. Sheehan in the Chicago *Post*, July 10–25, 1864; Nevins, *The Organized War to Victory 1864–1865*, IV: 87–88.

39. *Harper's Weekly*, July 9, 30, 1864.

40. Ibid., August 30, 1864.

41. Browning, *Diary*, 676; John Sherman to William Tecumseh Sherman, July 24, 1864, John Sherman Papers, Library of Congress; Mason Weld to Benjamin Butler, July 26, 1864; Edgar Conkling to Butler, July 18, 1864, in Butler, *Correspondence*, IV: 464, 512, 546–47; Zornow, *Lincoln & the Party Divided*, 109–10.

42. *Daily Illinois State Register*, July 20, August 12, 18, 19, 1864; David McDonald, "Hoosier Justice: The Journal of David McDonald, 1864–1868," Donald O. Dewey, ed., *Indiana Magazine of History* 62 (1966), 205–7.

43. Roy P. Basler, ed., *Collected Works of Abraham Lincoln* (New Brunswick, NJ, 153), VIII: 459, 499–501, 501n, 506–8, 514nn, 517, 517nn; Dana, *Recollections of the Civil War*, 188–89.

44. James G. Randall and Richard N. Current, *Lincoln the President: Last Full Measure* (Chicago, 1955), IV: 213.

45. Basler, ed., *Collected Works*, VII: 517.

46. Ibid.

47. McClellan to Mary Ellen McClellan, August 9, 1861, September 25, October 5, 1862, McClellan Papers, Library of Congress; Jacob D. Cox, *Military Reminiscences of the Civil War* (New York, 1900), I: 360; McClellan to Abraham Lincoln, July 7, 1862, *O.R.*, Ser. I, Vol. 11, Pt. 1, 73–74; *O.R.*, Ser. I, Vol. 19, Pt. 2, 549.

48. Basler, ed., *Collected Works*, VII: 514.

49. *CWL*, VII: 50ln.

50. Ibid., 500.

51. Ibid., 507.

52. Ibid., 517.

53. Ibid., 518n.

54. Nicolay and Hay, *Abraham Lincoln*, IX: 220.

55. J. B. Bingham to Andrew Johnson, June 26, 1864, Andrew Johnson Papers, Library of Congress; John Sherman to William T. Sherman, July 24, 1864, John

Sherman Papers, Library of Congress; Stanton to Lincoln, July 14, 1864, Stanton Papers, Library of Congress; Edgar Conkling to Butler, July 18, 1864, in *Correspondence of General Benjamin F. Butler*, Marshall, ed., IV: 512, 546–47; G. Coontz to Simon Cameron, August 15, 1864, Simon Cameron Papers, Library of Congress; Russell Everett to Cameron, August 23, 1864, Cameron Papers; Zornow, *Lincoln & the Party Divided*, 110.

56. James H. Ashley to Butler, July 24, 1864, in *Correspondence of Butler*, Marshall, ed., IV: 534–36; Shaffer to Butler, July 23, 1864, in *Correspondence of Butler*, IV: 513; Zornow, *Lincoln & the Party Divided*, 110–11.

57. Conkling to Butler, July 18, 1864, in *Correspondence of Butler*, IV: 510–11; Zornow, *Lincoln & the Party Divided*, 510–11.

58. Ibid.

59. Welles, *Diary*, Beale ed., II: 103.

60. Leonard Swett to "My Dear Wife," August [?] 1864, in Ida Tarbell, *The Life of Abraham Lincoln*, 3 vols. (New York, 1895; republished 1896, 1898, 1899), III: 200–201. This letter was lent to Tarbell by Leonard Herbert Swett of Aurora, Illinois. Though undated, it indicates that it was written on a Monday. Given the events described in the letter, this would have had to have been Monday, August 22, 1864.

61. Zornow, *Lincoln & the Party Divided*, 112.

62. Donnal V. Smith, *Chase and Civil War Politics*, 148–49; New York *Herald*, August 6, 1864; Shaffer to Butler, August 17, 1864, in *Correspondence of Butler*, Marshall, ed., V: 67–69; Stoddard, *Horace Greeley*, 227; Washington *Chronicle*, August 16, 1864; J. K. Herbert to Butler, August 27, 1864; Shaffer to Butler, August 29, 1864, in *Correspondence of Butler*, V: 116–17; Henry G. Pearson, *The Life of John A. Andrew: Governor of Massachusetts, 1861–1865*, 2 vols. (Boston, 1904), II: 159–61; New York *Sun*, June 30, 1889; as cited in Zornow, *Lincoln & the Party Divided*, 114–15.

63. New York *Sun*, June 30, 1889; George Wilkes to Elihu Washburne, August 31, 1864, Elihu Washburne Papers, Library of Congress; Francis Lieber to Sumner, August 31, 1864, in Frank B. Friedel, "The Life of Francis Lieber" (Ph.D. dissertation, 1941, Madison, WI), 630; Herbert to Butler, August 27, 1864, in *Correspondence of Butler*, Marshall, ed., V: 117–18; Gurowski, *Diary*, III, 329; as cited in Zornow, *Lincoln & the Party Divided*, 116–17.

CHAPTER ELEVEN
"The Fiery Trial through Which We Pass"

1. Augusta *Constitutionalist*, April 21, 1864; Second Inaugural Address, March 4, 1865, in *CWL*, VIII: 322.

2. Foote, *Civil War*, III: 125–26.

3. D. G. Crotty, *Four Years Campaigning in the Army of the Potomac* (Grand Rapids, IA, 1874), 117–18; Rufus R. Dawes, *Service with the Sixth Wisconsin Volunteers* (Marietta, OH, 1890), 235; *O.R.*, Ser. I, Vol. 33, 776; Charles E. Davis,

Jr., *Three Years in the Army: The Story of the 13th Massachusetts Volunteers* (Boston, 1893), 302–3; cited in Bruce Catton, *A Stillness at Appomattox* (Garden City, NY, 1953), 34–36.

4. *O.R.*, Ser. 1, Vol. 42, Pt. 2, 783.

5. Augusta *Constitutionalist,* January 22, 1864.

6. Augusta *Chronicle & Sentinel*, May 22, 1864.

7. *Lee's Dispatches*, edited by Douglas Southall Freeman and Grady McWhiney, (New York, 1915), 185.

8. *O.R.*, Ser. I, Vol. 32, Pt. 3, 588.

9. Clifford Dowdey, *Lee's Last Campaign: The Story of Lee and His Men Against Grant, 1864* (Boston, 1960), 60.

10. Shelby Foote, *The Civil War: A Narrative* (New York, 1974), III: 12

11. Ibid., III: 14-16.

12. *O.R.*, Ser. I, Vol. 51, Pt. 1, 369–70; McPherson, *Battle Cry of Freedom*, 333–34.

13. *O.R.*, Ser. I, Vol. 46, Pt. 1, 11, 20–21; Porter, *Campaigning with Grant*, 36–38; *O.R.*, Ser. I, Vol. 33, 827–28; *O.R.*, Ser. I, Vol. 32, Pt. 3, 246; Catton, *A Stillness at Appomattox*, 132–33; McPherson, *Battle Cry of Freedom*, 727–28.

14. Porter, *Campaigning with Grant,* 78–79; Foote, *Civil War*, III: 190–91.

15. Porter, *Campaigning with Grant*, 106–7, 110–12; Foote, *Civil War*, III: 221.

16. Thomas L. Livermore, *Numbers and Losses in the Civil War in America 1861–1865* (Dayton, OH, 1986, reprint 87 from an essay read before the Military Historical Society of Massachusetts, February 23, 1897, Boston), from the articles "Military Training," in the *Journal of the Military Service Institution of July 1893,* and "General Thomas in the Record," in vol. x of the *Military Historical Society of Massachusetts* (n.p., n.d.); Catton, *A Stillness at Appomattox*, 132; McPherson, *Battle Cry of Freedom*, 734.

17. Ulysses S. Grant, *Personal Memoirs of U. S. Grant*, edited by E. B. Long (New York, 1952), 419; George Templeton Strong, *The Diary of George Templeton Strong,* Allan Nevins and Milton Halsey Thomas, eds. 4 vols. (New York, 1952), II: 446; Gideon Welles, *Diary of Gideon Welles*, Howard K. Beale, ed., 3 vols. (Boston, 1909–11), III: 33.

18. Grant, *Memoirs*, 433–34.

19. Chamberlain, *The Passing of the Armies*, 3–6; Oliver Wendell Holmes, Jr., *Touched with Fire: Civil War Letters and Diary of Oliver Wendell Holmes, Jr.*, Mark DeWolfe Howe, ed. (Cambridge, MA, 1946), 126–52; Foote, *Civil War*, III: 294.

20. Oliver Wendell Holmes, Jr., to "Dear Parents," June 24, 1864, in Holmes, *Touched with Fire*, 149–50.

21. Brevet Major General William Farrar Smith, "The Eighteenth Corps at Cold Harbor," *Battles and Leaders of the Civil War*, Robert Underwood Johnson and Clarence Clough Buel, eds., 4 vols. (Secaucus, NJ, 1983), based on "The Century War Series," (New York, 1884–1887), IV: 225–28; Brevet Major General Martin T. McMahon, "Cold Harbor," *Battles and Leaders*, IV: 217–19; Foote, *Civil War*, III: 291–92.

22. Porter, *Campaigning with Grant*, 179.

23. Martin T. McMahon, "Cold Harbor," *Battles and Leaders*, IV: 219.

24. Grant, *Memoirs*, 443–44.

25. New York *World*, June 3–10, 1864; Philadelphia *Age*, June 3–10, 1864; *Ohio Daily Statesman*, June 3–10, 1864; Detroit *Free Press*, June 3–10, 1864.

26. New York *World*, June 3, 1864.

27. Ibid., June 4, 1864.

28. *O.R.*, Ser. I, Vol. 36, Pt. 3, 524.

29. Philadelphia *Age*, June 9, 1864; New York *World*, June 9, 1864.

30. Joshua Lawrence Chamberlain, *The Passing of the Armies* (based on various papers presented by Chamberlain between 1893 and 1905 and published in 1915 by G. P. Putnam Sons; a number of facsimiles were thereafter produced; this was based on Facsimile 21, reprinted 1974, 1981, 1982, 1985, 1986, 1991; new materials copyrighted 1982 by Morningside House, Inc., Dayton, OH, 1982), 3.

31. Military Order of the Loyal Legion of the United States, Commandery of the State of Maine, *In Memoriam: Joshua Lawrence Chamberlain, Late Major General U.S.V.* (1914), 11, reprinted in Chamberlain, *Passing of the Armies*.

32. McMahon, "Cold Harbor," 220; Ulysses S. Grant, *Personal Memoirs*, 2 vols. (New York, 1885), II: 276; Smith, "The Eighteenth Corps at Cold Harbor," 229; John Russell Young, *Around the World with General Grant*, 2 vols. (New York, 1879), II: 304.

33. P. G. T. Beauregard, "Four Days of Battle at Petersburg," *Battles and Leaders*, IV: 541, 544; *O.R.*, Ser. I, Vol. 40, Pt. 2, 86, 91, 117, 120, 156–57, 179, 205; Porter, *Campaigning with Grant*, 183–84; Catton, *A Stillness at Appomattox*, 194–99; McPherson, *Battle Cry of Freedom*, 740–41.

34. Holmes, *Touched with Fire*, Howe, ed., 150; Adam Gurowski, *Diary: 1863–'64–'65*, hereafter cited as *Diary III* (New York, 1868), 254; Strong, *Diary of the Civil War*, Nevins, ed., 458.

35. Welles, *Diary*, II: 44, 45.

36. Richmond *Examiner*, September 5, 1864; Lloyd Lewis, *Sherman: Fighting Prophet* (New York, 1932), 409; Augusta *Chronicle & Sentinel*, September 8, 1864; David Schenck, Diary, entry of September 15, 1864, in Southern Historical Collection, University of North Carolina; Augusta *Constitutionalist*, September 15, 1864; Mary Chesnut, *Mary Chesnut's Civil War*, edited by C. Vann Woodward, (New Haven, CT, 1981), 648.

37. Basil H. Liddell-Hart, *Sherman: Soldier, Realist, American* (New York, 1929), 402; Gilbert E. Govan and James W. Livingood, *A Different Valor: The Story of General Joseph E. Johnston, C.S.A.* (Indianapolis, IN, 1956), 274; Atlanta *Daily Intelligencer*, July 3, 1864; McPherson, *Battle Cry of Freedom*, 744–50; George Templeton Strong diary entry of July 23, 1864, in Strong, *Diary of the Civil War*.

38. Catton, *A Stillness at Appomattox*, 355; Govan and Livingood, *A Different Valor*, 169; Samuel Carter III, *The Siege of Atlanta, 1864* (New York, 1864), 125; McPherson, *Battle Cry of Freedom*, 735.

39. *Mary Chesnut's Civil War*, 266.

40. Basil Liddell-Hart, *Sherman: Soldier, Realist, American* (New York, 1979), 402; McPherson, *Battle Cry of Freedom*, 744.

41. *O.R.*, Ser. I, Vol. 38, Pt. 3, 616, 625, 818, 947–48; Jacob D. Cox, *Atlanta* (New York, 1882), 80–83; *O.R.*, Ser. I, Vol. 38, Pt. 4, 331; Albert Castel, *Decision in the West: The Atlanta Campaign of 1864* (Lawrence, KS, 1992), 221–42; McPherson, *Battle Cry of Freedom*, 747–48.

42. *O.R.*, Ser. I, Vol. 38, Pt. 4, 596–604; Jacob D. Cox, *Reminiscences of the Civil War*, 2 vols. (New York, 1900), 2: 263–65; Castel, *Decision in the West*, 303–16.

43. Few events of the war aroused such a feeling of mingled anger and anguish in the North as the April "massacre" at Fort Pillow. The facts of this incident, in which 231 Union soldiers, largely blacks, were killed while only fourteen Confederates fell, have provoked some dispute. Northerners saw only one side. They read headlines announcing "Attack on Fort Pillow—Indiscriminate Slaughter of the Prisoners—Shocking Scenes of Savagery"; dispatches from Sherman's army declaring that "there is a general gritting of teeth here"; reports from the Missouri *Democrat* detailing the "fiendishness" of rebel behavior; and editorials like that in the Chicago *Tribune* condemning the "murder" and "butchery." Senator Henry Wilson published in the New York *Tribune* a letter from a lieutenant colonel in the Army of the Tennessee giving gory particulars, while others poured in from survivors in the Mound City, Illinois, hospital. All this made a heavier impression because of the unquestionable facts that Confederates had previously killed some black soldiers after capture, and had exchanged not a single black private of the many captured at Battery Wagner, Port Hudson, and Olustee. Nevins, *The Organized War to Victory 1864–1865*, 60; Foote, *Civil War*, III: 111–12; McPherson, *Battle Cry of Freedom*, 748; Robert Selph Henry, *"First with the Most" Forrest* (Indianapolis, 1944), 248–49.

44. McPherson, *Battle Cry of Freedom*, 748.

45. Henry, 277.

46. *O.R.*, Ser. I, Vol. 39, Pt. 2, 121.

47. *O.R.*, Ser. I, Vol. 32, Pt. 2, 612–16, 778, 609; *O.R.*, Ser. I, Vol. 39, Pt. 2, 92–224; Henry, *"First With the Most,"* 285–304; *O.R.*, Ser. I, Vol. 39, Pt. 2, 121; *O.R.*, Ser. I, Vol. 39, Pt. 3, 464–66, 479, 484–85, 488–89, 494, 504, 517, 524; *O.R.*, Ser. I, Vol. 39, Pt. 2, 257–59, 302, 304, 316–19; Henry, *"First With the Most,"* 315; McPherson, *Battle Cry of Freedom*, 748–49.

48. *O.R.*, Ser. I, Vol. 38, Part 4, 507; Livermore, *Numbers and Losses in the Civil War*, 120–21.

49. New York *World*, July 12, 1864.

50. Strong, *Diary of the Civil War*, 467.

51. Jubal Early, *Autobiographical Sketches and Narratives of the War Between the States*, edited by Frank E. Vandiver (Bloomington, IN, 1960), 455–56; Frank E. Vandiver, *Jubal's Raid* (New York, 1960), 122–79; McPherson, *Battle Cry of Freedom*, 756–57; Nevins, *The Organized War to Victory*, 88–89.

52. Nevins, *The Organized War to Victory*, 88–89; Thomas W. Hyde, *Following*

the Greek Cross; or, Memories of the Sixth Army Corps (Boston, 1894), 222–23; *O.R.*, Ser. I, Vol. 37, Pt. 1, 231, 259; Welles, *Diary*, II: 75; Foote, *Civil War*, III: 60–61.

53. Strong, *Diary of the Civil War*, 474.

54. Robert Garlick Hill Kean, *Inside the Confederate Government: The Diary of Robert Garlick Hill Kean*, Edward Younger, ed. (New York, 1957), 165; Dunbar Rowland, *Jefferson Davis, Constitutionalist: His Letters, Papers, and Speeches*, 10 vols. (Jackson, MS, 1923), VI: 283; McPherson, *Battle Cry of Freedom*, 752.

55. John Bell Hood to Braxton Bragg, July 14, 1864, in *O.R.*, Ser. I, Vol. 38, Part 5, 879–80.

56. Robert E. Lee, *The Wartime Papers of Robert E. Lee*, edited by Clifford Dowdey (New York, 1961), 202.

57. Thomas L. Connelly, *Autumn of Glory: The Army of Tennessee, 1862–1865* (Baton Rouge, LA, 1971), 405; Sam R. Watkins, *"Co. Aytch": A Side Show of the Big Show* (New York, 1962), 172; William T. Sherman, "The Grand Strategy of the Last Year of the War," *Battles and Leaders*, IV: 253; Oliver O. Howard, "The Struggle for Atlanta," *Battles and Leaders*, IV: 314–17; John B. Hood, "The Defense of Atlanta," *Battles and Leaders*, IV: 337–42.

58. Howard, "The Struggle for Atlanta," 319–20; Hood, "The Defense of Atlanta," 341; Foote, *Civil War*, III: 472–92.

59. Livermore, *Numbers and Losses in the Civil War*, 122–26.

60. John Coddington Kenney, "Farragut at Mobile Bay," *Battles and Leaders*, IV: 380, 385–87; "The Opposing Forces at Mobile," *Battles and Leaders*, IV: 400; James D. Johnston, "The Ram 'Tennessee' at Mobile Bay," *Battles and Leaders*, IV: 401–6.

61. J. Crittenden Watson and Joseph Marton, "The Lashing of Admiral Farragut in the Rigging," *Battles and Leaders*, IV: 406–8; R. L. Page, "The Defense of Fort Morgan," *Battles and Leaders*, IV: 408–10; Kenney, "Farragut at Mobile Bay," 387–99; Foote, *Civil War*, III: 500–501; McPherson, *Battle Cry of Freedom*, 761.

62. McPherson, *Battle Cry of Freedom*, 761; Richard B. Irwin, "Land Operations Against Mobile," *Battles and Leaders*, IV: 410–11; James Russell Soley, "Closing Operations in the Gulf and Western Rivers," *Battles and Leaders*, IV: 412.

63. Jubal A. Early, "Early's March to Washington in 1864," *Battles and Leaders*, IV: 492–99; Grant, *Personal Memoirs*, 620–31; Grant to Henry W. Halleck, August 1, 1864, *Battles and Leaders*, IV: 615.

64. Theodore F. Rodenbough, "Sheridan's Richmond Raid," *Battles and Leaders*, IV: 188–92; A Private of the Sixth Virginia Cavalry, "The Death of General J. E. B. Stuart," *Battles and Leaders* (reprinted from *Southern Bivouac*, September 1884), 184.

65. Lee, *Wartime Papers*, 799–800.

66. *O.R.*, Ser. I, Vol. 38, Pt. 3, 661–68, 679–80, 689, 970–71; *O.R.*, Ser. I, Vol. 38, Pt. 5, 927, 930, 940, 949–51; Castel, *Decision in the West*, 448–50.

67. Castel, *Decision in the West*, 480–507; Foote, *Civil War*, III: 521.

68. "Sherman neckties" was the term Sherman's soldiers used for the sections of rail that were heated, then twisted around a tree or telegraph pole. Macon *Daily*

Telegraph, August 15, 1864, quoted in *New York Times*, August 26, 1864; Atlanta (Macon) *Daily Intelligencer*, August 19, 1864; *O.R.*, Ser. I, Vol. 38, Pt. 3, 692–93; Ibid., Pt. 5, 990–992; Ibid., Pt. 1, 164, 213, 512, 927; Ibid., Pt. 2, 518; Pt. 3, 42–43, 632–633, 693; Pt. 5, 993–996; Castel, *Decision in the West*, 485–88, 491–92.

69. *O.R.*, Ser. I, Vol. 38, Pt. 3, 764–65, 773–74, 822, 824, 835, 857–58; Arthur M. Manigault, *A Carolinian Goes to War: The Civil War Narrative of Arthur Middleton Manigault, Brigadier General, C.S.A.*, edited by R. Lockwood Turner (Columbia, SC, 1983), 246–47; Castel, *Decision in the West*, 496–521; McPherson, *Battle Cry of Freedom*, 774.

70. William Tecumseh Sherman, *Memoirs of General W. T. Sherman*, 2 vols. (Library of America edition that includes both volumes in one consecutively numbered text, New York, 1990, originally published 1875, 1885), 583.

71. Strong, *Diary of the Civil War* (diary entry September 3, 1864), 480–81.

72. Gurowski, *Diary*, III: 331.

73. Lloyd Lewis, *Sherman: Fighting Prophet* (New York, 1932), 409; McPherson, *Battle Cry of Freedom*, 775.

74. *Mary Chesnut's Civil War*, 648.

75. Ibid., (diary entry September 21, 1864), 645.

76. George to "Brother," September 8, 1864, published in Augusta *Constitutionalist*, September 15, 1864.

77. Richmond *Examiner*, September 6, 1864.

78. Augusta *Chronicle and Sentinel*, September 22, 1864.

79. Richmond *Sentinel*, September 16, 1864.

80. Augusta *Chronicle & Sentinel*, September 8, 1864.

81. John W. Graham to William A. Graham, September 5, 1864, in William A. Graham Papers, Southern Historical Collection, University of North Carolina.

82. Nelson, *Bullets, Ballots, and Rhetoric*, 121.

83. Merritt, "Sheridan in the Shenandoah Valley," 506–11.

84. Strong, *Diary of the Civil War*, (diary entry September 27, 1864), 494.

85. Ibid., 493–94.

86. *O.R.*, Ser. I, Vol. 40, Pt. 3, 223.

87. Thomas C. Leonard, *Above the Battle: War-Making in America from Appomattox to Versailles* (New York, 1978), 18; *O.R.*, Ser. I, Vol. 43, Pt. 1, 30–31; McPherson, *Battle Cry of Freedom*, 778.

88. *O.R.*, Ser. I, Vol. 43, Pt. 1, 30–31.

89. Merritt, "Sheridan in the Shenandoah Valley," 515–18.

90. Jubal A. Early, "Winchester, Fisher's Hill, and Cedar Creek," condensed from Jubal A. Early, *Memoir of the Last Year of the War for Independence in the Confederate States of America* (Lynchburg, VA, 1867), *Battles and Leaders*, IV: 528.

91. Merritt, "Sheridan in the Shenandoah Valley," 518–20; Bruce Catton, *Never Call Retreat* (New York, 1965), 393.

92. Merritt, "Sheridan in the Shenandoah Valley," 520–21.

93. McPherson, *Battle Cry of Freedom*, 780–81.

94. *Mary Chesnut's Civil War*, (diary entry September 29, 1864), 648.

CHAPTER TWELVE
"The Brave Men, Living and Dead"

1. Nevins, *War for the Union: The Improvised War 1861–1862*, 170–77; "James A. Leonard, Letters of a Fifth Wisconsin Volunteer," R. G. Plumb, ed., in *Wisconsin Magazine of History* III (1919–20), 63–64; "George Breck's Civil War Letters from the 'Reynolds Battery,'" in *Rochester in the Civil War*, Blake McKelvey, ed., (Rochester, NY, 1944), 140–41.

2. Joseph F. Linderman, *Embattled Courage: The Experience of Combat in the Civil War* (New York, 1987), 39–43; Bell Irwin Wiley, *The Life of Billy Yank: The Common Soldier of the Union* (New York, 1951), 20–28, 320–24.

3. Thomas Wentworth Higginson, "Regular and Volunteer Officers," in *The Blue and the Gray*, edited by Henry Steele Commager, 2 vols. (New York, 1950), I: 483; Henry Steele Commager, ed., *Illustrated History of the Civil War* (New York, 1971), 180.

4. Ibid.; Fitz John Porter to Manton Marble, September 30, 1862, Manton Marble Papers, Library of Congress; *CWL*, V: 442–43, 508–9; McPherson, *Battle Cry of Freedom*, 558–59.

5. James G. Blaine, *Twenty Years of Congress: From Lincoln to Garfield* (Norwich, CT, 1884–1886), I: 637; Philadelphia *Age*, August 24, 1864.

6. Ibid.

7. *The American Annual Cyclopaedia and Register of Important Events of the Year 1862* (New York, 1863), 706; Oscar Osburn Winther, "The Soldier Vote in the Election of 1864," in *New York History*, 25: 440.

8. *Acts of . . . the Legislature of Wisconsin . . . 1862, 1863* (Madison, 1863), 17.

9. *General and Special Laws of the State of Minnesota . . . 1862* (St. Paul, MN, 1862), 13–17, 267.

10. *American Annual Cyclopaedia . . . 1863* (New York, 1864), 330, 681.

11. *The Tribune Almanac and Political Register for 1863* (New York, 1864) 51–59; *CWL*, V: 494.

12. *American Annual Cyclopaedia . . . 1863*, 731; *Act of . . . West Virginia . . . 1863* (Wheeling, 1863), 119; Winther, "Soldier Vote in 1864," 441–42.

13. Though Delaware, New Jersey, Rhode Island, Nevada, and Oregon likewise did not enact enabling legislation, either because the voter verdict in those states was not considered to be in doubt or because their size made them less significant to the national canvass, the failure of such laws in those states would prove less critical.

14. William Dudley Foulke, *Life of Oliver P. Morton*, 2 vols. (Indianapolis, IN, 1877), I: 198–251.

15. *New York Times*, April 1, 1863; *General Statutes of New Jersey* (Jersey City, NJ, 1896), I: xxxvi, xxxviii.

16. *American Annual Cyclopaedia . . . 1864*, 504; *Laws of the State of Maryland for 1865* (Annapolis, MD, 1865), 187–89.

17. Winther, "Soldier Vote of 1864," 448.

18. *New York Times,* April 1, 1863; *Laws of the State of New York* (Albany, NY, 1864), 26; *American Annual Cyclopaedia . . . 1864,* 581.

19. Ibid., 581–84.

20. Ibid.

21. *New York Times,* October 29, 1864.

22. Winther, "The Soldier Vote," 444–45.

23. *Tribune Almanac . . . 1863,* 68–69.

24. Union League of Philadelphia, *Record of Hiester Clymer,* 20.

25. David H. Bates, *Lincoln in the Telegraph* (New York, 1907), 277–81.

26. *Tribune Almanac . . . 1864,* 54–59; Schuyler Colfax to Lincoln, July 25, 1864, Abraham Lincoln Papers, Robert Todd Lincoln Collection, 42960–61.

27. Ibid.

28. A Proclamation, July 18, 1864, in *CWL,* VII: 448–49.

29. General Robert McAllister to Ellen McAllister, July 21, 1864, *The Civil War Letters of General Robert McAllister,* edited by James I. Robertson (New Brunswick, NJ, 1965), 466.

30. Kenneth Stampp, *Indiana Politics during the Civil War* (Indianapolis, IN, 1949), 250–51; Lincoln Papers, RTL Collection, 36417.

31. William Dudley Foulke, *Life of Oliver P. Morton,* 2 vols. (Indianapolis, IN, 1899), I: 367.

32. Sherman to Stanton, September 17, 1864, *CWL,* VIII: 12n.

33. *O.R.,* Ser. III, Vol. 4, 732.

34. Lincoln to Sherman, September 19, 1864, in *CWL,* VIII: 11.

35. Lincoln to Morton, October 13, 1864, in *CWL,* 46nn.

36. Charles A. Dana, *Recollections of the Civil War* (New York, 1898), 227.

37. William Cannon to Edwin Stanton, Edwin Stanton Papers, Library of Congress; *The Civil War Papers of General Robert McAllister,* edited by James I. Robertson, Jr. (New Brunswick, NJ), 533.

38. McAllister to "my dear Family," September 23, 1864, in *McAllister Letters,* 507–8; Oliver Wendell Holmes, Jr., to parents, June 24, 1864, in *Touched with Fire,* 150; Charles S. Wainwright, *A Diary of Battle: The Personal Journals of Colonel Charles S. Wainwright 1861–1865,* Allan Nevins, ed. (New York, 1962), 461.

39. Evans Blake to Elihu Washburne, September 30, 1864, Elihu Washburne Papers, Library of Congress.

40. Chauncey B. Welton to parents August 4, September 19, 1864, in Southern Historical Collection, University of North Carolina.

41. Ibid., October 13, 1864.

42. Thaddeus B. Capron, "War Diary of Thaddeus H. Capron, 1861–1865," in *Journal of the Illinois State Historical Society* XII, no. 3 (October 1919), 394–95.

43. Edwin Hutchinson to "Dear Father," October 15, 1864, in Edwin Hutchinson Papers, Department of Archives and Manuscripts, Louisiana State University.

44. E. H. Kettell to McClellan, September 24, 1864, in McClellan Papers, Library of Congress.

45. *New York Times,* October 29, 1864; William T. Sherman, *Home Letters of*

General Sherman, edited by M. A. DeWolfe Howe (New York, 1909), 315–16; John R. Brumgardt, "Overwhelmingly for 'Old Abe': Sherman's Soldiers and the Election of 1864," *Lincoln Herald* 78, no. 4 (Winter 1976), 156–57.

46. Grant to Stanton, September 27, 1864, in Horace Porter, *Campaigning with Grant* (New York, 1897), 321–22.

47. Grant to Barnabas Burns, December 17, 1863, in Ulysses S. Grant, *Personal Memoirs of U. S. Grant and Selected Letters 1839–1865* (New York, 1990, reprinted from *The Papers of Ulysses S. Grant*, edited by John Y. Simon, 14 vols., 1967–85, by The Ulysses S. Grant Association, published by Southern Illinois University Press), 1039–40.

48. Ibid.

49. Grant to Elihu Washburne, September 21, 1864, in *Personal Memoirs*, 1069–70; Grant to John G. Thompson, August 29, 1863, in *Personal Memoirs*, 1032.

50. Grant to Lincoln, July 19, 1864, in *Personal Memoirs*, 1060–61; Grant to Washburne, August 16, 1864, in *Personal Memoirs*, 1064–65.

51. Grant, *Personal Memoirs,* 1065.

52. Ibid.

53. Porter, *Campaigning with Grant*, 322–23.

54. Ibid., 324.

55. Ibid., 321–23.

56. St. Paul (Minnesota) *Press*, September 4, 1864, as cited in Gray, *Hidden Civil War*, 189; Richmond *Examiner*, September 5, 1864; J. C. Devin to John Sherman, September 6, 1864, John Sherman Papers, Library of Congress; Bellefontaine (Ohio) *Republican*, September 23, 1864; Lieutenant Evans Blake to Washburne, September 30, 1864, Elihu Washburne Papers, Library of Congress.

57. *To the Soldiers of the Union* (Loyal Union League Publication), n.p., n.d., Library of Congress.

58. Ibid.

59. Ibid., 5–6.

60. Ibid., 8–9.

61. Ibid., 14.

62. James A. Connolly to "Dear wife," September 18, 1864, in *Three Years in the Army of the Cumberland: The Letters and Diary of Major James A. Connolly* (Bloomington, IN, 1959), 261.

63. Wainwright, *A Diary of Battle* (diary entry October 26, 1864), 476; McAllister to Ellen McAllister, October 10, 1864, in *McAllister Letters*, 518.

64. Chamberlain, *The Passing of the Armies*, 12.

65. *Tribune Almanac for 1865*, 46–67.

66. Ibid., 46–48.

67. Ibid., 47.

68. Harold M. Hyman, "Election of 1864," *The Coming to Power: Critical Presidential Elections in American History*, edited by Arthur M. Schlesinger, Jr., et al. (New York, 1971, 1972), 162.

69. Ibid.

70. Ibid.

CHAPTER THIRTEEN
"I Want to Finish This Job"

1. Zachariah Chandler to "My dear wife," September 8, 1864, Zachariah Chandler Papers, Library of Congress; Zornow, *Lincoln & the Party Divided*, 141.

2. Letter lent by Herbert Leonard Swett of Aurora, Illinois, to Ida Tarbell, quoted in Ida M. Tarbell, *The Life of Abraham Lincoln*, 3 vols. (New York, 1895; republished 1896, 1898, 1899, 1900), III: 202–3.

3. Ibid., 203.

4. Zornow, *Lincoln & the Party Divided*, 142.

5. Edward McPherson, *The Political History of the United States During the Great Rebellion*, 2nd ed. (Washington, DC, 1865), 419–20; Strong, *Diary of the Civil War*, 479; Charleston *Mercury*, September 5, 1864; Nelson, *Bullets, Ballots, and Rhetoric,* 113, 115.

6. Nicolay and Hay, *Lincoln*, IV: 367; Zornow, *Lincoln & the Party Divided*, 142–43.

7. G. B. Sedgwick to Forbes, September 5, 1864, in John Murray Forbes, *Letters and Recollections of John Murray Forbes*, Sarah F. Hughes, ed., 2 vols. (Boston, 1899), II: 101.

8. Henry G. Pearson, *The Life of John A. Andrew, Governor of Massachusetts, 1861–1865*, 2 vols. (Boston, 1904), II: 164–69.

9. Wilkes to Butler, September 15, 1864, in *Butler Correspondence,* Marshall, ed., V: 134–35; Zornow, *Lincoln & the Party Divided,* 143.

10. Weed to Seward, September 20, 1864, Abraham Lincoln Papers, Robert Todd Lincoln Collection, Library of Congress; Nicolay and Hay, *Lincoln*, IX: 366.

11. Pearson, *Life of John A. Andrew*, II: 171.

12. Nicolay and Hay, *Lincoln*, IV: 353–54.

13. Ibid., 360.

14. Ibid.

15. Hans L. Trefousse, "I Have Done My Share," *Civil War Times Illustrated*, reproduced from the winter 1968 issue of *Lincoln Herald* 9 (May 1970), 23–24; Winfred A. Harbison, "Zachariah Chandler's Part in the Re-election of Abraham Lincoln," *Mississippi Valley Historical Review* 25 (September 1935), 269.

16. Trefousse, "I Have Done My Share," 24.

17. Zachariah Chandler to "My dear Wife," August 27, 1864, Zachariah Chandler Papers, Library of Congress.

18. Chandler to Mrs. Chandler, August 28, 1864, Chandler Papers.

19. Ibid., September 2, 1864.

20. Ibid., September 8, 1864.

21. Trefousse, "I have Done My Share," 27.

22. Ibid.

23. Ibid., 27–28.

24. Ibid.; Lincoln to Blair, September 23, 1864, in *CWL*, VIII: 18.

25. Nicolay and Hay, *Lincoln*, IX: 332–84.

26. Sears, *Young Napoleon*, 381–81; Edward H. Wright to McClellan, March 15, 1864, McClellan Papers, Library of Congress; McClellan to Wright, March 19, 1864, Miscellaneous Collections, Huntington Library; Barlow to Marble, August 24, 1864, Marble Papers, Library of Congress; Randall Marcy to McClellan, September 13, 20, 1864, Marble Papers, Library of Congress.

27. Trefousse, "I Have Done My Share," 27–28.

28. Vallandigham to McClellan, September 4, 1864, McClellan Papers, Library of Congress; McPherson, *Battle Cry of Freedom*, 775.

29. Drafts of McClellan's acceptance letter, Samuel L. M. Barlow Papers, Henry E. Huntington Library; August Belmont to McClellan, September 3, 1864; S. L. M. Barlow to McClellan, September 3, 1864, McClellan Papers, Library of Congress.

30. J. Green to August Belmont, October 3, 1864, Manton Marble Papers, Library of Congress; S. S. Cox to Marble, October 8, 1864, Marble Papers; Edwin Stanton to McClellan, October 13, 1864, McClellan Papers, Library of Congress; Zornow, *Lincoln & the Party Divided*, 192–93; Dell, *Lincoln and the War Democrats*, 299–300; Foulke, *Life of Morton*, I: 253–72.

31. Dell, *Lincoln and the War Democrats*, 300.

32. Kenneth M. Stampp, "The Milligan Case and the Election of 1864 in Indiana," *The Mississippi Valley Historical Review* 31 (June 1944), 41–58; W. H. H. Terrell to General Wilder, September 6, 1864, cited in Stampp, "The Milligan Case and the Election of 1864 in Indiana," 55; New York *Tribune*, October 3, 1864; *CWL*, VIII: 11.

33. *CWL*, VIII: 11; Zornow, *Lincoln & the Party Divided,* 192; *The Tribune Almanac for 1865*, 58–59.

34. *Tribune Almanac for 1865*, 58–59.

35. Ibid.; *Tribune Almanac for 1863*, 56–57.

36. *Tribune Almanac for 1861*, 47–58; *Tribune Almanac for 1863*, 53–54.

37. *Tribune Almanac for 1863*, 53, 63.

38. Ibid.

39. *Tribune Almanac for 1861*, 47–48, 58–59; *Tribune Almanac for 1862*, 61; *Tribune Almanac for 1863*, 53–54, 55–57; *Tribune Almanac for 1864*, 58, 60–61.

40. *Tribune Almanac for 1865,* 54–55; Brillhart, "Election of 1864 in Western Pennsylvania," 22.

41. *Tribune Almanac for 1863*, 53, 63.

42. *Tribune Almanac for 1862*, 61; *Tribune Almanac for 1863,* 55.

43. *Tribune Almanac for 1863*, 55.

44. *Tribune Almanac for 1864,* 60–61; Porter, *Ohio Politics during the Civil War*, 109–21, 159–85.

45. *Tribune Almanac for 1865*, 56.

46. William Prime to McClellan, October 20, 1864, McClellan Papers, Library of Congress; Zornow, *Lincoln & the Party Divided*, 194.

47. *CWL*, VIII: 46; Zornow, *Lincoln & the Party Divided*, 194–95.

CHAPTER FOURTEEN
"Of the People, by the People, for the People"

1. Salmon P. Chase to John Sherman, October 2, 1864, John Sherman Papers, Library of Congress.

2. Ward Hill Lamon, *Recollections of Abraham Lincoln, 1847–1865* (Chicago, 1895), 205–8; Zornow, *Lincoln & the Party Divided*, 196–97.

3. Lamon, *Recollections of Lincoln*, 205–8.

4. Francis P. Blair to editor, October 5, 1864, printed in *National Intelligencer*, October 8, 1864.

5. Sears, *Young Napoleon*, 365–66; Grant to Lincoln, July 30, 1864, Lincoln Papers, Library of Congress; Edwin D. Morgan to Lincoln, July 27, 1864, Lincoln Papers, Library of Congress.

6. *CWL*, VII: 528.

7. Ibid.

8. Zornow, *Lincoln & the Party Divided*, 179–82; Anna Hardie, "The Influence of the Union League of America on the Second Election of Lincoln," (master's thesis, Louisiana State University, 1937), 68; William Frank Zornow, "Words and Money to Re-elect Lincoln," *Lincoln Herald* 54 (Spring 1952), 22–30; Frank Friedel, "The Loyal Publication Society: A Pro-Union Propaganda Agency," *The Mississippi Valley Historical Review* 26 (December 1939), 359–76; Henry J. Raymond to Elihu Washburne, November 20, 1864, Elihu Washburne Papers, Library of Congress; *Union Pamphlets of the Civil War 1861–1865*, Frank Friedel, ed., 2 vols. (Cambridge, MA, 1967), I: 7–8.

9. O. W. Smith to Samuel Morse, May 28, 1864, Samuel F. B. Morse Papers, Library of Congress, cited in Zornow, *Lincoln & the Party Divided*, 182–83.

10. Zornow, *Lincoln & the Party Divided*, 183.

11. Ibid., 183–84; Friedel, *Union Pamphlets*, 14–17.

12. Strong, *Diary of the Civil War*, 510.

13. Ibid.

14. *Conversations with Lincoln*, Charles M. Segal, ed. (New York, 1961), 234–35.

15. Strong, *Diary of the Civil War*, 512.

16. Nicolay and Hay, *Lincoln*, 375–76.

17. Nevins, *Organized War to Victory*, 66, 136.

18. Winther, "Soldier Vote," 440–58.

19. Ibid.

20. Brooks, *Washington, D.C., in Lincoln's Time*, 196.

21. Nicolay and Hay, *Lincoln*, X: 375–76.

22. Ibid., X: 377.

23. Oates, *With Malice Toward None*, 435.

24. Official manuscript (on microfilm) returns of 1864 election furnished by the State Librarian; Walter Dean Burnham, *Presidential Ballots, 1832–1896* (Baltimore, 1955), 368–90.

25. *Tribune Almanac for 1865*, 48.

26. Burnham, *Presidential Ballots*, 390–413; *Tribune Almanac for 1865*, 58;

Official manuscript returns of 1864 election at Indiana State Historical Library, Archives Division.

27. *Tribune Almanac for 1865*, 56–57.

28. *New York Times*, November 12, 1864; Zornow, *Lincoln & the Party Divided*, 206–21; Arthur Cole, *Era of the Civil War, 1848–1870* (Springfield, IL, 1919), 378–79; Joseph Schafer, "Who Elected Lincoln," *American Historical Review* 47 (October 1941), 57.

29. Cole, *Era of the Civil War*, 379–81.

CHAPTER FIFTEEN
"Shall Not Perish from the Earth"

1. Nicolay and Hay, *Lincoln*, X: 277–80.

2. Strong, *Diary of the Civil War*, 582–84.

3. Ibid.

4. Gurowski, *Diary III*, 398–99.

5. *CWL*, VIII: 332–33.

6. Albert G. Riddle, *Recollections of War Times* (New York, 1895), 323–24; George W. Julian, *Political Recollections 1840–1872* (Chicago, 1884), 250; Brooks, *Washington, D.C., in Lincoln's Time*, 185–87; Isaac M. Arnold, *The Life of Abraham Lincoln* (Chicago, 1885), 358–59; Oates, *With Malice Toward None*, 439–41.

7. *CWL*, VIII: 149, 254; Oates, *With Malice Toward None*, 439–41.

8. *CWL*, VIII: 149.

9. Ibid.

10. Ibid.

11. Ibid., VIII: 152.

12. Oates, *With Malice Toward None*, 440.

13. Ibid.

14. Hyman, "Election of 1864," 166.

15. Dudley Taylor Cornish, *The Sable Arm: Negro Troops in the Union Army, 1861–1865* (New York, 1966), 256–57, 264–65; James M. McPherson, *The Negro's Civil War* (New York, 1965), 223.

16. *The Wartime Papers of Robert E. Lee*, Dowdey, ed., 671–72, 892, 910, 918.

17. Foote, *Civil War*, II: 30–45, 87–103, 129–30, 169–170; McPherson, *Battle Cry of Freedom*, 571–74; 580–84; Nevins, *War Becomes Revolution 1862–1863*, 365–566, 405–7, 408–11.

18. S. L. M. Barlow to Manton Marble, August 24, 1864, S. L. M. Barlow Papers, Huntington Library; S. L. M. Barlow to McClellan, September 3, 1864; McClellan Papers, Library of Congress; James Harrison to Louis V. Bogy, August 24, 1864, Clement C. Clay Papers, National Archives, quoted in McPherson, *Battle Cry of Freedom*, 771.

19. August Belmont to McClellan, September 3, 1864, McClellan Papers, Library of Congress.

20. *CWL*, V: 426–40; VIII: 100–101.

21. *The Liberator*, February 10, 1865.

22. Carl Sandburg, *Abraham Lincoln*, 4 vols. (New York, 1939), 4: 244–45; William H. Crook, "Lincoln's Last Day," *Harper's Monthly Magazine* (September 1907), 519.

23. Crook, "Lincoln's Last Day," 519.

24. Welles, *Diary*, 283ff., reprinted in *The Blue and the Gray*, Commager, ed., 1103–4.

25. Tom Taylor, "Abraham Lincoln: Foully Assassinated April 14, 1865," *Punch*, reprinted in *The Blue and the Gray*, Commager, ed., 1104.

26. Nicolay and Hay, *Lincoln*, X: 302; Oates, *With Malice Toward None*, 471.

Bibliography

MANUSCRIPTS

Detroit Public Library
    Austin Blair Papers
    Zachariah Chandler Papers
Duke University, Durham, North Carolina
    Darius Starr Papers
Henry E. Huntington Library, San Marino, California
    S. L. M. Barlow Papers
    McClellan's Civil War Collection
    Charles Sumner Papers
Historical Society of Pennsylvania, Philadelphia
    Salmon P. Chase Papers
Illinois State Historical Library, Springfield
    Lyman Trumbull Papers
Indiana State Historical Society Library, Indianapolis
    Lyman Trumbull Papers
    William Henry Smith Papers
Indiana State Library, Indianapolis
    Departmental and General Telegrams, 18 vols.
    George W. Julian Papers.
    Letterbooks of General Henry B. Carrington, 5 vols.
    Letter Press Books of Governor Oliver P. Morton, 9 vols.
    Official manuscript returns of 1864 election
Indiana University, Lilly Library, Bloomington
    Henry S. Lane Papers

Library of Congress, Washington, D.C.
  Simon Cameron Papers
  Zachariah Chandler Papers
  Salmon P. Chase Papers
  Anna Dickinson Papers
  Joshua Giddings and George Julian Correspondence
  Horace Greeley Papers
  Samuel P. Heintzelman Papers
  Andrew Johnson Papers
  Daniel Read Larned Papers
  Abraham Lincoln Papers, Robert Todd Lincoln Collection
  Manton Marble Papers
  George B. McClellan Papers
  Samuel F. B. Morse Papers
  John G. Nicolay Papers
  Frederick Olmstead Papers
  John Sherman Papers
  Edwin M. Stanton Papers
  Thaddeus Stevens Papers
  Charles Sumner Papers
  Lyman Trumbull Papers
  Benjamin Wade Papers
  Elihu Washburne Papers
Lincoln National Life Foundation, Ft. Wayne, Indiana
  R. W. Thompson Papers
Minnesota Historical Society, Minneapolis
  Alexander Ramsay Papers
National Archives, Washington, D.C.
  Clement C. Clay Papers
New Jersey Historical Society, Trenton
  George B. McClellan Papers
Southern Historical Collection, University of North Carolina, Chapel Hill
  William A. Graham Papers
Ohio Historical Society, Columbus
  Samuel Medary Papers
  John P. Sanderson Papers

NEWSPAPERS

Atlanta *Daily Intelligencer*
Augusta *Chronicle & Sentinel*
Augusta *Constitutionalist*

Beaver Dam *Argus*
Bellefontaine (Ohio) *Republican*
Bloomington *Times*
Boston *Athenian*
Boston *Daily Journal*
Boston *Evening Transcript*
Cairo *City Democrat*
Cairo *City Gazette*
Charleston *Mercury*
Chicago *Post*
Chicago *Times*
Chicago *Daily Tribune*
Cincinnati *Daily Commercial*
Cincinnati *Daily Gazette*
Cincinnati *Daily Enquirer*
Cleveland *Leader*
Columbus *Crisis*
Concord (New Hampshire) *Patriot*
Davenport (Iowa) *Daily Gazette*
Dayton *Daily Empire*
Dayton *Daily Journal*
Dayton *Daily Ledger*
Detroit *Advertiser and Tribune*
Detroit *Free Press*
Detroit *Post and Tribune*
Detroit *Tribune*
Dubuque *Herald*
Evansville *Gazette*
Goshen *Democrat*
Harrisburg *Patriot and Union*
Huntington *Democrat*
Illinois *State Journal*
Illinois *State Register*
Indianapolis *Daily Journal*
Indianapolis *Daily Sentinel*
Indianapolis *State Sentinel*
Joliet *Signal*
La Crosse (Wisconsin) *Weekly Democrat*
Lawrenceburg (Indiana) *Democratic Register*
London *Morning Herald*
London *Times*
Macon *Daily Intelligencer*
Macon *Daily Telegraph*
Missouri *Democrat*

Missouri *Republican*
New Albany *Weekly Ledger*
New York *Daily News*
New York *Evening Post*
New York *Express*
New York *Herald*
New York *Journal of Commerce*
New York *Sun*
New York *Sunday Mercury*
New York Times
New York *Tribune*
New York *Weekly Day Book*
New York *World*
Newark *Journal*
Ohio *Daily Statesman*
Ottawa *Weekly Republican*
Paterson *Register*
Philadelphia *Age*
Philadelphia *Inquirer*
Philadelphia *Press*
Philadelphia *Evening Bulletin*
Providence *Journal*
Providence *Post*
Richmond *Dispatch*
Richmond *Enquirer*
Richmond *Examiner*
Richmond (Indiana) *Palladium*
Richmond *Sentinel*
Richmond *Whig*
Rockford (Illinois) *Register*
St. Paul *Press*
Sullivan (Indiana) *Democrat*
Terre Haute *Journal*
Vincennes (Indiana) *Gazette*
Washington *Chronicle*
Washington *National Intelligencer*

GOVERNMENT PUBLICATIONS

Acts of . . . the Legislature of Wisconsin [1862, 1863]. Madison: 1863.
Acts of . . . West Virginia. . .1863. Wheeling: 1863.
Congressional Globe, 37th Congress, 1st Session.
Congressional Globe, 37th Congress, 2d Session.

Congressional Globe, 37th Congress, 3rd Session.
Congressional Globe, 38th Congress, 1st Session.
Congressional Globe, 38th Congress, 2d Session.
Ex Parte Vallandigham. 68 U.S. 243, 251. Decision of the U.S. Supreme Court reported at *United States Reports*, Vol. 68.
General and Special Laws of the State of Minnesota . . . 1862. St. Paul: 1862.
General Statutes of New Jersey. Jersey City: 1896.
House Executive Documents. 39th Congress, 1st Session (December 1865).
Journal of the House of Representatives of the Twenty-Third General Assembly of the State of Illinois. Regular Session. Begun and Held at Springfield, January 5, 1863.
Journal of the Senate of the Twenty-Third General Assembly of the State of Illinois. Regular Session. Begun and Held at Springfield, January 5, 1863.
Laws of the State of Maryland for 1865. Annapolis: 1865.
Laws of the State of New York. Albany: 1864.
Official manuscript (on microfilm) returns of 1864 election at Indiana State Historical Library, Archives Division, furnished by the State Librarian.
Record of the Service of the Fifty-Fifth Regiment of Massachusetts Volunteer Infantry. Cambridge: 1968.
Records of the Judge Advocate General's Office, General Courts-Martial, 1812– 1939, NN 3409, box 1165.
Report of the Adjutant General of the State of Indiana. Edited by W. H. H. Terrell. 8 vols. Indianapolis: 1869.
U.S. Congress. Senate. *Report of the Joint Committee on the Conduct of the War.* 38th Congress, 2d Session. Sen. Rep. No. 142.
U.S. Navy Department. *Official Records of the Union and Confederate Navies in the War of the Rebellion.* 31 vols. Washington, DC: U.S. Government Printing Office, 1894–1927.
U.S. Statutes at Large. Washington, DC: U.S. Government Printing Office.
U.S. War Department. *The War of the Rebellion: Official Records of the Union and Confederate Armies.* 128 vols. Washington, DC: U.S. Government Printing Office, 1880–1901.

ARTICLES

Abrams, Roy H. "'The Jeffersonian,' Copperhead Newspaper." *Pennsylvania Magazine of History and Biography* 57 (July 1933): 260–83.
Birdsall, B. C. "McClellan and the Peace Party." *The Century Magazine* 17 (September 1890): 638–39.
Brillhart, Norman C. "Election of 1864 in Western Pennsylvania." *Western Pennsylvania History Magazine* 8 (January 1925): 23–36.
Brooks, Noah. "Lincoln's Re-election." *The Century Magazine* 49 (April 1895): 865–72.

————. "Two War-Time Conventions." *The Century Magazine* 49 (March 1895).

Brumgardt, John R. "Overwhelmingly for 'Old Abe': Sherman's Soldiers and the Election of 1864." *Lincoln Herald* 78 (Winter 1976): 153–59.

————. "Presidential Duel at Midsummer: The 'Peace' Missions to Canada and Richmond, 1864." *Lincoln Herald* 77 (Summer 1975): 96–102.

Capron, Thaddeus B. "War Diary of Thaddeus H. Capron, 1861–1865." *Journal of the Illinois State Historical Society* (October 1919): 330–406.

Castel, Albert. "The Fort Pillow Massacre: A Fresh Examination of the Evidence." *Civil War History* 4 (March 1958): 37–50.

Cimprich, John, and Robert C. Manfort, Jr. "Fort Pillow Revisited: New Evidence about an Old Controversy." *Civil War History* 28 (Decmember 1982): 293–306.

Dewey, Donald O., ed. "Hoosier Justice: The Journal of David McDonald, 1864–1868." *Indiana Magazine of History* 62 (1966): 175–232.

Dudley, Harold M. "The Election of 1864." *The Mississippi Valley Historical Review* 18 (March 1932): 500–18.

Eidson, William G. "Louisville, Kentucky, During the First Year of the Civil War." *Filson Club History Quarterly* 38 (July 1964): 224–38.

Fesler, Mayo. "Secret Political Societies in the North During the Civil War." *Indiana Magazine of History* 14, no. 3 (September 1918): 183–286.

Fried, Joseph P. "The Draft Riots." *Civil War Times Illustrated* 4, no. 5 (August 1965): 4–10, 28–31.

Friedel, Frank B. "The Loyal Publication Society: A Pro-Union Propaganda Agency." *The Mississippi Valley Historical Review* 26 (December 1939): 359–76.

Gilmore, James R. "The Chicago Conspiracy." *The Atlantic Monthly* 16 (July 1885): 108–12.

————. "Our Last Day in Dixie." *The Atlantic Monthly* 14 (September 1864): 715–26.

————. "Our Visit to Richmond." *The Atlantic Monthly* 14 (September 1864): 372–83.

————. "A Suppressed Chapter of History." *The Atlantic Monthly* 37 (September 1887): 425–48.

Glonek, James H. "Lincoln, Johnson and the Baltimore Ticket." *Abraham Lincoln Quarterly* 6 (March 1951): 255–71.

Harbison, Winfred A. "Zachariah Chandler's Part in the Re-Election of Abraham Lincoln." *Mississippi Valley Historical Review* 22 (September 1935): 267–76.

Hines, Thomas Henry. "The Northwestern Conspiracy." *Southern Bivouac: A Monthly Literary and Historical Magazine.* New Series (January 1885): 506–10.

Hubbart, Henry Claude. "Pro-Southern Influences in the Free West, 1840–1865." *The Mississippi Valley Historical Review* 20 (June 1935): 45–62.

Jones, V. C. "The Kilpatrick-Dahlgren Raid: Boldly Planned . . . Timidly Executed." *Civil War Times Illustrated* 4, no. 1 (April 1965): 12–21.

Kaplan, Sidney. "The Miscegenation Issue in the Election of 1864." *Journal of Negro History* 34 (July 1949): 274–343.

Leonard, James A. "James A. Leonard, Letters of a Fifth Wisconsin Volunteer." *Wisconsin Magazine of History.* Edited by R. G. Plumb. 2 (1919–20): 51–75.

Levine, Peter. "Draft Evasion in the North During the Civil War, 1863–1865." *Journal of American History* 67 (1981): 816–34.

Schafer, Joseph. "Who Elected Lincoln?" *American Historical Review* 47 (October 1941): 51–63.

Stampp, Kenneth M. "The Milligan Case and the Election of 1864 in Indiana." *The Mississippi Valley Historical Review* 31 (June 1944): 41–58.

Thomas, Emory M. "The Kilpatrick-Dahlgren Raid." *Civil War Times Illustrated* 17 (April 1978): 28–35.

Trefousse, Hans L. "I Have Done My Share." *Civil War Times Illustrated* 9, no. 2 (May 1970): 22–29.

Welles, Gideon. "History of Emancipation." *Galaxy* 14 (December 1872): 838–51.

Wiley, Bell Irwin. "Billy Yank and Abraham Lincoln." *Abraham Lincoln Association Quarterly* 6 (June 1950): 103–20.

Williams, T. Harry. "Voters in Blue: The Citizen-Soldiers of the Civil War." *Mississippi Valley Historical Review* 31 (September 1944): 187–204.

Winther, Oscar O. "The Soldier Vote in the Election of 1864." *New York History* 25 (October 1944): 440–58.

Zornow, William F. "Lincoln, Chase, and the Ohio Radicals in 1864." *Bulletin of the Historical and Philosophical Society of Ohio* 9 (January 1951): 3–32.

———. "Lincoln Voters Among the Boys in Blue." *Lincoln Herald* 53, no. 3 (Fall 1952): 22–25.

———. "Words and Money to Re-elect Lincoln." *Lincoln Herald* 54, no. 1 (Spring 1952): 22–30.

PUBLISHED LETTERS AND SPEECHES

Adams, Henry, *A Cycle of Adams Letters 1861–1865.* Edited by Worthington C. Ford. 2 vols. Boston & New York: Houghton Mifflin Company, 1920.

Breck, George, "George Breck's Civil War Letters from the 'Reynolds Battery.'" *Rochester in the Civil War.* Edited by Blake McKelvey. Rochester: n.p., 1944.

Butler, Benjamin F. *Private and Official Correspondence of General Benjamin F. Butler During the Period of the Civil War.* Edited by Jessie Ames Marshall. 5 vols. Norwood: Plimpton Press, 1917.

Chamberlain, Joshua Lawrence. *The Passing of the Armies.* Based on papers presented by Chamberlain between 1893 and 1905 and published in 1915 by G. P. Putnam Sons; based on Facsimile 21, reprinted 1974, 1981, 1982, 1985, 1986, 1991; new materials copyrighted Dayton: Morningside House, Inc., 1982.

Connolly, James A. *Three Years in the Army of the Cumberland: The Letters and*

Diary of Major James A. Connolly. Edited by Paul M. Angle. Bloomington: Indiana University Press, 1959.

Cox, Samuel S. *Miscegenation or Amalgamation. Fate of the Freeman.* Speech of Samuel S. Cox of Ohio delivered in the House of Representatives, February 17, 1864. Washington, DC: 1864.

Davis, Jefferson. *Jefferson Davis: Constitutionalist, His Letters, Papers, and Speeches.* 10 vols. Edited by Dunbar Rowland. Jackson, MS: Mississippi Department of Archives and History, 1923.

Forbes, John Murray. *Letters and Recollections of John Murray Forbes.* Edited by Sarah F. Hughes. 2 vols. Boston: Houghton, Mifflin, 1899.

Grant, Ulysses S. *Personal Memoirs of U. S. Grant and Selected Letters 1839–1865.* Reprinted from *The Papers of Ulysses S. Grant.* Edited by John Y. Simon. 14 vols. Carbondale, IL: The Ulysses S. Grant Association, published by Southern Illinois University Press, 1967–1985.

Holmes, Oliver Wendell, Jr. *Touched with Fire: Civil War Letters and Diary of Oliver Wendell Holmes, Jr.* Edited by Mark DeWolfe Howe. Cambridge, MA: Harvard University Press, 1946.

Johnson, Andrew. *The Papers of Andrew Johnson.* Edited by Leroy P. Graf and Ralph W. Haskins. 9 vols. Knoxville, TN: University of Tennessee Press, 1967.

Lee, Robert E. *Lee's Dispatches: Unpublished Letters of General Robert E. Lee, C.S.A., to Jefferson Davis and the War Department of the C.S.A., 1862–65.* Edited by Douglas Southall Freeman. New York: G. P. Putnam Sons, 1915.

———. *The Wartime Papers of Robert E. Lee.* Edited by Clifford Dowdey. New York: Da Capo Press, 1961.

Lincoln, Abraham. *Abraham Lincoln: Speeches and Writings 1859–1865: Speeches, Letters, and Miscellaneous Writings, Presidential Messages and Proclamations.* Edited by Don E. Fehrenbacher. New York: Library of America, 1989.

———. *Collected Works of Abraham Lincoln.* 9 vols. Edited by Roy P. Basler. New Brunswick, NJ: Rutgers University Press, 1955.

Locke, David Ross. *Divers Views, Opinions and Prophecies of Yoors Trooly Petroleum Vesuvius Nasby.* (pseud.) Cincinnati, OH: R. W. Carroll, 1866.

McAllister, Robert. *The Civil War Letters of General Robert McAllister.* Edited by James L. Robertson. New Brunswick, NJ: Rutgers University Press, 1965.

McClellan, George B. *The Civil War Papers of George B. McClellan: Selected Correspondence 1860-1865.* Edited by Stephen B. Sears. New York: Ticknor & Fields, 1989.

Military Order of the Loyal Legion of the United States, Commandery of the State of Maine, prep., *In Memoriam: Joshua Lawrence Chamberlain, Late Major General U.S.V.* (1914, reprinted in Joshua Lawrence Chamberlain, *Passing of the Armies,* based on papers presented by Chamberlain between 1893 and 1905 and published in 1915 by G. P. Putnam Sons; of the numerous facsimiles thereafter produced, this was based on Facsimile 21, reprinted 1974, 1981, 1982, 1985, 1986, 1991; new materials copyrighted 1982 by Morningside House, Inc., Dayton, OH).

Moore, Frank, ed., *The Rebellion Record: A Diary of American Events, with Documents, Narratives, Illustrative Incidents, Poetry, Etc.* 12 vols. New York: G. P. Putnam Sons, 1861–63 (v. 1–6); New York: D. Van Nostran, 1864–68 (v. 7–12).

Richardson, James D., ed. *A Compilation of the Messages and Papers of the Presidents, 1789–1897.* 10 vols. Washington, DC: Government Printing Office, 1896–1899.

Schurz, Carl. *Speeches, Correspondence, and Political Papers of Carl Schurz.* 6 vols. Edited by Frederic Bancroft. New York: G. P. Putnam Sons, 1913.

Segal, Charles M., ed. *Conversations with Lincoln.* New York: G. P. Putnam Sons, 1961.

Sherman, William T. *Home Letters of General Sherman.* Edited by M. A. DeWolfe Howe. New York: Scribner's Sons, 1909.

Sumner, Charles. *The Works of Charles Sumner.* 15 vols. Boston: Lee and Shepard, 1870–1873.

Tilden, Samuel J. *Letters and Literary Memorial of Samuel J. Tilden.* 2 vols. Edited by John Bigelow. New York: Harper, 1908.

The Tribune Almanac and Political Register for 1860. New York: Greeley & McElrath, 1861.

The Tribune Almanac and Political Register for 1861. New York: Greeley & McElrath, 1862.

The Tribune Almanac and Political Register for 1862. New York: Greeley & McElrath, 1863.

The Tribune Almanac and Political Register for 1863. New York: Greeley & McElrath, 1864.

The Tribune Almanac and Political Register for 1864. New York: Greeley & McElrath, 1865.

The Tribune Almanac and Political Register for 1865. New York: Greeley & McElrath, 1866.

U.S. Congress. House of Representatives. Address by Benjamin G. Harris. April 9, 1864. *Congressional Globe.* 38th Congress, 1st session, 1864, 1515–16.

U.S. Congress. House of Representatives. Address by Alexander H. Long. April 8, 1864. *Congressional Globe.* 38th Congress, 1st session, 1864, 1499–1508.

U.S. Congress. House of Representatives. Address by Clement L. Vallandigham. January 14, 1863. *Congressional Globe.* 37th Congress, 3rd Session, 1863, appendix, 52–60.

DIARIES, AUTOBIOGRAPHIES, MEMOIRS, AND REMINISCENCES

Adams, Charles Francis, Charles Francis Adams, Jr., and Henry Adams. *A Cycle of Adams Letters 1861–1865.* Boston: Houghton, Mifflin Company, 1920.

Appleton's *American Annual Cyclopaedia and Register of Important Events.* First series. 15 vols. New York: D. Appleton and Company, 1862–1876.

Arnold, Isaac M. *The Life of Abraham Lincoln.* Chicago: Clarke & Co., 1885.

Bates, Edward. *The Diary of Edward Bates.* Edited by Howard K. Beale. Washington, DC: U.S. Government Printing Office, 1933.

Blaine, James G. *Twenty Years of Congress: From Lincoln to Garfield.* Norwich: The Henry Bill Publishing Co., 1884–1886.

Brooks, Noah. *Washington, D.C., in Lincoln's Time.* New York: The Century Co., 1895. Edited by Herbert Mitgang and republished Athens, GA: University of Georgia Press, 1958, 1962, 1971, 1989.

Browning, Orville Hickman. *The Diary of Orville Hickman Browning.* Edited by Theodore Calvin Pearse and James G. Randall. 2 vols. Springfield, IL: Trustees of the Illinois State Historical Library, 1927.

Carpenter, F. B. *Six Months in the White House with Abraham Lincoln.* New York: Hurd and Houghton, 1867.

Castelman, John Breckenridge. *Active Service.* Louisville, KY: Courier-Journal Job Printing Co., 1917.

Chamberlain, *The Passing of the Armies.* Dayton: Morningside House, Inc., 1991. Originally published in New York, 1915.

Chase, Salmon P. *Inside Lincoln's Cabinet: The Civil War Diaries of Salmon P. Chase.* Edited by David E. Donald. New York: Longmans, Green and Co., 1954.

Connolly, James A. *Three Years in the Army of the Cumberland: The Letters and Diary of Major James A. Connolly.* Bloomington, IN: Indiana University Press, 1959.

Cox, Jacob D. *Atlanta.* New York: Charles Scribner's Sons, 1882.

———. *Military Reminiscences of the Civil War.* 2 vols. New York: Charles Scribner's Sons, 1900.

Cox, Samuel S. *Eight Years in Congress, from 1857 to 1865.* New York: D. Appleton and Company, 1865.

Crotty, D. G. *Four Years Campaigning in the Army of the Potomac.* Grand Rapids, MI: 1874.

Dana, Charles A. *Recollections of the Civil War.* New York: D. Appleton & Co., 1902.

Davis, Charles E., Jr. *Three Years in the Army: The Story of the 13th Massachusetts Volunteers.* Boston: Estes and Lauriat, 1894.

Davis, Jefferson. *Rise and Fall of the Confederate Government.* New York: D. Appleton and Co., 1881.

Dawes, Rufus R. *Service with the Sixth Wisconsin Volunteers.* Marietta, OH: E. R. Alderman & Sons, 1890.

Dicey, Edward. *Spectator of America.* Athens, GA: University of Georgia Press, 1971. Originally published in 1863 under the title *Six Months in the Federal States* by Macmillan and Company, London.

Early, Jubal. *Autobiographical Sketches and Narratives of the War Between the States.* Edited by Frank E. Vandiver. Bloomington, IN: Indiana University Press, 1960.

Eddy, T. M. *The Patriotism of Illinois.* 2 vols. Chicago: Clarke & Co., 1865–1866.

Emilio, Lewis F. *A Brave Black Regiment: History of the Fifty-Fourth Regiment of Massachusetts Volunteer Infantry, 1863–1865.* Boston: Arno Press, 1969, reprint of 1894 edition.

Fremantle, Lt. Col. Arthur J. *Three Months in the Southern States April–June 1863.* London: William Blackwood and Sons, 1863.

Gilmore, James R. *Personal Recollections of Abraham Lincoln and the Civil War.* Boston: L. C. Page and Company, 1898.

Grant, Ulysses S. *The Personal Memoirs of U. S. Grant.* 2 vols. Edited by E. B. Long. New York: Library of America, 1952.

Greeley, Horace. *The American Conflict: A History of the Great Rebellion in the United States of America, 1860–65.* 2 vols. Hartford, CT: O. D. Case & Co., 1867.

Gurowski, Adam. *Diary of Adam Gurowski, 1863–1864–1865.* New York: Burt Franklin, 1968. Originally published Washington, DC, 1866.

Hamilton, James A. *Reminiscences of James A. Hamilton or Men and Events, at Home and Abroad During Three Quarters of a Century.* New York: Charles Scribner's Sons, 1869.

Hay, John. *Lincoln and the Civil War in the Letters and Diaries of John Hay.* Edited by Tyler Dennett. New York: Dodd, Mead & Co., 1935.

———. *Letters of John Hay and Extracts from his Diary.* Edited by Mrs. John Hay. 3 vols. Washington, DC: printed but not published, 1908.

Headley, John W. *Confederate Operations in Canada and New York.* New York: The Neale Publishing Company, 1906.

Holmes, Oliver Wendell, Jr. *Touched with Fire: The Civil War Letters and Diaries of Oliver Wendell Holmes, Jr. 1861–1864.* Edited by Mark De Wolfe Howe. Cambridge, MA: Harvard University Press, 1947.

Hyde, Thomas W. *Following the Greek Cross; or, Memories of the Sixth Army Corps.* Boston: Houghton, Mifflin, 1894.

Johnston, Joseph E. *Narrative of Military Operations.* New York: D. Appleton & Co., 1874.

Jones, John B. *A Rebel War Clerk's Diary.* Philadelphia: J. P. Lippincott & Co., 1866.

Julian, George W. *Political Recollections, 1840–1872.* Chicago: Jansen, McClurg & Co., 1883.

Kean, Robert Garlick Hill. *Inside the Confederate Government: The Diary of Robert Garlick Hill Kean.* Edited by Edward Younger. New York: Oxford University Press, 1957.

Koerner, Gustav. *Memoirs of Gustave Koerner 1809–1896.* Edited by Thomas J. McCormick. 2 vols. Cedar Rapids, IA: The Torch Press, 1909.

Lamon, Ward Hill. *Recollections of Abraham Lincoln, 1847–1865.* Edited by Dorothy Lamon. Chicago: A. C. McClurg and Company, 1895.

Logan, Mary. *Reminiscences of the Civil War and Reconstruction.* Edited by George Worthington Adams. Carbondale: Southern Illinois University Press, 1970.

Longstreet, James. *From Manassas to Appomattox: Memoirs of the Civil War in*

America. Philadelphia: J. B. Lippincott Company, 1895.

McAllister, Robert. *The Civil War Letters of General Robert McAllister*. Edited by James L. Robertson. New Brunswick: Rutgers University Press, 1965.

McClellan, George B. *McClellan's Own Story*. New York: C. L. Webster & Co., 1887.

McClure, Alexander K. *Lincoln and Men of War Times*. Philadelphia: Times Publishing Co., 1892.

————. *Our Presidents and How We Make Them*. New York, London: Harper & Brothers, 1900.

————. *Old Time Notes of Pennsylvania*. 2 vols. Philadelphia: The John C. Winston Co., 1905.

McPherson, Edward. *The Political History of the United States of America During the Great Rebellion, from November 6, 1860 to July 4, 1864*. Washington, DC: Philip & Solomons, 1864.

Manigault, Arthur M. *A Carolinian Goes to War: The Civil War Narrative of Arthur Middleton Manigault, Brigadier General, C.S.A.* Edited by R. Lockwood Turner. Columbia, SC: University of South Carolina Press, 1983.

Meade, George Gordon. *The Life and Letters of George Gordon Meade*. 2 vols. New York: Charles Scribner's Sons, 1913.

Miers, Earl Schneck. *Lincoln Day by Day: A Chronology, 1809–1865*. 3 vols. Washington, DC: Lincoln Sesquicentennial Commission, 1960.

Nicolay, John G., and John Hay, *Abraham Lincoln: A History*. 10 vols. New York: The Century Co., 1949.

Porter, Horace. *Campaigning with Grant*. New York: The Century Company, 1897.

Powers, Frank. *Freedom: A Documentary History of Emancipation: The Black Military Experience*. Edited by Ira Berlin. Cambridge, MA: Cambridge University Press, 1985.

Raymond, Henry J. *The Life and Public Services of Abraham Lincoln*. New York: Derby and Miller, 1865.

Richardson, Albert D. *A Personal History of Ulysses S. Grant*. Hartford, CT: American Pub. Co., 1868.

Riddle, Albert G. *Recollections of War Times: Reminiscences of Men and Events in Washington, 1860–1865*. New York: G. P. Putnam Sons, 1895.

Ruffin, Edmund. *The Diary of Edmund Ruffin: The Years of Hope April, 1861–June, 1863*. Edited by William K. Scarborough. Baton Rouge, LA: Louisiana State University Press, 1976.

Schurz, Carl. *The Reminiscences of Carl Schurz*. 3 vols. New York: The McClure Company, 1908.

Seward, Frederick W. *Seward at Washington 1861–1872*. New York: Derby and Miller, 1891.

Sherman, William Tecumseh. *Memoirs of General W. T. Sherman*. 2 vols. New York: Library of America, 1990. Edition includes both volumes in one consecutively numbered text. Originally published by C. I. Webster & Company, 1891.

Stidger, Felix G. *Treason History of the Order of Sons of Liberty, Formerly Circle of Honor, Succeeded by Knights of the Golden Circle, Afterward Order of American Knights.* Chicago: n.p., 1903.

Strong, George Templeton. *Diary of the Civil War 1860–1865.* Edited by Allan Nevins. New York: Macmillan Company, 1962.

Sumner, Charles. *The Works of Charles Sumner.* 15 vols. Boston: Lee and Shepard, 1870–73.

———. *Memoirs and Letters of Charles Sumner.* Edited by Edward Lillie Pierce. 4 vols. Boston: Roberts Brothers, 1881–93.

Wainwright, Charles S. *A Diary of Battle, The Personal Journals of Colonel Charles S. Wainwright 1861–1865.* Edited by Allan Nevins. New York: Harcourt, Brace & World, 1962.

Watkins, Sam R. *"Co. Aytch": A Side Show of the Big Show.* New York: McCowat-Mercer, 1962 (first published in 1882 under title "1861 vs. 1882: 'Co. Aytch,' Maury Grays, First Tennessee Regiment").

Welles, Gideon. *Diary of Gideon Welles.* Edited by Howard K. Beale. 3 vols. Boston: Houghton, Mifflin Company, 1911.

Woodward, C. Vann, ed. *Mary Chesnut's Civil War.* New Haven, CT: Yale University Press, 1981.

Young, John Russell. *Around the World with General Grant.* 3 vols. New York: The American News Company, 1879.

BIOGRAPHIES

Baringer, William E. *Lincoln's Rise to Power.* Boston: Little, Brown, and Company, 1937.

Clarke, Grace. *George Julian.* Indianapolis, IN: Indiana Historical Commission, 1932.

Dictionary of American Biography. 22 vols. New York: Charles Scribner's Sons, 1928–36.

Donald, David. *Charles Sumner and the Coming of the Civil War.* New York: Alfred A. Knopf, 1970.

———. *Charles Sumner and the Rights of Man.* New York: Alfred A. Knopf, 1961.

Dowdey, Clifford. *Death of a Nation: The Story of Lee and His Men at Gettysburg.* New York: Alfred A. Knopf, 1958.

———. *Lee's Last Campaign: The Story of Lee and his Men against Grant, 1864.* Boston: Bonanza Books, 1960.

Elliott, Charles Winslow. *Winfield Scott: The Soldier and the Man.* New York: Macmillan Company, 1937.

Fessenden, Francis. *Life and Public Services of William Pitt Fessenden.* 2 vols. Boston: Houghton, Mifflin Company, 1907.

Foulke, William Dudley. *Life of Oliver P. Morton.* 2 vols. Indianapolis, IN, and Kansas City, MO: Bowen-Merrill Company, 1899.

Freidel, Frank. *Francis Lieber: Nineteenth-Century Liberal.* Baton Rouge, LA: Louisiana State University Press, 1947.

Govan, Gilbert E. and James W. Livingood. *A Different Valor: The Story of*

General Joseph E. Johnston, C.S.A. Indianapolis, IN: Bobbs-Merrill, 1956.

Hamlin, Charles Eugene. *The Life and Times of Hannibal Hamlin.* Cambridge, MA: Riverside Press, 1899.

Harris, Wilmer C. *Public Life of Zachariah Chandler, 1851–1875.* Lansing, MI: Michigan Historical Commission, 1917.

Henderson, G. F. R. *Stonewall Jackson and the American Civil War.* 2 vols. New York: Longman, Green, 1919.

Henry, Robert Selph. *"First With the Most" Forrest.* Indianapolis, IN: Bobbs-Merrill, 1944.

Klement, Frank L. *The Limits of Dissent: Clement Vallandigham & the Civil War.* Lexington, KY: University Press of Kentucky, 1970.

Krug, Mark M. *Lyman Trumbull: Conservative Radical.* New York: A. S. Barnes and Company, Inc., 1965.

Lamers, William M. *The Edge of Glory: A Biography of General William S. Rosecrans, U.S.A.* New York: Harcourt-Brace, 1961.

Lewis, Lloyd. *Sherman: Fighting Prophet.* New York: Harcourt-Brace, 1958.

Liddell-Hart, Basil H. *Sherman: Soldier, Realist, American.* New York: Dodd, Mead & Company, 1929.

Lindsey, David. *"Sunset Cox," Irrepressible Democrat.* Detroit: Wayne State University Press, 1959.

Mitchell, Stewart. *Horatio Seymour of New York.* Cambridge, MA: Harvard University Press, 1938.

Myers, William Starr. *A Study in Personality: General George Brinton McClellan.* 2 vols. New York: D. Appleton-Century, 1934.

Nicolay, Helen. *Lincoln's Secretary: A Biography of John G. Nicolay.* New York: Longmans, Green and Company, 1949.

Oates, Stephen B. *With Malice Toward None: The Life of Abraham Lincoln.* New York: Harper & Row, 1977.

———. *Abraham Lincoln, The Man Behind the Myths.* New York: Harper & Row, 1984.

Oberholtzer, Ellis P. *Jay Cooke: Financier of the Civil War.* 2 vols. Philadelphia: G. W. Jacobs & Company, 1907.

Pearson, Henry G. *The Life of John A. Andrew: Governor of Massachusetts, 1861–1865.* 2 vols. Boston, New York: Houghton, Mifflin Company, 1904.

Randall, J. G., and Current, Richard N. *Lincoln the President: Last Full Measure.* 4 vols. New York: Dodd-Mead, 1945–55.

Randall, J. G., *Lincoln the Liberal Statesman.* New York: Dodd-Mead, 1947.

Sandburg, Carl. *Abraham Lincoln.* 4 vols. New York: C. Scribner's Sons, 1941.

Schuckers, J. W. *Life and Public Services of Salmon Portland Chase.* New York: D. Appleton and Company, 1874.

Sears, Stephen W. *George B. McClellan: The Young Napoleon.* New York: Ticknor & Fields, 1988.

Smith, Donnal V. *Chase and Civil War Politics.* Columbus, OH: Ohio Archaeological and Historical Society, 1931.

Smith, Theodore C. *The Life and Letters of James Abram Garfield.* 2 vols. New Haven, CT: Yale University Press, 1925.

Stoddard, Henry Luther. *Horace Greeley: Printer, Editor, Crusader.* New York: G. P. Putnam Sons, 1946.

Swift, Lindsay. *William Lloyd Garrison.* Philadelphia: G. W. Jacobs & Company, 1911.

Tarbell, Ida. *The Life of Abraham Lincoln.* 3 vols. New York: S. S. McClure Company, Doubleday & McClure Company, and McClure, Phillips & Company, 1895–1900.

Thomas, Benjamin P., and Harold M. Hyman. *Stanton: The Life and Times of Lincoln's Secretary of War.* New York: Alfred A. Knopf, Inc., 1962.

Vallandigham, James L. *A Life of Clement L. Vallandigham.* Baltimore, MD: Turnbull Company, 1872.

Van Deusen, Glyndon G. *William Henry Seward.* New York: Oxford University Press, 1967.

Warden, Robert E. *Account of the Private Life and Public Services of Salmon Portland Chase.* Cincinnati, OH: Wilstach, Baldwin & Co., 1874.

White, Horace. *The Life of Lyman Trumbull.* Boston, New York, Houghton, Mifflin Company, 1913.

Wittke, Carl. *Against the Current: The Life of Karl Heinzen, 1809–80.* Chicago: University of Chicago Press, 1945.

Woodburn, James A. *The Life of Thaddeus Stevens.* Indianapolis, IN: The Bobbs-Merrill Company, 1913.

SECONDARY ACCOUNTS AND MONOGRAPHS

Alexander, DeAlva S. *A Political History of the State of New York.* 3 vols. Port Washington, NY: I. J. Friedman, 1969.

Ashworth, John. *"Agrarians" and "Aristocrats": Party Political Ideology in the United States, 1837–1846.* New York: Cambridge University Press, 1987.

Austin, Erik W. *Political Facts of the United States Since 1789.* New York: Columbia University Press, 1986.

Baker, Jean H. *The Politics of Continuity: Maryland Political Parties from 1858 to 1870.* Baltimore, MD: Johns Hopkins University Press, 1973.

Baringer, William E. *Lincoln's Rise to Power.* Boston: Little, Brown and Company, 1937.

Belden, Thomas Graham, and Marva Robins Belden. *So Fell the Angels.* Boston: Little, Brown and Company, 1958.

Belz, Herman. *Reconstructing the Union: Theory and Policy During the Civil War.* Ithaca, NY: Cornell University Press, 1969.

Burnham, Walter Dean. *Presidential Ballots, 1836–1892.* Baltimore, MD: Johns Hopkins University Press, 1955.

Carter, Samuel, III. *The Siege of Atlanta, 1864.* New York: St. Martin's Press, 1973.
————. *The Final Fortress: The Campaign for Vicksburg, 1862–1863.* New York: St. Martin's Press, 1980.
Castel, Albert. *Decision in the West: The Atlanta Campaign of 1864.* Lawrence, KS: University Press of Kansas, 1992.
Catton, Bruce. *Never Call Retreat.* Garden City, NY: Doubleday & Company, Inc., 1965.
————. *A Stillness at Appomattox.* Garden City, NY: Doubleday & Company, Inc., 1953.
Church, Charles A. *History of the Republican Party in Illinois, With a Review of the Aggressions of the Slave Power.* Rockford, IL: Wilson, 1912.
Cole, Arthur. *Era of the Civil War, 1848–1870.* Springfield, IL: Illinois Centennial Commission, 1919.
Commager, Henry Steele, ed. *The Blue and the Gray.* 2 vols. Indianapolis: Bobbs-Merrill, 1950.
————. *Illustrated History of the Civil War.* New York: Promontory Press, 1978.
Connelly, Thomas L. *Autumn of Glory: The Army of Tennessee, 1862–1865.* Baton Rouge, LA: Louisiana State University Press, 1971.
Conrad, Henry C. *History of the State of Delaware.* 3 vols. Wilmington, DE: Self-published, 1908.
Cook, Adrian. *Armies of the Streets: The New York City Draft Riots of 1863.* Lexington, KY: University Press of Kentucky, 1974.
Cornish, Dudley Taylor. *The Sable Arm: Negro Troops in the Union Army, 1861–1865.* Lawrence, KS: University Press of Kansas, 1966.
Coulter, E. Merton. *The Civil War and Readjustment in Kentucky.* Chapel Hill, NC: University of North Carolina Press, 1926.
Dell, Christopher. *Lincoln and the War Democrats: The Grand Erosion of Conservative Tradition.* Madison, NJ: Associated University Presses, Inc., 1975.
Faust, Patricia L., ed., *Historical Times Illustrated History of the Civil War.* New York: Harper & Row, 1986.
Foote, Shelby B. *The Civil War: A Narrative.* 3 vols. New York: Random House, 1974.
Gray, Wood. *The Hidden Civil War: The Story of the Copperheads.* New York: Viking Press, 1942, 1964.
Hanchett, William. *The Lincoln Murder Conspiracies.* Urbana, IL: University of Illinois Press, 1983.
Hassler, Warren W., Jr. *Commanders of the Army of the Potomac.* Baton Rouge, LA: Louisiana State University Press, 1962.
Hesseltine, William B. *Lincoln and the War Governors.* New York: Alfred A. Knopf, 1955.
Horan, James D. *Confederate Agent: A Discovery in History.* New York: Crown Publishing, 1954.
Hubbart, Henry C. *The Older Middle West, 1840–1880.* New York: Russell & Russell, 1963.
Johnson, Robert Underwood, and Clarence Clough Buel, eds., *Battles and Leaders*

of the Civil War. 4 vols. Secaucus, NJ: 1983, based on "The Century War Series," published 1884 to 1887 in New York.

Kinchen, Oscar A. *Confederate Operations in Canada and the North.* North Quincy, MA: Christopher Publishing House, 1970.

Kirkland, Edward C. *The Peacemakers of 1864.* New York: The Macmillan Company, 1927.

Klement, Frank L. *The Copperheads in the Middle West.* Chicago: University of Chicago Press, 1960.

————. *Dark Lanterns: Secret Political Societies, Conspiracies, and Treason Trials in the Civil War.* Baton Rouge, LA: Louisiana State University Press, 1984.

Lader, Laurence. *The Bold Brahmins: New England's War Against Slavery.* New York: E. P. Dutton, 1961.

Lee, Basil L. *Discontent in New York City 1861–1865.* Washington, DC: Catholic University Press, 1943.

Leonard, Thomas C. *Above the Battle: War Making in America From Appomattox to Versailles.* New York: Oxford University Press, 1978.

Linderman, Joseph F. *Embattled Courage: The Experience of Combat in the Civil War.* New York: Macmillan, Inc., 1987.

Livermore, Thomas L. *Numbers and Losses in the Civil War in America 1861–1865.* Dayton, OH: Morningside House, Inc., 1986, being reprint 87 from an essay read before the Military Historical Society of Massachusetts, February 23, 1897, at Boston from the articles "Military Training" in the *Journal of the Military Service Institution* of July 1893 and "General Thomas in the Record" in vol. 10 of the *Journal of the Military Historical Society of Massachusetts*, and thereafter published in 1900 under this title.

Long, E. B., and Barbara Long. *The Civil War Day by Day: An Almanac 1861–1865* Garden City, NY: Doubleday & Company, 1971.

Lorant, Stefan. *The Glorious Burden: The American Presidency.* New York: Harper & Row, 1968.

McCarthy, Charles H. *Lincoln's Plan of Reconstruction.* New York: McClure, Phillips & Company, 1901.

McCormick, Richard P. *The Second American Party System: Formation in the Jacksonian Era.* Chapel Hill, NC: University of North Carolina Press, 1966.

McPherson, James M. *Battle Cry of Freedom: The Era of the Civil War.* New York: Oxford University Press, 1988.

————. *The Negro's Civil War.* New York: Pantheon Books, 1965.

Milton, George Fort. *Abraham Lincoln and the Fifth Column.* New York: The Vanguard Press, 1952.

Morison, Samuel Eliot. *The Oxford History of the American People.* New York: Oxford University Press, 1965.

Nelson, Larry E. *Bullets, Ballots, and Rhetoric: Confederate Policy for the United States Presidential Contest of 1864.* University, AL: University of Alabama Press, 1976.

Nevins, Allan. *The Emergence of Lincoln: Prologue to Civil War 1859–1861.* 2 vols. New York: Charles Scribner's Sons, 1950.

————. *The War for the Union: The Improvised War 1861–1862.* 2 vols. New York: Charles Scribner's Sons, 1959.

————. *The War for the Union: War Becomes Revolution 1862–1863.* New York: Charles Scribner's Sons, 1960.

————. *The War for the Union: The Organized War 1863–1864.* New York: Charles Scribner's Sons, 1971.

————. *The War for the Union: The Organized War to Victory 1864–1865.* New York: Charles Scribner's Sons, 1971.

Nichols, Roy F. *The Disruption of American Democracy.* New York: The Macmillan Company, 1948.

Oates, Stephen B. *Our Fiery Trial: Abraham Lincoln, John Brown, and the Civil War Era.* Amherst, MA: University of Massachusetts Press, 1979.

Parish, Peter J. *The American Civil War.* New York: Holmes & Meier Publishing, 1975.

Perkins, Howard C., ed., *Northern Editorials on Secession.* 2 vols. Gloucester, MA: Peter Smith, 1964.

Pitman, Benn. *Assassination of President Lincoln, 1865.* Cincinnati, OH: Moore, Wilstach & Baldwin, 1865.

Pitman, Benn, ed. *The Trials for Treason at Indianapolis.* Cincinnati, OH: Moore, Wilstach, & Baldwin, 1865.

Porter, George H. *Ohio Politics During the Civil War Era.* New York: Columbia University Press, 1911. Reprinted in New York by the AMS Press, 1968.

Potter, David M. *Lincoln and His Party in the Secession Crisis.* New Haven, CT: Yale University Press, 1942, 1962.

Power, Richard Lyle. *Planting Corn Belt Culture: The Impress of the Upland Southerner and Yankee in the Old Northwest.* Indianapolis, IN: Indiana Historical Society, 1953.

Randall, James G. and David Donald. *The Civil War and Reconstruction.* 2d rev. Lexington, KY: Heath, 1969.

————. *Constitutional Problems under Lincoln.* Urbana, IL: University of Illinois Press, 1951.

————. *Lincoln the Liberal Statesman.* New York: Dodd, Mead, 1947.

Reid, Whitelaw. *Ohio in the War: Her Statesmen, Generals and Soldiers.* 2 vols. Cincinnati, OH: R. Clarke Company, 1898.

Rhodes, James Ford. *History of the United States from the Compromise of 1850.* New York: Macmillan Company, 1906.

Riddle, Albert G. *Recollections of War Times.* New York: G. P. Putnam Sons, 1895.

Schlesinger, Arthur M., Jr., ed. *History of U.S. Political Parties.* 4 vols. New York: Chelsea House Publishing, 1973.

Sifakis, Stewart. *Who Was Who in the Union.* New York: Facts on File, 1988.

Silbey, Joel H. *A Respectable Minority: The Democratic Party in the Civil War Era, 1860–1868.* New York: W. W. Norton & Company, 1977.

Smith, Donnal V. *Chase and Civil War Politics.* Columbus, OH: Ohio Archaeological and Historical Society, 1931.

Sprague, Dean. *Freedom under Lincoln.* Boston: Houghton, Mifflin, 1965.

Stampp, Kenneth M. *Indiana Politics During the Civil War*. Indianapolis, IN: Indiana Historical Bureau, 1949.

Stanwood, Edward. *A History of the Presidency*. 2 vols. Boston: Houghton, Mifflin, 1965.

Sulgrove, Berry R. *History of Indianapolis and Marion County Indiana*. Philadelphia: 1884.

Tidwell, William A., with James O. Hall and David Winfred Gaddy. *Come Retribution: The Confederate Secret Service and the Assassination of Lincoln*. Jackson, MS: University Press of Mississippi, 1988.

Tredway, G. R. *Democratic Opposition to the Lincoln Administration in Indiana*. Indianapolis, IN: Indiana Historical Bureau, 1973.

Trefousse, Hans L. *The Radical Republicans: Lincoln's Vanguard for Racial Justice*. Baton Rouge, LA: Louisiana State University Press, 1969.

Vandiver, Frank E. *Jubal's Raid*. New York: McGraw-Hill, 1960.

Wiley, Bell Irwin. *The Life of Billy Yank: The Common Soldier of the Union*. Indianapolis, IN: Bobbs-Merrill, 1951.

Williams, T. Harry. *Lincoln and the Radicals*. Madison, WI: University of Wisconsin Press, 1941.

———. *Lincoln and His Generals*. New York: Alfred A. Knopf, 1952.

Wood, Forrest G. *Black Scare: The Racist Response to Emancipation and Reconstruction*. Berkeley, CA: University of California Press, 1968.

Woodward, C. Vann, ed. *Responses of the Presidents to Charges of Corruption*. New York: Delacorte Press, 1974.

Zornow, William Frank. *Lincoln & the Party Divided*. Norman, OK: University of Oklahoma Press, 1954.

ELECTION PAMPHLETS

An Argument on the Ethical Position of Slavery in the Social System, and its Relation to the Politics of the Day. New York: 1864.

Chandler, William E. *The Soldier's Right to Vote. Who Opposes It? Who Favors It? Or the Record of the McClellan Copperheads Against Allowing the Soldier Who Fights, the Right to Vote While Fighting*. Washington, DC, 1864.

Croly, David Goodman and George Wakeman, *Miscegenation: The Theory of the Blending of the Races, Applied to the American White Man and Negro*. New York: 1864.

Democratic Campaign Document. *Bible View of Slavery*. New York: 1864.

Democratic Campaign Document. *Campaign Broadside No. 1—The Miscegenation Record of the Republican Party*. New York: 1864.

Democratic Campaign Document. *The Lincoln Catechism, Wherein the Eccentricities & Beauties of Despotism are Fully Set Forth*. New York: 1864.

Democratic Campaign Document No. 11. *Miscegenation Indorsed by the Republican Party*. New York: 1864.

Johnson, Reverdy. *Power of the President to Suspend the Habeas Corpus Writ.* N.p., n.d.

Loyal Union League. *To the Soldiers of the Union.* N.p., n.d.

Report of the Judge Advocate General on "The Order of American Knights," Alias "The Sons of Liberty." A Western Conspiracy in Aid of the Southern Rebellion. Washington, DC: 1864.

Society for the Diffusion of Political Knowledge. *Emancipation and its Results.* New York: 1864.

Train, George Francis(?) *A Voice From the Pit.* Washington, DC: 1864.

Tribune, Chicago. "To the Loyal Soldiers of the Union Look at This." Chicago: 1864.

Unionist Campaign Document. *The Real Chicago Platform, as Expounded by the Democratic Orators at Chicago.* Chicago (?): 1864.

Union League of Philadelphia. *Address by the Union League of Philadelphia to the Citizens of Pennsylvania, in Favor of the Re-election of Abraham Lincoln.* Philadelphia: 1864.

Union League of Philadelphia. *Record of Harister Clymer; and Historical Parallel Between Him and Major General John W. Geary. Also Official Returns on Elections on Constitutional Amendments Allowing Soldiers the Right to Vote.* Philadelphia: 1864.

Vallandigham, Clement L. *The Great Civil War in America.* New York: 1863. Reprinted in *Union Pamphlets of the Civil War.* Edited by Frank Friedel. 2 vols. Cambridge, MA: Harvard University Press, 1967.

Van Evrie, John H. *Subgenation: The Theory of the Normal Relation of the Races: An Answer to "Miscegenation."* New York: Van Evrie, Horton and Co, 1864.

DISSERTATIONS AND THESES

Friedel, Frank B. "The Life of Francis Lieber." Doctoral Dissertation. University of Wisconsin, 1941.

Hardie, Anna. "The Influence of the Union League of America on the Second Election of Lincoln." Master's Thesis. Louisiana State University, 1937.

Kamaras, Nicholas Paul. "George B. McClellan and the Election of 1864." Doctoral Dissertation. University of Delaware, 1976.

Perry, Marjorie Anita. "Opposition to the Civil War in Indiana." Master's Thesis. University of Washington, 1932.

Sterling, Robert E. "Civil War Draft Resistance in the Middle West." Doctoral Dissertation. Northern Illinois University, 1974.

Index

Other titles of interest

FREDERICK DOUGLASS
Benjamin Quarles
Introd. by James M. McPherson
408 pp., 9 illus.
80790-4 $15.95

ABRAHAM LINCOLN
His Speeches and Writings
Edited by Roy P. Basler
Preface by Carl Sandburg
888 pp., 6 illus.
80404-2 $19.95

THE ABRAHAM LINCOLN
ENCYCLOPEDIA
Mark E. Neely, Jr.
368 pp., more than 300 illus.
80209-0 $19.95

THE ANNALS OF THE
CIVIL WAR
Written by Leading Participants
North and South
New introd. by Gary W. Gallagher
808 pp., 56 illus.
80606-1 $21.50

THE ANTIETAM AND
FREDERICKSBURG
General Francis W. Palfrey
New introduction by
Stephen W. Sears
244 pp., 4 maps
80691-6 $13.95

BATTLE-PIECES AND
ASPECTS OF THE WAR
Herman Melville
New introduction by
Lee Rust Brown
282 pp.
80655-X $13.95

THE BLACK PHALANX
African American Soldiers
in the War of Independence,
the War of 1812, and the
Civil War
Joseph T. Wilson
New introduction by
Dudley Taylor Cornish
534 pp., 64 illus.
80550-2 $16.95

A BRAVE BLACK REGIMENT
The History of the 54th
Massachusetts, 1863–1865
Captain Luis F. Emilio
New introduction by
Gregory J. W. Urwin
532 pp., 89 photos, 9 maps
80623-1 $15.95

BY SEA AND BY RIVER
A Naval History of the
Civil War
Bern Anderson
344 pp., 20 illus.
80367-4 $13.95

CAMPAIGNING WITH GRANT
General Horace Porter
New introduction by
William S. McFeely
632 pp., 32 illus.
80277-5 $12.95

CHANCELLORSVILLE AND
GETTYSBURG
General Abner Doubleday
New introduction by
Gary W. Gallagher
269 pp., 13 maps
80549-5 $13.95

CHARLES SUMNER
David Herbert Donald
New introduction by the author
1152 pp., 49 illus.
80720-3 $24.95

THE CIVIL WAR DAY BY DAY
An Almanac 1861–1865
E. B. Long with Barbara Long
1,135 pp., 8 pages of maps
80255-4 $19.95

THE CIVIL WAR PAPERS OF
GEORGE B. McCLELLAN
Selected Correspondence 1860–1865
Edited by Stephen W. Sears
669 pp.
80471-9 $17.95

A CIVIL WAR TREASURY
Being a Miscellany of Arms and
Artillery, Facts and Figures,
Legends and Lore, Muses and
Minstrels, Personalities and People
Albert A. Nofi
431 pp.
80622-3 $15.95

**THE GENERALSHIP OF
ULYSSES S. GRANT**
J. F. C. Fuller
446 pp., 17 maps & plans
80450-6 $14.95

HERNDON'S LIFE OF LINCOLN
William Henry Herndon
and Jesse Weik
New introd. by Henry Steele Commager
650 pp.
80195-7 $14.95

JEFFERSON DAVIS
Private Letters, 1823–1889
Selected and edited by
Hudson Strode
604 pp., 1 photo
80638-X $16.95

LINCOLN AND THE CIVIL WAR
**In the Diaries and
Letters of John Hay**
Selected by Tyler Dennett
362 pp.
80340-2 $13.95

LINCOLN AND THE NEGRO
Benjamin Quarles
275 pp., 8 illus.
80447-6 $13.95

BLACK ABOLITIONISTS
Benjamin Quarles
310 pp.
80425-5 $13.95

**THE BOOKS OF AMERICAN
NEGRO SPIRITUALS**
Two volumes in one
J. W. and J. R. Johnson
384 pp.
80074-8 $14.95

THE COTTON KINGDOM
A Traveller's Observations on
Cotton and Slavery in the
American Slave States
Frederick Law Olmsted
Edited with an introd.
by Arthur M. Schlesinger
704 pp.
80723-8 $18.95

**FREDERICK DOUGLASS ON
WOMEN'S RIGHTS**
Edited by Philip S. Foner
200 pp.
80489-1 $13.95

SLAVERY
A World History
Updated Edition
Milton Meltzer
584 pp., 251 illus. 3 maps
80536-7 $22.50

LINCOLN THE PRESIDENT
J. G. Randall
New introd. by Richard N. Current
**Volume One: Springfield to
Gettysburg**
909 pp.   80754-8 $22.50
**Volume Two: Midstream to the
Last Full Measure**
956 pp.   80755-6 $22.50

THE LINCOLN READER
Edited by Paul M. Angle
608 pp., 40 photos
80398-4 $16.95

LINCOLN'S HERNDON
David Herbert Donald
442 pp., 11 photos
80353-4 $13.95

**THE MAKING OF AN
AFRO-AMERICAN**
Martin Robison Delany
Dorothy Sterling
368 pp., 3 illus.
80721-1 $14.95

**MEMOIRS OF GENERAL
WILLIAM T. SHERMAN**
New introduction by
William S. McFeely
820 pp.
80213-9 $17.95

THE VIRGINIA CAMPAIGN, 1864 and 1865
General Andrew A. Humphreys
New introduction by
Brooks D. Simpson
510 pp., 10 maps
80625-8 $15.95

WALT WHITMAN'S CIVIL WAR
Edited by Walter Lowenfels
Drawings by Winslow Homer
368 pp., 16 illus.
80355-0 $14.95

THE WARTIME PAPERS OF ROBERT E. LEE
Edited by Clifford Dowdey and
Louis H. Manarin
1,012 pp.
80282-1 $19.95

THE STORY OF THE CONFEDERACY
Robert Selph Henry
Foreword by
Douglas Southall Freeman
526 pp.
80370-4 $14.95

THOMAS MORRIS CHESTER, BLACK CIVIL WAR CORRESPONDENT: His
Dispatches from the Virginia Front
Edited by R.J.M. Blackett
375 pp., 3 photos, 1 map
80453-0 $13.95

TRAGIC YEARS 1860–1865
A Documentary History of the
American Civil War
Paul M. Angle and
Earl Schenck Miers
1108 pp.
80462-X $23.95

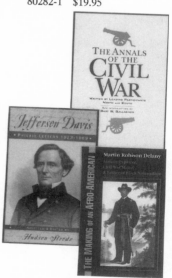

Available at your bookstore

OR ORDER DIRECTLY FROM

DA CAPO PRESS

1-800-321-0050